STRESS AND HEALTH
Principles and Practice for Coping and Wellness

STRESS AND HEALTH
Principles and Practice for Coping and Wellness

---◇---

Phillip L. Rice
Moorhead State University

Brooks/Cole Publishing Company
Pacific Grove, California

Brooks/Cole Publishing Company
A Division of Wadsworth, Inc.

Printed in the United States of America

10   9   8   7   6   5   4   3

Library of Congress Cataloging-in-Publication Data

Rice, Phillip L., (date)
   Stress and health.
   Includes bibliographies and indexes.
   1. Stress (Psychology) 2. Adjustment
(Psychology) 3. Stress (Psychology)—
Prevention. 4. Health. I. Title. [DNLM:
1. Stress, Psychological. WM 172 R497s]
BF275.S75R53   1987   155.9   86-26875
ISBN 0-534-07608-4

Sponsoring Editor: Claire Verduin
Marketing Representative: Neil Kelly
Editorial Assistant: Linda Ruth Wright
Production Editor: Candyce Cameron
Production Assistant: Sara Hunsaker
Manuscript Editor: Judith L. Hibbard
Permissions Editor: Carline Haga
Interior and Cover Design: Sharon L. Kinghan
Art Coordinator: Judith Macdonald
Interior Illustration: Scientific Illustrators, Champaign, Illinois
Photo Editor: Judith Macdonald
Typesetting: Omegatype Typography, Inc., Champaign, Illinois
Printing and Binding: Malloy Lithographing, Inc., Ann Arbor, Michigan

(Credits continue on page 380.)

To my mother and father,
who provided the foundation,
and Mike, who provided the focus

PREFACE

———————————◇———————————

Stress management and personal health programming are hardly modern topics, even though their mass appeal is relatively recent. The flood of books on stress, coping, time management, and personal health programming continues to grow. This suggests that unmet needs are still being identified and addressed. It is also a commentary on a field that continues to evolve both as a research and an applied discipline.

Much research still is needed to determine the factors that initiate, mediate, moderate, and maintain or divert stress. Work still needs to be done to develop better assessment programs and techniques appropriate to specific stress and health problems. Nowhere is this more evident than when self-help skills have been rushed to the commercial marketplace because of their proven effectiveness in a clinical setting, but without the benefit of equally convincing evidence of effectiveness when used by a novice at home without the benefit of a therapist.

A survey of the vast literature on stress management and personal health programming revealed what seems to be three general types of books. One group is simple to the point of being simplistic. These books are the type often regarded as pop or cult books. Most of these books are of the genre that reveal secrets to better living and a happier life through running, sex, cooking, primal screams, or some such notion. Many provide applications of stress management techniques but in an empirical and theoretical vacuum.

A second group of books are those written by health care professionals; these teach techniques of stress management and health programming. A few are described as comprehensive while others deal with a specialized technique. These books nonetheless tend to be applied books and provide very limited information on the principles, theory, and research behind the techniques.

Books of the third type summarize the large and growing body of research literature and discuss important methodological and theoretical issues. These books are certainly important to the stimulation of scholarly research, and they also fill a gap in the training of future health care professionals. But they are generally esoteric to the point of being inaccessible to the average reader, and thus seem unsuitable for introducing the beginning reader to the field of stress and health. In addition, they do not develop personal coping skills.

This book has been written to fill the middle ground between the second and third group of books. There is no illusion that it will be able to fill all needs. It has been necessary to make many decisions, some of which were painful, on what to include and what had to go. The treatment is thus selective rather than exhaustive.

Stress and Health: Principles and Practice for Coping and Wellness is intended to be an introductory book that can be used in first- or second-year college health and adjustment classes. It may also be helpful to those who want more substance than is provided in the popular literature. The book presents an accessible review of fact and fancy in stress and health research along with enough detailed instructions to permit a modestly motivated reader to develop useful stress and health skills. It is also intended to help readers become informed consumers, able to separate the chaff from the grain where extreme claims are made for the latest, hottest, state-of-the-art procedures. The reader may thus be able to match a particular technique to personal stress and health problems rather than trying a smorgasbord of practices in the hope that sooner or later something will work.

◆ TO THE INSTRUCTOR

If time permits using the entire book, the course will provide a fair balance between the principles and the practice of coping and wellness. If time does not permit covering all the topics in the book, some choices obviously will have to be made based on the needs of the typical student and the objectives of the course.

The book has been organized to permit the instructor to teach either a *principles syllabus* or an *applied syllabus*. No doubt other organizing schemes can be used, but these were the two primary "short courses" that were conceptualized. The principles syllabus covers major content areas of stress and health. The chapters that are intended to serve this focus include Chapters 2 through 10, covering the following topics: stress concepts, theories, and models; the physiology of stress; the cognitive stress system; personality and stress; stress in the family; social sources of stress; coping with victimization; environmental stress; and job stress.

The applied syllabus covers the major techniques that enable an individual to cope more effectively with stress, eliminate high-risk behaviors, and maintain better overall health. The chapters that serve this purpose are Chapters 1 and 2, 8, and 11 through 16. These chapters cover a number of topics and techniques central to self-help programs, as indicated by this list of topics: stress and personal health; stress concepts, theories, and models; coping with victimization; progressive muscle relaxation; cue-controlled and graduated relaxation; autogenics, desensitization, and stress inoculation; meditation and biofeedback; managing time-related stress; and behavioral health strategies.

◆ ACKNOWLEDGMENTS

There were many times when I wondered if this book would ever see the light of day. The constant support, patience, and encouragement of my family, friends, and colleagues made the task of writing much more enjoyable than it might have been otherwise. There are many who can only know from my personal expressions of thanks that they have contributed greatly to this work. Some expressions of gratitude cannot go unmentioned, however.

My research assistants, Sue Becker, Diane Myhre, Todd Huseby, and Grace Vomhof, logged many miles between my office and the library to obtain hundreds of books and articles that became the data base for this book. If they ever suffered from writer's cramp while filling out interlibrary loan requests they never complained. But they must have wondered when the revolving doors at the library would ever stop spinning. My secretary, Debra Lien, labored quietly and patiently to divert distractions and interruptions while also attending to many routine administrative duties that would have otherwise consumed much of my time.

My special friend, Dr. Richard Wielkiewicz, provided a sympathetic ear and a critical eye while editing several of the chapters written in the early stages of this project. It was a time of great excitement for both of us as he worked on his own book. We shared the responsibility of bolstering sagging spirits. We commiserated over chapters that just would not seem to fall in place and helped each other to persevere to the end.

Dr. Richard Kolotkin was the first to encourage my interest in health psychology. The many hours we spent exchanging ideas, developing seminar and workshop ideas, and so forth has had a lasting impact on the shape of this work. In addition, my colleagues, Dr. Gary Nickell and Dr. Willie Hallford, have provided critical comments on several chapters that helped make this a better work.

In the end, though, the shape of my work for the past few years began during a two-hour conversation with Professor Michael Wertheimer at the University of Colorado. I went to Colorado to work with Dr. Wertheimer on a project in the history of psychology. He could have confined his time and attention to providing insights for that project. But Mike took a personal interest in my career and helped me focus. There is little more that can be said to convey the profound sense of gratitude that is due him.

The staff at Brooks/Cole has provided support, encouragement and technical assistance above all my expectations. I want to thank editor Claire Verduin who believed in the project from the beginning and moved it from a dream to reality. Candy Cameron, production editor, kept the project on schedule and somehow got me to believe that there is joy in editing and life after proofreaders' marks. It was a special pleasure to work with Judith Hibbard, manuscript editor. Because of her efforts, sentences and phrases that I had struggled with took on new life and clarity. This work is undoubtedly better for her involvement. Also, thanks to Sharon Kinghan for the design of the book, to Judith Macdonald for coordinating the art work, and to Carline Haga, for managing the permissions. Through the many telephone conversations, there was always a special sense of warmth and personal regard. Thank you all.

Several people reviewed the manuscript at different stages in its development: Sandra Gallo, Niagara County Community College; Richard Fee, University of Louisville; Michael Stevenson, Ball State University; John Hall, St. Lawrence University; Stephen Germeroth, Catonsville Community College; Stella Wong, University of Hawaii; Donald Wagner, University of Cincinnati; and David Bush, Villanova University. Their many useful suggestions helped form the final manuscript.

Phillip L. Rice

CONTENTS IN BRIEF

—————————————◇—————————————

CONTENTS

◆ **PART 5**
RELAXATION, DESENSITIZATION, AND STRESS INOCULATION   235

Part 1

TAKING CONTROL OF STRESS AND PERSONAL HEALTH

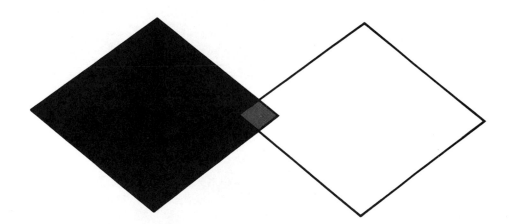

STRESS AND PERSONAL HEALTH: THE LIGHT AND DARK SIDES OF COPING

I'm an old man and have known a great many troubles, but most of them never happened.

Mark Twain

Stress, coping, time management, Type A behavior, personal health programming, diet, exercise, holistic health: These are buzzwords of the 1970s and 1980s. Whether you read scientific journals or the popular press, the themes are much the same.

And for every pound of journal article, there seems to be a pound of advice on how to apply the basic scientific discoveries. Indeed, few other issues have sparked such intensive efforts at translating laboratory findings into self-help tools. In this respect, the stress and health industries have taken on the appearance of fads. Fads skyrocket into public attention, live an intense but brief life, and pass into obscurity. It will be unfortunate if the central issues of stress and health suffer a similar fate.

Stress is not just a figment of someone's imagination any more than health is just a modern problem. Both are issues of extreme importance to everyday living and deserve all the attention devoted them. But unlike most fads, current coping and wellness applications are based on long-standing research programs. Together, they provide increased understanding of the intimate connection between physical and emotional resilience and suggest ways to improve the overall quality of life.

The importance currently attached to stress and health derives from two different but related concerns. One is the effort to improve the quality of life by increasing physical health and emotional well-being. The goal is not the mere absence of sickness and anxiety, but the positive joy of health and happiness.

The second concern has to do with certain characteristics widely attributed to modern technological societies. These include being fast-paced, time-driven, growth-oriented, and profit-obsessed. Recent evidence suggests that people who become trapped in this value scheme experience many pressures that exact a heavy toll both mentally and physically. The goal is for society to reduce the loss in human potential and for individuals to develop a sense of active mastery.

◆ STRESS SNAPSHOTS AND COPING CAMEOS

It is relatively easy to find people whose resistance has been severely tested by the strain of modern living. Pick up a daily newspaper or weekly magazine and you will usually see a collection of short but touching stories of people responding to stressful situations or health crises. The efforts of some of the actors in these coping cameos are at least humorous if not totally unique. Others show the near-tragic results of acting under pressure. Here are a few snapshots and cameos pulled from recent news sources.

Stress snapshot 1: An iron magnolia in academia.   When Jan Kemp blew the whistle on preferential treatment of athletes at the University of Georgia, she could not have anticipated the shock waves she would send through the academic and athletic communities. At the outset, it was a teacher's conscience asking for academic honesty and integrity. Along the way, it cost Jan her job, placed her career in jeopardy, nearly destroyed her family, and led to two suicide attempts. But Jan met the challenge, took on the giant of big-time college athletics, and grew a lot in the process.

During the trial of her suit against the university, Jan described herself as shy but courageous. A journalist referred to her as another "Iron Magnolia," after Rosalynn Carter's nickname. *Sports Illustrated* described her as tough and resilient.[1] In the end, Jan Kemp won a moral victory because the values she had placed above her own comfort and security were supported. She won a legal victory with reinstatement to her job and a major damage award. But she also won a personal victory, the satisfaction of knowing that she had met the challenge.

Coping cameo 1: Take this car, please!   The owner of a $12,000 lemon had already spent nearly $12,000 more just to keep the automobile running. The dealer and manufacturer seemed uncaring. So he painted a sign on the car and hoisted it into the air with a crane, creating a mechanical billboard to express his sense of futility. Over the next few weeks, he engaged in a heated battle trying to force the manufacturer to take the automobile back.

Stress snapshot 2: He has pulled a grenade pin!   Those words signaled the beginning of what was to be one of the severest tests of courage for the captain, crew, and passengers of TWA Flight 847. "He has pulled a hand-grenade pin and is ready to blow up the aircraft if he has to. We must, I repeat, we must land at Beirut. No alternative."

Moments after landing, the threats became even more intense. "They are threatening the passengers! . . . They are threatening to kill them now!

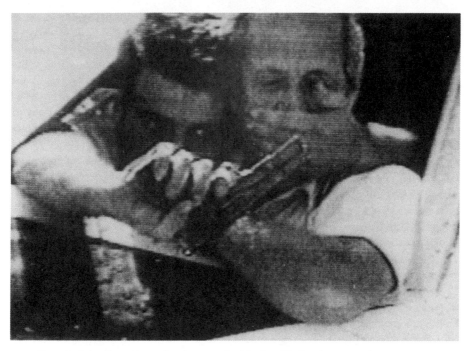

Captain John Testrake under the gun of a hijacker. Under the most adverse conditions and with the fate of the passengers on his shoulders, this pilot remained calm, cool, and collected. *(AP/Wide World Photo)*

They are threatening to kill them now! We want the fuel now! Immediately!"

The voice was that of Captain John Testrake. During the 17-day ordeal, he was the voice of the terrorists to the world, the man responsible for his aircraft and the lives of the 153 passengers on board. Captain Testrake showed how adversity and challenge can be confronted and overcome.

Coping cameo 2: Help! my mother is dying! A man called the Medevac hotline in a Texas town. His mother appeared to be dying of a heart attack. He expected to hear "An ambulance is on the way." Instead, he got a third degree from the dispatcher. As precious minutes passed, he grew increasingly tense and angry. A few profane words emphasized that this was a real emergency. On advice from her supervisor, the dispatcher hung up. Before help could arrive, his mother died.

◆ THE DARK SIDE OF STRESS

These anecdotes reveal how frustrated expectations and the perception of threat can influence judgment. They show how perceptions become distorted and communication is garbled under conditions of stress. But anecdotes do not reflect the extent of loss that results from unmanaged stress. A more accurate impression may be conveyed by the hard data that follow.

Every year, thousands of people seek medical or psychological help for emotional distress that exceeds their ability to cope. One of every three marriages ends in divorce.[2] Sixteen of every 100,000 Americans commit suicide apparently because they have found no lasting happiness.[3] Every year thousands of people burn out on the job. The result is often a personal crisis of shattering proportions that affects the family as well. There is the added toll of financial loss, which is shared by the employer. According to a survey conducted by the American Academy of Family Physicians, 80% of business executives, 66% of teachers and secretaries, 44% of garment workers, and 38% of farmers suffer work-related stress.[4]

Most stress is caused by the way we think about and interpret the events taking place around us. Some of it, however, is a response to very real time pressures, exorbitant work demands, and environmental hazards. And some of it is a direct result of sheer physical strain or danger from the job itself.

Over 100,000 Americans die each year from some type of occupational illness, while another 13,000 die from industrial injury.[5] According to one survey, 9 of every 10 American industrial workers are not adequately protected from commonly used hazardous industrial chemicals. And in 1978, 60,000 acts of violence, including rape and murder, were committed in our public schools, mostly against teachers.[6]

Even if the majority of workers escape accidental injury or violent attack, the mere potential produces stress and contains hidden psychological and physical health risks. The psychological effects of stress are ever present and fairly well recognized: insomnia, anger, irritability, inability to concentrate, self-pity, reduced capacity for decision making, depression, and impaired memory capacity.

But the other side of the coin is equally important: Stress can exact a heavy toll on physical health as well. The presence of life-threatening hazards, environmental hazards, family pressures, and social and psychological stressors all affect the way in which our bodies function. The end result can be a variety of physical health problems afflicting each of us in different ways and with varying degrees of severity.

The Stress–Health Connection

The reason for this stress–health connection lies in the way in which the brain interprets what is going on, how it responds to perceived threat, and how it translates those perceptions into body responses. The body systems involved in stress will be discussed in Chapter 3. However, it is important to note here that the brain works in a *literal* way.[7] Whether there is an actual threat or only an imagined threat is of no consequence to the literal brain. Perceived threat *is* threat. And when threat is present, the brain will sound the alert, and the body will respond by mobilizing its defensive systems.

In this way, the brain can induce many changes in vital life-sustaining functions. A few of these are increased output from the pituitary, elevated adrenal flow, increased blood pressure, and increased heart rate. The sole purpose of these changes is to restore balance to the body as quickly as possible, a process called **homeostasis.**

When the threat (real or imaginary) goes on for a long time, the body's defensive changes may be forced to work continuously at high speed. Then the body may begin to wear down, lose its resistance, and be unable to ward off added stress. Hans Selye called this the General Adaptation Syndrome (GAS), which begins with an *alarm reaction,* continues with mobilized *resistance,* and ends with *exhaustion* if the stress is not removed or relieved.[8]

In the first stages of stress, unfortunately, many bodily changes are so subtle they go undetected. Indeed, it may take a serious physical illness or some disturbing malfunction before the person recognizes what is happening. The fallout from overlooked and uncorrected stress can be a variety of ailments (see Figure 1–1).

It is estimated that over 25 million people suffer recurring headaches.[9] Another 7 million suffer lower back pain that is probably stress-related.[10] Hypertension affects the lives of 23–44 million Americans, leading to 60,000 deaths each year.[11] Cancer strikes down 750,000 people each year. More significant is the fact that most cancer victims successfully treated and no longer showing any signs of malignancy suffer reactivation of cancer after periods of severe stress.[12] Thus, it is suspected that life-style and psychosocial variables play an important role in starting the disease process. However, recent evidence shows that biological factors are most important once the disease is in process.[13]

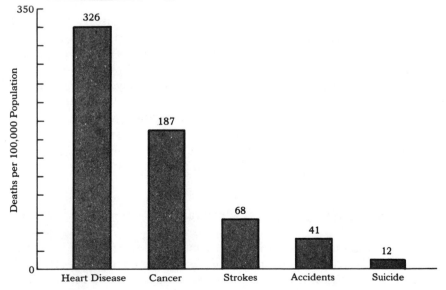

Figure 1–1. Five leading causes of death in the United States. Each has been connected in some fashion to stress.

The Damaging Effects of Behavioral Excesses

As if the mental and physical stressors described were not enough, people engage in behavioral excesses or self-defeating behaviors of an almost endless variety. Smoking, drug abuse, a sedentary life-style, overeating, improper diet, sheer neglect of the body, refusal to pay attention to many warning signals from the body, burying the signals under piles of over-the-counter drugs, and lack of appropriate medical checkups head the list.

The physical toll from these actions is alarming. The most optimistic assessment suggests that improper life-style may result in high blood pressure, atherosclerosis, reduced cardiovascular fitness, increased risk of coronary failure, diabetes, decreased respiratory capacity, lowered muscle tone, fatigue, and lowered resistance to illness.

On the pessimistic side, the costs are calculated in more concrete terms. Approximately 320,000 premature deaths occur each year as a result of smoking.[14] Misuse of alcohol leads to another 200,000 deaths per year, many of them teenage traffic fatalities.[15] Americans spent about $8 billion on 1.4 billion prescriptions in 1977.[16] This was in addition to nearly 13 billion tranquilizers, amphetamines, and barbiturates purchased as over-the-counter drugs.[17]

Poor health adds physical stress to the person's load. When the body is injured or functions improperly, information feeds back to the brain that something is wrong. When this information signals pain and/or potential life threat (as in a cardiac arrhythmia), the result is usually extreme anxiety for the person. If everything works correctly, stress will be a strong motivator for the person to seek some remedy (such as surgery, chemotherapy, geographic relocation, or exercise) that will start the body on its way to recovery.

There are, however, counterforces at work that can distort the normal tendency to avoid harming the body in the first place and to seek remedies in the second place. This is most clearly illustrated in the case of behaviors that enable the person to escape persistent tension. Tension or anxiety is usually viewed as unpleasant, and the general tendency is to try to avoid unpleasant things as much as possible. Tension may be reduced by smoking, anxiety by drinking, and boredom by eating. Even though escape is not the most effective means of dealing with the causes of the stress, the cycle of tension, escape, and strengthening of escape behaviors through tension reduction can go on and on. It is easily started but difficult to stop.

◆ STRESS–HEALTH EXCHANGES

The foregoing facts have been presented to make two main points. First, the relation between stress and health is a two-way street. Stress affects health and health affects the ability to deal with stress. Poor health reduces individual capacity for successful coping. It makes no difference whether poor health results from injury and environmental hazards, life-style and self-defeating behavior, or the gradual weakening of body resistance by prolonged emotional stress. Poor health puts more stress into the system.

On the positive side, engaging in adaptive coping and health behaviors conserves the body's defensive resources, increases resistance to stressors, improves both the mental and physical sense of well-being, and leads to increased productivity and satisfaction with living. Overall, the effect is one of enhanced personal functioning benefiting interpersonal, social, and professional areas of life. Energy that was formerly expended just trying to stay on top is available for concentration on problem solving, creative expressions, and personal relationships. As Charlesworth and Nathan have suggested, the end result is not just success but fun, since "wellness behaviors are known to be positively addicting."[18]

Second, efforts to maintain wellness should not be isolated activities, as though they had nothing to do with stress management. And conversely the effort to manage stress should incorporate sound health strategies. Books that take a one-sided view (solely stress texts or only health programming) perpetuate the illusion that treatment of the mind can be separated from treatment of the body. The balanced effort that gives proper and equal accord to both coping and wellness will yield the best overall result.

◆ THE BRIGHT SIDE OF STRESS

Among the more important discoveries since the 1970s is the extent to which the ill effects of unmanaged stress and poor health practices may be avoided by learning simple skills and by making modest adjustments in life-style. The most revealing evidence on this issue comes from two studies. One was conducted in Canada and the other was done in the United States but was based on the Canadian study.

The Canadian government was interested in determining the major contributing factors to disease and death. The study, published in 1974, identified four major factors. These are (1) inadequacies in the existing health care system; (2) behavioral factors or unhealthy life-styles; (3) environmental hazards, including occupational, industrial, and ecological hazards; and (4) human biological factors such as genetic defects, congenital defects, and acquired physical injury or weakness.[19]

The importance of this finding is not obvious until linked to the work done by a team of U.S. researchers.[20] Using the four factors supplied by the Canadian project, the U.S. group analyzed the 10 leading causes of death as they existed in 1976. They concluded that fully 50% of all deaths in the United States can be attributed to unhealthy behavior or life-styles (Figure 1–2). Another 20% can be related to environmental hazards. Human biological factors accounted for another 20% of the mortality rate, while the remaining 10% can be attributed to inadequacies in the health care system.

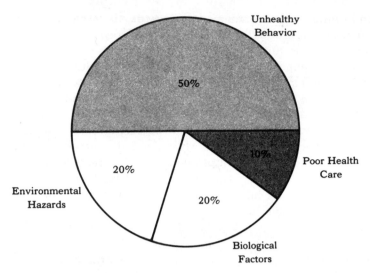

Figure 1–2. Major factors contributing to death in the United States. Fully 50% of deaths are related to life-style factors under the direct control of the person.

The silver lining in this dark cloud is that we might be able to reduce mortality by as much as 50% simply by changing life-style and health-risk behaviors.[21] Obviously, this does not mean that 50% of the population can be prevented from dying. But a significant number of *premature* deaths might be prevented—deaths that occur, for the most part, for no good reason except that people chose a self-defeating and self-limiting life-style. This they do in spite of the fact that alternative life-styles can be fashioned with only a modest amount of planning and effort.

Recent evidence suggests that many people have begun to make positive life-style changes. In spite of the increase in number of hours spent watching television,[22] more and more people are participating in exercise programs that improve overall physical fitness. They have discovered that the benefits of life-style change are worth the effort.

◆ MOTIVATION FOR LIFE-STYLE CHANGE

There are many good reasons to learn coping skills and work toward maintaining health. These include the likelihood of reducing physical discomfort and disease, increasing self-actualization, reducing stress, and improving conflict management in interpersonal relations. Practical reasons include reducing loss in wages due to stress-related illness, reducing the cost of health care, and bypassing the shortage of doctors. Changes in the values of society and the medical community have begun to support more self-managed health programs. Also, there is more concern about traditional methods of caring for the ill, which has started a trend toward holistic health practice. More emphasis is being placed on preventive methods and on the person as a total being. Finally, since the 1960s, the desire to reassert control of our personal lives and reduce dependence on outside help has resurfaced as a very powerful motive.

◆ HABIT AND REWARD: FORCES AGAINST CHANGE

In spite of the many positive reasons for learning coping and personal health skills, many people do not stick with their programs. The reasons for dropping out are relatively common. Both personal and social pressures can operate to weaken resolve. Internal pressures arise because learning new skills takes time, effort, sacrifice and maybe even some discomfort if not outright pain. New habits also have to replace old habits. And old habits do not give way easily. External pressures include lack of positive support from family or friends along with cultural values that frequently work against assuming personal responsibility for stress and health.

A Hard Habit to Break

Perhaps the hardest thing to counteract is the presence of a deeply entrenched living routine. Living routines reflect our preferences for eating, sleeping, exercising, working, playing, and so forth. This is what is usually called **life-style.** A life-style is comfortable, like the old pair of jeans we slip on when relaxing. Life-style is also habitual. Like brushing teeth in the morning, it is done without thinking. It takes no planning and little or no special effort to maintain. No matter how damaging the habit is, it is still there. And habits, especially old ones, are hard to break.

Changing life-style, on the other hand, requires planning and effort. It requires rethinking personal values and having a watchdog attitude for some time until the new habit is strong enough to maintain itself. And it is difficult to change, especially to *keep changed,* because of all those powerful cues that prompt old behaviors to occur without thinking.

Nature Hates Delay of Reward!

In addition to the problem of habit, there is also the problem of delay in rewards. What we are working toward (feeling better, being more in control of our emotions, reduced tension levels, for example) is often so intangible, distant, and slow to come that we are tempted to throw in the towel before the match has really started. The principle working against our will, defeating our motivation, is that *we have a very low tolerance for delays in reward.* But we respond very readily to rewards that are immediate.

Potato chips taste good. Who thinks about the fat they dump into the system when the bag is open? A salad with little or no dressing tastes bland. But in the long run it helps keep the body operating better. The problem is that the taste of the chips is here and now and pleasant, while the benefit of the salad is long-term and difficult to see.

◆ PRACTICAL SOURCES FOR PERSONAL MOTIVATION

The will to persevere may be bolstered by more immediate, tangible, and practical types of motivators. In fact, the socioeconomic situation since the 1960s has provided many powerful incentives for individuals to become involved in their own personal health programming.

Stress Doesn't Make Appointments

One of the most practical reasons for developing coping skills is to be able to deal with stress and personal health at the time a problem presents itself, not when the doctor can squeeze us in. Stressors certainly do not make appointments. When they crop up, they seem to require immediate attention. It goes without saying that a personal therapist cannot be available at the most convenient times.

The skills must be readily available to use at the most timely moment. Dealing with stress one week later in the privacy of a therapist's office is usually too late. The problem is that we continue to engage in a kind of mental shadow boxing. We fight through the old stress event over and over again.

There are several possible results of this secret struggle. One is that the irritation increases until it boils over in outright anger. Another possible outcome is that it festers inside, robbing us of energy, vitality, and spontaneity. It is also possible to find a solution to the problem and resolve the conflict.

In any case, coping skills need to be available to use *publicly,* wherever and *whenever* stress is occurring. As later chapters will reveal, this is indeed possible.

The Doctor Shortage

A second reason for developing personal health skills is related to the shortage of health care personnel. The array of mental and physical distress described earlier raises a serious question as to how clinical practitioners can deliver adequate health care, both mental and physical, to the millions in need.

More important, there is every indication that health practitioners already experience difficulty meeting the demands that patients put on them for time and services. Of the nearly 1 billion visits made to doctors each year, approximately 60% of those visits are made to office-based physicians.[23] These health practitioners work more than 51 hours per week,[24] yet they are able to provide no more than 18 minutes of contact time for each patient. These estimates do not even touch the mental health delivery system.

On that score, it is estimated that nearly 1.5–2 million men and women suffering from serious psychological problems are being overlooked for a variety of reasons, including a shortage of trained practitioners and para-professionals.[25] Society cannot possibly afford the size of professional work force that would be necessary to remedy problems of this scope and magnitude.

This suggests that taking responsibility for personal health is a practical necessity. It is probably also economically inevitable as more pressures mount on the health care delivery system. Further, it is personally desirable in view of the potential for developing an overall higher quality of life.

The Cost of Being Sick

A third incentive to develop coping and health skills is that failure to do so can lead to increased illness. The cost of being sick adds up in four ways. It costs each person in two ways. First, it costs financially from lost wages. Second, it costs physically in both the obvious discomfort but also in the increased toll on body reserves. Third, it costs business whenever illness interferes with work. For example, it increases absenteeism and increases the risk of injury due to workers below their peak efficiency trying to carry out dangerous jobs. Fourth, it costs the government when subsidies are involved either to a health agency or to the stricken in direct aid payments. These costs cannot always be translated to dollars and cents, but here are some estimates.

According to recent statistics, spending for health care ballooned from $27 billion dollars in 1960 to $387 billion in 1984.[26] This amounts to $1 billion per day in health care! Further, while we spent about 6% of our gross national product (GNP) for health care in 1960, we now spend about 10% of the GNP. The federal government now commits virtually 11 cents of every dollar to health spending. Tragically, almost 97% of this money goes entirely to caring for the sick and disabled. This leaves only 3% of the federal health dollar for the prevention of sickness.

Businesses lose nearly $17 billion each year in productivity because of mental stress on the job. In addition, they lose over $60 billion from stress-related physical illness. Each year, over $8.6 billion is lost in wages because of cardiovascular disease alone. These costs do not include insurance programs that businesses maintain to cover their employees and other health-related expenses. One company, Kimberly-Clark, spent $14.3 million for insurance premiums for 15,000 employees.[27] Multiply this figure by the number of major businesses carrying similar insurance programs, weight it for the number of employees in each business, and you will see a monumental cost to business for health care. These figures illustrate the high cost of taking care of the sick and injured. They also suggest why the prevention of even a small percentage of sickness and injuries translates into sizable financial savings for the person, for businesses, and for government.

◆ A GUIDE TO COPING AND WELLNESS

Stress and Health is intended to provide two essential ingredients for effective coping and personal health programming. The first is a foundation of principles and theory derived from current research on stress and health. Knowledge of the basic processes involved in stress and health generally permits a more ready identification of sources of difficulty. Without such information, much of the effort to cope and keep fit may be like looking for the proverbial black cat in a dark basement.

The second ingredient is a variety of techniques that can be used to manage stress and maintain wellness. In addition to teaching basic coping skills, some background will be provided on deciding what technique is most suited for particular stress symptoms and what limitations must be considered in using each technique.

Many different approaches have appeared for reducing stress, improving personal coping skills, detecting personal health risks, and maintaining health. In fact, there are far too many techniques to be discussed here. As a result, this book will concentrate primarily on applications that have been successfully translated into self-help techniques. Only those techniques with a fairly extensive body of supporting research have been included. Feedback provided by many students and clients has also influenced the selection process. Techniques for stress management, time management, prevention of job stress, and control over self-defeating behaviors such as overeating and lack of exercise will be covered.

In addition, techniques were selected for inclusion that have a relatively short learning curve. In general, each technique can be learned by most people in a matter of a few weeks with a few hours devoted each week. If you are motivated to assume responsibility for your health through modest life-style changes and can be diligent for short periods of time when deliberate attention to reading, rehearsal, and self-observation is necessary, you should find these skills becoming as much a way of life as eating and riding a bicycle. And you may want to take these skills, like those of eating or riding, to the level of gourmet or professional. Or, like many people, you may simply prefer to keep these skills at a functional and practical level to be called upon when needed.

◆ WHAT LIES AHEAD: AN OVERVIEW

The first three parts are largely devoted to principles and theory. The major focus is on the biological, psychological and social processes at work in stress and health management. Chapter 2 provides an overview of terminology and theory in stress and health. Chapter 3 describes the sequence of events that occurs in the body as it mobilizes to defend against perceived threat of both physical and psychological varieties.

Chapter 4 deals with the cognitions and attitudes that influence lifestyle and stress loads. This is an extremely important issue because we each see the world through a different pair of glasses, or psychological filters. The same situation can appear completely different to each of us. That is why one person's stress can be positive, arousing, and exciting, while to another person the same stress is negative, debilitating, and unbearable. Hans Selye used the term *eustress* to refer to the positive variety and *distress* to refer to the negative.[28]

Chapter 5 presents a discussion of the relationship between stress and personality. Subsequent chapters (Chapters 6–10) will describe the sources of stress existing in the family, in social settings, at work, and in the natural environment.

The last two parts provide the actual techniques of stress management and personal health programming. Chapters 11 and 12 provide the rationale and method for reducing tension with deep muscle relaxation. Chapter 13 describes how to manage specific fears with desensitization, a technique that builds on the relaxation procedure but also uses imagery. Autogenic techniques and a method of stress inoculation are also introduced in this chapter. Chapter 14 describes a number of meditation procedures including transcendental meditation. In addition, an analysis of the promise and pitfalls of biofeedback is provided. Chapter 15 discusses methods for managing time more efficiently. And finally, Chapter 16 discusses behavioral methods for managing diet and exercise.

◆ NOTES

[1]Nack, W. (1986, February 26). This case was one for the books. *Sports Illustrated*, pp. 34–42.

[2]Morrison, E. S., & Borosage, V. (1977). *Human sexuality: Contemporary perspectives*. Palo Alto, CA: Mayfield, p. 438.

[3]Schumer, F. (1983). *Abnormal psychology.* Lexington, MA: Heath, p. 256.

[4]Veninga, R. L., & Spradley, J. P. (1981). *Work stress connection*. Boston: Little, Brown, p. 11.

[5]Institute of Medicine (United States). (1979). *Healthy people: The Surgeon General's report on health promotion and disease prevention*. (Government Document No. HE20.2:H34/5, pp. 9-11–9-12). Rockville, MD: U.S. Government Printing Office.

[6]Veninga & Spradley, *Work stress connection,* p. 17.

[7]This term is borrowed from Kenneth Pelletier, who used it in his 1977 work *Mind as healer, mind as slayer* (New York: Dell).

[8]Selye, H. (1974). *Stress of life*. New York: McGraw-Hill.

[9]Veninga & Spradley, *Work stress connection*, p. 59.

[10]Veninga & Spradley, *Work stress connection*, p. 59.

[11]Yates, J. E. (1979). *Managing stress: A businessperson's guide*. New York: AMA-COM: Division of American Management Association, p. 6.

[12]Yates, *Managing stress*, p. 6.

[13]Cassileth, B. R., Lusk, E. J., Miller, D. S., Brown, L. L., & Miller, C. (1985). Psychosocial correlates of survival in advanced malignant disease? *The New England Journal of Medicine, 312,* 1551–1555.

[14]Institute of Medicine, *Healthy people*, pp. 10-6.

[15]Institute of Medicine, *Healthy people*, pp. 10-11.

[16]Veninga & Spradley, *Work stress connection*, p. 59.

[17]Charlesworth, E. A., & Nathan, R. G. (1982). *Stress management: A comprehensive guide to wellness*. Houston: Biobehavioral Press, p. 10.

[18]Charlesworth & Nathan, *Stress management*, p. x.

[19]Lalonde, M. (1974). *A new perspective on the health of Canadians, a working document*. Ottawa: Government of Canada.

[20]Institute of Medicine, *Healthy people*, pp. 1-9.

[21]Institute of Medicine, *Healthy people*, pp. 1-9.

[22]Thompson, J. K., Jarvie, G. J., Lahey, B. B., & Cureton, K. J. (1982). Exercise and obesity: Etiology, physiology, and intervention. *Psychological Bulletin, 91,* 55–79.

[23]Institute of Medicine—Division of Health. (1978). *A manpower policy for primary health care*. Washington, DC: National Academy of Sciences, p. 29.

[24]Institute of Medicine—Division of Health, *Manpower policy*, p. 41.

[25]National Institute of Mental Health. (1982). *A network for caring: The community support program of the National Institute of Mental Health* (DHHS Publication No. ADM 81-1063). Washington, DC: U.S. Government Printing Office, p. 25.

[26]Institute of Medicine, *Healthy people*, pp. 1-5; U.S. Bureau of the Census (1985). *Statistical abstract of the United States: 1986* (106th ed.). Washington, DC: U.S. Government Printing Office, p. 96.

[27]Yates, *Managing stress*, p. 2.

[28]Selye, *Stress of life*, p. 14.

STRESS CONCEPTS, THEORIES, AND MODELS

It's not the large things that send a man to the madhouse. . . . no, it's the continuing series of small tragedies . . . , not the death of his love but a shoelace that snaps with no time left . . .

Charles Bukowski

The concept of stress is somewhat like the elusive concept of love: Everyone knows what the term means but nobody would define it in exactly the same way. Commonsense definitions, dictionary definitions, and formal scientific definitions all point in the same general direction, but continue on different paths. Hans Selye, the grand master of stress research and theory, said that "stress, like relativity, is a scientific concept which has suffered from the mixed blessing of being too well known and too little understood."[1]

◆ COMMONSENSE AND NOT-SO-COMMON DEFINITIONS

When most people talk about stress, it is usually in terms of pressure they are feeling from something happening in their immediate environment. Students talk about being under stress because of poor exam performance or an impending deadline for a major paper. Parents talk about the stress and strain of raising teenagers and the financial burdens of running a household. Teachers talk about the pressure of maintaining professional currency while still keeping on top of the administrative duties connected with classroom teaching. Doctors, nurses, and lawyers talk about the strain of meeting the seemingly endless demands of their patients and clients.

In each case, it is obvious that several other terms could be used equally well in place of the term *stress*. Two such terms, *pressure* and *strain*, were already substituted without any forewarning. Most readers would probably not notice anything unusual about the substitutions. In fact, *Webster's New*

Hans Selye, the grand master of stress research and discoverer of the General Adaptation Syndrome. *(Courtesy of Karsh of Ottawa/Woodfin Camp)*

Twentieth Century Dictionary uses precisely those two terms to lead into a definition of stress which is "strain; pressure; especially, . . . force exerted upon a body, that tends to strain or deform its shape."

Stress or Distress: The Negative View

Selye used the term *distress* to refer to "damaging or unpleasant stress."[2] Expressed in these terms, stress is much the same as a state of anxiety, fear, worry, or agitation. The core of the psychological experience is negative, painful, something to be avoided. Unfortunately, *stress* and *distress* are used all too often as though they are interchangeable terms. Perhaps this is because the commonsense view of stress is weighted to the negative side. In fact, Selye introduced the terms *distress* and *eustress* in order to avoid this dilemma.

Stress or Eustress: The Positive View

Pleasurable and satisfying experiences come from what Selye calls *eustress*.[3] Participation in a wedding ceremony, anticipation of competing in a major sports event, or performing in a theatrical production are examples of eustress. This is positive stress. The "joy of stress" is now used by some writers to emphasize the good that may come from stress.[4] Eustress heightens awareness, increases mental alertness, and often leads to superior cognitive and behavioral performances. Eustress may supply the arousing motivation for one individual to create a work of art, another an urgently needed medicine, another a scientific theory. It is stress to be sought out and used as an ally for personal and professional growth.

The Yerkes–Dodson law, first formulated in 1908, summarizes the relation between arousal and performance.[5] The law states that, up to a point, performance will increase as arousal increases. Performance will be best when arousal is optimum (not maximum). Beyond the optimal level of arousal, performance begins to deteriorate. Figure 2–1 shows this relation. With exceptionally high levels of tension, performance may be as bad as when a person is not aroused at all. Compare the performance efficiency of someone who is about to fall asleep because of fatigue or boredom with the performance efficiency of someone who is hysterical. Both are inefficient and nonproductive.

The point is that people perform at their best when there is at least a moderate degree of pressure. Too little stress is just as bad as too much. *The aim of stress management is not to eliminate stress entirely, but to control it so that an optimal level of arousal is present.* Selye pointed out that "complete freedom from stress is death."[6] It is the extreme, disorganizing stress that we want to avoid.

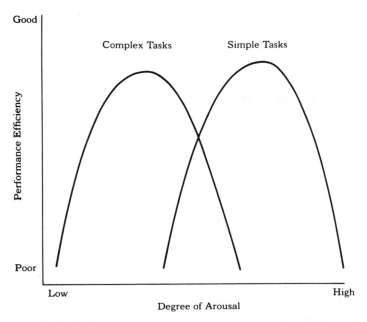

Figure 2–1. Effects of amount of stress or arousal on efficiency of performance.

◆ FORMAL DEFINITIONS OF STRESS

Even in the scientific literature, **stress** is used in three distinct ways. It is used first to refer to an event or to any environmental stimulus that causes a person to feel tense or aroused. In this sense, stress is something *external* to the person. Second, it is used to refer to a subjective response to what is going on. In this sense, stress is the *internal* mental state of tension or arousal. It is the interpretive, emotive, defensive, and coping processes occurring inside the person. Such processes may promote positive growth or produce mental strain. The particular outcome depends on factors that will be explained later when the cognitive model of stress is described. In its third stage, stress is viewed as the *physical reaction* of the body to demand or damaging intrusions. Demand promotes a natural arousal of the body to a higher level of activity, which can be positive and health promoting. Selye viewed it as analogous to the immune system's response to an invading germ.

Stress as External Cause

When speaking of stress as an external stimulus, it is more appropriate to talk of **stressors.** These may be likened to what an engineer means when talking about force, such as the force exerted by cars on a bridge or the pressure of wind against a skyscraper. We are all confronted with demands that put pressure on us: too much work, too little money, too many creditors, the arrival of a baby, the excitement of a new job, and so on. These are the stressors, not the stress. Just as the bridge is designed to withstand the load of cars and trucks, we must have some means of meeting or resisting the pressure of external stressors. We do this through defensive reactions or various coping strategies.

Stress as Psychological Resistance and Tension

Cognitive processes such as problem solving, planning, decision making, and introspective analysis are some of the positive methods for resisting stress. Other cognitive tools such as rationalization, denial, and fantasy have customarily been viewed as negative defenses. However, recent research suggests that these processes may play a very important role in helping people make it through the early stages of recovery from traumatic stress.[7]

Even when the resistance is effective, cognitive side effects are likely to occur during the period of stress. You can respond to stress passively or actively as far as your behavior is concerned. But the mental processes involved in meeting external demands are in some fashion always active, energy consuming, and tension producing.[8] Emotional reactions are likely to be more volatile, marked by increased irritability, explosiveness, and displacement of anger and frustration. Perceptual processes involved in the interpretation of external stimuli may be distorted. Situations previously treated as humorous or nonthreatening become ominous and threatening, and rational planning and decision making may deteriorate or fail to function at all.

It is interesting to note that people frequently use a variety of physical terms to report their personal batting average against stress. They may talk about being on the verge of a physical or emotional collapse. Or they may suggest that they are ready to snap or break down. When the feeling comes that their cognitive, physical, and behavioral coping resources have been taxed to the limit they may say things like "This is beyond me" or "I just can't keep up anymore." Some may even reach a point where they say "I just feel like giving up." These are signs of the cracks in the defensive armor, reflections of the *strain* that they accumulate while enduring stress.

Just as the term *stressor* is best used to refer to forces bearing on a person, *strain* is best used to refer to the effect of that pressure within the person. Selye made a very important point, however: Strain occurs whether the stressor is pleasant or unpleasant. All that "counts is the intensity of the demand for readjustment or adaptation."[9] Whether it is distress or eustress, the demand on coping resources is the same.

Stress as Bodily Defenses

The third definition of stress emphasizes the global biological reaction to stress. Selye stated rather emphatically that *"stress is not merely nervous tension."*[10] Stress is *"the nonspecific response of the body to any demand made upon it."*[11] The body responses are described as a three-part system of neural (hypothalamus), glandular (pituitary and adrenal), and hormonal (adrenaline, for example) reactions to the stressor. Selye rarely if ever dealt with psychological tension as described in the preceding section. But we could also respond to Selye that *stress is not just physical tension*.

To summarize, a **stressor** is defined as an external force. **Strain** has been defined as the wear and tear that are due to resisting the pressure. In this view, stressor is cause and strain is the combined psychological and physiological effect. When the term *stress* or *strain* is used without qualification, both the psychological and physiological defense reactions are implied.

◆ DISTINGUISHING STRESS FROM OTHER EMOTIVE STATES

Several related terms are frequently used in discussions of stress, sometimes almost as though interchangeable. These include *anxiety, conflict, frustration,* and *hassles.* Some clarification of their usage in stress literature may be helpful.

Anxiety

One term frequently used is **anxiety,** or "a specific, unpleasurable state of tension that indicates the presence of some danger to the organism."[12] A clinical definition (used for severe anxiety reactions) says that anxiety is a "sudden onset of intense apprehension, fear, or terror, often associated with feelings of impending doom."[13]

Anxiety is distinguished from fear in that anxiety is a general state of apprehension while fear has a specific object. A person is afraid of spiders or snakes or heights, for example. Anxiety, on the other hand, does not seem to be related to anything in particular, at least not that the person can point to directly.

Distinguishing anxiety from stress, though, is nearly impossible. In fact, one entire volume devoted to stress and anxiety never does make a distinction between the two.[14] Thus, stress and anxiety can both refer to the subjective psychological result of environmental pressure.

Conflict

Competition between two goals results in conflict.[15] Three types of conflict have been identified. **Approach—approach** conflicts occur when two equally desirable goals compete and only one goal can be obtained. A high school graduate who has been accepted to two equally attractive universities may go through some degree of conflict before making a decision.

Avoidance—avoidance conflicts occur when two goals have equally unattractive values. For example, a middle management employee given the choice of taking a demotion with a substantial cut in pay or taking an assignment in Dog Harness, Alaska, at the same rank and salary experiences this type of conflict.

Approach—avoidance conflicts exist when the same goal has both positive and negative features. For example, marriage is usually associated with such positive features as permanence and stability in personal relationships, a sense of teamwork and sharing, and the prospect of family, to name a few. But it is also associated with such negatives as the perception of loss of freedom and independence, sometimes overwhelming responsibility, and an uncertain yet seemingly irreversible commitment to one person. Most of life's day-to-day pressures are probably of an approach—avoidance variety.

Frustration

When some barrier comes between the person and the attainment of a goal, **frustration** occurs. The person who wants to begin a small business but cannot save enough money to get started experiences frustration. Similarly, the person who wants to impress a boss or a potential lover but finds someone else constantly interfering will likely feel frustration.

One of the possible, though not inevitable, outcomes of frustration is aggression. The person wanting to start the business may decide to steal in order to get the money. The person thwarted in an attempt to impress the boss or lover may become verbally or physically aggressive against the person who interferes.

Hamilton believed that anxiety "is the major and most fundamental source of strain in the person."[16] But he also suggested that "the greater the load from these sources [conflict, frustration, and anxiety], the greater the number and the severity of the stressors and the farther the movement towards a limit of 'stress' tolerance."[17]

Hassles

Most recently, Lazarus has suggested that we should adopt the term *hassles* in place of the frequently used and oft-abused *stress*. *Hassles* is used in every-day conversation to convey the sense that pressures are piling up ("I don't need this hassle") or that someone is pressing too hard ("Don't hassle me"). More formally, **hassles** are "the irritating, frustrating, *distressing* demands that in some degree characterize everyday transactions with the environment [italics added]."[18] The types of events used to illustrate hassles include losing the car keys, bills piling up with no end in sight, constant interruptions, not enough time for leisure, the shoelace that breaks with no time left. In comparing hassles with life-changes such as divorce or death of a spouse, Lazarus and his research team found a higher relationship between hassles and illness than between life-change and illness.[19]

◆ BUILDING THEORIES: EXPLANATORY STORIES OF SCIENCE

A variety of theories have been developed to explain what stress is and how it works. Even though the term *theory* tends to sound very formal, theories are really the explanatory stories of science. They provide an organized and coherent picture of some part of nature or some aspect of human behavior. Theories make it possible to predict that an event or behavior will occur under certain conditions. If the theory is proven correct, undesirable outcomes may be prevented in the future through some remedial action.

Some theories, such as Selye's, attempt to decipher the way in which the body responds to stress. Psychological theories attempt to understand the way in which personality, expectations, and interpretations turn a personal or social event into a situation of stress. Social theories provide explanations of stress based more on group conflict and unequal distribution of wealth. Holistic health theories espouse a set of social and personal values based on the idea that body and mind must be treated in unified fashion.

The theory that provides the unifying theme of this book is the *cognitive* or *transactional* model of stress. This model is capable of integrating diverse psychological and social processes that contribute to stress. At the same time, it can be viewed as compatible with the type of physiological analysis presented by Selye.

◆ VARIETIES OF BIOLOGICAL STRESS THEORIES

While there are many biological theories of stress, only two such theories will be discussed. The first is Hans Selye's theory. The second is the genetic–constitutional theory.

The General Adaptation Syndrome

Selye's theory may be summarized in four general statements. (1) All biological organisms have an innate drive to maintain a state of internal balance or equilibrium. The process that maintains an internal balance is called *homeostasis*. As it turns out, maintaining homeostasis is a life-long task. (2) Stressors, such as germs or excessive work demands, disturb internal equilibrium. The body responds to any stressor, whether pleasant or unpleasant, with a nonspecific physiological arousal. This reaction is defensive and self-protective. (3) Adjustment to stress occurs in stages. The time course and progress through the stages depends on how successful the resistance is relative to the intensity and duration of the stressor. (4) The organism has a finite reserve of adaptive energy. When depleted, the organism's ability to cope with continued stress is gone and death may follow.

The pioneer research program that led to this theory was already under way in the 1950s and 1960s. Selye observed that laboratory animals subjected to stress, as might be encountered in learning a difficult task, reacted with signs of physical stress up to and including acute traumatic ulcers of the stomach and subsequent death.[20]

The most celebrated study of this nature, conducted by J. V. Brady, is now referred to as the executive monkey study.[21] Two monkeys were put into a learning situation that involved the delivery of a punishing shock for incorrect responses. But each monkey faced a completely different situation. One monkey, the executive monkey, was solely responsible for engaging in behavior to *prevent* the punishment from being delivered to both himself and his cohort. The second monkey had no control whatsoever. His safety and comfort were solely dependent on the alertness and decision process of the executive monkey.

The outcome of this story is fairly well known. Virtually all of the executive monkeys developed ulcers. Some died. The cohort monkeys with no responsibility suffered little or no ill effects from the experience. It seemed that the demands of work, the responsibility placed on the executives, produced the stress and ultimately death.[22]

Observations based on this type of research led Selye to propose the existence of a three-stage process called the *General Adaptation Syndrome* or GAS (Figure 2-2). The syndrome consists of three stages, which can be summarized as follows.

1. *Alarm reaction.*   The alarm reaction occurs at the first appearance of a stressor. For a short period of time, the body has a lower-than-normal level of resistance. But the body quickly marshals defensive resources and makes self-protective adjustments. If the defensive reactions are successful, the body returns to normal activity and the alarm is past. Most short-term stress is resolved in this phase. Such stress may be called an *acute* stress reaction.

2. *Stage of resistance.*   If stress continues because of factors outside of the organism's control or because the first reaction failed to remove the emergency, the body will call for a full-scale mobilization. The problem is that the body has to expend a lot of resources to win the war. As a result, resistance will generally decrease. In addition, more serious physical symptoms, such as ulcers, may develop. These physical symptoms may reduce resistance even more.

3. *Stage of exhaustion.*   If the stressor is unusually severe or stays on for a long period of time, the body's reserves of energy are further depleted or totally exhausted. Resistance breaks down altogether and death follows shortly after.[23]

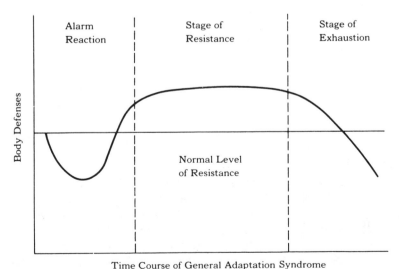

Time Course of General Adaptation Syndrome

Figure 2–2.   Reaction to stress varies with duration of the stressor.

As influential as Selye's theory has been, it must now be viewed as too narrow. One major weakness is that it does not encompass the psychosocial factors of critical importance to understanding human stress.[24]

Genetic–Constitutional Theories

The ability to resist stress is frequently related to coping strategies applied in the face of a current emergency. But a number of factors related to individual *genetic history* affect resistance as well. These factors are called *predisposing* factors. They determine how vulnerable the person is or what the risk is for certain diseases or breakdown. Predisposing factors may be likened to threshold or tolerance factors.

Genetic–constitutional research attempts to establish a link between the genetic makeup (genotype) and some physical characteristic (phenotype) that lowers the person's overall ability to resist stress. There are a number of ways in which genetic factors are thought to reduce resistance. For example, genetic makeup influences balance in the autonomic nervous system, the fight-or-flight emergency reaction system. General temperament is also genetically determined in part. *Temperament,* a very broad term, refers to differences in activity levels (active versus passive), differences in emotionality (pleasant versus unpleasant), and differences in reactivity (hypersensitive versus hyposensitive).[25]

Genes also control the codes for the structure and function of organs and body systems. Of most importance to stress resistance are the kidneys, the cardiovascular system (risks for coronary, high blood pressure, arteriosclerosis), the digestive system (risks for stomach and duodenal ulcers), and the nervous system (imbalance in autonomic system).

◆ THE DIATHESIS–STRESS MODEL

The debate on the relative contribution of inheritance and environment (nature and nurture) to personality and intelligence has raged for decades. While the debate may be far from over, there now is at least some agreement that the issue will never be resolved in favor of one *or* the other but in terms of some combination of the two. The diathesis–stress model has been offered to do just that.

The theory suggests that there is an interplay between *predisposing* and *precipitating* factors. The person's genetic map contributes predisposing factors, such as a lower threshold for stress or a physical weakness that makes the person vulnerable to some type of illness. However, whether that weakness ever shows up or not depends on the amount of stress the person actually experiences. In a relatively sheltered and stress*less* environment, even a very vulnerable person might never show signs of the strain. By the same token, a person under severe and continuous strain might respond poorly even though genetic predispositions are strong.

◆ VARIETIES OF PSYCHOLOGICAL STRESS THEORIES

The major psychological theories include the psychodynamic, learning, and cognitive–transactional models.

The Psychodynamic Model

Sigmund Freud's theory is undoubtedly the accepted standard for the psychodynamic model worldwide. Two kinds of anxiety were described in his revised theory. *Signal* anxiety occurs when there is an objective external danger. It corresponds most closely to the stressor–strain (danger–anxiety) relation. The second, *traumatic* anxiety, refers to instinctual, traumatic, or internally generated anxiety. Examples include anxiety aroused when coping with repressed sexual drives and aggressive instincts. These drives are more or less difficult to deal with depending on the load of unresolved conflicts carried over from early years. Anxiety puts a strain on psychic functioning, which is seen in a variety of "psychopathologies of everyday life"—to use Freud's term.[26] Traumatic anxiety is the dominant form of anxiety in Freud's theory.

The Learning Theory View

As an explanation of stress, learning theory is usually based on one of two models or a combination of the two. The first is the classical conditioning model pioneered by the Russian Nobel laureate in physiology I. P. Pavlov. The second is the operant conditioning model proposed by the American behaviorist B. F. Skinner.

Classical conditioning is illustrated in the famous (or infamous) experiment conducted by the father of behavioral psychology, John Watson. Watson showed 11-month-old Albert a pet rat. Initially, there was no fear of the animal. Later Albert was shown the rat just as a very loud noise was made. Predictably, he responded with fear to the loud sound. After just seven repetitions, however, Albert was afraid of the rat even when no loud sound was present. Fear was also present with a variety of other objects similar to the rat—for example, a rabbit, a sealskin coat, and a Santa Claus mask.

In classical conditioning, the loud noise is viewed as one of a general class of stimuli called **unconditional stimuli** (UCS).[27] These are biologically powerful and unlearned signals most often related to survival needs of the organism. Responses to unconditional stimuli, such as fear, are unlearned and called reflexes or **unconditional responses** (UCR). The stimulus of the rat was from another class of signals called **conditional stimuli** (CS). Prior to any experience with them, conditional stimuli may be regarded as novel or simply neutral stimuli. In order to have any power, they must be associated with a powerful UCS. When a conditional stimulus brings about the response previously produced only by the UCS, the response is called the learned or **conditional response.** When the stimuli are emotionally loaded, as was the case with the rat, the CS may be called the stressor while the state of anxiety and physical arousal may be called the strain.

Two aspects of the conditioning process are important for stress theory. First, emotional responses such as fear and anxiety are complex, including (1) behavioral, (2) psychological, and (3) physiological components. Escape and/or avoidance behaviors serve to keep the person as far away as possible from stressful stimuli. Subjectively, the person experiences a state of internal tension when confronting a feared object or event. Finally, the body becomes physiologically aroused, as reflected by increased blood pressure, heart rate, and body temperature. When conditioning occurs, as in Albert's case, the CS (the rat) is associated with all three components. Thus, very low levels of the stimulus (a picture of a rat) can result in subjective tension and physiological arousal, even though the person does not show it outwardly.

Second, anxiety may become anticipatory after the original conditioning has occurred. Anxiety can be aroused just by talking or thinking about the feared stimulus, even when there is no immediate pressure to confront it. Think of a person who is afraid of snakes. When the subject of snakes is introduced into the conversation, the person may visibly tense, even physically shudder, and then ask that the topic be dropped. If the person has previously failed to control the anxiety while confronting a fear-laden situation, the anxiety can be disabling, keeping the individual from enjoying normal pleasures.

Operant conditioning theory proposes that behavior changes because the behavior produces either good or bad outcomes. When the behavior produces pleasant outcomes, or rewards, the behavior increases. When the behavior produces unpleasant outcomes, or punishment, the behavior decreases. Explanations of stress from an operant perspective place most emphasis on the acquisition of avoidance behavior and the discriminative control of symptomatic behavior.

Avoidance behavior is viewed as an operant behavior engaged in to reduce learned fear or anxiety. For Albert, associating the rat with the loud noise served to condition a fear response to the rat. Fear is an unpleasant emotion that increases internal tension. People generally try to reduce or remove unpleasant tension. Since running away from the rat will reduce the tension, the behavior of running away is strengthened. In other words, if the rat appears again, the most likely response is flight. In general, any stressful situation that produces high or unmanageable levels of anxiety is likely to motivate some form of escape or avoidance.

This model may explain why people have difficulty in certain types of interpersonal relationships. For example, a supervisor is given the unpleasant task of telling an employee that his or her work is below expectations. Confronting the employee with such information can be very stressful, especially if the supervisor has had difficulties in the past. This may lead to any number of escape or avoidance behaviors such as putting the confrontation off as long as possible, writing the employee a note instead of talking face to face, couching the information in terms that obscure or distort the important information, or delegating the responsibility to someone else. The original reasons for anxiety are not really important. Once anxiety is conditioned, some type of avoidance behavior is likely to occur.

◆ THE COGNITIVE–TRANSACTIONAL MODEL OF STRESS

The way in which people perceive and label events, store information about their experiences, and retrieve and use that information in confronting new experiences is important to the arousal of stress and to the coping strategies employed to deal with stress. Cognitive researchers attempt to understand stress mechanisms in terms of the way in which information is processed at different stages in its pathway through the brain.

Cognitive theorists assume that humans are active, reasoning, and deciding beings. They also assume that people construct schemata, or mental blueprints. **Schemata** represent what the person has learned about how the world works and how to relate to it. Certain schemata may be almost universal, such as the schema for gravity. Other types of schemata, such as a schema for teacher–student relationships, always show a high degree of personal uniqueness.

Over the years, there have been a number of so-called transactional theories. The model that will be developed in more detail in Chapter 4 was developed by Richard S. Lazarus.[28] The theory is sometimes known as the cognitive–phenomenological approach. As explained by Lazarus, the theory has roots deeply planted in a number of scientific soils such as the cognitive sciences, personality theory, attitude research, social research, health research, and behavioral medicine. Lazarus accepts the fact that stress can have a powerful impact on health and conversely that health can change the person's resistance or coping ability. The theory is thus not a one-sided stress theory or a one-sided health theory.

The central point of the transactional model is that stress is "neither an environmental stimulus, a characteristic of the person, nor a response but a relationship between demands and the power to deal with them without unreasonable or destructive costs."[29] It is obvious that a *relational* analysis is the key to this theory. There are some important implications to be drawn from this statement.

First, the same environmental event may be interpreted as stressful by one person but not another. This indicates that most external stimuli cannot be defined in any absolute sense as stressful. What makes the event stressful or not depends on some cognitive appraisal by the person. Second, the same person may interpret an event as stressful on one occasion but not on another. This may be due to changes in physical condition or changes in psychological states. For example, the person might be physically relaxed or rested at one time and tense or tired at another time. Also, emotional and motivational states can differ from one time to another affecting the appraisal process.

◆ VARIETIES OF SOCIAL STRESS THEORIES

A number of social theories focus on the integration of the individual into society and the numerous tensions that are part of any society. These are called *conflict theories*. A major source of tension is that society has to engage in some degree of coercion to get members to adhere to social norms. One conflict theorist believes that a crucial problem is affording members of society more *life chances,* or opportunities for individual growth.[30] In addition, conflict theories look at such variables as the stability of social relationships, the distribution of economic goods and services in the society, and the distribution of interpersonal power and personal control. The general relationship of each of the conflict variables to stress is fairly obvious. Stress is theoretically associated with less stable social relationships, with poverty and lack of access to necessary social services, and with low power and personal control.

Evolutionary theory views social change and tension as the inevitable result of social development. People must simply accept the fact of social change and accommodate to it rather than fight against it. Another type of theory, *environmental–ecological,* explains stress in terms of conditions such as crowding, pollution, health hazards from industrialization, and environmental accidents. Finally, *life-change theory* explains stress by reference to life-changes that require major adaptations by the person. Such events as the death of a spouse, bankruptcy, being fired, or being informed of life-threatening illness fit in the category of major events requiring substantial adjustments by the person.

◆ THE HOLISTIC HEALTH MODEL

Holistic theory has many faces. It has come to be regarded as a movement with political and economic overtones, a religion of life-style and self-sufficiency practiced ardently by a group of true believers, a humanistic philosophy with seemingly antiscientific sentiments, or a counterculture with antimedical establishment themes. It is all of these, and yet goes beyond any of these.

The term has unfortunately come to encompass every type of health practice from herbal medicine, acupuncture, and organic gardening to yogic meditation, laying on of hands, and biofeedback. It is to some extent a reaction to biological reductionism and medical specialization in Western medicine but it reacts without being antiscientific. The holistic movement sees Western medicine as dehumanizing and devaluing the role of mental processes in health and healing. Holistic health has also been seen as a synthesizing movement trying to regain a sense of humane medical treatment and respect for the whole person, a medical tradition that has existed without interruption since ancient times and is most visible in Eastern medical tradition.

In his edited volume *Ways of Health,* David Sobel stated that the word *holistic* "more precisely and most simply describes an *attitude* or *mode of perception* that attempts to view *the whole person in the context of the total environment.*"[31] According to Alvin Burstein and Sandra Loucks, there are three trademarks of the holistic health movement. These are "(1) a recognition of human complexity and diversity, (2) an emphasis on the importance of mental events and personal value systems, and (3) a recognition of the desirability of responsibility for oneself."[32] Daniel Girdano and George Everly propose that *holistic* is "the concept underlying an approach to controlling stress and tension that deals with the complete lifestyle of the individual, incorporating intervention at several levels—physical, psychological, and social—simultaneously."[33]

Properly speaking, however, the holistic health model cannot be regarded as a scientific theory. While research can be presented to support what the holistic model preaches, it does not generate research itself and does not have the formal properties of scientific theory. Holistic health thus seems to be oriented more toward attitude change than toward explaining stress and health.

◆ SUMMARY

This overview has provided working definitions for basic terms to be used throughout the book. The external source or cause of stress has been defined as the *stressor.* The internal tension, be it psychological tension (such as anxiety) or a physical defense reaction, has been defined as *stress* or *strain.*

Several theories commonly encountered in stress and health research have been reviewed. This review has been representative and summarizing rather than exhaustive and intensive. It is presented primarily to provide a context and reference point for materials to be presented in subsequent chapters.

◆ NOTES

[1]Selye, H. (1980). The stress concept today. In I. L. Kutash, L. B. Schlesinger, & associates (Eds.), *Handbook on stress and anxiety.* San Francisco: Jossey-Bass, Chapter 7, p. 127.

[2]Selye, H. (1974). *Stress without distress.* Philadelphia: Lippincott, p. 31.

[3]Selye, H. (1979). The stress concept and some of its implications. In V. Hamilton & D. M. Warburton (Eds.), *Human stress and cognition: An information processing approach.* New York: Wiley, Chapter 3, p. 70.

[4]Hanson, P. G. (1986). *The joy of stress*. Fairway, KS: Andrews, McMeel & Parker.

[5]Yerkes, R. M., & Dodson, J. D. (1908). The relation of strength of stimulus to rapidity of habit formation. *Journal of Comparative and Neurological Psychology, 18*, 459–482.

[6]Selye, *Stress without distress*, p. 32.

[7]This material with full references will be reviewed in more detail in Chapter 4, "The Cognitive Stress System."

[8]*Tension* should be taken here in its most natural sense of "aroused and straining." When you get involved in a TV murder mystery, you may actively try to figure out who did it. You are then in a state of mental tension. But it has no implication of overload or negative strain. It does not mean the system is undergoing extreme strain like a rope tensed to the point of breaking.

[9]Selye, *Stress without distress*, pp. 28–29.

[10]Selye, *Stress without distress*, p. 30.

[11]Selye, *Stress without distress*, p. 27.

[12]Budzynski, T. H., & Peffer, K. E. (1980). Biofeedback training. In Kutash, Schlesinger, & associates, *Handbook on stress*, p. 413. Budzynski and Peffer are themselves citing the accepted definition of Weiss and English given in 1957.

[13]American Psychiatric Association. (1980). *Diagnostic and statistical manual of mental disorders* (3rd ed.). Washington, DC: Author, p. 230.

[14]This is a reference to the book by Kutash, Schlesinger, & associates, *Handbook on stress*.

[15]The literature on conflict is generally traced to the following sources: Miller, N. (1944). Experimental studies in conflict. In J. McV. Hunt (Ed.), *Personality and the behavior disorders* (Vol. 1). New York: Ronald Press, pp. 431–465; Dollard, J., Doob, L. W., Miller, N. E., Mowrer, O. H., & Sears, R. R. (1939). *Frustration and aggression*. New Haven, CT: Yale University Press; Lewin, K. (1948). *Resolving social conflicts*. New York: Harper & Row.

[16]Hamilton & Warburton, *Human stress*, p. 86.

[17]Hamilton & Warburton, *Human stress*, p. 80.

[18]Kanner, A. D., Coyne, J. C., Schaefer, C., & Lazarus, R. S. (1981). Comparison of two modes of stress measurement: Daily hassles and uplifts versus major life events. *Journal of Behavioral Medicine, 4*, 3.

[19]Life-change research will be reviewed in detail in Chapter 7. While Lazarus's argument has merit, what can be learned from a study of life-change research is still of great importance.

[20]Selye, H. (1974). *The stress of life*. New York: McGraw-Hill.

[21]Brady, J. V., Porter, R. W., Conrad, D. G., & Mason, J. W. (1958). Avoidance behavior and the development of gastroduoedenal ulcers. *Journal of the Experimental Analysis of Behavior, 1*, 69–72.

[22]One interesting sidelight to this line of research was discovered by other investigators attempting to follow up on Brady's famous executive monkey study. Essentially, it was determined that it was during the period of time off—in other words, the vacation time—that the ulcers developed in the executive monkeys, not during the working time.

[23]Selye, H. (1980). The stress concept today. In Kutash, Schlesinger, & associates, *Handbook on stress,* Chapter 7, p. 129. This chapter may be one of the most precise statements of Selye's theory available. Also, the research supporting the theory will be presented in more detail in Chapter 3, "The Physiology of Stress."

[24]Vernon Hamilton echoed this point of view when he suggested forthrightly that Selye's "level of analysis does not immediately help, however, when considering traditional conceptions of emotional tension or strain, their relationship to social vulnerability or to successfully completed, adaptive behaviour, *and the cognitive structures* which must mediate between them." See Hamilton, V. (1979). "Personality" and stress. In Hamilton & Warburton, *Human stress,* Chapter 3, p. 70.

[25]Fuller, J. L., & Thompson, W. R. (1978). *Foundations of behavior genetics.* St. Louis, MO: Mosby. Chapter 10 offers a review of the research in this area.

[26]Freud, S. *The psychopathology of everyday life* (A. Tyson, Trans.). New York: Norton.

[27]I am departing from the American convention of using *conditioned* in each of the four basic terms. This was an unfortunate error in translating the terms from Pavlov's Russian texts into English. It is more accurate to say *conditional,* which also makes it much plainer what the terms mean: *conditional* meaning "dependent upon" and *unconditional* meaning "not dependent upon." Thus, the UCS does not depend on anything for its power while the CS depends on prior association with the UCS in order to acquire power.

[28]Lazarus, R. S., & Launier, R. (1978). Stress-related transactions between person and environment. In L. A. Pervin & M. Lewis (Eds.), *Perspectives in interactional psychology.* New York: Plenum Press.

[29]Coyne, J. C., & Holroyd, K. (1982). Stress, coping, and illness: A transactional perspective. In T. Millon, C. Green, & R. Meagher (Eds.), *Handbook of clinical health psychology,* New York: Plenum Press, Chapter 6, p. 108.

[30]Dahrendorf, R. (1979). *Lebenschancen.* Frankfurt: Suhrkamp,. p. 92, cited in H. Strasser & S. Randall (1981). *An introduction to theories of social change.* London: Routledge & Kegan Paul, p. 49.

[31]Sobel, D. S. (1979). *Ways of health: Holistic approaches to ancient and contemporary medicine.* New York: Harcourt Brace Jovanovich, pp. 15, 16.

[32]Burstein, A. G, & Loucks, S. (1982). The psychologist as health care clinician. In Millon, Green, & Meagher, *op. cit.,* Chapter 9, p. 179.

[33]Girdano, D. A., & Everly, G. S. (1979). *Controlling stress and tension: A holistic approach.* Englewood Cliffs, NJ: Prentice-Hall, p. 20.

Part 2

THE STRESS RESPONSE

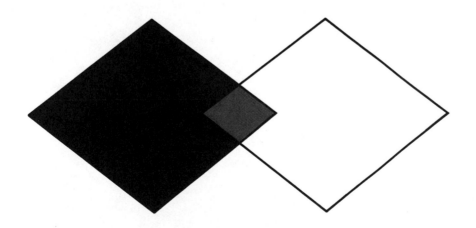

3

THE PHYSIOLOGY OF STRESS: THE BRAIN, BODY, AND IMMUNE SYSTEMS

It is highly dishonorable for a Reasonable Soul to live in so Divinely built a Mansion as the Body she resides in, altogether unacquainted with the exquisite structure of it.

Robert Boyle

The body is perhaps the most beautiful, intricate, yet efficient machine ever devised. The more we come to understand its design, the more we stand in awe of its perfection. At the same time, the more we understand its intricacies, the more mystery seems to unfold. For every door opened in the labyrinth of the body, more doors appear that still need to be opened.

The next few pages will provide a tour through the body beautiful, the body functioning as it was intended to function. Six systems have been singled out for discussion. These are the nervous, respiratory, endocrine, immune, cardiovascular, and digestive systems. These systems were selected because they (1) are implicated by stress research as central to the defensive reactions of the body, (2) are most frequently abused through misbehavior, or (3) can be influenced through modest behavioral and/or attitudinal life-style changes.

◆ CHARTING THE BACK ROADS OF THE MIND

Tracking the flow of information through a system as complex as the body is not an easy job. The problem is made all the more difficult because of an intricate system of checks and balances, duplicate pathways and feedback circuits, which serve to keep everything running in harmony . . . most of the time. Duplication of pathways (referred to as *redundancy*) makes it possible to keep in communication with other parts of the brain and body, even when there is a traffic jam in one pathway. Feedback circuits allow the brain to regulate or modify (or *attenuate*) new input at different stages of processing. In spite of this complexity, exciting progress has been made in recent years that provides some understanding of the body's most complex organ. Because this chapter is intended only to provide the basics necessary to understand stress and health physiology, the actual relations have been simplified to some extent.

◆ MIND, BRAIN, AND BODY: SOME DEFINITIONS

The terms *mind, brain,* and *body* will be used frequently in the course of this and later discussions. Because the issue of mind–body relationships has been a thorn in the flesh of science for a long time, there is some need to make clear how these terms will be used.

The term **mind** will be used to mean all the processes of the brain, whether we are aware of these processes as they occur or not. It is what is going on when we remember, make decisions, solve problems, reason, reflect, and observe our own reflections. **The mental system** will be used to refer to the interconnected operations of the mind—for example, perceiving, evaluating, reflecting on, and responding to external stimuli. The term **brain** refers to the mass of neural tissue housed in the skull.

There is no dispute that the brain is a physical organ. But it seems safe to say that the way in which it behaves and our awareness of some of this behavior makes the brain difficult to talk about without considering its uniqueness. That uniqueness is still conveyed best through using such terms as *mind* and *mental process.* There is no need to become bogged down in a dispute over mind–body relationships. This dispute has not been resolved in centuries of debate. In addition, no empirical data or logic will serve to resolve the issue to everyone's satisfaction.[1]

◆ THE BRAIN: ITS ROLE IN STRESS AND HEALTH

Of all the systems of the body, the brain probably still holds more mysteries than all others. It may be one of the last frontiers in the quest for understanding how the body works. Learning how the brain works has been likened to climbing a ladder with 100 rungs on it. In spite of the amount that we now know, and no matter how far we think we have come, we are still no further than the first or second rung on the ladder.

The nervous system is divided into two parts, the *central nervous system* (CNS) and the *peripheral nervous system* (PNS). The central nervous system is further divided into the brain and spinal cord. The peripheral nervous system is also divided into two subsystems. These are the *autonomic nervous system* and the *somatic nervous system.* Finally, the autonomic nervous system has two major parts, the *parasympathetic* and the *sympathetic nervous systems.* Figure 3–1 summarizes these divisions. The brain and the autonomic systems are most important to the discussion of how the body reacts to stress.

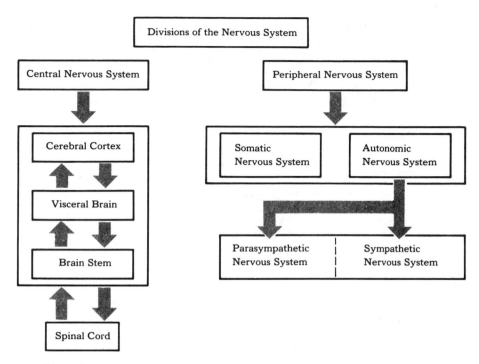

Figure 3–1.   Major divisions of the nervous system.

Neuroanatomists, scientists who specialize in mapping the structure of the brain, now recognize several layers of tissue in the brain. Each layer marks a distinct stage in the development of the brain. These layers from oldest to newest are the brain stem, the visceral brain (made up of many different parts), and the new brain (neocortex) or cerebral cortex.

The Brain Stem

The **brain stem** is a bulblike outgrowth at the top of the spinal column. It houses many structures that keep vital life functions (such as breathing and heart activity) going without any deliberate attention on our part. The brain stem structures of concern here include the medulla and the reticular activating system. Figure 3–2 shows these structures.

The medulla is like Grand Central Station. It contains all of the nerve fibers both arriving from the body and departing the brain through the spinal cord. Two types of nerve fibers leave the brain through this concourse. These are the autonomic nerves, which control many visceral activities, and the motor nerves (corticospinal tract) for control of muscles.[2]

In addition to the sensory and motor nerves, the brain stem contains many separate nuclei, which are called *autonomic nuclei.* These nuclei carry on life-supporting processes such as respiration, heart action, and digestion. For example, the rhythmic nature of breathing is regulated by the brain stem respiratory center. In normal states, there is a relatively even rate of

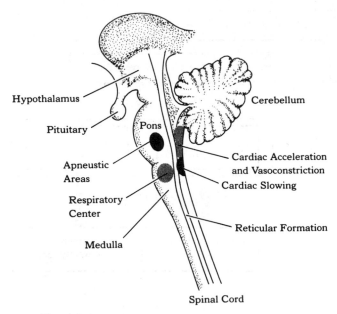

Figure 3–2.   Brain stem and reticular system with cardiovascular and respiratory control centers.

breathing (about 12 breaths per minute)[3] and good balance between inhalration and exhalation (about 2 seconds and 3 seconds, respectively).[4] However, stress can alter this balance, as illustrated by a variety of everyday situations. Stress in public speaking may result in the appearance of being out of breath. Stepping into a cold shower, having a loud firecracker go off unexpectedly, or having someone run a red light in front of you may cause a catch in your breath followed by a more rapid rate of breathing for a short period.

During such events, the cortex signals the autonomic respiratory nuclei, which in turn signal the respiratory system itself. The balance of inhalation and exhalation may be tipped in the direction of more inhalation or very deep breathing, which puts more oxygen in the blood than normal. There may also be an increase in the actual rate of breathing.

Anxiety Hyperventilation

A condition called *anxiety hyperventilation* shows what can happen under extreme stress. In **hyperventilation,** there is an excessive ventilation of the blood supply as it tries to release carbon dioxide. When this happens, the person may feel dizzy to the point of blacking out. Shortness of breath may occur and the heart may feel as though it is pounding. The person may also experience **parathesia,** a numbness or tingling in parts of the body. This can heighten anxiety since it is generally perceived as a sign of a heart attack. Thus, in addition to being very uncomfortable, the experience can be frightening.

Hyperventilation is regarded as psychogenic in origin. In other words, it is a condition that comes from phychological traits and social circumstances rather than from physical pathology. The condition can be relieved in one of two ways. One is to breathe voluntarily at a measured slow pace or to hold the breath for short periods. The other is to breathe into a paper bag and rebreathe the same air.

Control over the activity of the heart also comes from autonomic nuclei in the brain stem. Both the sympathetic and parasympathetic sides of the autonomic system operate to keep the heart pumping smoothly. The sympathetic system drives the heart to higher rates when necessary. Sometimes it can drive the heart to beat as many as 250 beats per minute (normal is 70). But the action of the sympathetic system also increases the strength of the heartbeat. On the other hand, the parasympathetic system tends to moderate the strength of the beat as well as decrease the rate.

The Reticular Activating System

The **reticular activating system** (RAS) is a bundle of fibers that runs like a great rope through the middle of the brain stem upward into the hypothalamus and thalamus. It may be viewed as the great sentry system of the brain. In general, the work of the RAS is threefold: two-way communication between brain and body, selection of sensory information for processing by the cortex (gating), and vigilance or arousal.

Brain–body communication.   The reticular formation serves as one of the primary two-way streets for communication between the brain and the rest of the body. In fact, one way to divide the RAS is on the basis of the descending reticular pathway and the ascending reticular pathway. The descending pathway relays signals from the hypothalamus to a number of organs controlled by the autonomic system. It also relays involuntary motor impulses to voluntary muscles.

Psychosocial stressors are communicated to the body via the descending pathway and the hypothalamic–pituitary pathway. These connections are shown in Figure 3–3. In this way, nonphysical stressors are able to initiate major changes in physical systems. The most important changes occur in the cardiovascular, glandular, and immune systems. With prolonged stress, these changes may produce undesirable effects.

On the other hand, physical stressors, such as extreme temperatures and body injury, are communicated to the brain via the ascending RAS. These stressors may be translated into a variety of emotional states producing psychological discomfort and tension. Awareness of pain is jointly overseen by the reticular and thalamic centers. Because pain usually produces negative emotions, an amplification effect may occur that increases sensitivity to the pain itself. However, normal healing processes are also stimulated. In fact, the body can produce its own analgesiclike substances to reduce the level of pain experienced while healing is in process. More will be said about this later.

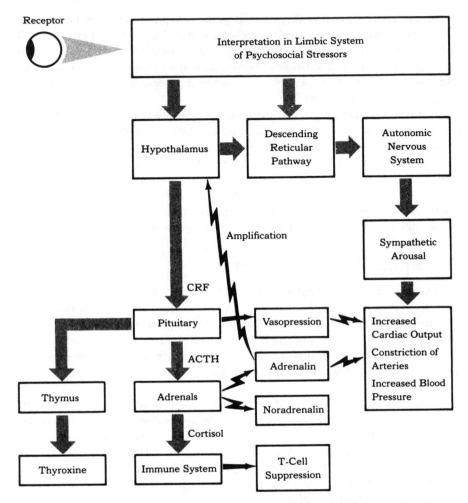

Figure 3–3. Effects of prolonged stress in the hypothalamic–pituitary–adrenal complex and autonomic systems.

Gating.   The RAS receives inputs either directly or indirectly from all of the sensory systems of the body. In turn, it can influence the sensitivity of receptors (such as the eyes and ears) and relay stations for any of the senses. The general outcome of this changing sensitivity is to help the flow of information through one sensory channel while restricting the flow in another. Because of this, a great amount of information initially sent to the brain may be lost or distorted. This may not seem like a very efficient way of doing business, but it actually serves to ensure that really important information gets where it is needed.

To borrow some terms from communication theory, the RAS works to increase the ratio of signal to noise. If every bit of sensory information were allowed to enter the brain, the brain would quite simply be overwhelmed. Think of what it would be like having every radio and every TV running full blast while every member of your family is talking at once. That is noise! When the radios and TVs are turned down to background level, the sound from only one person talking is signal. By being more selective in what gets through, the brain can maintain its overall operation at a higher level of efficiency.

One very important issue is, How does the RAS know what information is important and what is not? At present, only the most general answers can be given to this question. The RAS has inputs from virtually every part of the brain including centers responsible for motivation, emotion, attention, and associative processes. Changes in any of these internal states can bias the way in which the RAS selects information. An example will illustrate this point.

Think of a parent who puts the baby in its crib for a nap and then takes a brief nap also. The TV is on and there is a moderate level of street noise. In spite of this, the parent rests comfortably, blocking the noise out effectively. Then the baby whimpers softly, its cry not as loud as the other sounds. The parent gets up and immediately tends to the child. The motivational strength attached to the baby's cry permits it to get through and awaken the sleeping parent.

Vigilance and arousal.   The third function of the RAS, vigilance or arousal, is most important to the way in which the higher brain centers work. As described earlier, the RAS looks out for important information reaching the senses. Then it provides an alerting signal to higher centers of the brain, warning that something important is coming. Additional evidence of its function comes from surgical procedures that isolate the cortex from the RAS and from clinical observations when damage has occurred from the RAS. If it is damaged in a certain area, activity in the cortex is depressed. In some cases, coma will occur.

The Visceral Brain

The **visceral brain** is a complex set of structures lying virtually in the center of the brain. It is called the *visceral brain* because of its many connections with the hypothalamus, which itself controls most of the visceral processes having to do with basic biological survival. Because potentially emotional stimuli are interpreted in this complex, it must be considered central to any explanation of the way in which the brain responds to stress. The most important structures are the thalamus, the hypothalamus–pituitary complex, and additional centers associated with the limbic system. These structures are diagrammed in Figure 3–4.

The thalamus.   The **thalamus** is the major relay center for every sensory system except the sense of smell. It is in an excellent position to evaluate the emotional content of information provided by the senses. The first

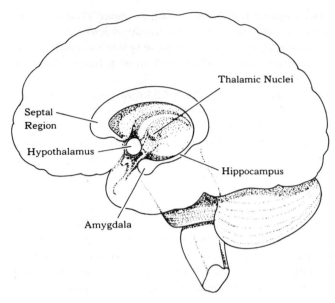

Figure 3–4.   Cross section of the cerebral cortex showing the major limbic system nuclei for control of emotions.

clinical observations supporting this view were based on patients who had physical damage to the thalamus. Such people were observed to overreact to emotional stimuli. Other patients also showed uncontrollable weeping or laughing without any accompanying subjective experience.[5]

One of the more interesting recent discoveries is the role the thalamus plays in the perception of pain. Pain researchers commonly identify three types of pain: pricking pain, which comes from a knife cut or a needle, for example; burning pain; and aching pain, which is a deep muscle or bone pain.[6] Each of the specialized neural pain pathways terminate in the thalamus. Burning and aching pain also have connections to the RAS.

The potential for exercising cognitive control over the perception of pain, through such mechanisms as shutting the neural gates that communicate pain[7] or increasing the level of *endorphins* (literally, the morphine within) in this region, is not yet fully understood. But some promising steps are being taken to provide therapies for people with chronic pain. Stimulation techniques have been developed that depend on this knowledge. These have enabled terminally ill patients to control the level of their pain without the use of drugs.

The limbic system.   The **limbic system** is part of the primitive brain concerned with survival. It includes the thalamus, hypothalamus, amygdala, hippocampus, and septum. Refer again to Figure 3–4 for details. The functions most often associated with the limbic system include anger, aggression, punishment, reward, sexual arousal, and pain.

For example, when the amygdala is damaged, greatly increased appetite frequently appears. Damage to the septum generally results in an overall increase in emotionality. Extreme irritability and rage responses with unprovoked aggression may occur. The amygdala produces the opposite type of reaction, suggesting that these two serve to balance aggressive tendencies: the amygdala starting and the septum moderating aggressive tendencies. The septum and hypothalamus have also been implicated as major reward or pleasure centers in the brain.

Damage to the hippocampus can cause deficits in long-term memory and may slow down or block several types of learning. Most often, these are learning processes that require some kind of avoidance or discrimination response. Because of its intimate connections with the entire emotional–motivational complex, it is possible that many distortions in memory from emotionally loaded content are related to the way the hippocampus works.

The hypothalamus.   The general location of the hypothalamus is just above the roof of the mouth, toward the back. It is directly connected to the pituitary gland, which is also called the master gland of the body. Through this connection, the hypothalamus has very powerful effects on nearly every visceral system in the body. Another measure of the significance of the hypothalamus is that virtually every part of the brain has some type of connection to it. For example, the hypothalamus is highly integrated with the RAS and the limbic system.

Because of this connection, it can respond directly to psychological and emotional stimuli. It also responds to cognitive stressors originating in the cortex. Sexual behavior originates in the limbic region but depends on the hypothalamus for control. The limbic system is also able to influence the operation of the autonomic system through this same arrangement. Sleep appears to be jointly controlled by centers in both the hypothalamus and the RAS. Finally, the hypothalamus is very richly supplied with blood so that it can monitor such things as the level of nutrients in the blood, body fluid volume, and concentration of hormones originating in other parts of the body. The latter is very important in amplifying and moderating stress reactions.

But the role of the hypothalamus in stress is most clearly revealed in four specific functions. These are (1) initiating activity in the autonomic nervous system, (2) stimulating the secretion of ACTH (adrenocorticotrophic hormone) from the anterior pituitary, (3) producing ADH (antidiuretic hormone) or vasopressin, and (4) stimulating the thyroid glands to produce thyroxine. To accomplish these tasks, the hypothalamus has two dedicated centers that regulate the stress response. One center (the anterior lateral, meaning to the front and side) slows down sympathetic activity. It also inhibits the production of pituitary stress hormones. The second center (the posterior medial, or toward the back and middle) stimulates the sympathetic system and the production of pituitary stress hormones. Understanding these four functions is central to understanding how the stress response begins.

The Autonomic Nervous System

The **autonomic nervous system** (ANS) is the primary control system for three different types of tissues. These include cardiac muscle, most of the glands, and all smooth muscle.[8] It controls heart activity, blood pressure, digestion, urinary and bowel elimination, and many other body functions. The ANS is controlled from the brain stem, hypothalamus, and spinal cord.

The ANS has two parts, the parasympathetic and the sympathetic. These two systems exist in a state of dynamic but antagonistic tension. When one is active the other is relatively quiet or passive, and vice versa. It is not possible for both systems to be working at a high level at the same time.

The parasympathetic system is in control when we are in a quiet and relaxed state. Most of the positive reconstructive processes occur during this time. Blood is concentrated in the organs of the body for such important work as digestion and storage of energy reserves. Breathing tends to be slow and balanced. Heart rate and blood pressure are both reduced. Body temperature also drops and muscles are generally relaxed.

The sympathetic system is called the fight-or-flight system. It is in control in emergency situations or in states of heightened emotionality. This alarm or stress response originates within the hypothalamus. Guyton has identified eight effects of sympathetic arousal. Paraphrased, these are

1. increased blood pressure,
2. increased blood flow to the large active muscles coupled with decreased blood flow to internal (for example, digestive) organs not needed for rapid activity,
3. increased energy consumption throughout the body,
4. increased blood glucose concentration,
5. increased energy release in muscles,
6. increased muscle strength,
7. increased mental activity, and
8. increased rate of blood coagulation.[9]

When the emergency is over, the hypothalamus activates the parasympathetic system again. In this way, repair of destructive effects from the emergency period is begun.

You have probably heard more than once that you are not supposed to eat while angry—that you should engage only in pleasant conversation while eating. The reason is that anger changes salivary and digestive processes. Indigestion can occur because the body is not prepared to work on food in the stomach during an aroused emotional state. Most of the blood needed for this work has been redistributed to the muscles. Some other undesirable effects of prolonged sympathetic arousal include elevated blood pressure and ulcers.

The Master Gland

The **master gland,** or pituitary, secretes six important hormones (and several less important hormones) from its anterior region and two from its posterior section. Virtually all of its secretions are under the direct control of the hypothalamus. The hypothalamus produces its own hormones to accomplish this. One hormone, the corticotropin-releasing factor (CRF), tells the anterior pituitary to release ACTH. Release of ACTH moves the adrenal glands to action. Almost any kind of stress, whether physical or psychological, will lead to a nearly instantaneous increase in the level of ACTH. This is followed shortly after by the secretion of several hormones from the adrenals including cortisol, epinephrine, and norepinephrine.

Cortisol is also known as hydrocortisone. In general, the effect of this hormone is to provide more energy to the body through conversion of body stores into glucose. Recently, cortisol has been implicated in suppression of the immune system. The outcome of immune suppression is reduced resistance to infections and disease. But the major concern is the possible role immune suppression has in the development of cancer.[10] This will be discussed in more detail later in this chapter. The general relationship to stress is diagrammed in Figure 3–5.

The other two major hormones secreted by the adrenal glands are epinephrine (also called adrenaline) and norepinephrine (also called noradrenaline). The general effect of these hormones is the same as that of the sympathetic nervous system. In fact, the action of the adrenal glands amplifies the action of the sympathetic nervous system. The levels of epinephrine and norepinephrine vary with the intensity of stimulation of the system. Under conditions of high stress, the system can be virtually flooded with epinephrine and norepinephrine.

Epinephrine has a very powerful effect on the heart. It increases both the rate and the strength of contractions. It also has a general tendency to increase blood pressure. By a feedback loop to the hypothalamus, it tends to increase the secretion of ACTH and other hormones. This amplifies the effect of changes in other visceral systems as well as increasing the level of activity in its own loop. This is why activation of the hypothalamic–pituitary–adrenal (HPA) complex can have have such powerful effects under conditions of prolonged stress.

For a short period, many psychologists believed that specific emotions would someday be linked to specific physical processes. In this view, love might be a specific neural–hormonal pattern that is always the same for any person feeling love. Some other emotion—for example, happiness—might be associated with a much different neural–hormonal pattern. Up to now, the only reliably proven association between a neural–hormonal pattern and a specific emotion involves epinephrine and norepinephrine. In general, epinephrine is found in connection with fear while norepinephrine is found when anger occurs.

Recently, the respective roles of epinephrine and norepinephrine in stress reactions have been clarified. In general, early work led researchers to suspect that epinephrine is most important when stress is of a mental variety. Such tasks as mental arithmetic, continued vigilance, and public speaking were all presumably associated with increased levels of this hormone in the bloodstream. On the other hand, norepinephrine was believed to be

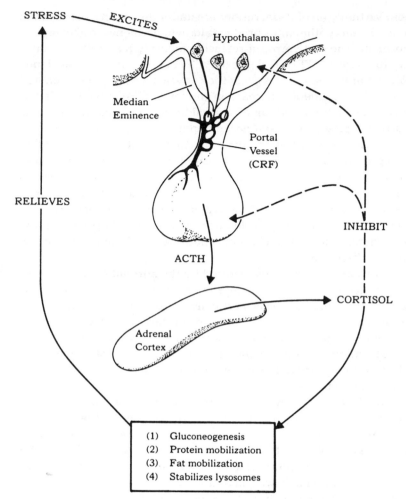

Figure 3–5. Stress excitation and adrenal inhibition in the hypothalamic–pituitary–adrenal complex.

associated with physical stressors such as being immobilized,[11] being submerged in ice water,[12] isometric stress, and physical exercise. However, the evidence supporting this division of duty was often inconclusive, if not contradictory.

Using a rather sophisticated continuous blood-sampling technique along with a high-power statistical procedure called time-series analysis, a team of Stanford researchers verified the long-suspected relationship.[13] They also discovered the reason for the early confusing results. It appears that the two hormones behave much differently in speed of reaction and the speed at which they clear out of the bloodstream. Epinephrine is very fast acting and also gets out of the bloodstream quickly. Norepinephrine, however, appears to clear out of the bloodstream much more slowly. When mental and physical tasks were mixed in testing procedures, especially with the mental tasks coming later, norepinephrine appeared to be related to mental activity. But it was because the norepinephrine was not leaving fast enough to give a clear reading.

Vasopressin

Vasopressin (ADH) is one of the two major hormones produced in the hypothalamus but released by the posterior section of the pituitary gland. In addition to regulating fluid loss through the urinary system, vasopressin influences heart activity and blood pressure. Both volume and pressure of blood in the venous cavities of the heart are monitored by receptors that feed information to the hypothalamus. If volume and pressure are low, vasopressin in increased. If the volume and pressure are high, vasopressin production is reduced. In this way the output of the heart is regulated. More importantly, when blood pressure is low, vasopressin exerts a very powerful effect by constricting arteries—thus causing an increase in blood pressure. A severe loss of blood volume, such as occurs in a traumatic injury, leads to immediate and dramatic increases in the production of ADH to preserve pressure and restore volume. In addition, vasopressin can have a direct effect on vasoconstriction. In periods of severe stress, its release from the hypothalamus may serve to elevate already high blood pressure caused by other neural and hormonal processes.[14]

The Thyroid Glands and Thyroxine

Physical and psychological stress can have powerful effects on the rate of **metabolism,** the rate at which fuel for the body is burned. Such changes influence mood, energy, nervous irritability, and mental alertness. These changes are regulated in a three-step sequence from the hypothalamus, through the pituitary, and to the thyroid where the hormone *thyroxine* is released.

When a demand is placed on the system, such as psychosocial stress or strenuous physical exercise, the hypothalamus releases a neural hormone called thyrotropin-releasing factor (TRF). Release of TRF stimulates the pituitary gland, which in turn tells the thyroid to release thyroxine. As demand increases, output of TRF also increases, and consequently metabolic rate increases. A feedback circuit is built in, though, that enables the hypothalamus to adjust the level of TRF. When the demand is over, the output of TRF is also reduced and metabolism swings back to normal.

A side effect of this is that high levels of thyroxine make the system more responsive to adrenaline. Thus another amplification effect takes place. It appears that adrenaline serves as a short-term stress hormone while thyroxine serves as a long-term stress hormone.

There are other behavioral effects stemming from high levels of thyroxine. Mental activity seems to be aroused and there is a tendency to feel more nervous and anxious. The person may feel constantly tired yet sleep may come only with great difficulty. Blood flow also increases greatly, which results in higher blood pressure. Usually respiratory rate and intensity are also increased. Finally, increased secretion of gastric juices and stomach motility occur, with resulting diarrhea. All of these may be recognized as symptoms that occur during periods of stress.

◆ NATURAL DEFENSES: THE IMMUNE SYSTEM

One of the most sophisticated body systems is the immune system. It has one primary function and that is to provide immunity to disease. **Immunity** is defined as "the power of an individual to resist or overcome the effects of a particular disease or other harmful agent."[15] When the body is invaded by foreign agents such as poisons, germs, or toxic substances, the body takes defensive actions by producing antibodies to attack and destroy the invaders. Or it may use its innate immunity system to fight battles against a number of other agents such as bacteria, viral infections, and blood poisons.

Among the types of cells produced to provide immunity are the *T-cell* and the *B-cell*. T-cells are produced (preprocessed) in the thymus gland, sometimes called the master organ of the immune system. They are very important in fighting bacterial infections, such as tuberculosis, and some viral infections. Also, T-cells combat cancer cells, fungi, and cells from transplanted organs. B-cells are produced in an unknown part of the body, possibly the spleen. They are able to neutralize foreign agents.

Until recently, the immune system was regarded as a largely autonomous system, operating only to recognize what is self and what is not-self. The sole purpose was seen as to attack and kill what is not-self. But, in a review of the scientific literature, Robert Ader has argued that "the immune system is integrated with other physiological systems and, like all such systems operating in the interests of homeostasis, is sensitive to regulation or modulation by the brain."[16] Ader has provided convincing evidence for (1) the influence of conditioning on the immune function, (2) the relation between psychosocial factors, such as life stress, and immunocompetence, and (3) the relationship between use of psychoactive drugs and immunocompetence.

Stress and the Immune System

Uncovering the processes involved in the relation between stress and immunity has not been easy for scientific sleuths. But now a body of research on the relation between psychosocial stress and immunity has suggested that stress alters the way in which the immune system operates.[17] In general, the effect of stress is to lower the body's resistance to disease by suppressing the number of disease-fighting cells available. The net outcome for the person may be an increase in the frequency or intensity of afflictions. Lowered resistance may also slow down recovery from existing disease.

In particular, laboratory research with animals using a variety of stressors shows that T-cell circulation is suppressed.[18] Observations of human reactions to stress generally confirm this result.[19] Plaut and Friedman, for example, have shown that the risk for contracting infectious diseases, allergic reactions, and autoimmune disease is related to life stress in humans.[20] Other researchers have shown that grief following the death of a spouse[21] and after an abortion[22] can lower the number of lymphocytes available to fight disease.

It is also known that prenatal exposure to alcohol can be toxic to the immune system. While this conclusion is based on studies with animal populations, a fairly high likelihood exists that similar effects occur in humans. The implications of this research include better education of pregnant women and improved prenatal care techniques to reduce or eliminate potential harm. Perhaps one day society will look on ingestion of alcohol during pregnancy as another form of child abuse.

The Brain and the Immune System

As more and more evidence accumulates, one major neuralhormonal system emerges with a central role in influencing the immune system. That is the hypothalamic–pituitary–adrenal (HPA) system. The centrality of this system in stress reactions has already been described at some length. When stress occurs, the hypothalamic–pituitary system activates the adrenal glands. Output from the adrenal glands stimulates the immune system.[23] This has the desired effect of initiating defensive reactions, increasing resistance, and speeding recovery.

Unfortunately, some hormones (especially cortisol) put out by the adrenals tend to suppress or damage both T-cells and B-cells. As a result, resistance to many infectious diseases declines and the person may have increased susceptibility to common ailments such as colds and flu. In addition, especially under conditions of prolonged stress, certain people may be more susceptible to the development of cancer.

One critical question is, How can stress produce a health-promoting response at one time and a health-defeating response at another? The overall mechanism is not yet known. It may be related to the type of stress confronting the person. But there is some evidence to suggest that it may also be related to the time course of the stress itself.[24]

Two central factors seem to be chronicity and intensity.[25] **Chronicity** simply refers to a condition that goes on seemingly without end. Under conditions of prolonged stress, the health-promoting response becomes fatigued, the vital hormones needed from the adrenal glands are depleted, and the immune system response is weakened. This is parallel to Selye's stage concept of alarm, reaction, and exhaustion.

Intensity, of course, has to do with the strength or power of the stressful conditions. What determines intensity, however, may reside as much with the person as with the stressor itself. Even different stressful situations can produce quite different neural-hormonal reactions.

This is most clearly revealed in a study at the University of California, Los Angeles (UCLA), where the predictability of the stressor was manipulated.[26] The investigators were concerned with the role of *opioid peptides* in stress-related immune deficiency, especially as it relates to *natural killer cells*.

Opioids are constructed by neural cells in the brain and pituitary. They are found concentrated in many of the lower and middle centers of the brain, such as the thalamus and limbic system. Opioids produce analgesia for pain by blocking the transmission of pain signals. In fact, natural opioids produce an analgesic effect roughly comparable to morphine.[27]

Natural killer cells are a type of lymphocyte specialized to recognize and kill tumor cells along with other foreign bodies. Previous investigations showed that natural killer cells are reduced in animals by stressors such as surgery, starvation, and transportation. Also, suppression of killer cell activity occurs in college students who have poor coping skills for life-change.[28]

In the UCLA study, the investigators used two groups of rats exposed to two different stress (shock) conditions. The crucial difference was that one group received shock on an unpredictable schedule, while the other group received shock continuously. Both groups showed an analgesic, or pain-blocking, response as expected. But the group that received unpredictable shock blocked pain through activation of the natural opioid mechanism in the brain.

The results showed clearly that natural killer cell activity was suppressed in the opioid analgesia group but not in the other group. The investigators suggested that the production of opioid peptides is one of the mechanisms that mediates the relation between certain types of stress and suppression of natural killer cells. They further suggested that the primary ingredient in the stressful condition is similar to *learned helplessness* situations, which are marked by inescapable punishment, unpredictability, and lack of personal control. Experiments in learned helplessness have shown a similar release of opioids.

The Body at War with Itself

One side effect of the way in which the immune system works is the development of allergies. **Allergies** may be described as wars between special antibodies and external agents called allergens. The warfare results in the rupture of two different white blood cells and release of toxic materials into the bloodstream. One of these is the substance histamine.

Hives and hay fever.   The most common allergies are hay fever, asthma, urticaria, and anaphylaxis. Anaphylaxis, though relatively rare, is extremely serious since it can lead to circulatory shock and death within a few minutes of onset. Urticaria is a type of anaphylaxis localized in the skin.

The skin becomes inflamed and swollen, a condition most commonly called hives. Hay fever occurs when the allergic reaction occurs in the nasal area. This leads to increased capillary pressure and rapid fluid leakage into the nose. Antihistamines are commonly prescribed for both urticaria and hay fever since histamine is the primary cause of the difficulty. Antihistamines are not used for asthma since other products of the allergic reaction are known to be involved. Psychological factors have been alleged in the origins of some allergic reactions—for example, urticaria and asthma.

A Japanese team has provided evidence for the relation of stress to skin diseases.[29] Using a clinical sample, the investigators found that life-style changes and substantial daily stress preceded the appearance of urticaria. Life-style changes occurred most frequently in schools, residence, type of work, marriage, promotion, and so forth. The stressors most frequently experienced were overwork, interpersonal difficulties, or family difficulties. An interesting sidelight to the study was that autogenic training (described in Chapter 13) seemed to be effective in reducing the levels of histamine in the blood.

Asthma.   **Asthma** is defined as "an intermittent, variable, and reversible obstruction of bronchial airways."[30] Relative to the other allergies, asthma has received the most attention. This is probably because of the sheer number of victims and the cost of treatment. Asthma afflicts about 4% of the population at any given time, and costs several billion dollars each year for treatment and care.

Explanations have been provided that suggest a psychosocial origin. At this point, though, there is no convincing evidence that either family stress or personality is important in the origin of asthma. Such psychosocial factors might play a role in the day-to-day level of reaction, however. And even though conditioning has been shown to affect the immune system, which could then produce the asthmatic attack, no proof of such a mechanism has been provided to date. More importantly, behavioral treatment programs have had little or no success. Perhaps the most important observation is that life-style serves to intensify symptoms and/or defeat medical treatment.

Acquired immune deficiency syndrome.   A great deal of attention, both professional and public, has been devoted to the disease of the 1980s, acquired immune deficiency syndrome (AIDS). AIDS has been called "a modern-day black plague."[31] Even though the numbers involved bear little resemblance to the plagues of the past, the toll in human life and suffering is growing. Based on statistics compiled through April 7, 1986, there were 18,907 adult cases of AIDS in the United States,[32] of which nearly 50% have died.[33] These figures do not include cases known to exist in Haiti or in Africa where the situation is described as epidemic.[34] In the United States, AIDS seems to attack specific at-risk groups including male homosexuals, intravenous drug abusers, and people who require blood products for a variety of medical reasons. Figure 3–6 shows the distribution of AIDS in these high-

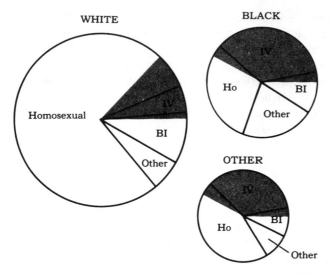

Figure 3–6. Proportions of AIDS cases represented by various risk groups in the United States, shown separately for whites, blacks, and other nonwhites (92% of whom are Hispanic). The circles are proportional to the number of cases reported for the three racial or ethnic groups. The group at risk because of intravenous (IV) drug use is indicated by shading in order to show the overlap between it and the homosexual (Ho) and bisexual (Bi) groups. (Data based on the 18,907 adult cases of AIDS reported to the Centers for Disease Control as of April 7, 1986).

risk groups. In spite of this predominant pattern, recent evidence has suggested that AIDS can be transmitted through heterosexual contact as well.[35] On a brighter note, another study provided evidence that members of the family of an AIDS victim are at minimal or no risk of infection.[36]

As recently as 1984, the Centers for Disease Control defined AIDS as "characterized by opportunistic infections and malignant diseases in patients without a known cause for immunodeficiency."[37] It is now known that AIDS is caused by a virus, which is most commonly known as the HTLV-III/LAV virus. An international committee has proposed that the virus be designated as the human immunodeficiency virus or HIV.[38] The virus attacks "the human T4 lymphocyte, a key cell of the immune response."[39]

Perhaps one of the most overlooked issues is the stress that the threat of AIDS places on certain groups, especially the gay community. Because of the tendency for members of this group to be among the high-risk groups, they appear to suffer from increasing anxiety, panic attacks, loss of self-esteem, fear of isolation from friends and loved ones, and loss of self-sufficiency.[40]

Because of extensive publicity, widespread antigay sentiment, and the public tendency to isolate gays as though they were lepers, gays diagnosed and found free of AIDS are still exposed to high levels of stress. They are among the "worried well," people who have no disease but are so worried that they engage in a variety of behaviors not conducive to their own physical or mental well-being. These include the extremes of denial and repression or obsessional thinking about all of the possible bad things that are about to happen. It may also extend to severe restrictions in personal and social mobility or the other extreme of repeated visits to doctors and medical facilities. The long-term impact on health may be nearly as detrimental as if the person had contracted AIDS. In such cases, a type of social victimization may be in process that subjects a person to negative consequences due largely to being part of one of society's less favored groups.

◆ THE CARDIOVASCULAR SYSTEM

The heart is a miracle organ by any standard. It works day and night, seldom missing a beat as it pumps life-giving blood through the entire body. In the newborn child, the pulse rate is around 120–140 beats per minute. In the mature adult, the heart beats 60–70 times per minute. At this rate, the average heart beats 3,900 times per hour, or 93,600 beats each day. During exercise, the pulse rate can go up to around 100, and in strenuous exercise it can go even higher. Astronauts have been observed to have pulse rates at about 140 beats per minute during the most stressful periods of liftoff and reentry.

Stress and the Heart

While a great deal of attention has been devoted to the physical origins of heart failure, more and more attention has been shifting to psychosocial factors and life-style forces that contribute to cardiovascular problems. The major focus has been on stress, personality, diet, exercise, and abstinence or temperance.

Several pathways used by the brain to influence other organs have already been noted. Events interpreted as stressful or emotionally loaded are translated into changes in the rate, intensity, or balance of processes in a number of physical systems including the cardiovascular,[41] respiratory, and digestive. Tracing this influence from the limbic through the HPA complex and the sympathetic division of the autonomic system provides convincing evidence that stress has far-reaching effects on the cardiovascular system.

Hypertension

Hypertension is an elevation in blood pressure above accepted levels, regardless of what produced it. It is the usual diagnosis given when systolic blood pressure exceeds 160 and diastolic exceeds 120. Serious danger exists when the systolic pressure reaches 200.[42] **Essential hypertension** is the term given to hypertension of unknown origins. Activation of the sympathetic nervous system, as in stress–anxiety reactions, will increase cardiac output with a resulting increase in blood pressure. Under normal circumstances this condition will last only a matter of a few hours. However, given the right situation, continued sympathetic arousal, and prolonged constriction of the arteries supplying the kidneys, a more long-term hypertension may appear.

In addition to sympathetic arousal, control from the HPA complex initiates release of the two adrenal hormones, adrenaline and noradrenaline, and of renin from the kidneys. Besides increasing cardiac output and elevating blood pressure, adrenaline and noradrenaline are known to speed up the rate of damage to the arteries. Renin is a chemical that results in the production of a peptide called angiotensin, "the most potent vasoconstrictor known."[43] The result of these three hormones is to duplicate and amplify the effect of the sympathetic system. Thus cardiac output and blood pressure can increase to even higher levels than occur with only sympathetic arousal.

Atherosclerosis

In medical terms, **atherosclerosis** is a disease of the large arteries "in which yellowish patches of fat are deposited, forming plaques that decrease the size of the [opening]."[44] The yellowish patches of fat, called arterial plaques, are actually deposits of cholesterol and other lipids. A variety of factors including genetic risk, diet, lack of exercise, and stress can all contribute to the formation of arterial plaques. Rosenman and Friedman were among the first to note the relation between stressful events and the appearance of cholesterol.[45] They reported, for example, that tax accountants in the two weeks prior to the April 15 deadline had greatly increased serum cholesterol relative to either February or March.

Another effect of stress and sympathetic arousal is to increase the tendency for blood to coagulate. Even when no injury has occurred, the effect in the bloodstream is the same. There is a buildup of blood platelets (also called thrombocytes), which are incorporated into the arterial plaques. Since plaques reduce the physical space that blood has to pass through, pressure is increased.

But plaques also cause a breakdown in the wall of the artery itself. The body, of course, tries to repair this breakdown. The platelets are supposed to help in this process but instead contribute to the problem by making the plaques even thicker. At this point, it is mostly irrelevant how the plaques got there. Stress only adds to the problem.

In the later stages of atherosclerosis, fibrous cells also infiltrate the plaques and add to the scar tissue on the artery wall. Calcium deposits further harden the cell walls and narrow the corridor. Blood must be squeezed through a much smaller space than is normal. The heart then has to work much harder to produce the blood flow. But just as a weight lifter develops larger muscles with increasing workouts, heart muscle also grows as it works harder. Unfortunately, the muscle grows faster than the supply network grows to keep blood flowing to the heart. The muscle that pumps all the blood to the rest of the body does not have enough of its own resource to stay healthy. The heart then may deteriorate further and more serious coronary problems may follow.

◆ THE DIGESTIVE SYSTEM AND ULCERS

One of the first conclusions derived from Selye's stress research was that stress could produce ulcers. The executive monkey study described earlier demonstrated this outcome convincingly by showing that stress can have disastrous effects on the digestive system, including perforated ulcers and death. Aside from these laboratory simulations of stress, a number of observations support the contention that psychosocial factors play an important role in the origin of ulcers. For example, urban populations have a higher prevalence of ulcers than rural populations. In addition, the prevalence of ulcers increases in wartime. Certain occupational groups known to have much higher levels of psychological stress, such as air traffic controllers, are also more subject to ulcers.[46]

There are several different types of ulcers. Peptic ulcers are produced when the gastric juices used to digest food are produced at too high a level. In the absence of neutralizing secretions, these juices attack the lining of the stomach causing irritation, bleeding, and, in severe cases, a break in the stomach wall itself. Peptic ulcers may be acute or chronic. The acute ulcer is also known as the stress ulcer. There are probably a number of physical causes for the stress ulcer. The most likely include excess production of hydrochloric acid and pepsin under control of the parasympathetic system and excess secretion of adrenal hormones under the control of the HPA complex.

Gastric ulcers are deeper erosions in the stomach lining that occur most frequently on the bottom curved surface of the stomach, just below the outlet to the intestines. They are known to be caused by excessive use of aspirin and alcohol. Also, they seem to be associated with chronic anxiety and depression.[47]

◆ SUMMARY

In this chapter we have seen how the brain translates emotional or stressful stimuli into specific physical processes. In general, the process begins when the older *visceral brain* interprets an external stimulus as emotionally loaded. Resulting outputs from the brain via the autonomic system and the hypothalamic–pituitary–adrenal complex mobilize the natural defenses of the body to fight the stress. The physical response is a general state of arousal with increased cardiac volume, higher blood pressure, faster formation of arterial plaques, accelerated wear and tear on the heart, altered respiratory response, and suppression of the immune system. These physical changes in organ or system function can have negative consequences for the organism if maintained over a long period.

◆ NOTES

[1]William Uttal makes this same point but goes on to say that "in almost all cases, [the debate] will necessarily be based on softer criteria including ones based on emotion, values, and intuitive and aesthetic judgments of consistency, completeness, or productiveness." Uttal, W. R. (1978). *The psychobiology of mind.* Hillsdale, NJ: Erlbaum, p. 81.

[2]Liebman, M. (1979). *Neuroanatomy made easy and understandable.* Baltimore: University Park Press.

[3]Guyton, A. C. (1977). *Basic human physiology: Normal function and mechanisms of disease.* Philadelphia: Saunders, p. 399.

[4]Guyton, *Basic human physiology,* p. 424.

[5]Grossman, S. (1973). *Essentials of physiological psychology.* New York: Wiley. Grossman provides a review of some of this early work in his chapter on affective behavior, Chapter 12. See especially pp. 285ff.

[6]Guyton, *Basic human physiology,* p. 504.

[7]Melzack, R., & Wall, P. (1965). Pain mechanisms: A new theory. *Science, 50,* 971–979.

[8]Liebman, *Neuroanatomy made easy,* p. 38.

[9]Guyton, *Basic human physiology,* pp. 600–601.

[10]Riley, V. (1981). Psychoneuroendocrine influences on immunocompetence and neoplasia. *Science, 212,* 1100–1109.

[11]Tanaka, M., Kohno, Y., Nakagawa, R., Ida, Y., Takeda, S., Nagasaki, N., & Noda, Y. (1983). Regional characteristics of stress-induced increases in brain noradrenaline release in rats. *Pharmacology, Biochemistry and Behavior, 19,* 543–547.

[12]Aslan, S., Nelson, L., Carruthers, M., & Lader, M. (1981). Stress and age effects on catecholamines in normal subjects. *Journal of Psychosomatic Research, 25,* 33–41.

[13]Ward, M. M., Mefford, I. N., Parker, S. D., Chesney, M. A., Taylor, C. B., Keegan, D. L., & Barchas, J. D. (1983). Epinephrine and norepinephrine responses in continuously collected human plasma to a series of stressors. *Psychosomatic Medicine, 45,* 471–486.

[14]Blessing, W. W., Sved, A. F., & Reis, D. J. (1982). Destruction of noradrenergic neurons in rabbit brainstem elevates plasma vasopressin, causing hypertension. *Science, 217,* 661–663.

[15]Memmler, R. L., & Wood, D. L. (1977). *The human body in health and disease* (4th ed.). Philadelphia: Lippincott, p. 281.

[16]Ader, R. (1983). Developmental psychoneuroimmunology. *Developmental Psychobiology, 16,* 251–267.

[17]Locke, S. E. (1982). Stress, adaptation, and immunity: Studies in humans. *General Hospital Psychiatry, 4,* 49–58.

[18]Keller, S. E., Weiss, J. M., Schleifer, S. J., Miller, N. E., & Stein, M. (1981). Suppression of immunity by stress: Effect of a graded series of stressors on lymphocyte stimulation in the rat. *Science, 213,* 1397–1400.

[19]Locke, S. E., et al. (1978, April). *The influence of stress on the immune response.* Paper presented at the annual meeting of the American Psychosomatic Society, Washington, DC.

[20]Plaut, S. M., & Friedman, S. B. (1981). Psychosocial factors, stress, and disease processes. In R. Ader (Ed.), *Psychoneuroimmunology.* New York: Academic Press, pp. 3–29.

[21]Bartrop, R. W., Lazarus, L., Luckhurst, E., Kiloh, L. G., & Penny, R. (1977). Depressed lymphocyte function after bereavement. *Lancet, 1,* 834–836.

[22]Assael, M., Naor, S., Pecht, M., Trainin, N., & Samuel, D. (1981). *Correlation between emotional reaction to loss of loved object and lymphocyte response to mitogenic stimulation in women.* Paper presented at the Sixth World Congress of the International College of Psychosomatic Medicine, Quebec, Canada.

[23]These include cortisol, aldosterone, and desoxycorticosterone. Paradoxically, cortisol can also act to suppress the immune system. The crucial variable seems to be dosage level. At low levels, cortisol is a stimulant to the immune system. At higher levels, it is suppressive. For a review, see Comsa, J., Leonhardt, H., & Wekerle, H. (1982). Hormonal coordination of the immune response. In R. H. Adrian et al. (Eds.), *Reviews of physiology, biochemistry and pharmacology.* New York: Springer-Verlag, pp. 115–191.

[24]Comsa et al., Hormonal coordination, p. 149.

[25]Ader, Developmental psychoneuroimmunology, pp. 253–256.

[26]Shavit, Y., Lewis, J. W., Terman, G. W., Gale, R. P., & Liebeskind, J. C. (1984). Opioid peptides mediate the suppressive effect of stress on natural killer cell cytotoxicity. *Science, 223,* 188–190.

[27]Stephens, G. J. (1980). *Pathophysiology for health practitioners.* New York: Macmillan, p. 555.

[28]See Shavit et al., Opioid peptides, for a number of studies documenting this relation.

[29]Teshima, H., Kubo, C., Kihara, H., Imada, Y., Nagata, S., Ago, Y., & Ikemi, Y. (1982). Psychosomatic aspects of skin diseases from the standpoint of immunology. *Psychotherapy and Psychosomatics, 37,* 165–175. Their work with animal subjects confirmed suppression of the immune system, as other investigations have shown.

[30]Pinkerton, S. S., Hughes, H., & Wenrich, W. W. (1982). *Behavioral medicine: Clinical applications.* New York: Wiley, p. 234.

[31]Batchelor, W. F. (1984). AIDS: A public health and psychological emergency. *American Psychologist, 39,* 1279.

[32]Bakeman, R., Lumb, J. R., Jackson, R. E., & Smith, D. W. (1986, July 17). AIDS risk-group profiles in whites and members of minority groups. *The New England Journal of Medicine, 315,* 191–192.

[33]Osborne, J. E. (1986, March 20). The AIDS epidemic: Multidisciplinary trouble. *The New England Journal of Medicine, 314,* 779–782.

[34]Kreiss, J. K., et al. (1986, February 13). AIDS virus infection in Nairobi prostitutes. *The New England Journal of Medicine, 314,* 414–418.

[35]In addition to the evidence provided by Kreiss et al., AIDS virus, a documented case study shows transmisson via traditional heterosexual practices: Calabrese, L. H., & Gopalakrishna, K. V. (1986, April 10). Transmission of HTLV-III infection from man to woman to man. *The New England Journal of Medicine, 314,* 987.

[36]Friedland, G. H., et al., (1986, February 6). *The New England Journal of Medicine, 314,* 344–349.

[37]Seligmann, M., et al. (1984). AIDS—An immunologic reevaluation. *The New England Journal of Medicine, 311,* 1286–1292.

[38]Coffin, J., et al. (1986, May). What to call the AIDS virus? *Nature, 321,* 10.

[39]Burny, A. (1986, May). More and better trans-activation. *Nature, 321,* 378.

[40]Morin, S. F., Charles, K. A., & Malyon, A. K. (1984). The psychological impact of AIDS on gay men. *American Psychologist, 39,* 1288.

[41]Gliner, J. A., Bedi, J. F., & Horvath, S. M. (1979). Somatic and non-somatic influences on the heart: Hemodynamic changes. *Psychophysiology, 16,* 358–362.

[42]Blood pressure is measured both at the peak of output of the heart, the *systolic* pressure, and at the resting phase of the heart, the *diastolic* pressure. In the normal heart, these pressures are 120/80, respectively.

[43]Guyton, *Basic human physiology,* p. 231. Technically, the steps from renin to the actual formation of angiotensin II involve an intermediate conversion process involving three other chemicals. But it is angiotensin II that initiates vasoconstriction and increased arterial pressure.

[44]Memmler & Wood, *The human body,* p. 299.

[45]Rosenman, R. H., & Friedman, M. (1974). Neurogenic factors in pathogenesis of coronary heart disease. *Medical Clinics of North America, 58,* 269–279.

[46]Pinkerton et al., *Behavioral medicine,* pp. 185–188.

[47]Stephens, *Pathophysiology,* p. 337.

Part 3

PSYCHOLOGICAL SOURCES OF STRESS

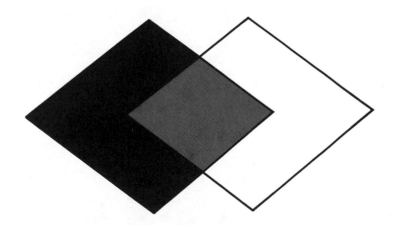

4

THE COGNITIVE STRESS SYSTEM: ATTITUDES, BELIEFS, AND EXPECTATIONS

If pleasures are greatest in anticipation, just remember that this is also true of trouble.

Elbert Hubbard

The appointment with your doctor ends with arrangements made for a two- or three-day stay in the hospital. "We have to run some tests," the doctor says. "What do you mean by tests?" is your reply. "For what? What do I have? Tell me what's going on. I need to know."

Your supervisor stops by to summon you to a meeting with management in one hour. "We have to discuss the production record of your group" is the only clue. "What's wrong with our work?" is the reply. "I can't say anything more until the meeting. See you then."

Your teenager calls to say, "I don't know how to tell you this, . . . but, ah, . . . I just wrecked the car." "You did what? Were you hurt? Was anyone with you? How did it happen? Where are you now?"

What all of these very different events have in common is that each is ripe for many different interpretations. The hospital diagnostics may be welcomed for rest, discovery, and the end of uncertainty. The tests may be dreaded because of what might be found or because of the expectation that the procedures will be very uncomfortable, if not painful. The production record may be good or bad; the supervisor's comments do not suggest which. The youngster who has to relay the unwelcome information to parents also faces a variety of uncertainties. The wrecked car may be just scratched, or it might be totaled. "What will my parents say?"

◆ LABELS, GUESSES, AND GAPS

The most common first response in situations filled with uncertainty is the process of **labeling,** or assigning meaning to the event. Hospital tests mean a serious health problem. A meeting with management spells trouble, reprimands, probably less of a chance for promotion, and so forth. Labeling will occur very early, even prior to having all of the possible information. The process is for the most part private and goes unnoticed. But it plays a vital role in transactions with the people we deal with on a daily basis. It sets the stage for a distress reaction or a positive encounter.

A second process is going on at the same time, though. That is, people tend to fill in gaps in the available information with **guesses,** or inferences about what is happening. "What's wrong with our work?" not only labels the supervisor's summons as a threat, it indicates that the person has already guessed at what the meeting is about. The inference is that the news is bad and the group will probably be dressed down for bad production. In fact, the outcome of the meeting might be much different. The real information might be that the group is being considered for a special project that needs their production ability. But the pessimistic guess about what is going on nudges the process to the negative side of stress.

Most events have some uncertainty because only a small amount of information is available at any given point. People actively seek more information to fill in these gaps. And obtaining information is a time-dependent process. The doctor does not know what to expect or what will be found. It may be several days before test results are available. The supervisor has been ordered not to talk. That gives you at least an hour of worry, fretting, and thinking before the full story is told. The teenager can relay only bits and pieces of the total picture verbally. In the meantime, the mind will work overtime making up its own pictures of what has happened or what will happen. These three processes—assigning meaning, filling in gaps, and seeking information—will continue in cycles until the event has been evaluated and integrated.

◆ ANTICIPATIONS: HOPE AND DESPAIR

One of the most dramatic examples of the powerful effect of labeling was related by Herbert Lefcourt. A woman had been mute and socially withdrawn for nearly 10 years. She was in a psychiatric hospital, confined to a ward known to patients as the chronic hopeless ward. Then the hospital needed to do some redecorating. In order to facilitate the work, the hospital staff moved all of the people, including the mute woman, to a new location. The new ward was known to patients as the exit ward. It was for those who would be going home shortly. Just after being moved to the new unit, the mute woman started talking and seemed quite happy with her increasing social contacts. However, the work on the old chronic hopeless ward was soon done, and all the previous residents were returned. In Lefcourt's words, "Within a week after she had been returned to the 'hopeless' unit, the patient . . . collapsed and died. The subsequent autopsy revealed no pathology of note, and it was whimsically suggested at the time that the patient had died of despair."[1]

◆ COGNITIVE SCIENCE: PROBING THE MYSTERIES OF MIND

Observations of voodoo deaths and the action of placebos provide very strong supporting evidence that thoughts, labels, and expectations influence stress reactions and health processes in very powerful ways. In fact, a great many of the slings and arrows of modern living probably would never really happen if it were not for the way we think about our daily transactions.

Stress is not a physical property of a situation like heat, or weight, or length. It is more a product of our cognitive processes, the way in which we think about and evaluate the situation. In much the same way, how we cope and how effective our coping is depends to a great extent on how we think about our resources and skills for coping.

Labels, thinking, and expectations are the province of the mind. They fall within the domain of **cognitive science,** a new science of the mind that looks at all the ways in which humans know, think, reason, and decide. Considered private and inaccessible for decades, the mysteries contained in the hidden recesses of the mind are now the subject of intense discussion and investigation. Slowly but surely, these mysteries are opening up to the probing eyes of cognitive scientists in laboratories around the world. Their discoveries may hold the key to understanding why one person's distress is another's challenge.

Early on, the bulk of cognitive research was concerned with identifying basic processes in cognition. But now, more and more attention is being devoted to cognitive processes involved in stress and health. In addition, more and more work is going into developing cognitive approaches to therapy and self-help programs that focus on the fallibility and distortions introduced by the cognitive system. That is what this chapter is about. In the following pages, such cognitive processes as perception, attention, appraisal, and information seeking will be discussed. Then a widely accepted model of cognitive processing will be described. Finally coping styles and strategies will be presented.

◆ A MODEL OF MIND: INFORMATION PROCESSING

Cognition has been defined as all the ways of knowing, thinking, reasoning, and deciding. It includes the processes of attention, perception, memory, problem solving, and creativity, in short all of the things we have come to associate with intelligence. Cognitive scientists have adopted a model of how the mind works, a model borrowed from the three separate fields of computers, communication, and language. This model is called the *information-processing model.* It states that the person's transactions with the environment can be viewed as somewhat like an elaborate computer data processing task. For each task, there are no less than three stages: input, throughput, and output. There is also usually a *feedback system* to allow for correction of error and to make other necessary adjustments.

In human terms, senses such as the eyes and ears serve as the input channels for all information. Virtually everything from there on—attention, memory, reasoning, planning, problem solving, and so forth—is regarded as part of the throughput process. These mental functions, however, depend on an internal organization. Where computers are dependent on someone outside to write and organize a program for them, people build their own programs using organizational schemes based on rules acquired from many transactions with the environment. Speaking and acting are output processes. The task of the cognitive scientist is to identify what goes on at each stage, what parts of the brain serve each function, and how feedback is incorporated at different stages in the process.

◆ SCHEMATA AND PERSONAL CONSTRUCTS

As experiences accumulate, some notions about how the world operates become a part of the core of memory. These notions are organized in files in the mind containing as much information about a certain event or class of events as is available. In addition, the organization within a file is meaningful and coherent, and allows the person to predict with some accuracy what the outcome of personal action should be. In the short time that scientists have been trying to decipher how the mind works, two theoretical notions have been advanced that address this issue. One comes from the arena of personality theory, the *personal construct* theory of George Kelly.[2] The other comes from the area of developmental theory, the concept of *schema* advanced by the great Swiss thinker Jean Piaget.[3]

Both personal constructs and schemata are subjective constructions of some part of reality. Thus, both can influence perceptions and reactions. According to Kelly, constructs are not part of reality. Rather, constructs are imposed on reality to give meaning to it. They are predictive guesses that are meant to be tested: The world is just or unjust. Bosses, spouses, and acquaintances are bad or good, happy or sad, friendly or hostile, warm or aloof, accepting or rejecting, healthy or sick. Any construct that refers to others can also refer to self. Some constructs become rigid and impermeable to new information, while other constructs remain flexible and permit a wide range of new information.

A key concept in Kelly's thinking is that people become mentally channeled by the way in which they anticipate events.[4] To use an analogy, expectations of events are like putting on blinders so that only a very narrow range of the track can be seen at any one time. It is as though other interpretations simply do not exist because they cannot be seen. An example is a couple who came near to divorce because the husband thought she was being unfaithful. She had been engaging in some rather mysterious and secretive behavior for a period of time. As it turned out, she had engaged in an elaborate ruse in order to surprise him with a special gift. But his construct of reality allowed him to see only one interpretation: "She must be running around with someone else." Recall the employee summoned to the meeting with management. The employee's construct of reality could well tip the balance of emotions in the meeting toward tension and confrontation.

In Piaget's theory, changes are made to sensory input in order to make it fit into available schemata (assimilation). As new information is made available, the schema grows and becomes more elaborate (accommodation). We have schemata for cars: what they are like, how they operate, and how we can operate them. We have schemata for houses, food, different groups of people, social behavior, virtually any and all parts of our environment that are important to our ability to function and survive. Schemata seem to function as the primary *meaning systems* in cognition. Our schemata for bosses probably carry much different meanings from our schemata for peers or employees. Schemata for mothers are different from schemata for fathers. Schemata for situations contain the rules for what behavior is appropriate. And a very personal schema keeps a type of file on ourselves. As will be seen in the following pages, perceptual and memory processes draw upon schemata in virtually every transaction we have with our environment.

◆ PERCEPTION: STRESS IS IN THE EYE OF THE BEHOLDER

If schemata are the central organizing files of the mind, perception is the selective and organizing gateway to the mind. In fact, Ulric Neisser, the dean of cognitive scientists, states that perception is the most fundamental cognitive act.[5] This may indeed be appropriate where stress and health are concerned. As one review of stress in work environments noted, employee perceptions of stressful situations are related to employee health and well-being. This finding has been duplicated many times.[6]

Perception may be defined as the interpretation and organization of all information provided to the brain by the senses. *Interpretation* suggests that some meaning has been attached to the information and that a value judgment, no matter how primitive, has been made. One basic judgment made is whether the event is positively regarded (it is pleasant and valuable to the person) or negatively regarded (it is unpleasant or possibly even painful to the person). *Organization* implies that connections have been made to experiences stored in long-term memory. The new information is then classified, or put in the same memory bin along with similar information. It adds to the person's store of experiences, and in the future will add its own color to the interpretation and organization of new information.

Even from the first moments after birth, the positive and negative evaluations are not random. Evidence points to the existence of perceptual biases related to inherited emotional sets and to the cumulative effect of experience.[7] These sets lead some people to see most things in a negative way and react accordingly. Other people seem to view almost any event, even those that are catastrophic, as positive. As one cognitive scientist put it, these biases, whether inborn or acquired, appear to cause a person "to label events of one type as personally or subjectively acceptable and those of another type as aversive."[8]

Misperceptions and Stress

One basic problem is that perception is not perfectly veridical. In other words, mental representations of what happened do not always square with external reality. Indeed, the process of perception falls prey to a number of errors that produce distortions or subtle alterations in the message. Two of the best known and most severe forms of perceptual distortions are delusions and hallucinations. A **delusion** is a mistaken belief, such as "I am Jesus" or "Everyone is out to get me." **Hallucinations** are tricks the brain plays on some people. They firmly believe they have seen or heard something that does not in actuality exist.

What about something less extreme, such as an imagined threat or the thought that a doctor's examination could be negative? A very interesting research project sheds some light on this issue. The experiment was actually designed to answer some questions on how the brain works in responding to a real physical object. The crucial point in the experiment came when the scientists stopped presenting the geometric forms that had been seen earlier. At this time, they simply asked the subjects to imagine that the geometric forms were on the blank screen in front of them. The results were unexpected. There were no differences in the brain waves from when the real object was shown and when the object was just imagined! To the brain, in other words, the perception of the object was indistinguishable from its own thought of the object.[9] Similar observations led Kenneth Pelletier to refer to the brain as the *literal brain*.[10]

Such observations help to explain how people can get upset all over again when they recall an emotionally upsetting event. It also explains why people may go into a state of virtual panic when merely thinking about surgery or an upcoming major exam. The thought is as real to the mind as the actual event. And the effect on the body is just the same!

Perceptual Vigilance and Attention

The perceptual system appears to have some fairly elaborate processes built in to insure continued alertness or attention to changes in the environment. As defined by cognitive scientists, **attention** is the process by which a person chooses what to attend to. This "choosing" may be involuntary, impulsive and automatic, or voluntary, deliberate, and selective.

A car crash in front of the house, a firecracker placed under a chair by a mischievous friend, the shout of "fire" in a theater, will almost certainly lead to an automatic attending response. The features of physical stimuli that demand attention generally have to do with size, intensity, and motion. In addition, surprise, novelty, and complexity shift the process in the direction of involuntary attention.

A process called *selective attention* serves to protect against overload, to help focus on relevant information thus improving efficiency, and to block out unacceptable information. But when selective attention is combined with voluntary sustained attention, it is *perceptual vigilance*. This requires extreme concentration and deliberate control over competing irrelevant information. Vigilance is vital to certain jobs, such as air traffic control and medical practice. A number of serious accidents and near misses have been attributed to the pressure on air traffic controllers, especially in high-density airports such as Boston, New York, and Chicago. In medical settings, medical staff must monitor life signs of patients over long periods of time. Anesthesiologists must be alert every instant to any sign of change in vital functions during prolonged surgery.

Sustained attention can produce a variety of problems. For example, vigilance tends to suffer greatly over even rather short periods of time. Just hours into a shift, an air traffic controller may begin to lose the high level of concentration required for optimal accuracy. In addition, the level of arousal required to sustain vigilance appears to take a toll physically and psychologically. Controllers working in congested airports have a much higher rate of such physical illnesses as high blood pressure and gastric difficulties. They also report more migraines and subjective stress.

Another vigilance problem is encountered when patients are given disturbing news of a serious disease or treatment that will affect their future for some time. Some people prefer the path of least resistance, using some form of denial to protect themselves. Some get aroused, vigilant, and actively seek all kinds of information about their disease and prognosis. They seem to prefer being active and participating in their treatment to sitting back passively. But others become vigilant to the extreme. Janis called it *hypervigilance*.[11] In such cases, the person seems to be on guard all the time, as though the smallest signal must be detected to keep on top of the disease.

Unfortunately, too much of a good thing, such as apple pie or ice cream, usually turns out in the long run to do more harm than good. And that is the case here. Hypervigilance tends to interfere with decision making. It also generally keeps the person in a state of high physical and emotional arousal, which may actually hinder the healing process.

Perceptual Defense: Hear No Evil, See No Evil?

When attention serves to protect the individual from personally sensitive or undesirable information, it is called *perceptual defense*. The notion of perceptual defense goes back to work done in 1948 spearheaded by Leo Postman.[12] Postman's group observed that people were much slower to respond to "bad" or obscene words than to neutral or good words.

Research has shown more clearly how perceptual defense might work when people are confronted with stressful information. One research team asked people to view a rather unpleasant film. It appears from this study that people allocate even more time to process negative information than positive. But, in addition, the people in this study turned away in order to avoid confronting a threatening exposure. Whether they are tied up with thinking or with physically avoiding, they are taken out of perceptual circulation for a short period, and thus are unable to attend to any new information.[13]

Evidence of this type supports the notion of a perceptual defense process. But it also points to an added danger not previously suspected, the probability of missing new information. This process may account for gaps that occur in memory for anxiety-filled transactions. At the scene of a hit-and-run accident, for example, a person might be transfixed by the horror of the scene just long enough to miss out entirely on any identifying information that would enable the police to locate and prosecute the culprit.

◆ PERCEPTION, DEPRIVATION, AND OVERLOAD

A rather large body of research built up over nearly 50 years indicates that the amount of stimulation we are subject to can have a significant impact on activity and emotionality. Thus it can directly influence levels of stress and reactions to chronic stress. In essence, we each have a preferred level of stimulation. We try to avoid the extremes of deprivation and overload. Both seem to be very aversive. In the middle preferred ground, the emphasis is on novelty and quality. Sameness and sheer quantity are less desirable.

Stimulus Deprivation: Boredom and Stress

A study on stimulus deprivation conducted at McGill University in 1954 has become almost legendary.[14] Volunteers were paid $20 per day simply to lie in bed and sleep. For most students, this seemed like an easy buck. They could quit whenever they wanted to, and in the meantime their basic bodily needs would be satisfied. There was only one catch. They had to lie in a cubicle with hands and arms padded and with translucent goggles on their eyes. Even external sounds were blocked out by a masking sound presented through a speaker system.

The outcome of the experiment was quite unexpected. Nobody was willing to go beyond 72 hours and most of the volunteers quit in the first 24–36 hours. They slept for the first few hours, and enjoyed it to be sure. But after that, most of the volunteers experienced boredom, restlessness, and increasing anxiety. They tried to provide their own input by singing, whistling, and talking to themselves. But there was a gradual deterioration of intellectual efficiency, followed by some unsettling, if not terrifying, experiences. That is, many of the students began to have hallucinations. Some of the hallucinations were mild, but they seemed to increase in bizarreness and intensity with time. Most were simple geometric forms but some were more grotesque, such as eyeglasses that turned into deformed long-legged people walking on the horizon of a small world. Almost all of the students noted that the experience was emotionally disturbing and unpleasant. It was just too much of too little input.

Is there any way to explain this result? One possible explanation has to do with the reticular formation. The brain has a built-in arouser in the reticular formation. It keeps activity going most of the time, even when the brain is cut off from external input. Contact with the outside world, though, is necessary for reality testing. When external input is cut off, the brain improvises. It generates its own activity and makes up its own images. As these internal forms stray farther and farther from the norm, they take on the appearance of hallucinations. To use a metaphor, there are no quality controls to ensure that the internal production is what the external blueprint called for.

This evidence suggests that a minimum level of input is needed in order to keep the cognitive system operating smoothly and that reduction in input below the minimum preferred level may produce stress. The results of this study are supported by reports from people who function in stimulus-deprived environments such as under water exploration, polar expeditions, radar operation, and long-distance truck driving. Formal research in this area has been helpful in preparing people to work in such conditions.

Stimulus Overload: Too Much Equals Chaos

Too much stimulation may be perceived as a psychological overload. The oft-heard expression "This place is a zoo" is probably a statement that too much is going on at a pace too fast for the individual to keep up. The simple solution, of course, is to get away, be alone, reduce the rate of stimulation even if for just a short time. When this is feasible, it may be all the coping strategy necessary. When not feasible, other measures may be called for such as family problem solving (Chapter 6), more effective management of space and reduction of noise (Chapter 9), and cognitive coping strategies (Chapter 13).

◆ PERCEPTIONS OF SELF, OTHERS, AND SITUATIONS

Most of the perceptual processes described to this point deal with primary perception, or organizing tendencies that take place at the time of input. But there are secondary or derived perceptions also. Secondary perceptions depend more on schemata or constructs as described earlier. The schemata in question here contain a wide range of personal norms, subjective biases, stereotypes, and normative rules for behavior in specific social settings. Three of the most important derived perceptions are self-perception, person perception, and situation perception.

Self-perception: The Real and the Ideal

Self-perception is a type of composite image of ourselves that combines physical as well as mental features. We see ourselves as beautiful or plain, strong or weak, fairly intelligent or less intelligent, highly capable or less capable. This picture enters into the appraisals we make of situations, how we evaluate our relationships to others, how we assess our ability to deal with a new challenge. A positive view of self usually goes with more positive or neutral interpretations of situations. Even demanding situations are more likely to be treated as challenges than as threats. On the other side, poor regard for self is usually associated with a tendency to evaluate situations as threatening and to respond to them as stressful.

One of the most comprehensive studies of stress and coping resources discovered a very important relationship to self-concept. Leonard Pearlin and Carmi Schooler, of the National Institute of Mental Health, interviewed 2300 people from urban Chicago.[15] In this group, three psychological traits turned out to be crucial in protecting against stress. These were self-esteem, self-denigration, and mastery. Of these three, the most important was self-denigration. The more the person had a tendency to engage in negative thoughts about self, the greater the stress. Most significant is the fact that self-denigration was the strongest variable for all four of the major life arenas assessed in the study, which were marital stress, parenting stress, family financial stress, and work stress. Exercise 4-1 is intended to help you look at and possibly get rid of negative views of self.

The relationship between self-concept and stress is a two-way street, however. Just as a low self-regard can increase the tendency to view a situation as stressful, so too a very stressful situation can threaten self-regard.[16]

Self-Study Exercise 4–1.   Rooting out Negative Thoughts About Self

If you have a tendency to think of yourself in negative terms it would be useful to carry out a brief exercise. For a period of approximately a week, keep a daily diary of negative things you say to yourself about yourself. Here are a few examples of negative thoughts: "I know I can't do that." "I don't have any friends." "I'm a real loser." "Everybody else is getting ahead but me." Also make a note of what your mood is at the time. Finally, note any personal conflicts or daily hassles that have occurred either prior to or following the negative thoughts.

At the end of the week, scan the diary to see if there is a pattern to the thoughts about yourself. Do they have to do with your work, skills, or competencies? Do they have to do with your body, personality, relationships? Then look at any changes in moods and stressors. Did they tend to follow or precede the negative thoughts? If you can decipher a pattern, you may have one key to dealing with daily mood and stress.

For example, imagine someone running alone on a jogging trail about to overtake another lone runner. Suddenly, the runner ahead collapses, gasping for breath. There are a number of decisions that have to be made in a relatively short period of time. "What should be done? Should I try to figure out what's wrong and do my best to help until somebody else comes? Maybe I should just get to the nearest phone and call for help?" The decision to be made may have life or death consequences. If the decision is wrong, feelings of guilt, intense periods of self-doubt, and questions about personal adequacy can result. Janis noted that the more the person's self-esteem is at stake as a competent decision maker, the greater the stress is likely to be.[17]

It may be that the better copers are able to deny, rationalize, or in some other way neutralize failures. The defense mechanisms proposed by Freud were viewed in this way. Defenses enable a person to "define an event filled with negative implications and consequences in such a way that it does not detract from [a] . . . sense of worthiness, ability, or power."[18] Positive self-regard is increased with successes and pressures resulting from negative feedback are minimized by denial. This is probably very acceptable as long as the denial does not distort reality. Accuracy in self-perception is just as important as veridical perception of the world.

Several years ago, the famous psychotherapist Carl Rogers devised a means to help people get more accurate self-portraits. The exercise provided in Exercise 4–2 follows the concept begun by Rogers. First, write down all of the things that *most* describe the real "you." Use descriptive terms such as *submissive, assertive, shy.* Put down the first response that comes to mind without editing, and then think of the next most characteristic trait. When you cannot think of any more traits that describe you, go on to the second step.

The second step asks you to write down how you think other people see you. Be candid even if it hurts at times. Again, try not to stifle your first impressions. Let the first thoughts flow on to the page. After you are done, compare your first list with the second list. What are the major differences between the two lists? Do these differences suggest any areas of needed change? If so, how might you go about making changes?

The last step is to write down all the traits that would make up your ideal self, how you would be if you could make any changes you wanted. Space is provided in the worksheet to do this. There is just one limit on the process. The ideal self should be realistic and attainable, not a dreamlike fantasy that has no likelihood of happening. For example, you might want to be well-disciplined in weight control or exercise, especially if you now view yourself as undisciplined. This would be a realistic goal. On the other side, if you are of average or even above-average intelligence, it would be unrealistic to describe the ideal self in terms of intellectual prowess that would rival Einstein. But you might still aspire to be more mentally active than you are now. This would be a worthwhile goal.

As you are constructing this picture of the ideal self, try not to think about what you put down for the real you. By the same token, list any traits

Self-Study Exercise 4–2.   Cross-Checking Perceptions of Self

How I See
Myself

_____   _____

_____   _____

_____   _____

_____   _____

_____   _____

_____   _____

How Others
See Me

_____   _____

_____   _____

_____   _____

_____   _____

_____   _____

_____   _____

How I Would
Like to Be

_____   _____

_____   _____

_____   _____

_____   _____

_____   _____

_____   _____

that you want to be part of the ideal you even if they were also part of the real you. Once you have completed this ideal picture, compare the real you with the ideal you. The same questions can be asked as before. What are the major differences between the real you and the ideal you? Do the differences suggest any things that you might be doing for self-improvement? If so, how might you go about making changes?

Person Perception

Just as self-perception is important to stress transactions, so is perception of others. Two of the most important influences in person perception are implicit personality theories and attributions.

Implicit personality theories.   Virtually every interaction with another person adds some kind of information to the memory store about what people are like and what they do in certain situations. In this way we build up schemata for people. Schemata for people take on all the markings of a personality theory, but they function as *implicit theory* rather than formally stated theory. Basically, they connect emotional, behavioral, and intellectual traits to certain labels. When we encounter someone who has a pattern of traits seen previously, the schema for that type of person is called up. Then, there is a tendency to assign the same label for future reference. The schemata enable us to predict, to some extent, what the other person will do and to adjust our own behavior accordingly. The labels enable us to assign some degree of meaning to personal transactions and to communicate with others about our personal encounters with certain types of people.

Some problems occur, however, when we assign a label too quickly. Here is an example. Say that you have had a brief encounter of the nasty kind with someone, a store clerk who has been rude and abrupt, or someone who rushes out of a door nearly knocking you down without so much as a "Sorry," or a pause to see if you are all right. The tendency is to form a very quick first impression of the person, search for a schema that adds meaning, and attach a label summarizing what you think the person is like.

This process is loaded with many opportunities for error. First impressions are based on very limited information. There was no way of knowing that the manager had just sent a pink slip giving notice of termination. You didn't give the clerk the benefit of the doubt. That is one source of error.

First impressions also are very difficult to eliminate. They keep a shadowy presence on the backroads of the mind. That is another source of error.

Finally, first impressions tend to function as halos. That is, they tend to color interpretations of the other person's behavior in future encounters.

In the meantime, you discover that the merchandise has to be returned. This leads to a full-length mental feature anticipating the confrontation with the clerk that is surely going to occur. As the epigram at the beginning of this chapter stated, "If pleasures are greatest in anticipation, just remember that this is also true of trouble." In this case, it is faulty person perception based on implicit personality theory and hasty impressions based on limited contact that create a stressful situation.

Attributions and person perception.   The second influence, attribution, has to do with assigning cause or blame for outcomes of behavior. When we are at fault for some outcome, we have a tendency to attribute the cause of the problem to forces outside of our control. If we are late for an appointment, it is because the alarm didn't go off or the car wouldn't start. Even though we could have prevented the problem, we blame it on something outside. This is *external attribution*. However, if someone else is late for an appointment, the attribution is totally different. Then it is a flaw in that person's character. This is *internal attribution*. The general conclusion of many studies of attribution is that "we tend to overestimate the degree to which behavior is caused by traits of the individual and underestimate the degree to which it is caused by external factors."[19] Think again of the rude clerk.

The fact that we attribute blame to the environment when the problem is within our control is a fundamental cognitive error that makes it more difficult first to avoid conflict and second to correct behaviors contributing to conflict. Conversely, our tendency to attribute the error to personal weakness when it involves somebody else sets the stage for more tension. "Surely they should be able to see that the problem is within their control?" Realize though that when you are the one in error, this is exactly the type of attribution your peers are making about you!

On the surface, it seems difficult to eliminate this basic way of looking at causes. No research has looked at ways of changing attribution errors. However, awareness that such errors can contribute to stress may help track down problems if you are motivated to look for them. Let's assume for the moment that you are having frequent tension-filled interactions with a certain person or group of people. You have tried to understand why but you keep running into a brick wall. Look at the implicit personality theory you have used to describe the person or persons. Maybe you have been unfair to one or more of the people. Check your perceptions with others, but do so with people who don't have an ax to grind. If that doesn't seem to hold any keys, then look at the kinds of attributions that are being made from both your side and the other side. In fact, if the interactions are often loaded with accusations of blame, you may do well to start here. It may be that the self–other frame of reference that leads to different attributions is the source of the difficulty. As an exercise, easy to recommend but more difficult to carry out, put yourself in the other position and determine if you would make the same attributions. If so, you may be able to come to a better understanding of the difficulty and obtain a resolution of the conflict.

Perception of Situations

Perceptions of self and others influence the flow of every social transaction. But the situation, the context of the transaction, has a meaning which is added to the interpersonal. Such meaning is provided by situation schemata, very descriptively also called *event scripts*.[20] Event scripts are mental rule books, or step-by-step guides to what actions are called for in any situation as the event unfolds. Just as we have schemata for typical people, we have schemata for stereotypic events. The restaurant, a bus, a cab, a church service, the congressional gallery, each has a different script, rules, and expectations. What to do at Tiffany's is a much different script from what to do at MacDonald's!

One of the most interesting observations on the perception of situations came from the work of Beecher.[21] He compared reactions to pain among 215 soldiers seriously wounded in battle with those of civilians undergoing surgery for similar wounds. Only 25% of the soldiers wanted a narcotic for pain relief. On the other hand, 80% of the civilians wanted relief. Beecher concluded that in the context of battle the wound meant a ticket out, while to the civilians surgery was tantamount to disaster.

◆ MEMORY: I DON'T REMEMBER IT THAT WAY

In the middle of a domestic squabble, how many times have you heard one of these statements: "I don't remember it happening that way." "No, you were the one who said . . ." "Your memory is really messed up. It was nothing like that." Each of these comments reflects on one of the fundamental vagaries of human existence, the fragility of human memory. Perhaps it would be fairer to say the vulnerability of human memory because research over the past century suggests that human memory is not only very powerful but also quite permanent. But it is also subject to a number of forces that can selectively discard, suppress, or creatively reconstruct memory to fit personal motives and needs.

Two important memory processes are redintegration and reconstruction. **Redintegration** means to reunite or restore to a new condition. In memory, it means that a set of related bits of information are recalled as a unit when one item is recalled. For example, on the witness stand, a person may be prompted to recall some element of a hit-and-run accident or a murder scene. At that moment, a flood of information related to the prompted recollection may occur. For the most part, redintegration can be viewed as valuable. But there is one problem. Some of what is recalled really amounts to inferences or guesses about what must have occurred. This process fills in the gaps through a logical refabrication to make complete what is otherwise incomplete. In the heat of battle, it is all the more difficult to distinguish fact from fiction because what is recalled does make sense.

In **reconstruction,** a memory is shaped or molded to fit the person's expectations, beliefs, knowledge, or schemata. A classic study, which has stood the test of time, shows how schemata can influence the reconstruction of memory. Before World War I, an English psychologist by the name of Frederic Bartlett presented subjects with a story called "The War of the Ghosts."[22] The story was part of the oral tradition of Indians who lived on the west coast of Canada a century ago. It fit very well with the Indian schema of how the world works, but obviously had little to do with English schemata of cosmic order. Bartlett asked his subjects to recall the story anywhere from several hours to several years later. All of the records show evidence of distortions in recall. Details were omitted. Facts were changed. New bits of information cropped up that had nothing to do with the story as it was first told. This outcome is really not very startling in and of itself. But the systematic changes that occurred were very revealing of the way in which memory operates.

First, each successive recall of the story produced a shorter story, a process called *leveling*. In addition, some details were made more prominent, a process called *sharpening*. Changes in the story were made in the direction of personal culture. *Hunting seals* became *fishing* and *canoe* became *boat*. Elements of the story that were basically incomprehensible without knowledge of the Indian culture were simply discarded or completely changed.

This indicates that memory can change selectively to fit personal schemata. Many misunderstandings that lead to interpersonal conflict (marital disputes, for example) may result from these inferential, redintegrative, and reconstructive processes. It may be helpful in such cases to ask yourself the simple but hard question, "Is my memory serving me correctly?" In some cases an external reference may be available. There may be a friend or partner who was privy to the original conversation, a secretary or a tape recording of the meeting where the conversation was held. If so, it might prevent further escalation of the conflict to consult these sources.

◆ APPRAISAL PROCESSES IN STRESS

Probably the most influential model of the role of cognitive processes in stress comes from the work of Richard Lazarus and his group. The basic tenets of this model were introduced in Chapter 2. **Stress** is defined as a mismatch between demands and coping resources. Two cognitive processes are important to the person–environment transaction. These are *appraisal* and *coping*. **Appraisal** is used in the dictionary sense of the term, that is, to set a value on or judge the quality of something. **Coping** is defined as behavioral and cognitive efforts by the person to deal with both environmental and internal demands and conflicts between the two.[23]

Lazarus proposed that there are three appraisals that provide meaning and influence the course of coping when a situation has been appraised as stressful. The three appraisals are primary, secondary, and reappraisal. **Primary appraisal** provides the initial evaluation of the type of situation. **Secondary appraisal** considers the match between coping skills and the demands of the situation. Primary appraisal answers the question "Am I in trouble or not?" Secondary appraisal answers the question "What can I do about it?" **Reappraisal** is based on feedback from transactions that occur after the first two appraisals. Additional adjustments are made to the primary appraisal, which may in turn influence the perception of the skills available to deal with it.

There are three types of primary appraisal. Some events are simply *irrelevant* to the person. They contain no threat and require no response. Other events are *benign-positive*. They are evaluated as desirable or, at worst, neutral and present no real demands to personal skills. Events evaluated as *stressful,* however, vary in at least two ways. First, they vary in the nature of the threat to the person. Second, they vary in the nature of the demand placed on personal coping resources and skills. The beginning of stress occurs when the person perceives (primary appraisal) that a situation presents some physical or psychological harm, either real or imagined, for which no effective response is available (secondary appraisal). Stress ends when the person either reevaluates the event in such a way that the threat is no longer present or a coping reaction eliminates or effectively neutralizes the threat.

Lazarus proposed three stressful appraisals. The first type of stressful appraisal is that of *harm-loss*. Events of this nature usually involve the real or anticipated loss of something of great personal significance. The loss of a friend, lover, or spouse through death or separation is one type of harm-loss. Loss of a job, prestige, or money is another type. Damage to self-esteem is a psychological loss. Some losses inflict both real and ego losses. As Coyne and Lazarus noted, "There is no self-esteem threat more powerful than rejection by an intimate partner."[24] The diagnosis of long-term or terminal illness, mastectomy for breast cancer, loss of eyesight or hearing—any of these is a type of physical harm-loss.

The appraisal of *threat* occurs when a situation demands more coping capacity than is available. The emotional tone of the evaluation is negative. Challenge refers to a situation that is evaluated as demanding and potentially risky, but in which the emotional tone is one of excitement and anticipation. In addition, the person believes the demands can be met whatever they are. The distinction between threat and challenge is still somewhat muddy and not resolved to everyone's satisfaction.[25] An example might help to clarify. A novice climbs small mountains but becomes incapacitated by fear if asked to climb a sheer rock face. An experienced climber, on the other hand, not only relishes the thought of tackling a very demanding climb, but feels honored to be involved.

◆ FACTORS CONTRIBUTING TO STRESSFUL APPRAISALS

What determines whether a situation is appraised as stressful or not? There are at least three factors that seem to most critically influence the appraisal process. These are the *emotionality* associated with the event, *uncertainty* resulting either from the objective lack of necessary information to evaluate all aspects of the situation or from personal traits having to do with ability to deal with ambiguity, and *evaluation of meaning*.

Emotionality

The relationship between emotions and cognitive processes has been the subject of much controversy for quite some time. One camp adopts the point of view that emotions are primary and influence the form and focus of cognitive processes. Another camp takes the view that the cognitive system is primary and gives rise to emotions. Consistent with a transactional view, Lazarus considered cognitions and emotions as linked in an ongoing flow of negotiations with the environment. They are thus interdependent.[26] In this view, however, emotions can influence the adaptive transactions and coping process in four ways.

First, emotions serve a very important signal function that something is wrong. These emotional evaluations are rather primitive and related to survival themes. But as transactions with the environment turn out positively or negatively, emotional tones are paired with memory for the events. In this way, when the same situation or a very similar situation develops, it is highly likely that one of the first factors influencing the perception of the event will be the emotional tone stored previously.

Second, emotions serve to interrupt ongoing behavior. In this sense, emotional evaluations are attention getters. They redirect attention to something that is more important because of the danger or threat involved. If the situation is so powerful that it "demands" attention, then the likelihood is that it will also be appraised as stressful.

Third, emotions can interfere in other cognitive events, disrupting many cognitive tasks and initiating those tasks that are most relevant to whatever has been found emotional. This is why concentration or focus can be so difficult in certain highly emotional circumstances. For example, the death of a loved one frequently disrupts many thought processes for a long period of time. Concentration on other mental tasks can be very difficult. One extreme example of this is when the person becomes obsessed with thoughts of the deceased and cannot carry out any meaningful activities.

Finally, emotions can become motivators. Some emotions are unpleasant. We will do whatever we can to get rid of them. On the other side, some emotions are pleasant. We will engage in a variety of behaviors to maintain such an emotion or put ourselves in situations where there is hope that it will be recreated. Stress is generally associated with an unpleasant emotional state. Thus emotions can serve to increase behaviors that are aimed at controlling, eliminating, or reducing the internal tension.

Uncertainty

The second factor contributing to a stress appraisal is uncertainty. When a situation is presented for which existing knowledge is inadequate, or the situation is very complex, a condition of uncertainty exists. The Lazarus group considered uncertainty to be confusion over meaning.[27] No schemata are available to provide interpretations. In essence, the situation is not predictable and thus the person does not know what behavior is appropriate. Given this unpredictability, a feeling of helplessness or futility may overwhelm and lead to a stress reaction.

Mishel studied a group of 100 patients in a Veterans Administration hospital.[28] He found that lack of clarity and lack of information about the medical events that were to transpire accounted for the patients' evaluation of the events as stressful, rather than the event itself. Thus, there was a strong relationship between uncertainty and stress.

Two factors seem to determine whether uncertainty will result in a stress reaction or not. The first is *tolerance for ambiguity.* The second has to do with *information-seeking* skills. Formally, **ambiguity** is defined as "having two or more meanings" or "susceptible to more than one interpretation, vague or obscure." **Tolerance** means the ability to withstand or endure. Thus, whether an uncertain situation will result in stress or not depends on one's ability to endure while possible meanings are considered and the situation becomes predictable or certain.

When uncertainty occurs, one can engage in a search for new information that will remove the uncertainty. A number of investigators have come to the conclusion that information seeking is one of the most important coping strategies a person can develop. Notice, however, that engaging in a search for relevant information assumes that ambiguity can be tolerated for whatever period of time is required to obtain the necessary information. In addition, successful coping depends on both the ability to predict, to some extent, what will happen and the ability to engage in controlling behaviors. The ability to predict itself depends on having relevant information available. Belief in the ability to control, both in terms of locus of control and self-efficacy, are important at this point.

One study obtained a very interesting result in this regard.[29] The research team of Jerry Suls and Brian Mullen wanted to know if perceptions of control and desirability of life events would have any effect on subsequent health in a college sample. They found that undesirability of life change and lack of control over life-change could not produce change in later illness alone. However, if undesirable and uncontrollable events occurred together or undesirable events of uncertain control occurred, there was a significant impact on illness in the following month. The results suggest that information may be important to the extent that it both reduces uncertainty and increases the perception of personal control.

Meichenbaum suggested the use of a strategy called *perspective taking* when unalterable stress occurs.[30] This strategy involves such things as remembering that most all problems are time-limited, that other areas of life are still providing many rewards, and that bad outcomes can still be bearable. More will be said of cognitive strategies later and in Chapter 13.

Changing Meanings

The final factor influencing stress appraisal is evaluation of meaning. A wide variety of information has already been presented on how meaning is added during appraisals. Primary perceptual processes and schemata called up related to self, other, and situation perceptions all contribute. As the situation unfolds, new information may lead to some change in perception that calls up a new schema or a new event script. The meaning assigned because of the new schema may change the definition of the situation from stress to irrelevance or benign-positive.

◆ SECONDARY APPRAISAL, SELF-EFFICACY, AND MASTERY

Self-efficacy

As defined earlier, secondary appraisal deals with the issue of whether skills are available to meet the demands of the situation. A related concept introduced by Albert Bandura is self-efficacy.[31] Bandura considered it to be a form of self-perception or self-appraisal. It is a self-schema containing beliefs about personal competency and mastery. **Self-efficacy** refers to the perception of capability, the belief that personal skills and performance abilities are available that will enable the person to act appropriately and successfully in given situations.

In Bandura's theory, efficacy expectations are distinguished from outcome expectations. Briefly, each time we engage in a behavior it has some good or bad consequence. These outcomes are normally called rewards or punishments. As we mature, we learn to anticipate which behaviors are most likely to lead to which outcomes. These are outcome expectations. An **efficacy expectation** is the belief that the behavior that will produce the outcome can be successfully performed. In Bandura's words, "expectations of personal mastery affect both initiation and persistence of coping behavior. The strength of people's convictions in their own effectiveness is likely to affect whether they will even try to cope with given situations."[32]

Belief that one's skills are poor (low self-efficacy) would lead to the appraisal (secondary) that a given situation is unmanageable and thus stressful. Belief in one's ability to deal with anything that comes along is more likely to lead to the appraisal that the event is irrelevant or benign. A number of studies indicate that more successful coping behavior is related to increases in self-efficacy.[33]

Stress Reappraisals

According to the transactional model, every stress situation is an ongoing series of negotiations, as it were, that does not end until the stress is controlled through coping or the stress ends spontaneously. Feedback related to coping actions and from people who may be part of the situation provide information on both the successfulness of coping behaviors and on the meaning of the event itself. As feedback goes on, the person continues to reevaluate the situation, possibly adjusting both coping strategies and meanings in the process.

There seem to be three ways in which people deal with stressful events during reappraisal. These are rationalizing, changing the meaning of the event, and reducing the significance of the event. In rationalizing, a personally desirable meaning is attached to the event even though a completely objective analysis would show that the meaning is not appropriate. For example, after the first shock of being fired, a person might suggest that this is the long-awaited sign to go into private business, even though everyone else would consider the chances of the person being a successful business entrepreneur nonexistent.

Changing the meaning of the event may be warranted if new information provides a basis for it. For example, a manager is told of an impending reassignment to an office in a different region of the country. The first reaction is negative, hurt, a feeling of being shipped out and shuffled aside. Later on, as additional talks focus on responsibility, projects, pay, and locale, it becomes obvious that the new arrangement will mean a freer hand, more creative opportunities, a larger work force, and a more relaxed life-style for the family in a less overwhelming city. All of this may lead to a significant change in the meaning of the new assignment. In fact, it may be reassigned a positive meaning of challenge and opportunity instead of threat and loss.

Another process that occurs in reappraisal is reduction of the meaning of the event. To illustrate, assume that the union has been negotiating a new contract and the initial talks hint at a sizable pay increase. Plans begin already for new investments, perhaps even some luxury purchases that have been held off for a long time. Then the contract is settled, but the anticipated pay raise is cut drastically, providing little more than a token increase. Initially, there may be a great deal of frustration and anger directed toward both the union negotiators and the management. After a period of time, though, the planned investments and purchases may be gradually and quietly reduced in significance. "Well, we really didn't need that anyway." "We got along without it all this time, we can make it a while longer." This type of cognitive process seems to operate most frequently in cases where outcomes are essentially out of personal control.

◆ COPING RESOURCES, STYLES, AND STRATEGIES

Once a stressful appraisal has been made, there are a number of factors that influence the course of coping itself. These include the personal resources available, the particular style of coping the person has developed over the years, and specific strategies the person feels most comfortable in using. **Coping** has been defined as both the mental acts and the physical actions that are taken to control, manage, reduce, or make tolerable the effects of stress stemming from either external or internal demands.[34]

In general, coping is aimed at one of two outcomes. First, coping may be intended to alter the relationship between self and the environment. This may be accomplished by any one of the reappraisal processes already mentioned or through direct action. Problem solving is considered the most mature direct action, but in some cases escape or avoidance might be used instead.

Second, coping must deal with emotions aroused by stress. Therefore, at least part of the coping effort will be directed to managing unpleasant emotions.

Cognitive Control of Unpleasant Emotions

People engage in a variety of control procedures to eliminate unpleasant emotions. **Defense mechanisms,** made popular in Freud's theory, are a type of cognitive control. Two of the most important defenses used are denial and intellectualization.

Denial. **Denial** is a refusal to accept objective reality for what it is. It is one of the major stages, possibly necessary, in the process of grieving. It makes no difference whether grieving is due to news about a long-term life-threatening illness or to the death of a loved one.

Mardi Horowitz has written extensively on psychological responses to serious life events.[35] He summarized the signs and symptoms of denial that occur in stress reactions, as shown in Table 4–1. Extreme denial can prevent healthy coping and slow down the progression to other stages in the adjustment to and recovery from emergency situations.

Table 4–1.   Signs and Symptoms of Denial Phase of Stress Response Syndromes

Signs	Symptoms
Perception and attention	Daze
	Selective inattention
	Inability to appreciate significance of stimuli
Consciousness	Amnesia (complete or partial)
	Non-experience
Ideational processing	Disavowal of meanings of stimuli
	Loss of reality appropriacy
	Constriction of associational width
	Inflexibility of organization of thought
	Phantasies to counteract reality
Emotional	Numbness
Somatic	Tension–inhibition-type symptoms
Actions	Frantic overactivity to withdrawal

Note. From "Psychological response to serious life events" by M. J. Horowitz, in *Human Stress and Cognition: An Information Processing Approach* (pp. 235–263) by V. Hamilton and D. M. Warburton (Eds.), 1979, New York: Wiley.

Intellectualization. **Intellectualization** refers to the process of translating all feelings into some type of thought process. It is a means of blocking out feelings so that they do not have to be dealt with at all or at least not until the person is ready to do so. While denial is regarded as a primitive defense, intellectualization is regarded as a more mature means of defending against unwanted emotions.[36] The major difficulty is when intellectualization is used to such an extreme that all feelings are filtered through the rational net and thus never expressed.

In general, there must be a balance between the control and the expression of emotions. Extreme or inappropriate emotions need to be controlled or kept in check to some extent, while the less extreme and appropriate emotions can be expressed more openly. In fact, the process of *ventilating* emotions can have a therapeutic effect and can reduce stress for a period of time. Otherwise, the person can become somewhat like a time bomb waiting to go off when some situation triggers an emotional explosion.

Avoidance. Strictly speaking, avoidance is not one of the defense mechanisms. But it is commonly used to protect against unwanted emotions. People frequently avoid the banker for fear of being pressured about a loan or an overdrawn account. They skip class for fear of bad news on a test. Avoidance is not reality oriented, and when used to the extreme, it can interfere with effective coping.

Resources for Coping

Resources include the personal traits or characteristics that buffer the person against stress. The most important appear to be self-esteem, self-denigration, perception of control, and self-efficacy. Physical health and energy reserves can also be regarded as resources. In addition, such things as social supports in family and friends, at work, and in the community are important as stress buffers and facilitate active coping.

Coping styles refer to general patterns of behavior used to deal with stress. Elizabeth Menaghan defined coping styles as "typical, habitual preferences for ways of approaching problems."[37] For example, some people tend to be active when confronted by stress, while others are quite passive. One person feels that doing something is better than nothing, while another seems to feel that you can wait it out before you can beat it out. One author made the distinction between the *proactive* and the *reactive* styles.[38] The proactive person tries to act before stress to prevent it from ever developing; the reactive person takes few preventive measures and just reacts whenever stress occurs. Another difference has to do with cognitive styles. That is, some people may depend heavily on denial of problems, while others may depend much more on thinking and mental problem solving. Some people are more reflective, while others are more impulsive.

The terms *coping strategies* and *coping efforts* may be used somewhat interchangeably. They refer to the direct plans and actions used by the person to reduce or eliminate the stress. The number of strategies available and apparently in use appears virtually limitless. The brief description of coping strategies provided here is intended only to be representative.

The most commonly listed strategies are **attention diversion** strategies, used when the person engages in some other activity in order to not think about the source of stress. This is frequently encountered in situations that involve uncertainty, such as waiting for an all-important call on a job or dealing with a member of the family with a long-term illness. *Ventilating emotions* surrounding stress may also be a useful strategy. *Information seeking* or reading material devoted to the type of situation or person that seems to be the source of the stress is also a frequently adopted strategy.

Irving Janis described five different patterns of coping associated with certain preceding conditions and specific levels of stress:[39]

1. *Unconflicted adherence.* For want of a better term, this could be called the bulldozer or submarine strategy: Put the blade to the wall and just keep pushing, or damn the torpedoes, full speed ahead. The person decides just to go on doing what had been done previously. There seems to be no interest in outside information and no regard for risks.

2. *Unconflicted change.* The person would rather switch than fight. It doesn't make a lot of difference what is recommended, only that it is strongly suggested. The person immediately and uncritically takes on the recommended new course of action.

3. *Defensive avoidance.* In general, the person uses a number of cognitive and behavior schemes to avoid confronting the situation. This may involve denial, procrastination, blaming someone else, rationalization, and selective inattention.

4. *Hypervigilance.* More commonly referred to as panic, hypervigilance is evident when the person engages in frantic searches for solutions. Impulsive decisions may be made that are later regretted and that only add to the problem. There is evidence of deterioration in cognitive skills, probably a result of extreme emotional arousal. Deterioration is seen in repetitive thinking, reduction in the pool of available ideas, and appearance of simplistic ideas.

5. *Vigilance.* In vigilance, the most mature form of coping, the person uses rational problem-solving skills, engages in systematic information searches, considers alternative hypotheses about the source of the difficulty, and also evaluates alternative solutions in a relatively flexible and unbiased fashion.

Coping patterns 1 through 4 are associated with increasing severity of stress, while the last pattern may be used in any situation.

◆ SUMMARY

In principle, the cognitive system encompasses everything that has to do with mental activity, from the simplest to the most complex, from the most primitive to the most evolved. For many obvious reasons, the whole variety of mental processes could not be discussed. This review has focused on those parts of the cognitive system most known to be influential in stress and health. These include primary perception, attention, self, other, and situation perception. A central theme is that cognitive schemata serve to organize information from the myriad transactions with our environment. These schemata in turn provide the basic means whereby meaning is assigned during new transactions. The transactional view of stress was reviewed along with supporting information. Some relevant principles to aid in managing stress were presented but more details on cognitive techniques will be presented in Chapter 13.

◆ NOTES

[1] Lefcourt, H. M. (1976). *Locus of control: Current trends in theory and research.* Hillsdale, NJ: Erlbaum, p. 10.

[2] Kelly, G. A. (1955). *The psychology of personal constructs* (Vols. 1 and 2). New York: Norton.

[3] Ginsburg, H., & Opper, S. (1979). *Piaget's theory of intellectual development* (2nd ed.). Englewood Cliffs, NJ: Prentice-Hall.

[4] Kelly, *Psychology of personal constructs,* p. 46.

[5] Neisser, U. (1976). *Cognition and reality: Principles and implications of cognitive psychology.* New York: Freeman, p. 4.

[6] Beehr, T. A., & Newman, J. E. (1978). Job stress, employee health, and organizational effectiveness: A facet analysis, model, and literature review. *Personnel Psychology, 31,* 655–699, p. 682.

[7] Buss, A. H., & Plomin, R. (1975). *A temperament theory of personality development.* New York: Wiley; Thomas, A., Chess, S., & Birch, H. (1970). The origin of personality. *Scientific American, 223,* 102–109.

[8] Hamilton, V. (1979). Human stress and cognition: Problems of definition, analysis, and integration. In V. Hamilton & D. M. Warburton (Eds.), *Human stress and cognition: An information processing approach* (pp. 3–8). New York: Wiley, p. 6.

[9] John, E. R. (1967). *Mechanisms of memory.* New York: Academic Press.

[10] Pelletier, K. (1977). *Mind as healer, mind as slayer: A holistic approach to preventing stress disorders.* New York: Delacorte/Delta.

[11] Janis, I. L. (1982). *Stress, attitudes, and decisions.* New York: Praeger, pp. 85, 147–149.

[12] Postman, L., Bruner, J. S., & McGinnies, E. (1948). Personal values as selective factors in perception. *Journal of Abnormal Psychology, 43,* 142–154.

[13] Suedfeld, P., Erdelyi, M. H., & Corcoran, C. R. (1975). Rejection of input in the processing of an emotional film. *Bulletin of the Psychonomic Society, 5,* 30–32.

[14] Bexton, W. H., Heron, W., & Scott, T. H. (1954). Effects of decreased variation in the sensory environment. *Canadian Journal of Psychology, 8,* 70–76.

[15] Pearlin, L. I., & Schooler, C. (1978). The structure of coping. *Journal of Health and Social Behavior, 19,* 2–21.

[16]Coyne, J. C., & Lazarus, R. S. (1980). Cognitive style, stress perception, and coping. In I. L. Kutash, L. B. Schlesinger, and associates (Eds.), *Handbook on stress and anxiety* (pp. 144–158). San Francisco: Jossey-Bass, p. 162.

[17]Janis, *Stress, attitudes,* p. 147.

[18]Coopersmith, S. (1967). *The antecedents of self-esteem.* San Francisco: Freeman, p. 37.

[19]Bem, D. J., & Allen, A. (1974). On predicting some of the people some of the time: The search for cross-situational consistencies in behavior. *Psychological Review, 81,* 506–520, p. 508.

[20]Schank, R. C., & Abelson, R. (1977). *Scripts, plans, goals, and understanding.* Hillsdale, NJ: Erlbaum.

[21]Beecher, H. K. (1956). Relationship of significance of wound to the pain experienced. *Journal of the American Medical Association, 161,* 1609–1613.

[22]Bartlett, F. C. (1932). *Remembering: A study in experimental and social psychology.* London: Cambridge University Press.

[23]Coyne, J. C., & Holroyd, K. (1982). Stress, coping, and illness: A transactional perspective. In T. Millon, C. Green, & R. Meagher (Eds.), *Handbook of clinical health psychology* (Chapter 6). New York: Plenum Press, p. 109.

[24]Coyne & Lazarus, Cognitive style, p. 163.

[25]Coyne & Lazarus, Cognitive style, p. 151.

[26]Folkman, S., Schaefer, C., & Lazarus, R. S. (1979). Cognitive processes as mediators of stress and coping. In V. Hamilton & D. M. Warburton (Eds.), *Human stress and cognition: An information processing approach* (pp. 265–298). New York: Wiley.

[27]Folkman et al., Cognitive processes, p. 276.

[28]Mishel, M. H. (1984). Perceived uncertainty and stress in illness. *Research in Nursing and Health, 7,* 163–171.

[29]Suls, J., & Mullen, B. (1981, June). Life events, perceived control and illness: The role of uncertainty. *Journal of Human Stress,* pp. 30–34.

[30]Meichenbaum, D., & Jaremko, M. E. (1983). *Stress reduction and prevention.* New York: Plenum Press, p. 135.

[31]Bandura, A. (1977). Self-efficacy: Toward a unifying theory of behavioral change. *Psychological Review, 84,* 191–215.

[32]Bandura, Self-efficacy, p. 193.

[33]Bandura, A., Reese, L., & Adams, N. E. (1982). Microanalysis of action and fear arousal as a function of differential levels of perceived self-efficacy. *Journal of Personality and Social Psychology, 43,* 5–21.

[34]Lazarus, R. S., & Launier, R. (1978). Stress-related transactions between person and environment. In L. A. Pervin & M. Lewis (Eds)., *Perspectives in interactional psychology.* New York: Plenum Press.

[35]Horowitz, M. J. (1979). Psychological response to serious life events. In V. Hamilton & D. M. Warburton (Eds.), *Human stress and cognition: An information processing approach* (pp. 235–263). New York: Wiley.

[36]Vaillant, G. E. (1977). *Adaptation to life.* Boston: Little, Brown.

[37]Menaghan, E. G. (1983). Individual coping efforts: Moderators of the relationship between life stress and mental health outcomes. In H. B. Kaplan (Ed.), *Psychosocial stress: Trends in theory and research* (pp. 157–191). New York: Academic Press, p. 159.

[38]Adams, J. H., Hayes, J., & Hopson, B. (1976). *Transition: Understanding and managing personal change*. London: Martin Robertson, p. 24.

[39]Janis, I. L. (1982). *Stress, attitudes, and decisions: Selected papers*. New York: Praeger, pp. 148–149.

PERSONALITY AND STRESS: TRAITS, TYPES, AND BIOTYPES

> *Bodily traits are not merely physical, nor mental traits merely psychic. Nature knows nothing of those distinctions.*
> *[Paraphrased]*
>
> C. G. Jung

The notion that personality is somehow related to coping and health has almost the status of an idée fixe in Western society. It is so ingrained in Western philosophy, medicine, and psychology that many people probably would believe a link exists even if scientific evidence disputed it. Recent research, however, has shown that personality does correlate with both the type and the intensity of the stress response. It is related to certain types of health problems. In addition, personality may be related to a variety of sick-role behaviors that affect the time course and prognosis for recovery from illness.

Before delving into these issues, however, it is necessary to understand how the term *personality* is used by those who study it most. We all have some idea of what it means to have a pleasant personality. We may also feel quite confident that we know what we are talking about when we describe someone as having a rotten disposition. However, if pressed to define personality precisely and then to measure differences in personality accurately, we would find the job much tougher. That is the problem investigators face in trying to pin down the relationship between personality and stress or health. In the next few pages, we will examine the concept of personality and the major theories of personality that pertain to stress and health. Evidence will then be presented linking personality types to a variety of stress reactions and health problems. In some cases, the evidence seems quite strong and indisputable. In other cases, however, the claims are still based on shaky grounds and should be accepted only with great caution and skepticism.

◆ PERSONA: WHAT LIES BEHIND THE MASK

Over the centuries, the concept of personality has changed its face many times. As originally used by the ancient Greeks, the term *persona* meant a mask such as one that an actor would wear on stage for theatrical plays of that time. Later on, *persona* came to mean more generally the roles played by an individual associated with different aspects of life.

More recently, *persona* has come to mean some characteristic or a set of characteristics within the person. To put it in figurative terms, personality is the essence of the person behind the mask. It makes the person both real and uniquely different from anyone else. Personality is also stable and enduring, providing a private reference point in the midst of constant flux and change. Presumably, this same durability also allows an outsider to look inside somehow and predict with some accuracy how the person typically behaves.

◆ CLASSIC AND CONTEMPORARY DEFINITIONS OF PERSONALITY

Definitions of personality are relatively easy to come by. But agreement on what personality really refers to is more difficult. The most commonly encountered definition is provided by Gordon Allport, who said that **personality** is "the dynamic organization within the individual of those psychophysical systems that determine his characteristic behavior and thought."[1] Personality so defined is the hub or meeting point for all the various forces that come to bear on the individual during the course of development. These forces include genetic, emotional-conflictual encounters, learning experiences, family interactions, and social influences that have occurred throughout the person's life.

In spite of disagreement on what personality is, most definitions share common themes such as *uniqueness, organization,* and *style of adapting or coping.* The perceptions, thoughts, feelings and behaviors of each individual are organized in different patterns. This difference in patterns makes each person in some way uniquely different from every other person and determines the characteristic style of responding.

Theodore Millon has been more concerned with personality in relationship to stress and health. His view is roughly consistent with the psychodynamic view, which is that personality summarizes the person's style of defending against anxiety, resolving interpersonal stress, and dealing with psychological conflicts. Similarly, Millon views personality as the coping style used by the individual to deal with stressful situations.[2]

◆ VARIETIES OF PERSONALITY THEORY

Several distinct types of personality theories have been popular at one time or another. These include (1) the psychoanalytic, (2) the dispositional, (3) the phenomenological, and (4) the behavioral-cognitive. In the next few pages these approaches will be summarized and the relevance of each to current concerns in stress and health research indicated.

Psychoanalytic Theory in Stress and Health

Psychoanalytic theories such as those Sigmund Freud proposed describe personality by reference to some type of intrapsychic conflict. The nature of the conflict and the developmental stage during which the conflict first occurred are presumably important in determining the formation of the person's personality.

During the heyday of psychoanalysis, many attempts were made to interpret stress responses and health problems in terms of psychoanalytic theory. Most of these attempts were part of the early work in *psychosomatics*. A **psychosomatic disorder** is one in which a real physical ailment (such as ulcers, asthma, colitis, or cardiac arrhythmia) is caused by or influenced by a psychological process, such as ongoing stress or anxiety.

As one example a prominent psychoanalyst, Franz Alexander, proposed that the asthmatic person is a victim of three correlated events. There is, first a genetically determined weakness in one organ in the body that makes it likely that it will break down when stress occurs. This can be likened to a "weak link" theory. Second, there is a specific psychological conflict that weakens the person's defense system if and when stress occurs. And, third, there is some threatening situation. Presumably, life stress (the threat) arouses the unresolved conflict (the psychological risk) and the person is not able to defend against it. As a result, the weakest link in the body, the lungs, expresses the stress in asthmatic attacks. However plausible this sounds, the psychoanalytic orientation has not been widely accepted.

Also, there has been very little evidence to support the psychological origins of asthma. There may be a relationship between personality and the person's reaction to asthma[3] as well as to the course of recovery.[4] One review of the evidence for personality factors in allergy cases discovered one pattern that might be linked. This is the presence of strong dependency needs combined with maternal domination or paternal weakness in allergy patients.[5] Overall, however, the evidence is not convincing.

Dispositions, Personality Types, and Traits

The second type of theory is the *dispositional theory*. Dispositional theories accept a definition of personality that is very much like the third personality concept discussed earlier. That is, **dispositional theories** generally propose that there are "enduring, stable personality differences which reside within the person."[6] There are varieties of dispositional theories, but the two most commonly encountered are the typology approach and the trait approach. A **typology** approach looks for a small number of dispositional clusters that occur with some frequency. A **trait** approach looks for a large number of dispositions that allow description of an individual on each of the dispositions. Presumably, people may have many traits, but fit only one type.

Jung's typology.   Perhaps the best-known contemporary version of a typology was proposed by the Swiss psychiatrist Carl Jung. There are only two types of people in Jung's theory, the *introverted* and *extraverted*. The **introvert** is described as socially withdrawn, reflective, not given to displays of emotion, and somewhat closed off from the external world. The **extravert** is characterized as outgoing, socially active, free in the expression of emotions, and rather open.

Biotypes.   In contemporary stress and health research, attempts have been made to relate certain personality traits to particular diseases. As the reasoning goes, there are genetic mechanisms that determine constitution, temperament, and intellect in each person. The interplay of these factors in turn leads to the emergence of a unique personality, which may be as strong and resilient as genetic endowment can provide. Or it may be a personality given to weakness or excess. In the latter case, the nature of the genetics-personality link may produce risks for stress and health-related problems. One personality type might be more prone to heart attacks, while another personality type might be more prone to ulcers, and so on.

Based on this type of reasoning, a number of investigators now suggest that there are particular personality characteristics, **biotypes,** that can be associated with cancer, heart attacks, ulcers, arthritis, and headaches, among other conditions. Other investigations have linked such problems as depression, alcoholism, and smoking to personality. One of the most commonly encountered syndromes, or biotypes, in current stress research is the Type A behavior pattern.

One major difficulty in trying to establish this connection is the proverbial chicken-and-egg problem. In other words, health problems may change personality or personality disorders may contribute to health problems. But in any given situation, which came first?

Another problem is that biotype theories tend to convey the impression that genetics is destiny or—a very closely related misperception—that personality types are irreversible. Both of these notions are unfortunate. Personality was described earlier as the hub of all the influences—whether biological, psychological, or social—that weave their way into the fabric of personality from conception. Thus, genetic factors may be pushed or shoved in different directions, to more extreme or less extreme expressions, depending on the forces that come into play after birth. In addition, while the stability of personality is often emphasized, there are many indications that changes in personality function can and do occur throughout life. The Type A personality pattern is proof of this. Type A people can and do change their time-driven behavior and thereby reduce their risks of coronary problems.

The Difference Between Types and Traits

Trait theorists focus on a larger number of characteristics and avoid global categories such as those found in type theories. According to most trait theories, people have differing amounts of each trait. It is the combination of traits that differs greatly. Presumably, though, *profiles,* or patterns of traits, will emerge. Profiles basically show where a person is high on some traits, average on others, and low on still other traits. Even though there could be virtually infinite variation, most trait researchers assume there are a small number of profiles that describe a large percentage of people.

Trait Anxiety and State Anxiety

A related idea of great importance to stress research has been proposed by Charles Spielberger.[7] Spielberger believes that there is a basic difference between *trait anxiety* and *state anxiety*. **Trait anxiety** tends to be relatively stable across time and place. People who are high in trait anxiety have a much greater tendency to be anxious whatever the situation and relatively more anxious all the time compared to those low in trait anxiety. For these people, it takes relatively less external stress to trigger a stress reaction. On the other hand, people who are low in trait anxiety are more relaxed all the time, regardless of the situation. It takes relatively higher levels of stress to trigger an anxiety response in them.

On the other hand, **state anxiety** is specific to a situation. Job interviews, driving tests, and solo music performances are examples of situations that can produce high anxiety. State anxiety can vary a great deal within a person. For example, a person might be relatively low in trait anxiety but experience an extreme degree of state anxiety when confronted with a robber. The same person caught in a dangerous winter storm might handle the situation very calmly.

As another example, many students experience a form of state anxiety called *test anxiety.* People in a variety of professions have to take certifying or licensing exams periodically. Careers can hinge on passing qualifying or entrance exams. A person high in trait anxiety combined with high test anxiety would probably be overwhelmed or panicked by the test. On the other hand, someone with low trait anxiety would probably manage the situation without difficulty, as long as test anxiety did not become extreme.

The concept of state–trait anxiety has become more important in stress research because of the belief that stress reactions, especially chronic stress, may be related to trait anxiety. Trait anxiety has been associated with illness behavior in patients with myocardial infarction, while state anxiety has been related to willingness to admit to the presence of a serious illness. As the authors of one study suggested, recognition of the presence of a serious heart problem is mostly related to state anxiety, which itself seems to be related to the seriousness of the symptoms. On the other hand, acceptance of the role that being a heart patient entails (a more severely regimented life-style of exercise, diet, medication, and checkups) is mostly related to the enduring trait anxiety characteristic of the patient.[8]

◆ CORONARY HEART DISEASE, TYPE A BEHAVIOR, AND HYPERTENSION

Are there coronary-prone, depression-prone, and cancer-prone personalities? Are there special dispositions that predispose a person to alcoholism, drug dependency, or smoking? If so, what are the special traits that make people vulnerable to their own brand of illness or addition? And what is the hope to be offered that the risks can be reduced? These are some of the questions tackled in the next few pages.

The Coronary-Prone Personality

Perhaps the most widely publicized and popularly discussed biotype is the Type A or coronary-prone personality. The idea of Type A behavior pattern was first described by two doctors, Meyer Friedman and Ray Rosenman.[9] There are several popular tales of how Friedman and Rosenman came to discover the connection between Type A behavior and coronary thrombosis attacks. According to their own story, however, they were led to the discovery by an upholsterer who came to their office to repair some furniture. He apparently commented that the doctors must treat a lot of worried people. They questioned the basis of his opinion. He in turn pointed out the excessive wear on the leading edge of the couches and chairs. This was a sign to him that many of the doctors' clients were literally on edge. Following this bit of serendipity, they launched the line of research that was to lead to innumerable studies, several ways to tell how strong Type A tendencies are in a person, hundreds of popular articles, and workshops to intervene in the Type A behavior pattern.

What are the basic characteristics of the Type A personality? Most frequently, the **Type A person** is described as one who is time-driven, impatient, insecure of status, highly competitive and aggressive, generally hostile, and incapable of relaxing, even while on vacation. Time urgency is always prominent in the list of symptoms. Type A people seem to run with a faster internal clock. Compared to other people, they estimate that time passes more quickly. In addition, they tend to work more rapidly, pushing themselves to complete things at a faster pace than other people do.[10]

Rosenman and Friedman referred to the pattern as the *hurry sickness*. They listed 13 characteristics that are the most important trademarks for Type A behavior. These trademarks or criteria have been translated into a question format in Table 5–1. You might want to answer these questions yourself. In doing so, though, use your first impression of how you know you behave most of the time. Try not to edit your answers and try not to answer based on what you know a Type A should or should not be.

If you answered virtually all of these questions yes, you would be described as a Type A person. If you answered yes to over half of them, you might still be regarded as Type A, but not an extreme Type A.

Table 5–1.   Criteria Used to Identify Type A Behavior Pattern

1. Do you overemphasize some words in speech and hurry the last words in your sentences?	Yes _____	No _____
2. Do you always move, eat, and walk rapidly?	Yes _____	No _____
3. Are you generally impatient and get irritated when things do not move fast enough for you?	Yes _____	No _____
4. Do you frequently try to do more than one thing at a time?	Yes _____	No _____
5. Do you generally try to move the topic of conversation to your own interests?	Yes _____	No _____
6. Do you feel some sense of guilt when you are relaxing?	Yes _____	No _____
7. Do you frequently fail to take note of new things in your environment?	Yes _____	No _____
8. Are you more concerned with getting than becoming?	Yes _____	No _____
9. Do you constantly try to schedule more activities in less time?	Yes _____	No _____
10. Do you find yourself competing with other people who are also time-driven?	Yes _____	No _____
11. Do you engage in expressive gestures, clenching a fist or pounding the table to emphasize a point, while engaged in conversation?	Yes _____	No _____
12. Do you believe that your fast pace is essential to your success?	Yes _____	No _____
13. Do you score success in life in terms of numbers, numbers of sales, cars, and so on?	Yes _____	No _____

Note. Adapted form *Type A Behavior and Your Heart* by M. Friedman and R. H. Rosenman, 1974, New York: Knopf.

Over the years, the concept of the Type A behavior pattern has changed very little. At one time, it was viewed as a set of personality traits that set the Type A person apart from non–Type A people. A little later, the non–Type A person was described more carefully and called Type B. The Type B person would respond no to most of the questions given in Table 5–1. In addition, two positive traits are regarded as central to the Type B pattern. These are the ability to relax without feeling guilty and the ability to have fun for the sake of it, to play without the need to win at any cost.

In more recent years, it has become customary to distinguish four groups on the continuum from extremely time-driven Type A1 people to extremely laid back Type B4 people. In between are two additional categories. Type A2 people have a moderate amount of the hurry syndrome, but it is muffled, to use Jenkins's term, or not full-blown as in the true Type A1 group.[11] Type B3 people are more relaxed and free of the hurry syndrome but not as laid back as the extreme Type B4.

Type A and Coronary Risk

Is Type A behavior related to increased risk for coronary heart disease, as Friedman and Rosenman suggested? A rather large and still-growing body of literature has provided convincing evidence that people with the Type A behavior pattern have a much greater risk for heart attacks than people who do not display the hurry sickness. In the normal population, approximately 1 out of every 162 Americans will suffer a heart attack. In the age bracket of 39–49 years of age, Type A men are 6.5 times as likely to have a heart attack.[12]

In the past, a number of risk factors have been identified which are associated with high risk for coronary. These include (1) age, (2) sex, (3) high cholesterol levels, (4) hypertension, (5) smoking, (6) inactivity, (7) diabetes mellitus, (8) parental history of heart disease, and (9) obesity.[13] As David Glass pointed out, no matter what combination of these factors is used, they still fail to detect most new cases of coronary disease. The presence of the Type A behavior pattern is capable of predicting coronary disease better than all of the other risk factors put together. This relationship was established in a classic research project called the Western Collaborative Group Study, which was begun in 1965. The study was carried out over nearly eight years and involved some 3,500 subjects.[14]

Other studies point to the existence of a coronary-prone personality which can be identified long before an attack occurs.[15] The most important trait in the coronary-prone person is the existence of the Type A pattern, especially the impatience and overactivity factors. However, a second cluster seems to be very important. This is the presence of depression and high levels of anxiety, which seems to indicate an overreactive sympathetic nervous system.[16] In addition, it has been suggested that victims of coronary attacks experience no more stressful events than healthy subjects. However, they appear to translate their emotional upsets into bodily symptoms more frequently. As a result they seem to suffer more from digestion and sleep disturbances, which may compound or add to problems at work.

Several researchers have observed this sympathetic reactivity and have suggested that Type A people have an increased risk for a wide variety of stress-related illnesses, not just coronary disease.[17] There is some evidence to support this notion. For example, in the Western Collaborative Group Study, more people died from noncoronary causes than died from coronary causes. This included Type A people as well. Unfortunately, the authors do not report exactly what those other deaths resulted from.

Type A people reveal both physical and behavioral traits besides the hurry syndrome that set them apart from their Type B counterparts. In general, Type A people show greater sympathetic arousal, more clotting of blood, higher cholesterol levels, and increased triglyceride levels under stress.[18] While Type A people do have a higher risk for coronary disease, they do not necessarily have hypertension. In women, however, Rosenman and Friedman reported a three-to sevenfold higher rate of diastolic hypertension in Type A women (34.8%) as compared to Type B women (4.5%).[19]

Type A people do report more stress symptoms than Type B people. They appear to set higher performance standards for themselves.[20] In interpersonal relationships with Type B people, Type A people are much more dominant,[21] and they are impatient in competitive situations.[22] They also smoke more and exercise less.[23] Most of these characteristics are, of course, part of a pattern that increases risk for coronary attacks.

Attempts to relate Type A behavior to demographic factors have been somewhat more confusing. However, a better base of information has become available in the recent past. A history of parental coronary disease is not strongly related to Type A behavior.[24] Type A behavior tends to increase with socioeconomic status.[25] For some time, Type A was thought of as primarily a male pattern. But now it seems that whether Type A appears in men or women depends more on such variables as age, employment, and marital status than on gender. One study did find more men than women with Type A behavior, but mostly in the 18–25-year age range.[26] Women showed higher Type A scores in the better educated, working 25–39-year-old group. In most cases, as the authors of this study surmised, these were women who were working and rearing a family as well. This same study compared whites with blacks and found that whites had higher Type A scores than blacks. Finally, Type A scores tend to decrease with age.

Intervening in Type A Behavior

The techniques used to change Type A behavior run the gamut from Rosenman and Friedman's philosophical reeducation[27] to rather detailed behavior management programs focused on very narrowly defined aspects of the Type A pattern. While few firm conclusions can be drawn as yet, there is some basis for hope.

Many individuals identified as Type A have been able to change their life-styles dramatically in the direction of a more temperate approach to life. One of the reasons for caution in interpreting these results is that many of the studies have worked with people who had already experienced the trauma of a coronary attack. In many cases, these attacks were regarded as life threatening. The intrinsic motivation in such a scare may be all that is necessary to get people to change their life-style. Thus, how much the treatments really contributed to the change is not clear. It may be that the motivation to change and information on what to change is more important than the specific means of addressing the change.

The Hypertensive Personality

Closely related to the concept of Type A personality is the notion that there is a hypertensive personality. The idea originated with Franz Alexander, the psychiatrist mentioned earlier. According to Alexander, hypertensive patients fight an internal struggle between two strong but incompatible feelings. On the one hand, the person feels passive and dependent. On the other hand, there are very strong aggressive and hostile impulses. Expression of hostility is very threatening, though, so the person has to fight constantly to keep it under control. Theoretically, this internal conflict should produce long-term autonomic arousal, constriction of blood vessels, and increased blood pressure. Over a period of time, permanent arterial changes occur and hypertension is the result.[28]

Alexander's theory was largely speculative in nature and based on clinical observations of patients, as opposed to carefully thought out and controlled studies. More recently, attempts have been made to identify a specific pattern of traits common to hypertensives, but the results are not consistent.[29] For example, one study looked at the relationship between blood pressure and scores on several widely used personality scales. The research team reported that hypertensives tended to demean themselves while suppressing their own emotional feelings. In addition, they were described as neurotic, emotionally immature, guilt-prone, and tense.[30] Unfortunately, there were a number of flaws compromising the usefulness of this information. The study did not use a control group. The sample of hypertensives was small. Most important, the procedure used in the experiment involved a rather stressful catheter implant, which could have influenced the outcome.

After a rather lengthy review of evidence on this issue, Iris Goldstein concluded that there is no support for the notion that hypertensives are psychologically different from normals. Goldstein could find no sound evidence that hypertensives are any more neurotic than people with normal blood pressure. Further, there seems to be little or no support for Alexander's idea that hypertensives are struggling to inhibit aggression.[31]

◆ DEPRESSION

Depression is the common cold of mental illness.[32] It afflicts literally hundreds of thousands of people. At any moment, about 1 of every 15 American suffers moderate to severe depression. The chances are one in three that sometime in your life you will have a depressive episode severe enough to require clinical treatment.[33] For some, the affliction is barely noticeable, a blue Monday that lasts a little longer. For others, it is an unhappiness with self and all that life has to offer that colors all their waking perceptions. And for others, depression is the beginning of the end, the bottomless pit of sorrow and despair leading to hospitalization, attempted suicide, or death from suicide.

As this description suggests, depression seems to run on a continuum of severity. But there is also a growing body of evidence pointing to the existence of quite distinct types of depression. In fact, a genetic mechanism may play a major role in distinguishing less severe depression from severe depression. The most severe form of depression, called *bipolar depression,* is present in no more than 5–10% of the cases of depression. It appears to be genetically determined, while most other forms of depression appear to result from pressures from daily living.

To say that a person is depressed describes the emotional tone, to be sure. But there is so much more than that. It is a condition that is so pervasive it can change virtually all the activities normally considered a part of daily life. Depression is a disturbance in mood, a prolonged emotional state that colors all mental processes. The most significant mood seems to be a feeling of hopelessness coupled with helplessness. The person may lose weight because of a general loss of pleasure in eating. Sleep disturbances also occur frequently. Some people sleep a great deal when they become depressed, but at odd hours so that normal activities such as family routines are disrupted. Others may go to sleep readily but wake up early and not be able to get back to sleep. With both eating and sleeping problems, the person tends to feel fatigued and run down all the time. Normal reserves of energy are depleted and motivation suffers.

Depression also says something about how the person thinks. It is more than just sluggish thinking. The person has feelings of personal worthlessness to one degree or another. There may be a vague feeling of being guilty of some type of transgression. In the depressed person's mind, this sin accounts for why people don't care. Concentration suffers, so sticking to any kind of task that requires sustained attention becomes difficult if not impossible. In some serious cases thought disturbances may occur, including suicidal thinking and delusions of persecution or delusions of serious illness such as cancer.

There are several observations that make the study of depression most relevant to the study of stress and health. First, physical illnesses seem to be more commonly associated with depression. Risk for illness may increase because of a direct suppression effect on the immune system. Or it may be the cumulative effect of the problems that occur in loss of appetite, poor eating habits, lack of exercise, fatigue, and sleep disturbances. Second, many illnesses are accompanied by depression as a result of dealing with the illness. For example, chronic low back pain usually results in serious depression when the pain has lasted for more than two years.[34] Depression occurs in this case even when there is no evidence of depressive episodes before the back pain. Third, depression seems to be one major reaction to personal crises or failure to cope with a crisis. Depression also seems to be a common reaction to a number of stressors such as loss of work, loss of savings and investments, and divorce or separation. Finally, depressed people experience more stress in their daily lives yet seem to have fewer personal resources and social supports to deal with the stress than their nondepressive counterparts.[35]

The Depression-Prone Personality

In recent years, some attention has been given to the *depression-prone personality*. Richard Sword describes the depression-prone person as a hardworking, responsible, conscientious, and ambitious person. There is a strong sense of duty, and the person sets very high standards for others but even higher personal standards. The depression-prone person also has a high sense of personal integrity and honesty. Anger is rarely shown, and the person is generally pleasant and outwardly happy, even when inwardly sad.[36]

Stress, Depression, and Suicide

Suicide and depression are often linked in folklore. There is good reason to be concerned about the potential for a suicide when depression has dragged on for some time. What is often overlooked is that people rarely commit suicide while in a state of depression. This is because both the mental processes required to plan and execute the act and the physical stamina to carry out the act are not available. The most dangerous period is when the person is swinging back to a more normal mood state. Unfortunately, it tends to make the impact even more devastating for the family.

The increase in suicide among teenagers and young adults has led to many questions about the pressures contemporary society puts on our young people. Suicide is the second leading cause of death in college students. In white adolescent males, suicide increased by 64% during the time from 1970 to 1977.[37] In 1980, one out of every five suicides involved a 15–24-year-old male.[38] In one study of gifted high school students, it was discovered that stress and suicidal thoughts tend to go together. That is, the more stress builds up, the more likely the person is to think about suicide and self-destructive behavior. There does not appear to be any difference in this tendency, however, when the gifted are compared to normally intelligent adolescents. Gifted students do appear to be more sensitive to stress but actually experience less stress than their average counterparts.[39]

◆ THE CANCER-PRONE PERSONALITY

Cancer is probably one of the most terrifying diseases of our time. Approximately one in four people will be diagnosed with cancer at some time in their lives, while two in three families will have to deal with the disruption, pain, and suffering caused by cancer. The search for a cure has led in all directions—to medicines, surgery, radiation therapy, vitamins, diet, carrot juice, and apricot pits. Many people, desperately seeking to hang on to life and loved ones, grasp any straw that seems to offer a hope of understanding and beating the dread disease.

But treatment looks beyond just controlling or curing to the elimination of the threat of cancer. In turn, eliminating cancer depends on identifying more precisely the causes of cancer. This is all the more problematic, since cancer is not a single disease but an array of nearly 100 different types. The search for causes has led through many genetic, biochemical, physiological, and environmental studies to a partial understanding of what happens *after* abnormal cell growth is triggered. In some cases, it is even possible to trigger a cancerous growth process in the cell experimentally. But the real reasons for cancer are still largely unknown.

In recent years, more attention has been devoted to the possible connection between psychosocial stressors and cancer. Some of this work is worthy of consideration and shows promise of filling in additional pieces of the puzzle. But much of it is flawed, some of it probably worthless, and some possibly even dangerous. Barofsky pointed out that evidence linking stress, psychological conflicts, and personality characteristics to cancer has been extensively reviewed and found methodologically and empirically deficient.[40] The next few paragraphs will present evidence on the cancer-prone personality and identify the psychosocial processes that have been reliably linked to cancer.

The personality characteristics most frequently attributed to the cancer patient are internalized anger and aggression. A number of studies have shown that cancer patients tend to have higher levels of depression, anxiety, anger, hostility, denial, and repressed emotionality.[41] Suggestions that these emotional problems are linked to some childhood trauma, an unhappy childhood, or family maladjustment abound. Separation from or death of a parent or sibling has been found in cancer patients more frequently than in other patients.[42] One person has even gone so far as to suggest that vulnerability to cancer relates to lack of breast feeding in infancy.[43] Also, family histories of cancer patients reveal more unhappy home lives, domestic strife, and neglect during childhood. This may contribute to the feelings of loneliness, desertion, and denial seen in many cancer patients.

Unfortunately, most of the studies that provided the evidence for these statements suffered from one or more inadequacies. They lacked control groups, used patients who already knew of their diagnosis, and/or analyzed the data improperly.

Among the better-controlled studies, there is still conflicting information. One team found more repression and less "self-reported" depression relative to a control group.[44] One of the better controlled studies was carried out using women with breast cancer. The pattern of suppressed anger and abnormal release of emotions was verified in this group. None of the other personality traits previously attributed to cancer patients was observed.[45]

Even granted that this difference in anger and release of emotions is the crucial difference between cancer-prone and noncancer-prone people, there is still the issue of how the differences could be physically translated into cancer. One general model proposed by Barofsky is shown in Figure 5–1.

The path from psychological conflict to tumor production may actually involve any one of a number of different mechanisms. The most frequently suggested path is via elevated adrenocortical production resulting from stress. This presumably produces a suppression in the immune surveillance system, which controls the production of Killer-T cells involved in the detection of cancer cells. As a result of this suppression, tumors form with little or no resistance. (Information was presented about this in Chapter 3.) Sooner or later, the tumor presents a threat that is medically diagnosed and treated.

As the model shows, diagnosis of cancer and the resulting treatment add to the load of stress. Additional conflict, anger, hostility, denial, and depression generally occur as a result of cancer. The intensity and duration of such conflict is itself related to personal coping resources. But even the strongest will go through some period of disruption as they integrate the information about their uncertain future. Many of the early studies have been criticized,

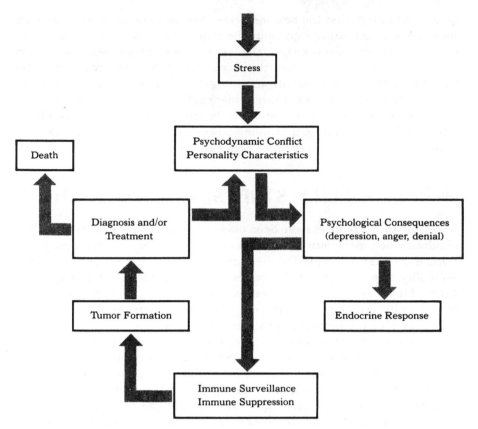

Figure 5–1. A theoretical model of how psychosocial stress and personality may influence the production of tumors.

however, because of using patients with already diagnosed cancer. It is impossible under such circumstances to separate the psychological characteristics that are due to the illness from those that have led to the illness.

As already noted, the patient's defensive coping reactions can significantly influence the course of a disease process. Katz and his colleagues provided some insight on this issue in their study of a group of women hospitalized for breast biopsy. At the end of the study, they concluded that being in a stress situation alone does not account for arousal of either the emotions or the physical emergency reactions so often expected from a stressor. Rather, both emotional defenses and physical arousal of the adrenal system appear to be dependent on how the stress is perceived, interpreted, and defended against. They found that high rates of adrenal reactivity were associated with apprehension, worry, fear, dejection, discouragement, and despair. On the other hand, low adrenal reactivity was associated with hope, faith in God, fate, and pride in one's ability to handle a life-threatening situation.[46]

A final issue has to do with the attitudes and emotions that are most curative and enable one to survive the threat of cancer. It is well known, if quietly admitted, that the best medicine may be to no avail when given to someone who has already given up the struggle for life. Even if there is no strong relationship between the origins of cancer and some personality type, the evidence does suggest that the way in which a person responds to the threat may have a lot to do with surviving the physical insult of cancer. The Katz study is one example of this evidence. Chronic worry, fear, hopelessness, and despair generally hasten the destructive disease process. On the other hand, hope, faith in a supreme power, and personal courage all generally operate to marshal the best body defenses available.

◆ PERSONALITY, STRESS, AND INFERTILITY

Many medical advances have been made to help couples conceive and bear children where previously there was little or no hope. While medical solutions have been welcome for the most part, there has been concern that infertility may result as much from psychological stress as from physiological problems. A number of investigators have suggested that heightened emotionality, stress, and depression can produce functional infertility. To date, however, the evidence is not very convincing.

One team of researchers attempted to obtain information on the issue by taking direct measures of autonomic reactions such as pulse volume, heart rate, skin resistance, and muscle tension.[47] Their rationale was quite simple. Emotional stress produces some rather powerful effects through the hypothalamic–pituitary–adrenal complex. In women, one of the important connections controlled by this complex is the production of follicle-stimulating hormone (FSH) and luteinizing hormone (LH). Both of these are critical to the development of the ovaries and thus to fertility and ovulation. Stress might inhibit the production of FSH and LH or in some other fashion interfere with what is necessary for ovulation and conception. Since the autonomic system and the adrenal system mimic each other, the researchers decided to measure the pattern of reactivity in the autonomic system.

Three groups of women were used from a hospital infertility clinic. One group was diagnosed as functionally infertile. A second group was organically infertile, while a third group was regarded as normally fertile. The conclusion of the study showed no differences whatsoever among the groups on any measures of autonomic reactivity.

Unfortunately, there are two flaws in the experiment that leave open the question of stress and fertility. First, the stressor tests used were of a very mild variety. The tests could be viewed as not very arousing for anybody and thus very insensitive to any differences that might exist. Second, not only was the fertile group very small (only five women), but the women were married to partners with abnormal sperm production. This indicates that concern about conception could still be present in these women, a conclusion that is further supported by the fact that they were patients at the infertility clinic. Thus, the supposedly normal group might have had a degree of emotional arousal present that could have tipped the autonomic balance in the direction of higher reactivity than normal. Again, differences would not be detected even if they existed.

◆ PREMENSTRUAL SYNDROME AND PERSONALITY

A great deal of attention has been focused on the premenstrual syndrome (PMS) in the recent past. There is even a rather lively controversy as to the legitimacy of the syndrome itself. Leaving that controversy for others to deal with, some researchers have tried to determine whether there is a personality profile that distinguishes women who complain of PMS from women who do not. One research team believes there is.

A personality profile was developed for 110 women, all of whom were in their eighth month of pregnancy.[48] The authors' choice of this sample was based on the belief that pregnancy places a load on both body and personality and that the characteristics alleged to occur with PMS would be more apparent in this group. They claimed to have assessed PMS ad hoc from menarche to pregnancy. The general profile associated with PMS was tension, rejection of sex role, anxiety, depression, and a variable called reduced parental aptness. The overall rate of PMS was 82%, with the highest percentage occurring in the group with the most extreme scores on these personality variables.

Thomas Plante and Douglas Denney approached the issue from a slightly different point of view.[49] They took several physiological measures related to autonomic arousal while women were engaged in stressful laboratory tests. Two groups of women were compared, those who had reported premenstrual stress and those who had no such complaints. The measures were taken at three different phases in the menstrual cycle, the first related to early growth (follicular), the second related to ovulation (luteal), and the third the menstrual phase.

The general outcome was very clear. The women's stress reactivity did not change during the three phases of the cycle. There was also no difference in recovery from stress. An interesting sidelight was that Plante and Denney confirmed a finding reported in the previously mentioned study; that is, women who complain of premenstrual stress tend to endorse personality items that reflect anxiety and depression even though their physiological patterns do not differ from noncomplainers.

◆ PERSONALITY AND SMOKING

Smoking is considered a high-risk, self-defeating behavior that probably serves to reduce tension for many people. It is thus of great significance in considering both health and stress. Concern about smoking has increased rather dramatically in recent years. Because of the potential harm, more programs have been designed to help people quit smoking or to try to reduce the number of people, especially adolescents, starting. The first type of treatment has to do with the forces that keep people smoking once they have started. The second type of program has to do with what gets people started.

There are many theories about what maintains smoking. These include that smoking is physically or psychologically addictive or both. Another theory suggests that smoking is primarily a tension release for people who are overly anxious. Support for this notion comes from reports that frequency of smoking increases and decreases with the rise and fall of stress. Theories on what motivates people to start smoking point to peer pressure and peer reinforcement, parental modeling, some set of personal traits, or some combination of all of these.

To this point, only a small amount of research has been done relating personality traits to smoking. In general, the smoker is described as extraverted, somewhat neurotic, and tense. There is a sex difference, however, in that higher anxiety is found in female smokers than in male smokers. Of greatest importance is the fact that these findings relate to the factors causing people to begin smoking, not to those that keep people smoking.[50]

From the standpoint of stress research, the findings are consistent with an interaction model. They suggest that people with higher levels of tension and anxiety may be more vulnerable to pressures to start smoking. Given stress of the right type and intensity, they are more likely to get trapped in the smoking habit. On the other hand, strong parental models, suitable outlets for tension, guidance for constructive emotional release, and educational programs that enable teenagers to cope with pressure from peers may prevent the habit from ever starting.

Getting people to quit smoking is just as problematic but involves another level of complexity. As indicated earlier, there is no evidence of personality factors related to sticking with the habit. But there is mounting evidence that smoking is a physically addictive process.[51] Much of the rhetoric on smoking has either ignored this issue or has denied it outright. It may be part of the societal consciousness, or unconsciousness as the case may be, that seeks to legitimize this vice. To admit that smoking is addictive would make it much more difficult to argue in favor of smoking—so many smokers don't admit it.

◆ THE ALCOHOLIC PERSONALITY

The same concerns that have prompted research on personality and smoking have led to a great deal of research on the alcoholic personality. Alcoholics generally have higher risks for illness, more rapid mental and physical deterioration,[52] and a higher death rate than nonalcoholics. The personal and social costs of drinking are staggering. The slaughter that occurs on our roads each year because of alcohol-related auto accidents is enough to suggest that society must come to grips with this major killer.[53]

Drinking seems to be related to a variety of stress reduction and escape behaviors that indicate ineffective coping skills. Drinking tends to increase and decrease relative to the amount of stress in the individual's life. For all these reasons, it is important to try to understand the factors that contribute to alcoholism.

It is now generally accepted that alcoholism has a substantial genetic component,[54] which may be expressed in a different basal metabolism or some other physical system. Presumably, this makes the person more vulnerable to the addictive properties of alcohol. In addition, a pattern of *positive assortative mating* has been identified (alcoholics marry alcoholics), which increases the risk of alcoholism for their offspring.[55] But there is also recognition that a variety of factors intervene in the person's development to determine whether the person actually becomes alcoholic or not.

The diathesis–stress model, described in Chapter 2, may be one of the best theoretical models available to describe the overall mix of factors contributing to alcoholism. This model states that predisposing (risk) factors will be expressed only if a precipitating (stress) event of sufficient intensity is encountered. According to one reviewer, the predisposing factors include a genetically transmitted psychological vulnerability. These include conduct disorders in childhood, hyperactivity, and attentional problems. The stress factors include such things as a disordered family and disturbed family interactions, type of peers associated with, ethnic background, and deprived environment.[56]

The emerging portrait of the alcoholic is of a person with chronic distress, externally controlled,[57] combined with weak or ineffective psychosocial skills.[58] Difficulty in psychosocial skills usually revolves around feelings of personal inadequacy, higher levels of fear than normal, and problems with concentration. These traits are revealed in conflict with authority, more frequent and intense expressions of hostility, and aggressiveness. This combination of factors may serve to reduce effectiveness on the job and in a variety of interpersonal relationships from casual social to intimate personal relationships.

When the alcoholic hits the road, some of these characteristics may be intensified. This only serves to increase the likelihood that something bad will happen. A model integrating personality factors with behavior leading to high-risk driving has been proposed by one research team.[59] This model is reproduced in Figure 5–2.

◆ CONTROL, HARDINESS, AND SELF-ESTEEM

Three traits will be discussed here that have been linked to stress and health. These are locus of control, psychological hardiness, and self-esteem.

Locus of Control, Coping, and Mastery

The concept of **locus of control** originated with the work of Julian Rotter in the early part of the 1960s. It refers to the expectancy that personal

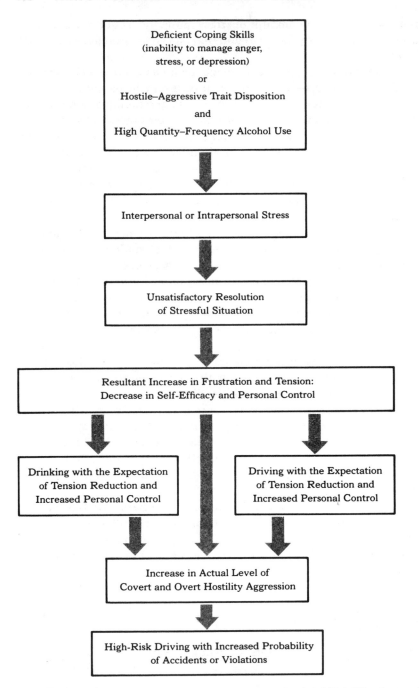

Figure 5–2. Hypothetical model of the effects of social skill deficits, heavy alcohol use, and hostile–aggressive disposition on high-risk driving.

actions will be effective to control or master the environment. In Rotter's model, people vary on a continuum between the two extremes of external and internal locus of control.[60] H. M. Lefcourt defined **external control** as the perception that positive or negative events are unrelated to one's own behavior and thus beyond personal control.[61] Most events are viewed as dependent on chance or controlled by powers beyond human reach.

The internal person, on the other hand, feels that few events are outside the realm of human influence. Even cataclysmic events may be altered for good through human action. H. M. Lefcourt defined **internal control** as the perception that positive or negative events are a consequence of personal actions and thus may potentially be under personal control.[62] If the theme song of the external is "Cast Your Fate to the Winds," the theme of the internal is "I Did It My Way."

Internal people as a group seem to have more efficient cognitive systems. They expend a substantial amount of mental energy obtaining information that will enable them to influence events of personal importance. In addition, internal people expend greater efforts to cope with or achieve mastery over their personal, social, and work environments.[63] In this way, a sense of mastery may develop that enables them to cope more successfully with stressful events.

What happens when personal weaknesses are pointed out? Some people respond by ducking their head, lowering their sense of personal worth, and resigning themselves to their fate. Other people say, "I'm going to work on that and lick it." One study approached this issue by giving negative feedback to people presumably based on personality tests they had taken earlier. Subsequently, when given the opportunity to engage in a program to correct the alleged personal shortcomings, internal people showed a much greater tendency to implement a specific plan of action.[64] As the author of the study noted, "Whether one terms it action taking, confronting, or mastery, internals seem to be more disposed toward behavior that will enhance their personal efficacy, even in the sense of rectifying inadequacies."[65]

A number of investigations have linked locus of control to coping with stress and dealing with family or personal health problems.[66] One review of personal control outlined three major types. These are behavioral control, which involves some direct action; cognitive control, which primarily reflects a personal interpretation of events; and decisional control, which means that the person has a choice among several different courses of action. The author stated that

> each type of control is related to stress in a complex fashion, sometimes increasing it, sometimes reducing it, and sometimes having no influence at all. . . . the relationship of personal control to stress is primarily a function of the meaning of . . . control . . . for the individual.[67]

Locus of control seems to be quite important in health behavior. For example, one study of tubercular patients showed that internally oriented patients had much more knowledge about their disease than externally oriented patients. This is noteworthy, since the information they obtained was very negative. Results such as this are interpreted as consistent with the idea that internals are knowledge seekers. It may also be related to their belief that they can do something positive to influence the outcome of the disease process. But in order to act on their own behalf, they must have appropriate information.[68]

Among the more difficult problems facing health service providers are the facts that people (1) are not highly motivated to engage in effective preventive health care and (2) do not follow prescribed medical programs very carefully when sick. One research team guessed that the problem might be related to locus of control. That is, people who are internally oriented might be motivated to control aspects of their environment related to their own health. On the other hand, externally oriented people might not be, since personal actions are perceived to be unrelated to either positive or negative outcomes. The outcome of the study suggests that it is the person who both values health and has an internal locus of control who is most likely to engage in preventive health behavior.[69]

Before this discussion is concluded, one important point needs to be made. There is a tendency to regard locus of control as a personality trait that is fixed at an early age and is thus difficult to change. This notion is most unfortunate. It appears that locus of control is a dynamic characteristic that can be changed with even modest desire and effort.

Psychological Hardiness

Some people seem to be especially resilient and unflappable. Stress rolls off with little or no apparent disruption to their actions or feelings. Suzanne Kobasa conducted research during the 1970s suggesting that personality can indeed play a significant role in helping a person resist illnesses associated with stress.[70] She has said that the resilient ones have *psychological hardiness*.[71] According to her work, there are three major traits that contribute to hardiness. These are control, commitment, and challenge. **Control** is defined and measured as locus of control, described in the previous section. **Commitment** is a sense of self and purpose. **Challenge** reflects the degree to which safety, stability, and predictability are important. Those with high hardiness are described as having a well-integrated sense of self and purpose. In addition, they will see change as stimulating and providing them with opportunity for growth.

In one study of 137 male business executives, Kobasa and her colleagues looked at both hardiness and exercise as buffers against illness. They found that stressful life events increased illness, while both hardiness and exercise reduced illness. In this sample, the more stress increased, the more exercise and hardiness proved their worth as buffers. Executives who were lowest on hardiness and exercised the least had the highest rate of illness. Conversely, those who were high on hardiness and exercised the most had the lowest rate of illness.[72] The positive buffering effect of hardiness has been observed in a sample of lawyers as well.[73]

Self-esteem, Stress, and Coping

The term **self-esteem** is frequently used to refer to a sense of positive self-regard. In the simplest possible terms, it is feeling good about yourself. *Self-esteem* is sometimes confused with *self-concept*. Actually, self-concept is a very broad term including all of the ways in which people compare and evaluate themselves (physically, mentally, and socially) compared to others. Self-esteem thus feeds into self-concept. Recent research suggests that self-esteem is made up of three psychosocial factors and two physical factors. The three psychosocial factors are self-regard, social confidence, and school ability. The two physical factors are appearance and ability.[74]

The relationship of self-esteem to coping is a complex one. It includes feedback from many previous successful or unsuccessful attempts at coping. In this sense, self-esteem is part of and feeds a long-term cycle. When people feel good about themselves, they are less likely to respond to or interpret an event as emotionally loaded or stressful. In addition, they even cope better when stress does occur. Because they cope better, it feeds back positive information that further increases self-esteem. Since self-esteem is a complex factor, however, many investigators have been trying to determine what specific aspects of self-esteem are more related to coping failure and success.

When low-esteem people are put in a threat situation, they tend to show poorer overall coping and lower overall competency. According to one investigation, the difficulty with coping in low-esteem people can be traced to two basic negative self-perceptions. First, low-esteem people have higher levels of fear under threat then high-esteem people. Second, low-esteem people perceive themselves as having inadequate skills to deal with the threat.[75] They are less interested in taking preventive steps and seem to have more fatalistic beliefs that they cannot do anything to prevent bad things from happening. They are a step behind from the start because of belief in their inability to cope.

A number of programs have been developed to help high-school students improve their self-esteem and their coping. One such program showed a generally positive outcome in increasing interpersonal coping skills.[76] An interesting note is that there seems to be a relationship between locus of control and self-esteem. Specifically, low–self-esteem subjects tended to score as externals. In the programs that have been developed to increase locus of control, it may be that self-esteem improves with reeducation in locus of control. This would be consistent with the idea that as people learn that stress can be controlled and that they can do the controlling, they feel better about themselves.[77]

◆ SUMMARY

In this chapter, a variety of personality theories have been reviewed that are specifically related to issues of stress and health. Several biotypes have been shown to have at best only weak links to health, while others appear to be very strongly related to vulnerability to stress or specific health problems. The Type A personality was reviewed at some length.

◆ NOTES

[1]Allport, G. W. (1961). *Pattern and growth in personality.* New York: Holt, Rinehart & Winston, p. 28.

[2]Millon, T. (1982). On the nature of clinical health psychology. In T. Millon, C. Green, & R. Meagher (Eds.), *Handbook of clinical health psychology* (pp. 1–27). New York: Plenum Press, p. 11.

[3]Jones, N. F., Kinsman, R. A., Dirks, J. F., & Dahlem, N. W. (1979). Psychological contributions to chronicity in asthma: Patient response styles influencing medical treatment and its outcome. *Medical Care, 17,* 1103–1118.

[4]Kaptein, A. A. (1982). Psychological correlates of length of hospitalization and rehospitalization in patients with acute, severe asthma. *Social Science and Medicine, 16,* 725–729.

[5]Kutash, I. L., Schlesinger, L. B., & associates. (1980). *Handbook on stress and anxiety.* San Francisco: Jossey-Bass.

[6]Liebert, R. M., & Spiegler, M. D. (1982). *Personality: Strategies and issues.* Homewood, IL: Dorsey Press.

[7]Spielberger, C. D. (1966). Theory and research on anxiety. In C. D. Spielberger (Ed.), *Anxiety and behavior* (pp. 1–22). New York: Academic Press.

[8]Byrne, D. G., & Whyte, H. M. (1983–1984). State and trait anxiety correlates of illness behavior in survivors of myocardial infarction. *International Journal of Psychiatry in Medicine, 13,* 1–9.

[9]Friedman, M., & Rosenman, R. H. (1974). *Type A behavior and your heart.* New York: Knopf, pp. 82–85.

[10]Yarnold, P. R., & Grimm, L. G. (1982). Time urgency among coronary-prone individuals. *Journal of Abnormal Psychology, 91,* 175–177.

[11]Jenkins, C. D., Rosenman, R. H., & Friedman, M. (1967). Development of an objective psychological test for the determination of the coronary-prone behavior pattern in employed men. *Journal of Chronic Disease, 20,* 371–379.

[12]Suinn, R. M. (1975). The cardiac stress management program for Type A patients. *Cardiac Rehabilitation, 5,* 13–15.

[13]Glass, D. C. (1977). Stress, behavior patterns, and coronary disease. *American Scientist, 65,* 177–187.

[14]Rosenman, R. H., et al. (1964). A predictive study of coronary heart disease. The Western Collaborative Group Study. *Journal of the American Medical Association, 189,* 15–22.

[15]Lloyd, G. G., & Cawley, R. H. (1983). Distress or illness? A study of psychological symptoms after myocardial infarction. *British Journal of Psychiatry, 142*, 120–125.

[16]van Doornen, L. J. P. (1980). The coronary risk personality: Psychological and psychophysiological aspects. *Psychotherapy and Psychosomatics, 34*, 204–215.

[17]Goldband, S. (1980). Stimulus specificity of physiological response to stress and the Type A coronary-prone behavior pattern. *Journal of Personality and Social Psychology, 39*, 670–679; Irvine, J., Lyle, R. C., & Allon, R. (1982). Type A personality as psychopathology: Personality correlates and an abbreviated scoring system. *Journal of Psychosomatic Research, 26*, 183–189.

[18]Lovallo, W. R., & Pishkin, V. (1980). A psychophysiological comparison of Type A and B men exposed to failure and uncontrollable noise. *Psychophysiology, 17*, 29–36.

[19]Rosenman, R. H., & Friedman, M. (1961). Association of specific behavior pattern in women with blood and cardiovascular findings. *Circulation, 24*, 1173–1184.

[20]Grimm, L. G., & Yarnold, P. R. (1984). Performance standards and the Type A behavior pattern. *Cognitive Therapy and Research, 8*, 59–66.

[21]Yarnold, P. R., & Grimm, L. G. (1982). *Interpersonal dominance and coronary-prone behavior.* Paper presented at the Third Annual Meeting of the Society of Behavioral Medicine, Chicago.

[22]van Egeren, L. F., Fabrega, H., & Thornton, D. W. (1983). Electrocardiographic effects of social stress on coronary-prone (Type A) individuals. *Psychosomatic Medicine, 45*, 195–203.

[23]Howard, J. H., Cunningham, D. A., & Rechnitzer, P. A. (1976, March). Health patterns associated with Type A behavior: A managerial population. *Journal of Human Stress*, pp. 24–31.

[24]Newlin, D. B., & Levenson, R. W. (1982). Cardiovascular responses of individuals with Type A behavior pattern and parental coronary heart disease. *Journal of Psychosomatic Research, 26*, 393–402.

[25]Shekelle, R. B., Schoenberger, & Stamler, J. (1976). Correlates of the JAS Type A behavior pattern score. *Journal of Chronic Disease, 29*, 381–394.

[26]Waldron, I., Zyanski, S., Shekelle, R. B., Jenkins, C. D., & Tannenbaum, S. (1977, December). The coronary-prone behavior pattern in employed men and women. *Journal of Human Stress*, pp. 2–18.

[27]Rosenman, R. H., & Friedman, M. (1977). Modifying Type A behaviour pattern. *Journal of Psychosomatic Research, 21*, 323–331.

[28]Alexander, F. (1939). Emotional factors in essential hypertension. *Psychosomatic Medicine, 1*, 173–179.

[29]Sparacino, J., Ronchi, D., Brenner, M., Kuhn, J. W., & Flesch, A. L. (1982). Psychological correlates of blood pressure: A closer examination of hostility, anxiety, and engagement. *Nursing Research, 31*, 143–149.

[30]Pilowsky, I., Spalding, D., Shaw, J., & Korner, P. I. (1973). Hypertension and personality. *Psychosomatic Medicine, 35*, 50–56.

[31]Goldstein, I. B. (1981). Assessment of hypertension. In C. K. Prokop & L. A. Bradley (Eds.), *Medical psychology: Contributions to behavioral medicine* (pp. 37–54). New York: Academic Press, pp. 45, 46.

[32]Rosenhan, D. L., & Seligman, M. E. P. (1984). *Abnormal psychology.* New York: Norton, p. 307.

[33]Rosenhan & Seligman, *Abnormal psychology,* p. 317.

[34]Garron, D. C., & Leavitt, R. (1983). Chronic low back pain and depression. *Journal of Clinical Psychology, 39,* 486–493.

[35]Mitchell, R. E., Cronkite, R. C., & Moos, R. H. (1983). Stress, coping, and depression among married couples. *Journal of Abnormal Psychology, 92,* 433–448.

[36]Sword, R. O. (1977). The depression-prone personality: Almost "too good" to be true. *Dental Survey, 53,* 12.

[37]United States Department of Commerce, Bureau of the Census. (1979, September). *Statistical abstract of the United States* (100th ed.). Washington, DC: U.S. Government Printing Office.

[38]Subcommittee on Juvenile Justice. (1985). *Teenage suicide* (Serial No. J-98-143). Washington, DC: U.S. Government Printing Office.

[39]Ferguson, W. E. (1981). Gifted adolescents, stress, and life changes. *Adolescence, 16,* 973–985.

[40]Barofsky, I. (1981). Issues and approaches to the psychosocial assessment of the cancer patient. In C. K. Prokop & L. A. Bradley, *Medical psychology: Contributions to behavioral medicine.* New York: Academic Press, pp. 57, 58; Derogatis, L. R., Abeloff, M. D., & Melisaratis, N. (1979). Psychological coping mechanisms and survival time in metastatic breast cancer. *Journal of the American Medical Association, 242,* 1504–1508; Fox, B. H. (1978). Premorbid psychological factors as related to cancer incidence. *Journal of Behavioral Medicine, 1,* 45–133; Fox, B. H. (1980). Behavioral issues in cancer. In S. M. Weiss, J. A. Herd, & B. H. Fox (Eds.), *Perspectives on behavioral medicine* (pp. 101–133). New York: Academic Press.

[41]For a brief overview and summary of these studies see Morrison, F. R., & Paffenbarger, R. A. (1981). Epidemiological aspects of biobehavior in the etiology of cancer: A critical review. In S. M. Weiss, J. A. Herd, & B. H. Fox (Eds.), *Perspectives on behavioral medicine* (pp. 135–161). New York: Academic Press.

[42]Kissen, D. M. (1967). Psychosocial factors, personality and lung cancer in men aged 55–64. *British Journal of Medical Psychology, 40,* 29–43.

[43]Booth, G. (1969). General and organ-specific object relationships in cancer. *Annals of the New York Academy of Sciences, 164,* 568–577.

[44]Dattore, P. J., Shontz, F. C., & Coyne, L. (1980). Premorbid personality differentiation of cancer and noncancer groups: A test of the hypothesis of cancer proneness. *Journal of Consulting and Clinical Psychology, 48,* 388–394.

[45]Greer, S., & Morris, T. (1975). Psychological attributes of women who develop breast cancer: A controlled study. *Journal of Psychosomatic Research, 19,* 147–153.

[46]Katz, J., et al. (1970). Psychoendocrine aspects of cancer of the breast. *Psychosomatic Medicine, 32,* 1–18.

[47]Brand, H. J., Roos, S. S., & van der Merwe, A. B. (1982). Psychological stress and infertility. Part 1: Psychophysiological reaction patterns. *British Journal of Medical Psychology, 55,* 379–384.

[48]Foresti, G., et al. (1981). Premenstrual syndrome and personality traits: A study of 110 pregnant patients. *Psychotherapy and Psychosomatics, 36,* 37–42.

[49]Plante, T. G., & Denney, D. R. (1984). Stress responsivity among dysmenorrheic women at different phases of their menstrual cycle: More ado about nothing. *Behaviour Research and Therapy, 22,* 249–258.

[50]Spielberger, C. D., & Jacobs, G. A. (1982). Personality and smoking behavior. *Journal of Personality Assessment, 46,* 396–403.

[51]Russell, M. A. H. (1976). Tobacco smoking and nicotine dependence. In R. J. Gibbins et al. (Eds.), *Research advances in alcohol, and drug problems* (Vol 3, pp. 1–47). New York: Wiley.

[52]Porjesz, B., & Begleiter, H. (1982). Evoked brain potential deficits in alcoholism and aging. *Alcoholism: Clinical and Experimental Research, 6,* 53–63.

[53]Donovan, D. M., Marlatt, G. A., & Salzberg, P. M. (1983). Drinking behavior, personality factors and high-risk driving: A review and theoretical formulation. *Journal of Studies on Alcohol, 44,* 395–428.

[54]Stabenau, J. R., & Hesselbrock, V. M. (1983). Family pedigree of alcoholic and control patients. *The International Journal of the Addictions, 18,* 351–363.

[55]Hall, R. L., Hesselbrock, V. M., & Stabenau, J. R. (1983). Familial distribution of alcohol use: I. Assortative mating in the parents of alcoholics. *Behavior Genetics, 13,* 361–372.

[56]Alterman, A. I., & Tarter, R. E. (1983). The transmission of psychological vulnerability: Implications for alcoholism etiology. *Journal of Nervous and Mental Disease, 171,* 147–154.

[57]Apao, W. K., & Damon, A. M. (1982). Locus of control and the quantity-frequency index of alcohol use. *Journal of Studies on Alcohol, 43,* 233–239.

[58]Nerviano, V. J., & Gross, H. W. (1983). Personality types of alcoholics on objective inventories: A review. *Journal of Studies on Alcohol, 44,* 837–851.

[59]Donovan et al., Drinking behavior, p. 416.

[60]Rotter, J. B. (1966). Generalized expectancies for internal versus external control of reinforcement. *Psychological Monographs, 80* (1, Whole No. 609).

[61]Lefcourt, H. M. (1976). *Locus of control: Current trends in theory and research.* Hillsdale, NJ: Erlbaum, p. 29.

[62]Lefcourt, *Locus of control,* p. 29.

[63]Phares, E. J. (1976). *Locus of control in personality.* Morristown, NJ: General Learning Press, p. 78.

[64]Phares, *Locus of control in personality,* p. 78.

[65]Phares, *Locus of control in personality,* p. 66.

[66]Donham, G. W., Ludenia, K., Sands, M. M., & Holzer, P. D. (1983). Personality correlates of health locus of control with medical inpatients. *Psychological Reports, 52,* 659–666; Ludenia, K., & Donham, G. W. (1983). Dental outpatients: Health locus of control correlates. *Journal of Clinical Psychology, 39,* 854–858.

[67]Averill, J. R. (1973). Personal control over aversive stimuli and its relationship to stress. *Psychological Bulletin, 80,* 286–303, p. 286.

[68]Lefcourt, *Locus of control*, p. 52. Lefcourt cites a study by Seeman and Evans (1962) that supports this contention.

[69]Abella, R., & Heslin, R. (1984, May). *Health locus of control, values, and the behavior of family and friends: An integrated approach to understanding preventive health behavior.* Paper presented at the Midwestern Psychological Association Conference, Chicago.

[70]Kobasa, S. C. (1979). Personality and resistance to illness. *American Journal of Community Psychology, 7,* 413–423.

[71]Kobasa, S. C. (1979). Stressful life events, personality and health: An inquiry into hardiness. *Journal of Personality and Social Psychology, 37,* 1–11.

[72]Kobasa, S. C., Maddi, S. R., & Puccetti, M. C. (1982). Personality and exercise as buffers in the stress-illness relationship. *Journal of Behavioral Medicine, 5,* 391–404.

[73]Kobasa, S. C. (1982). Commitment and coping in stress resistance among lawyers. *Journal of Personality and Social Psychology, 42,* 707–717.

[74]Fleming, J. S., & Courtney, B. E. (1984). The dimensionality of self-esteem: II. Hierarchical facet model for revised measurement scales. *Journal of Personality and Social Psychology, 46,* 404–421.

[75]Rosen, T. J., Terry, N. S., & Leventhal, H. (1982). The role of esteem and coping in response to a threat communication. *Journal of Research in Personality, 16,* 90–107.

[76]Silbergeld, S., & Manderscheid, R. W. (1976). Comparative assessment of a coping model for school adolescents. *Journal of School Psychology, 14,* 261–274.

[77]Phares, *Locus of control in personality,* p. 122.

FAMILY, SOCIAL, AND WORK STRESS

6

STRESS IN THE FAMILY: ADJUSTMENT, CONFLICT, AND DISRUPTION

> *Most of the complaints about the institution of holy matrimony arise not because it is worse than the rest of life, but because it is not incomparably better.*
>
> *John Levy and Ruth Munroe*

The night of November 16, 1982, was a night that would bring the Jahnke family national notoriety. On that night, 16-year-old Richard Jahnke, Jr., shot and killed his father with six blasts from a shotgun. Richard had waited hours in the darkness of the garage for his parents to return home from their anniversary outing so he could carry out an action he had apparently planned for some time. This sounds very much like a story of cold-blooded murder by a budding psychopathic criminal. But the details of this episode are very different, or so they seemed to many. Indeed, once the motives for the murder were laid bare in the press, there were pleas for Richard to be absolved of all responsibility for the crime.

The facts were that Richard, his 17-year-old sister Deborah, and his mother were victims of a brutal man who knew little of affection and even less of human decency. The man frequently beat Richard's mother, sexually molested Richard's older sister, and abused Richard himself. Richard became terrified of his father and anguished about what he saw happening to his sister and mother. The social service agency contacted in May had done nothing to stop the abuse. Richard decided that he must stop it himself.

This is stress in the family at its extreme. And while most family stress does not come from this extreme end of the continuum, family stress is a problem of substantial proportions. The following pages will provide a perspective on what we know about stress in the family and how to deal with it. First, some working definitions will be presented. Next, a comprehensive theory of family stress will be described. Later, stress from marital disruption, child abuse, and sexual abuse will be discussed. Finally, some useful coping and problem-solving strategies for the family will be discussed.

◆ FOCUS ON THE FAMILY

The largest volume of research in stress and health has chosen to focus on the ways in which various forces affect the individual for good or for ill. It has become increasingly obvious, however, that this approach is limited to some extent. The equation of stress involves the family in both destructive and constructive ways. Stress is seldom, if ever, an isolated event affecting only one person in one remote situation. More often than not, stress comes home from the job. It is routinely transplanted from the classroom and social events to the confines of the home. Virtually any type of negative experience from the outside world can make its presence felt in family life sooner or later.

Searching for the sources of stress in the family is really a search for the interplay of forces between the family unit and its members. The appearance of stress in anyone is likely to affect the functioning of the family during at least a portion of the time stress is present. A middle-management executive passed over for a promotion will in all probability display some signs of stress that will affect the family. A teenage girl suffering with anorexia will undoubtedly generate a number of disruptive influences in the family.

On the other hand, the way in which a family responds to stress as a group affects the burden each family member bears. Consider a family that has just suffered some economic loss. Family leaders are normally expected to keep their emotions in check to some extent and use rational problem-solving behavior. But assume that they display hysterical, irrational, and "catastrophizing" behavior instead.[1] The rest of the family may then interpret the situation as much worse than it actually is. As a result, some of the more vulnerable family members, such as young children, may develop feelings of anxiety and insecurity. Worse yet, they may learn that this is the "adult" way to respond to stressors and carry the style with them into their own adult life.

Another reason for increasing emphasis on stress in the family is because the family itself provides many opportunities for the emergence of stress. The family cycle has distinct phases of mate selection, marital adjustment, family planning, childbearing, childrearing, career decline, and retirement. Each phase has its peaks and valleys, joys and sorrows, harmony and stress, from the very first breath of commitment to the dying breath of one of the partners. It is not within the scope of this book to detail all of the stressors that exist at each stage. Several authors have already taken such an approach with fairly thorough treatments of stress in marriage and the family.[2]

Finally, attempts to resolve stress will most frequently occur at home first. People do not usually turn to the outside for help until after their own resources have failed and the privacy of home has failed to provide consolation and resolution. The normal course is for a spouse or parent to serve as confidante to the stressed member. Sometimes, however, the problem is just unloaded on the whole family in an emotional outburst. In other cases, the person may not be able to open up about what is causing the conflict. Nonetheless, the burden is carried so visibly and heavily that the family is affected without knowing why or, worse still, without knowing how to help.

In some cases, involvement in one member's stress consumes so much of the family's energies and resources that the family becomes distressed and maladjusted. When this happens, it is unlikely that anyone in the family will be able to obtain the support needed from other members to bear the strain and resolve his or her own feelings of helplessness, guilt, loneliness, neglect, or anger. There is probably no better illustration of the long-term effects of stress in the family than what has been happening in the last few years in the American farm family.

◆ A CASE STUDY IN FAMILY STRESS

For many American farmers, the 1970s was a decade of frustration, unsteady prices for farm commodities, increasing costs of production, staggering indebtedness for many, foreclosures for others, and the outright demise of many family farms. Projections in one state are that as many as 40% of the farmers could stand to lose their farms. In one small Iowa community of 8,000, three farmers committed suicide in an 18-month span because of despair over the prospect of losing their farms.[3]

For many farmers, the prospect of loss is more than just an economic matter. It is psychological and social, signifying a personal failure that the entire family, including the extended family, is watching. In addition, many farms have been in the family for years. Their loss signifies a separation and enforced detachment from all that has carried family pride and tradition for so many years.

If the economic load carried by the head of the family is immense, the emotional load apparently can be unbearable, as suggested by the reports of suicide. But the family suffers emotionally as well. Some members, especially the children, have little or no direct control over the situation and no responsibility for the origins of the difficulty. They become victims of the family disturbance. The incidence of depression, poor school work, and suicide among children of farm families has increased along with pressures on the farm family. The problems described are not necessarily confined to the farm family. The type of stressors will vary from rural to suburban to urban families, but the general outcome is much the same.

One body of evidence has accumulated showing that stress in the family increases the vulnerability of individual members to physical and emotional distress.[4] But a number of factors unique to the family may *increase* resistance to distress by providing **social buffers,** or social insulation against the storms and stresses of daily life.[5] Which occurs, vulnerability or resistance, depends on the psychosocial traits of individual family members and on dynamic factors having to do with the nature of family interactions, communication patterns, and problem-solving strategies established by the family.

◆ FAMILY STRESS: PROBLEMS IN DEFINITION

The term *family stress* as used by some authors has not been used to this point for a reason.[6] That is because the concept of stress as defined previously is not necessarily appropriate when referring to groups. In other words, a group of people cannot experience stress in the same way that a single person does. Qualitative differences exist that require a different level of analysis and different strategies for intervening.

Personal Versus Family Stress

First, it seems intuitively acceptable to say that a family is under stress. Common language frequently uses just this type of expression. One example came during the hijacking of TWA Flight 847 from Athens, Greece. Televised interviews with families who had husbands or brothers being held hostage on the plane during the 17-day ordeal amply documented the torment, frustration, and anger many of them felt. In a similar vein, studies of families who have lost loved ones, homes, or investments because of some natural catastrophe also show the terrible stress families sometimes have to endure. Virtually no one would quibble with the notion that families in any of these situations are families under stress.

Nonetheless, there is a problem when the concept of stress is used in this way. To put it simply, we speak of families under stress, but it is really individuals who are grieved, depressed, frustrated, or angry. Family stress theory is thus found straddling a fence between "the hazard of blatant reductionism to the level of individual behavior" and "the hazard of assuming that groups have the properties of individuals."[7]

In order to talk about family stress, then, a shift in focus is necessary. This can be done by looking at what a family is, how it is organized, and how it functions. Such a view treats the *family as a system* that can be disrupted. A **system** is defined as a set of connected elements that function as a whole.

The term **family** is a descriptive term used to refer to a unique social cluster of people who enjoy a special relationship by reason of love, marriage, procreation, and mutual dependence. They share certain common goals and values. They work cooperatively to realize those goals and usually become more united when threats to family integrity appear.

In order to meet the needs of individual members, the family system is organized with adult leaders and child followers. There is also some division of labor for productive earning and household management. And there is a type of natural division in terms of teachers and learners. Stress on the family can cause the system to malfunction, disrupting harmony and destroying the organization of the family. Efficiency in management of family resources is reduced, earning productivity is lowered, and socialization of the child is interrupted. When this happens, the family may be referred to as a *maladaptive system*. On the other hand, a family that functions as an organized, coherent and integrated unit may be referred to as an *adaptive system*.

To summarize, family stress is viewed as qualitatively different from personal stress. Where the person experiences emotional distress, the family suffers a loss of harmony. Where the person suffers from lack of concentration and loss of fluid thinking, the family has reduced resources for collective problem solving. Where the person suffers from ulcers or migraine, the family may physically break up in separation or divorce. For the person, stress is an insult to a biopsychological system. For the family, stress is an insult to a social system.

Stressors, Stress, and Crises

Formal definitions of terms used in the family stress literature have been offered by any number of writers to help deal with this difference between personal and family stress. The term **stressor** is defined by McCubbin and Patterson as "a life event or transition impacting upon the family unit which produces, or has the potential of producing, change in the family social system."[8] The death of a parent, long-term hospitalization of a family member, loss of income, or imprisonment of a family member would qualify as stressors in this view.

The same authors define stress in terms of the family's response to the event. The family's response is dependent on how the event is interpreted—in other words, what meaning the event has for the family and how serious the threat is. Finally, a **crisis** or **distress** is defined as the disorganization or incapacity that results from the family's lack of resources and problem-solving skills to manage the stress.

◆ A TRANSACTIONAL THEORY OF FAMILY STRESS

Over the years, a number of different theories of family stress have been proposed. Yet the most comprehensive theory was first proposed in the 1940s by Reuben Hill, a family sociologist from the University of Minnesota.[9] To its credit, the model is still highly respected today.

The theory has a sterile title devoid of any clue as to what is contained within—the ABCX model. David Klein referred to it and related theories as *stress–crises–coping* (SCC) theories.[10] In more formal terms, the ABCX theory states that some *event* (A) interacts with the family's *resources* for meeting crises (B) and the family's *definition* of the event (C) to produce a *crisis* (X).

One interesting feature of the ABCX model is the similarity between it and the cognitive–transactional model of personal stress proposed by Richard Lazarus. While Hill did not choose to call his theory transactional, the summary statement just provided suggests that it can be viewed as a transactional theory. Indeed, McCubbin and his colleagues noted this similarity.[11]

Only minor changes in wording are required to make the ABCX model read virtually identically to a statement of the cognitive–transactional model. In the family, a stressor exists only if the family has appraised (defined) the event as threatening and the family's resources (secondary appraisal) are inadequate to meet the demands.

Components of Family Stress and Coping

Two concepts are central to Hill's model. One is the *amount of change* induced by the stressor event. The second is the family's *vulnerability* to stress. The general model is shown in Figure 6–1. The amount of change is the extent of adjustment required of the family as a result of the event. Death of the major wage earner produces a substantial change in the family structure, as does divorce. Taking on a new assignment for the company that requires relocating to a new region of the country may also necessitate changes for the family, but not of the same magnitude as those involved in death or imprisonment. On the other hand, imprisonment of a family member might be welcomed if it removes a child molester or wife beater from the home. Thus, the influence of change is still dependent on how the family appraises or defines the change.

Family vulnerability.   In Hill's model, family vulnerability is really the most complex and crucial factor for the production of family stress. In essence, a stressor event interacts with family vulnerability to produce a crisis. The more loaded with threat an event is, regardless of vulnerability, the more likely the family will have a crisis on its hands. Similarly, the more vulnerable the family is, regardless of the potency of the threat, the more likely the family will experience stress.

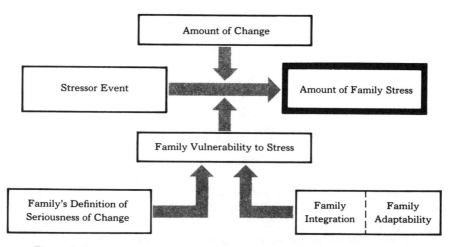

Figure 6–1. Modified Hill ABCX model of family stress.

This relationship holds true when the event produces short-term or acute stress. However, stress can pile up, one stressor after another. Or one stressor will just not go away, continuing to wear on the family. In this case, the effect is the same as an intense short-term stressor. The likelihood that a stressor will produce a crisis can be described as a relationship between the degree of vulnerability and the power of the stressor, as shown in Figure 6–2.

Family appraisals.   A number of factors are involved in family vulnerability. As shown in Figure 6–1, vulnerability is related to the family's definition (appraisal) of the seriousness of the change and to the overall integration and adaptability of family.[12] The family's definition of seriousness is a mixture of personal assessments (what it means to each person individually) and group assessments (what it means to the family as a social unit). The actual stress felt by each member is probably related to awareness of the implications of the change and the extent to which the person has influence or power to help alter the course of the stressor event or reduce the impact of the change.

Family resources.   Another factor contributing to family vulnerability is the resources of the family for meeting the demands of the stress event. Resources of the family are a combination of personal resources possessed by the individual family members and those resources that are a part of the family system. Family stress research has focused on four personal resources. These are financial status or economic well-being, health status or physical well-being, psychological resources usually assessed as personality variables, and educational level. Educational level serves as an indirect measure of cognitive skills, which presumably aid realistic appraisals and contribute to problem-solving ability.

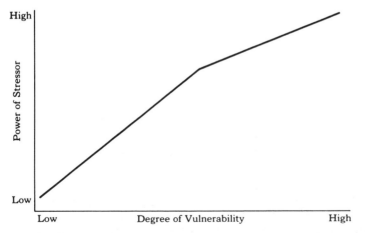

Figure 6–2.   Probability of a crisis occurring as a hypothetical relationship between power of the stressor and degree of vulnerability in the family.

Family decision making and problem solving.   Perhaps the most significant family resource is the family's pattern of decision making and competence in problem solving. David Klein has written extensively on this topic and addressed a number of the issues in family problem solving.[13] Concern exists not only for how the family addresses stress, but also for how the family socializes children to become competent problem solvers and mature adults able to withstand stress.

Karl Weick has identified 11 aspects of family problem-solving that distinguish families from other problem-solving groups.[14] These properties were summarized by David Klein.

1. Families work at solving problems when the energy levels of members are relatively low (such as at the beginning or end of the day).
2. Family members tend to mask expert power and allocate responsibility for problem solving on the basis of legitimate power.
3. Necessary knowledge for family problem solving is distributed unevenly among family members, as is investment in the outcome; the most informed member values acceptance more than the quality of outcome and is, therefore, able to control the flow of information selectively to maximize acceptance at the expense of quality.
4. Since affection in families tends to be noncontingent (constant at a high, positive level), family problem solving is relatively independent of learning through reinforcement.
5. The discussion of family problems often occurs in cascading fashion (one problem hitchhikes along with another), indicating that family members can be more interested in releasing emotional tension than in bringing up concerns that they want attacked instrumentally or rationally.
6. Families have both a voluntary (psychic) and involuntary (biological, legal) membership component; psychic withdrawal is a potential threat and thus an instrument of power.
7. Family problem solving is embedded in ongoing activity rather than occurring in a readily separated event, such as a council meeting; as a result it is difficult to know when problem solving is occurring.
8. Family problem solving occurs in relative isolation from outside influences and thus is likely to become stylistically rigid within a given family group.
9. Many family problems contain a developmental confound; that is, they are best left untreated and relegated to normal, natural trouble that will pass with time.
10. Families carry over large amounts of unfinished business and members lack consensus on criteria of satisfactory problem resolution; thus presumed solutions to one problem evoke new problems.
11. The ecology of families is relatively disorderly and gestural, and body cues are cryptic at best.[15]

Coping with Family Stress

McCubbin and his colleagues have identified four general hypotheses of how family coping actions work to protect the family from stress. The first is the notion that coping behaviors will reduce the vulnerability of the family itself. For example, if a family member is emotionally disturbed or threatens to leave the family unit, the family needs to allocate time and energy to this matter. Dealing with issues in a satisfactory way may remove the threat, thus restoring balance to the family and reducing vulnerability.

Second, coping actions may serve to strengthen or maintain family cohesiveness and organization. Third, coping may reduce or eliminate stressor events. Fourth, coping may actively operate on the environment to change it.

At the same time, investigators have acknowledged that coping activities can produce stress for the family because the coping strategies used are inferior, misguided, or non-reality-oriented strategies. There are at least three ways in which coping can damage the family system, according to the analysis of McCubbin. First, coping may produce indirect harm to the family unit or members of the family. One example is compensating for rising inflation by cutting back in health care. Second, coping efforts may produce direct damage to the family, as when a family members abuses alcohol or attempts suicide as a way out of current problems. Third, coping may increase family risks by retarding adaptive behaviors. This is most obvious when the family engages in denial or refuses to accept reality. For example, when a child becomes ill, possibly terminally ill, the family may reorganize realistically or unrealistically. When the latter is the case, the long-term picture is usually bleak.

Stages in Family Coping

In studies of families with fathers missing in action in the Vietnam War, the McCubbin group observed three stages in the family's adjustment. These were resistance, restructuring, and consolidation. Resistance was the initial reaction of most family members as they tried to deny or avoid the reality that was being forced on them. As the reality became more accepted, the family began to reorganize their lives around the new reality of a partial family. Family roles were redefined, children assumed more of the responsibilities for day-to-day maintenance of the household, and the mother looked for work. In addition, the mother became more independent while exercising a stronger authority in the family. One interesting note was that the extended family (for example, in-laws) frequently had difficulty adjusting to this new strength in the mother. They expressed disapproval, which only served to increase stress for her and her family. Finally, the family consolidated its gains by making the reorganization permanent and using this growth as a springboard for more changes in family life. A part of this final stage included new meanings assigned to the crises and a newly structured life-style for the entire family.[16]

◆ SEPARATION AND DIVORCE

Life in a family unit where everything is going smoothly has enough day-to-day tensions. No matter how devoted the parents are to each other, there are bound to be disagreements at times. Even the most loving of brothers and sisters fight once in a while. And there are all those active minds devoted to finding creative ways to spend money. Indeed, a study based on a rather large sample of Chicago-area people found that the one family stressor most consistently identified was financial pressures on the family.[17]

If it is this way in the best of families, families that are presumably tight-knit, think what it must be like in those families in which quarreling and fighting are the rule rather than the exception, alternating periods of separation and reconciliation keep everyone off guard, and no one ever knows if Dad is walking out the door for the last time before divorce breaks the family up for good. A rather large body of evidence, starting with the work of Holmes and Rahe on life-change, shows that the three most potent family stressors are death of a spouse, divorce, and marital separation.[18] These events are capable of producing both emotional and physical health problems in the family.

In 1976, there were 2,133,000 marriages and 1,077,000 divorces. These figures show a major change in the ratio of divorce to marriage in recent years. Some of the change is related to changing ideas about marriage itself, such as the fact that more people establish homes now without the sanction of legal marriages. But there is still cause for alarm about the growing trend to end marriages so frequently and even casually, in some cases with little effort to salvage the relationship. Because of this trend, a number of efforts have been mounted to identify the factors that contribute to marital conflict and divorce. The goal is not just to stem the tide of divorce but more importantly to reduce the toll on victims of divorce.

Personal Traits and Divorce

One of the most comprehensive reviews of stress and marital conflict was carried out by a team of community psychologists from the University of Colorado, headed by Bernard Bloom. They report that divorced and separated people are disproportionately represented among psychiatric patients, whereas married people are underrepresented. In addition, according to statistics supplied by the National Center for Health Statistics, divorced, separated, or widowed persons had much higher rates of illness and disability than married or never-married persons.[19] It may well be, if one research group is correct, that people who have serious difficulty with their health are less likely to get married, have more problems maintaining their marriages, and are less likely to get remarried.[20] There is also a higher rate of alcoholism in divorced and separated groups. One obvious question is whether the reported difficulties come after marital disruption or cause marital disruption. The evidence suggests that the seeds of these difficulties are present prior to marriage and probably contribute to marital disruption in the first place, whereas the disruption intensifies the problems in the second place.

Sluggers, Attackers, and Threateners

Suzanne Steinmetz conducted one of the most revealing studies to date on how people deal with conflict in marriage.[21] She obtained responses from 78 college students and their older friends. One of the more disturbing findings was that fully 30% of these young families had used physical violence of some type to resolve marital conflicts. Steinmetz identified four approaches to conflict in marriage. *Screaming sluggers* were the couples who made both verbal and physical attacks on each other. The *silent attackers* avoided quarreling at first. Sooner or later, however, they released their pent-up anger through physical assault. Then there were *threateners,* the ones who attacked each other verbally and threatened violence but never followed through with their threats. Finally, there was the group of *pacifists,* the people who were able to resolve their marital conflicts without the use of either verbal or physical attacks.

The Aftermath of Marital Disruption

In addition to these problems, which seem to contribute to marital disruption, the stress of marital disruption produces a variety of additional problems. Divorced people are involved more frequently in suicide and homicide and have a higher incidence of specific diseases, such as cancer, than married people.[22] In addition, divorced people are more frequently involved in motor vehicle accidents than other groups of people, and they average about three times the death rate from auto accidents that married people do.[23]

◆ THE SINGLE-PARENT FAMILY

When marital conflict ends in divorce or separation, the troubles are often only beginning, especially for the partner who retains custody of the children. Schlesinger studied a group of single parents, 90% of whom were women.[24] These single parents reported a common set of problems that confronted them in their struggles to keep the family intact. Some of the problems were difficulty in managing the children, having to go to work, financial problems, difficulties with sexual expression, and feelings of failure and shame. Nancy Colletta compared low-income families with moderate-income families and found that the major problem was a result of low income.[25] Low-income mothers had more problems related to childrearing practices, babysitters, health crises, and so forth. This was not the case in moderate-income families, in which stress was lower for both mother and child. One variable not assessed in this study, however, was educational level of the families. This could have influenced the reported stress levels as well.

In general, single-parent families tend to be more disorganized, which adds more stress onto individual members.[26] One group of investigators found that divorced parents felt more anxious, angry, rejected, and depressed than married persons.[27] While the mother and children were frequently able to stay in the original home, retaining some sense of continuity and stability, fathers were forced to abandon the homes they had worked so hard to provide. This appeared to contribute to the fathers' feeling of being more isolated and rootless at the beginning.

Children in the Single-Parent Family

Just as the parents of divorce feel a great number of stressors associated with changing their life-styles to accommodate to the reality of being single, so do children. According to statistics compiled by the Bureau of the Census, the number of children living in single-parent homes has doubled in the last decade and there has been a fourfold increase in the number of children living with mothers who have never married.[28] Many children are forced to accept adult responsibility while they have not had time to enjoy their childhood. As Avis Brenner suggested, they may enjoy being treated as equals but they still miss being treated as children.[29]

It appears, however, that children of divorce and separation may create as much stress as they suffer. Single mothers tend to have more difficulty with their sons, while single fathers tend to have more difficulty with their daughters. Since roughly 90% of the single-parent families are led by women, the difficulties encountered frequently result from problems in dealing with boys. Mothers apparently come to suffer additional anxiety and feelings of helplessness and incompetence as a result of trying to manage their sons. The long-term cycle may be one of escalating tensions between the two, eroding the relationship and resulting in loss of self-confidence for the mother.

One of the most frequent problems for children is the continued hopes and dreams that Mommy and Daddy will get back together again. It appears that this dream is especially unshakable, lasting for years in some children. It takes a gentle but persistent effort to help the child accept reality without adding greatly to inner turmoil.

This problem can carry over into postdivorce and remarriage as well. All too often, adults expect children to accept remarriage as though it is a blessing. What many adults do not seem to realize is that remarriage shatters the child's hopes and dreams of reconciliation. In addition, there is little time for the child to mourn the death of the dream when the parent remarries. Single parents contemplating remarriage would do well to consider this source of stress for their children and include them as much as possible in the decision process while also helping them to put to rest whatever hopes were still present for the dissolved marriage.

Postdivorce Conflict and Stress

Even after the divorce is done, there are many factors forcing the separate families to interact. Continued interest in the development of the children by both partners, sharing the children for visitation or moving them from one home to another in joint custody arrangements, financial obligations for the father and mother's concern when payments are inconsistent all add up to many opportunities for the old conflict to begin anew.

One research team has identified five different patterns that seem to mark postdivorce conflict.[30] These are listed with explanatory comments.

1. *Hostilities over parenting.* Research has shown that fathers tend to change more in parenting styles than mothers, which may contribute to some of the conflict. They are more easygoing[31] and spend more time with their children after obtaining custody than single mothers do.[32]

2. *Hostilities over matters not related to the children.* For example, bitterness and acrimony regarding the cause of the divorce may be carried over. Frequently, there is also continued anger over perceived injustices in the terms of the divorce settlement.

3. *Pressures from the children to maintain contact between mother and father.* This pressure is largely a part of the child's continued dream that the parents will get back together.

4. *Tugs of war, choosing sides, and shifting alliances* in which the parents may use one or more of the children as pawns to wage a war of nerves against the other parent. This pattern can be especially destructive to everyone. But more frequently than not, it is the children who end up the real losers. A wide variety of research shows that children of divorce fare best when the parents are able to carry on an amicable relationship,[33] share the children with warmth and regard for each other's rights,[34] and help the children understand that the love of both parents is not dependent on a marriage contract alone.

5. *Continued interaction caused by the extended family, grandparents,* and so forth. One of the most overlooked aspects of divorce is that divorce does not just shatter the dreams of the nuclear family. It shatters the dreams of many members of the extended family as well. Parents of the divorced couple have to explain to their friends why their son's or daughter's marriage failed. They may, in fact, perceive it as a failure in their own parenting. But they also have a vested interest in their grandchildren and frequently want to retain some contact. Making arrangements for this can be a source of much stress to both the mother and father.

◆ VIOLENCE IN THE FAMILY

Of all the family stressors receiving attention today, none rates higher than spouse and child abuse. Statistics reveal a frightening number of physical injuries and deaths due to either family quarrels or an ongoing pattern of family violence. Unfortunately, just counting the physical scars ignores the real toll, life-long emotional scars that the abused carry with them wherever they go. At the least, abused children tend to suffer a damaged self-image, poorer emotional adjustment if not mental disturbance, more disturbed family relationships, lower impulse control, and inferior coping skills.[35]

Violence in the family is not a modern invention, and it may not even be as rare as some would like to think. One investigative team took the position, based on the sheer frequency of violence in the family, that it is *normal*. They also suggested that conflict is "an inevitable and necessary part of social relationships," even though physical violence is not.[36] Police records do not help dispel this notion, since nearly 20% of all homicides are a direct result of family violence.

Stress and Child Abuse

The National Center on Child Abuse and Neglect conducted a study on child abuse from May 1979 to June 1980. They defined **child abuse and neglect** as follows:

> A child maltreatment situation is one where, through purposive acts or marked inattention to the child's basic needs, behavior of a parent/substitute or other adult caretaker caused foreseeable and avoidable injury or impairment to a child or materially contributed to unreasonable prolongation or worsening of an existing injury or impairment.[37]

In spite of the fact that instances of abuse or neglect caused by siblings or institutional staff were ignored, a total of 652,000 maltreated children were found. In this group, 207,000 had been physically assaulted, 138,400 had been emotionally abused, and 1,000 had been killed.

After all of this, add another 329,000 children whose care fits the criterion of neglect. While there are many formal definitions of **neglect,** Brenner described it best: "Children live with caretakers who are unwilling or unable to become involved with them and who are emotionally and sometimes physically absent."[38] Brenner's description of the neglected child is close to nauseating and reveals the silent and insidious tragedy of neglect.

> Households . . . cluttered with garbage, piles of clothing, excrement, dirty dishes, and stained mattresses lacking sheets and blankets. Drugs, liquor, poisons, and matches are discarded wherever they have been used last. It is not unusual to find a baby lying naked in a crib covered with feces and next to it a bottle of soured milk.[39]

Having witnessed many of these things and more (for example, chickens sharing the baby's area, perching on the crib, and adding their excrement to that of the humans), this can only suggest that however horrifying, words cannot do justice to the actual experience.

Attempts to identify the factors contributing to abuse and neglect have turned up some leads. Still, the path to constructive programs to prevent child and spouse abuse are a long way down the road. For the moment, consider these major contributors to abuse and neglect.[40]

Abuse and Developmental History

Parents who maltreat their children have had a developmental history that predisposes them to do so. Both retrospective and prospective studies confirm this conclusion. This does not mean that all abusive parents were themselves abused as children. Suffering personal abuse or neglect as a child is only one of the factors that sets the stage for becoming an abusive parent.

Another factor is the powerful influence of observing aggression. Starting with the classic work of Albert Bandura and his colleagues, a large number of studies have supported the idea that watching one's parents engage in acts of aggression toward each other and/or being rewarded for engaging in similar aggressive actions within one's own family contributes to becoming abusive in adult relationships.[41]

Parental rejection also may be a key factor. The evidence suggests that abusive parents are looking for the love and acceptance from their children that they did not get from their own parents.[42] In effect, a role reversal is created in which the parents are the "cared for" and the children are the longed-for "caregivers." When the parents do not receive the care they expected from their children, they turn to abuse.

Equally important are development experiences that enable the person to pass into adulthood with suitable skills and values for the task of parenting. This includes experience with childcare during childhood and adolescence. One line of evidence suggests that parents who abuse their children are woefully ignorant of the most rudimentary information on the sequence and timing of a child's growth and maturation.[43] Without the knowledge, it may be difficult for some to comprehend that the way a child thinks and behaves is natural and not contrived especially to irritate.

Life-change, Stress, and Abuse

The fact that many adults who were abused as children nonetheless rear their own children with love, sensitivity, and regard indicates that development history alone cannot account for being abusive as an adult. There must be other forces adding to the developmental influences. One likely factor is stress within the family that precedes the abuse. Quite simply, stress may be either the cause of maltreatment or an effect of maltreatment or both. Certainly, abuse of spouse or child tends to create an overwhelming amount of stress for any family, especially when the attack was unexpected. But some investigators have tried to determine if stress itself can prompt the abuse.

One research team has observed that life-change (such as death of a spouse, divorce, loss of a job, or economic hardships, among others) is highly correlated with child abuse and neglect *when the developmental history previously described is also present.*[44] Stress that causes maltreatment, however, may be only the beginning of a vicious cycle in which abuse creates even more stress which then perpetuates abuse.

One of the most powerful stressors in the family is marital conflict. Studies of the relationship between marital conflict and abuse find that the degree of conflict tends to be very high in families where abuse of children is present.[45] Caution must be exercised in interpreting some of these studies because it is not always clear whether the conflict came before or after the child abuse. However, Steinmetz showed that husbands and wives who use physical and verbal aggression in resolving marital conflict also used the same tactics in disciplining their children.[46] Finally, the transition to parenthood may be a stressor beyond the coping capacity of some people. The disruption caused by the child's presence and the lack of preparation for the responsibilities of parenting may be enough to tip some parents over the edge into abuse of the child.

Conflict between parents is also associated with diminished skills in mothers feeding young infants. Another cycle of interactions between the two parents and between the parents and the child may take stress levels in the home to new heights. A worst-case scenario would go something like this. Problems in feeding the baby lead to stomach upsets and colic. The baby gets more uncomfortable and vocal about its displeasure. On the other side, mother's confidence in her ability to take care of her baby begins a slow downward spiral. Father helps to erode mother's confidence by directly questioning the mother's skills while threatening drastic action if the child cannot be "shut up." The mother then finds herself in a bind between a husband who has little patience for the baby's disrupting influence and a baby who seems to be at best ungrateful for all of mother's efforts to meet its needs. In this climate, either one of the parents or both may turn on the child, scapegoating their frustrations and venting their anger against the most helpless member of the family unit.

Finally, disorganization in the family appears to be related to a pattern of abuse. Disorganization disables the family's coping capacity, which generally leads to increased levels of stress. It is possible that the most important disorganizing influences are unemployment and economic privation. Research in both the United States and Great Britain shows that unemployment could well be the single most important factor related to abuse and neglect.[47]

Children As Causes of Stress and Abuse

Another factor receiving more attention is the role the child plays in raising levels of tension and stress in the family. According to this view, the infant is still an innocent and probably unwitting provocateur. But older children may be both less than innocent and at least partially aware of what they are doing. Starting with this notion, investigators have begun to look for evidence to link patterns of physical and/or psychological traits of children to aggression in adults.

First, it has been noted that a large percentage of maltreated children are premature babies.[48] In general, premature and maltreated infants lack social responsiveness.[49] Parents may see this as a source of mild irritation at first. But, should the pattern continue, a feeling of rejection may build that leads to questions about competence as a parent. Soon, the parent may feel a strong sense of frustration followed by anger and ultimately aggression. Another line of evidence indicates that parents find the crying and appearance of their premature babies aversive and disagreeable.[50] As Jay Belsky pointed out, however, "child maltreatment must be considered an interactive process; although children may play a role in their own abuse or neglect, they cannot cause it by themselves."[51] In Belsky's view, the interaction is between traits of the parent and characteristics of the child.

Older children may prompt abuse through misbehavior. Evidence based on observations of family interactions shows that when parents punish or discipline a child, there is a tendency for the child to react with more coercive action toward the parent.[52] The interaction tends to deteriorate into a war of wills as each one of the combatants seeks either to control or to resist control. The situation may further deteriorate with each side escalating the level of punitiveness and counteraggression. The interaction may end only when the more powerful adult physically attacks the less powerful child.

Sibling Abuse

One of the overlooked aspects of child abuse is physical injuries caused by siblings. It is now recognized that sibling rivalry can take on some sinister twists leading to traumas equaling anything that parents are able to inflict. Tooley described children abused by siblings as "weaponless and without safe refuge" in their own homes.[53] One study found that sibling abuse had occurred in over half of the families studied.[54] Since the National Center on Child Abuse and Neglect Study specifically ignored sibling abuse, we must consider their estimates of the frequency of abuse to be conservative.

Perhaps the most sinister aspect of sibling abuse is that it can occur in the presence of the parents who are supposed to be the protectors and guardians. Tooley described three different parental patterns that suggest how sibling abuse can occur. First, some parents simply choose to ignore or deny that abuse is going on. Second, some parents apparently are either unable to manage a violent child or they are intimidated by the child. Thus, they placate him or her by allowing attacks on the other children to occur without interference. Third, some parents may actually encourage sibling aggression as a means of acting out their own violent impulses.

◆ BATTERED WIVES

Many of the factors related to child abuse are part of the pattern in spouse abuse as well. For example, men who batter their wives and battered women are more likely to come from families with the pattern of violence already established.[55] In addition, the more frequently a woman has been struck by her parents as a child, the more likely she was to be in a violent intimate relationship.[56]

One of the more unsettling issues, however, is why an abused adult will not only tolerate the abuse but also seems to keep coming back for more. While children may be forced to stay because they are dependent on adults for their basic biological needs, no such necessity exists for most adults. Most adults should be able to act in their own behalf to protect themselves from repeated abuse, even if it means walking away from the abusive partner. But time and again adults stay in an abusive relationship even at great risk to their own safety or until some more traumatic episode breaks the relationship.

Traumatic Bonding and Battered Women

Don Dutton and Susan Painter felt that the explanation for this paradox lies in the process of *traumatic bonding*.[57] There is no simple definition of traumatic bonding. It can only be described as a complex process in which personal, familial and social forces operate in consort and collusion to lock the woman into the abusive relationship. In the interest of brevity, only an outline of the process is provided here.

First, as Dutton and Painter noted, domestic violence is more often than not a series of events in which periods of quarreling and abuse alternate with almost equally passionate attempts on the part of the battering male to make amends. This pattern may in fact lead women to regard the abuse as somehow an exceptional part of the relationship or to ignore it altogether.[58] As reported in their review, a variety of clinical and laboratory results with both human and animal subjects support the contention that these alternating conditions increase the likelihood of traumatic bonding. Another investigative team reviewed emotional bonding in infants and concluded that inconsistent treatment by the source of affection (for example, punishment by a parent who also bestows love) intensifies the child's attempts to get even closer to the parent.[59]

A second factor involved in traumatic bonding is the power imbalance between the abuser and the abused. This imbalance may mask mutual dependency needs in which the abused identifies with the abuser and gains some sense of power. On the other side, the abuser needs the submission of the abused in order to satisfy his own needs.[60]

◆ SEXUAL ABUSE OF CHILDREN

Sexual abuse of a child may be the most despicable violation of the trust given parents as guardians of their children. In 1981, there were 17,880 reports of sexually abused children, all under the age of 12 years. More than 2,000 of this group were under the age of 5.

Most instances of sexual abuse take place within the family. Statistics indicate that nearly 80% of all cases of child abuse involve the stepfather

(30%), father (28%), mother's lover (11%), or mother (10%). When this is not the case, the offender is usually someone from among the extended family, friends, or acquaintances of the family. The offenders appear to be operating from one of three motives: They are seeking tenderness, they are exercising power not available in other aspects of their life, or they are venting sadistic rage.[61]

Physical and Psychological Symptoms of Sexual Abuse

A variety of physical and psychological problems have been reported in sexually abused children. These include sleep disturbances with nightmares, general restlessness, sometimes hyperactivity, eating problems that may include stomachaches and vomiting, and a *failure-to-thrive* syndrome. There may also be genital irritation, painful discharge of urine, bed-wetting, and soiling.

Avis Brenner summarized the long-term psychological effects that may occur in sexually abused children.[62] These include:

1. poor self-concept,
2. poor social skills,
3. depression,
4. hostility and suicidal feelings,
5. inability to get along with family,
6. inability to trust others, and
7. inability to experience sex as satisfying.

Hostility, guilt, and feeling unworthy are frequently associated with suicidal thoughts and actions. This appears to be true of children victimized by parental sexual abuse as well.

Major Warning Signs of Sexual Abuse

The following list is a composite of the types of behaviors that children may display after having experienced sexual abuse.

1. Appearance of new and rather strong fears, such as fear of the dark, of being alone, of sleeping alone, of strangers, or of men.
2. Insistence on having mother present all the time and refusal to go to places formerly favored by the child.
3. Changes in emotionality such as increased irritability, worry about staying clean, withdrawal from normal activities and circle of friends, crying, and sleep disturbances.
4. Changes in habitual behaviors such as appearance of bed-wetting, loss of appetite, and excessive bathing.
5. Appearance of more "adultlike" behaviors including overt interest in and expressions of sexuality, seductive talk and actions, and so on. This may include intense acting-out behaviors including sexual acting out such as promiscuity or prostitution.

6. Sudden changes in school performance, inability to concentrate, falling grades, or indirect attempts to communicate with teacher about sexual actions and fears.
7. Major changes in relationships, such as parents becoming overprotective or jealous of other friends, or inordinate attention and control by one of the parents. Such changes may be a clue to the offender.
8. Increased attempts by the perpetrator to "buy" the child's loyalty and silence through gifts of money, trips, favors, and clothes, among other things.
9. Appearance of more clandestine contacts between the perpetrator and the child, such as contriving to be alone and being secretive.

All of these signs do not appear in any given child. The most important and easily detected signs are those associated with physical injury, such as irritation, bruises, swelling, and bleeding in the genital region. Also, the appearance of any signs of venereal disease is indicative of sexual contact. Beyond these physical signs, the most important clues are marked changes, usually for the worse, in behaviors or performances that are normally expected from the child.

Effects on the Family

The effects of sexual abuse on the family are legion. Basic familial relationships become strained, natural family roles are changed, and patterns of affection are distorted.[63] The unhealthy alliances frequently shift the balance of power in the family to the abused daughter if she is old enough to recognize the power she wields. As Mary de Young pointed out, the daughter holds power over the offender because his security depends on her willingness to keep silence.[64] In fact, the offender may resort to a variety of forms of bribery or threats to keep the victim silent. At the same time, he may try to interpret morality and reality for the child in a way that prevents the child from developing a sense that the sexual activities are wrong. This is aided greatly by the child's lack of fully matured cognitive structures for interpreting the meaning of the interaction.[65] This same deficit probably contributes to the child's self-blame, and feelings of guilt and shame.

These problems carry over for sexually abused children into the adult years. They tend to experience disturbances in their relationships to their own husbands, seemingly looking for the father figures they never had as children. They continue to harbor negative or, at best, confused feelings about their own family. There is a mixture of hate, sympathy, understanding, and some affection for the father, but mostly ambivalence. Surprisingly, 38 (79%) of the victims in de Young's study felt more strongly negative toward their mothers than toward their fathers. After interviewing the victims, de Young concluded that:

> the origin of these commonly noted negative feelings toward the mothers is in the recognition that the mothers, above anyone else, had the power to

stop the incest from continuing or to prevent it from occurring in the first place. Most of the mothers of the victims in the clinical sample chose not to exercise that power. Therefore, feelings of anger toward the offending father or stepfather ("How could he do this to me?") are easily transferred to the nonparticipating mother ("How should she *let* him do this to me?").[66]

◆ POSITIVE COPING IN THE FAMILY

There are positive and constructive aspects of coping in the family. Since the family is a social system, it provides a variety of intimate contacts and supports that are not available in society at large. In this sense, the family serves as a major source of social support.

The Family As a Social Support System

A major moderator of stress is the extent of social support available. Social support may be defined simply as help given by spouses, parents, and friends. Pearlin's group defined **social support** as the "access to and use of individuals, groups, or organizations in dealing with life's vicissitudes."[67] Gerald Caplan viewed social support as attachments to individuals and groups that serve to reduce vulnerability to stress and improve the person's ability to cope with "short-term challenges, stresses, and privations."[68]

Within the family context, social support functions at two levels. First, there is the fact that the family itself is a social support network for family members. Second, there is a community in which the family is embedded. The extent to which the community provides a social network for the family as a unit is also important in moderating stress. Unfortunately, some communities serve as a source of major stressors rather than as a support network.

One of the most systematic statements on social support is that provided by Sidney Cobb. According to Cobb's analysis, social support conveys three types of information to a person. First, social support leads a person to have a sense of being cared for and loved. Second, social support leads a person to a sense of being esteemed and valued by other people. Third, social support leads the person to a sense of belonging to a communication network with mutual obligations.[69]

Cobb's analysis is extended to the whole gamut of social systems from small to large. In essence, it makes no difference whether the frame of reference is the family or a mutual interest group. In fact, social support groups will wax and wane in importance as different stages of the life cycle are encountered. There is a time, for example, when the teenage peer group is the most important, perhaps the only, support network for the teenager. Later on, as the young adult looks for employment and seeks to become a respected member of the community, the social network will probably be supervisors, work associates, and community leaders. Thus, many different social groups can provide support to moderate the effects of stress.

Evidence is available from a number of sources to show that social support is important to early development, recovery from surgical procedures, and to health. For example, one study was conducted with children born after their mothers had requested an abortion. The results showed that unwanted children were more likely to get in trouble with the law and were more likely to require some form of psychiatric treatment in their youth than matched control children who were presumably wanted by their parents.[70]

It is well known that children experience less stress from hospital procedures when parents and staff are able to provide a warm, supportive environment. This is why many hospitals now make arrangements for parents to stay in the hospital with their child. Also, parents now have the legal right to stay with their infant or young child.[71]

In addition to social support, there appears to be a very important cognitive element involved in the child's acceptance of a hospital procedure. Children can be prepared for their hospitalization through presurgical visits to meet their hospital care-givers. They can view films in which similar-age and same-sex children model the hospital procedure.[72] When this is done at the child's level of cognitive development, the child is much better able to deal with the anxiety of hospitalization or out-patient surgical procedures.

An extensive study of 10,000 men with angina pectoris showed the importance of support in the marital relationship. Men who had a satisfying love relationship were significantly less likely to present symptoms of angina even when physical risk factors were present.[73] Social support is also very important to compliance with medical prescriptions and treatment programs. One review of the literature found that of 19 projects that studied social support, all observed that social isolation and/or lack of affiliation were/was highly related to dropping out of treatment.[74] Other research shows the centrality of social support to minimizing the impact of stress from job loss,[75] long-term illness and recovery, grief after the loss of a loved one, and retirement. Finally, social support may moderate the effects of essential hypertension, increase the chances of surviving a heart attack, and increase the expected length of survival in cancer patients.[76]

Avoiding Pitfalls in Family Problem-Solving

A few suggestions based on Weick's analysis of the way in which family problems are dealt with can be advanced that may help families organize problem solving for better outcomes.

First, try to schedule problem-solving activities at times when energy levels are adequate. Right after work will probably not be the best, but some time in the early evening would be suitable. This time is most likely to be associated with recovery from the strain of the day and a feeling of being reenergized.

Second, try to separate problem solving clearly from other family activities. Some families even schedule family conferences so that it is clear the time is devoted to an issue that needs to be discussed. In our own family, the time right after the evening meal is used for this purpose. This also takes care of the problem of the energy lags that normally occur after busy days.

Third, try to identify what each family member knows about a particular problem. This will provide any "experts" with more of a role in suggesting ways to resolve the problem.

Fourth, accept suggestions from any family member without any threat of withdrawal of love and acceptance. Emphasize that affection and mutual respect are unrelated to the solutions offered, no matter how good or bad the suggestions might be. This is not done by lectures but by actions. Also emphasize that finding a high-quality solution is important and generally will benefit everyone.

Fifth, try to keep the family focused on one and only one problem at a time. When other problems hitchhike along, there is a tendency for energy to be diverted and the original problem may become more blurred and confused. Emotions are aroused and the problem-solving session degenerates into a gripe session. Worse yet, increasingly strident accusations may be made about perceived wrongs done by one member to another. In fact, it may be the unfinished business Weick talked about that is clouding the issue. In such an atmosphere, the outcome can be more destructive than constructive. Solutions that normally come to mind do not. Even more likely, the original problem is simply forgotten and left unresolved.

Sixth, if family problem solving seems to be getting in a rut, try some imaginative alternatives. With some more complex issues, for example, it might help to have a field trip to the local library to find information relevant to the issue. Public and cable television also have a wide range of programs devoted to issues of personal and family stress, family management, and health, among other topics. These programs can be a source of useful information and insights that will help the family think more clearly about a problem. Changing the approach to problem solving may also help the family avoid tunnel vision or repeated attempts to solve new problems with old, worn-out solutions. It might thus prevent family problem solving from becoming isolated and rigid, as Weick suggested.

Finally, recognize that all problems do not really need a solution. That is, they are related to developmental stages in the life cycle that will pass with time and patience. This is true of both adults and children, though we tend to think of it more often in connection with children. Adults go through developmental changes during the course of rearing their children. It is helpful for parents to teach their children to learn to recognize the signs of change and to adjust their thinking about people accordingly. It is also desirable for them to come to think of people as always growing and changing no matter how rapidly or slowly they grow and no matter what the direction.

◆ SUMMARY

Family stress was defined as pressure that disrupts or changes the family system. The effects of such stress are to reduce harmony and resources for collective problem solving. A model of family stress proposed by Reuben Hill was described stating that an event interacts with the family's resources for meeting crises and the family's definition of the event to produce a crisis.

Several types of family stress were discussed, including separation and divorce, the single-parent family, family violence, and abuse. Single-parent families tend to be more disorganized and children in such families tend to be put in a position of conflict. They are neither truly child nor adult. They also tend to maintain their hopes that the parents will reunite, a hope that is often dashed when the parent remarries.

Abuse tends to occur most in families in which the parents had a developmental history predisposing them to neglect or abuse. The parents may have been abused themselves or they may have witnessed abuse. Stress in the family increases the likelihood that abuse will occur. When the wife is abused, there may be a traumatic bonding that serves to keep the person in the family in spite of the suffering.

When the family functions in its intended way as a sensitive social support system, many stressors from outside can be minimized. Families can structure their problem solving to avoid common pitfalls and increase the chances that useful solutions will be obtained.

◆ NOTES

[1]*Catastrophizing* is a favorite term of Albert Ellis, the developer of rational emotive therapy.

[2]The following is a selective list of references that take a life cycle view of stress: Hobbs, D., & Cole, S. P. (1976). Transition to parenthood: A decade replication. *Journal of Marriage and the Family, 38*, 723–731; Menaghan, E. (1982). Assessing the impact of family transitions on marital experience: Problems and prospects. In H. McCubbin (Ed.), *Family stress, coping and social support.* New York: Springer; Rollins, B. C., & Feldman, H. (1970). Marital satisfaction over the family life cycle. *Journal of Marriage and the Family, 32*, 20–28.; Russell, C. (1974). Transition to parenthood: Problems and gratifications. *Journal of Marriage and the Family, 36*, 294–302.

[3]Turkington, C. (1985). Farmers strain to hold the line as crisis uproots mental health. *APA Monitor, 16*, pp. 1, 26, 27, 38.

[4]Bloom, B. L., Asher, S. J., & White, S. W. (1978). Marital disruption as a stressor: A review and analysis. *Psychological Bulletin, 85*, 867–894.

[5]Cobb, S. (1976). Social support as a moderator of life stress. *Psychosomatic Medicine, 38*, 300–314.

[6]McCubbin, H. I., et al. (1980). Family stress and coping: A decade review. *Journal of Marriage and the Family, 42*, 855–871.

[7]Klein, D. M. (1983). Family problem solving and family stress. *Marriage and Family Review, 6*, 93.

[8]McCubbin, H. I., & Patterson, J. M. (1983). The family stress process: The double ABCX model of adjustment and adaptation. *Marriage and Family Review, 6*, 7–37.

[9]Hill, R. (1949). *Families under stress.* New York: Harper & Row, Publishers.

[10]Klein, Family problem solving.

[11]McCubbin & Patterson, The family stress process.

[12]Burr details eight different factors related to vulnerability. The other five variables are amount of positional influence of the family, amount of personal influence (discussed briefly in the text), externalization of blame for change, amount of time changes anticipated, and amount of anticipated socialization. Space does not permit a full discussion of each of the factors in the model.

[13]See, for example, the following two summary articles: Klein, D. M., & Hill, R. (1979). Determinants of family problem-solving effectiveness. In W. R. Burr, R. Hill, F. I. Nye, & I. L. Reiss (Eds.), *Contemporary theories about the family* (Vol. 1, pp. 493–548). New York: Free Press; Klein, D. M. (1983). Family problem solving and family stress. *Marriage and Family Review, 6,* 85–112.

[14]Weick, K. E. (1971). Group processes, family processes, and problem solving. In J. Aldous et al. (Eds.), *Family problem solving: A symposium on theoretical, methodological, and substantive concerns.* Hinsdale, IL: Dryden Press.

[15]Klein, Family problem solving, pp. 511–512.

[16]McCubbin et al., Family stress and coping.

[17]Pearlin, L. I., & Schooler, C. (1978). The structure of coping. *Journal of Health and Social Behavior, 19,* 2–21.

[18]Holmes, T. H., & Rahe, R. H. (1967). The Social Readjustment Rating Scale. *Journal of Psychosomatic Research, 11,* 213–218.

[19]Bloom et al., Marital disruption.

[20]Carter, H., & Glick, P. C. (1976). *Marriage and divorce: A social and economic study.* Cambridge, MA: Harvard University Press.

[21]Steinmetz, S. K. (1977). The use of force for resolving family conflict: The training ground for abuse. *The Family Coordinator, 26,* 19–26.

[22]Kitagawa, E. M., & Hauser, P. M. (1973). *Differential mortality in the United States: A study in socio-economic epidemiology.* Cambridge, MA: Harvard University Press.

[23]National Center for Health Statistics. (1970). *Mortality from selected causes by marital status* (Series 20, Nos. 8A & 8B, USDHEW). Washington, DC: U.S. Government Printing Office.

[24]Schlesinger, B. (1969). The one-parent family in perspective. In B. Schlesinger (Ed.), *The one-parent family: Perspectives and annotated bibliography.* Toronto: University of Toronto Press.

[25]Colletta, N. D. (1983). Stressful lives: The situation of divorced mothers and their children. *Journal of Divorce, 6,* 19–31.

[26]Hetherington, E. M., Cox, M., & Cox, R. (1976). Divorced fathers. *Family Coordinator, 25,* 417–428.

[27]Hetherington, E. M., Cox, M., & Cox, R. (1977). The aftermath of divorce. In J. H. Stevens, Jr., & M. Matthews (Eds.), *Mother-child, father-child relations.* Washington, DC: National Association for the Education of Young Children.

[28]U.S. Department of Commerce, Bureau of the Census. (1982). *Marital status and living arrangements: March 1982* (Population Characteristics Series P-20, No. 380). Washington, DC: U.S. Government Printing Office.

[29]Brenner, A. (1984). *Helping children cope with stress*. Lexington, MA: Lexington Books, p. 26.

[30]Cline, D. W., & Westman, J. C. (1971). The impact of divorce on the family. *Child Psychiatry and Human Development, 2,* 135–139.

[31]Smith, R. M., & Smith, C. W. (1981). Child rearing and single-parent fathers. *Family Relations, 30,* 411–417.

[32]Orthner, D. K., Brown, T., & Ferguson, D. (1976). Single-parent fatherhood: An emerging family life style. *The Family Coordinator, 25,* 429–437.

[33]Rofes, E. E. (Ed.). (1982). *The kids' book of divorce: By, for and about kids*. New York: Vintage Books.

[34]Wallerstein, J. S., & Kelly, J. B. (1980). *Surviving the breakup: How children and parents cope with divorce*. New York: Basic Books.

[35]Hjorth, C. W., & Ostrov, E. (1982). The self-image of physically abused adolescents. *Journal of Youth and Adolescence, 11,* 71–76.

[36]Gelles, R. J., & Straus, M. A. (1979). Determinants of violence in the family: Toward a theoretical integration. In W. R. Burr, R. Hill, F. I. Nye, & R. L. Reiss (Eds.), *Contemporary theories about the family* (Vol. 1, pp. 549–581), p. 549.

[37]National Center on Child Abuse and Neglect. (1981). *Study findings: National study of the incidence and severity of child abuse and neglect* (OHDS 81-30325). Washington, DC: U.S. Government Printing office, p. 4.

[38]Brenner, *Helping children cope*, p. 115.

[39]Brenner, *Helping children cope*, p. 117.

[40]The major points included in the summary may be found in this review: Belsky, J. (1980). Child maltreatment: An ecological integration. *American Psychologist, 35,* 320–335.

[41]Bandura, A. (1973). *Aggression: A social learning analysis*. Englewood Cliffs, NJ: Prentice-Hall.

[42]Rohner, R. (1975). Parental acceptance-rejection and personality: A universalistic approach to behavioral science. In R. Brislin et al. (Eds.), *Cross-cultural perspectives on learning*. New York: Halsted Press.

[43]Blumberg, M. (1974). Psychopathology of the abusing parent. *American Journal of Psychotherapy, 28,* 21–29.

[44]Conger, R., Burgess, R., & Barrett, C. (1979). Child abuse related to life change and perceptions of illness: Some preliminary findings. *Family Coordinator, 28,* 73–78.

[45]Smith, S. M., & Hanson, R. (1975). Interpersonal relationships and childrearing practices in 214 parents of battered children. *British Journal of Psychiatry, 127,* 513–525.

[46]Steinmetz, The use of force.

[47]Light, R. (1973). Abuse and neglected children in America: A study of alternative policies. *Harvard Educational Review, 43,* 556–598.

[48]Klein, M., & Stern, L. (1971). Low birth weight and the battered child syndrome. *American Journal of Diseases of Childhood, 122,* 15–18.

[49]Egeland, B., & Brunnquell, D. (1979). An at-risk approach to the study of child abuse: Some preliminary findings. *Journal of the American Academy of Child Psychiatry, 18*, 219–235.

[50]Frodi, A., et al. (1978). Fathers' and mothers' responses to the faces and cries of normal and premature infants. *Developmental Psychology, 14*, 490–498.

[51]Belsky, Child maltreatment, p. 324.

[52]Patterson, G. (1977). A performance theory of coercive family interaction. In L. G. Cairns (Ed.), *Social interaction: Methods, analysis, and illustration.* Chicago: University of Chicago Press.

[53]Tooley, K. M. (1977). The young child as victim of sibling attack. *Social Casework, 58*, 25–28, p. 26.

[54]Straus, M. A., Gelles, R. J., & Steinmetz, S. K. (1980). *Behind closed doors: Violence in the American family.* Garden City, NY: Anchor Books/Doubleday.

[55]*San Francisco Family Violence Project Handbook* (1980).

[56]Straus, M. A. (1977). Sociological perspective on the prevention and treatment of wifebeating. In M. Roy (Ed.), *Battered women: A psychosociological study of domestic violence.* New York: Van Nostrand Reinhold.

[57]Dutton, D., & Painter, S. L. (1981). Traumatic bonding: The development of emotional attachments in battered women and other relationships of intermittent abuse. *Victimology: An International Journal, 6*, 139–155.

[58]Rounsaville, B. (1978). Theories of marital violence: Evidence from a study of battered women. *Victimology: An International Journal, 3*, 11–31.

[59]Rajecki, P., Lamb, M., & Obmascher, P. (1978). Toward a general theory of infantile attachment: A comparative review of aspects of the social bond. *The Behavioral and Brain Sciences, 3*, 417–464.

[60]Dutton & Painter, Traumatic bonding, p. 147.

[61]Groth, A. N., & Burgess, A. W. (1977). Motivational intent in the sexual assault of children. *Criminal Justice and Behavior, 4*, 253–264.

[62]Brenner, A. *Helping children cope*, p. 131.

[63]Muldoon, L. (Ed.). (1979). *Incest: Confronting the silent crime.* St. Paul: Minnesota Program for Victims of Sexual Assault.

[64]de Young, M. (1982). *The sexual victimization of children.* Jefferson, NC: McFarland, p. 52.

[65]Orzek, A. M. (1985). The child's cognitive processing of sexual abuse. *Child and Adolescent Psychotherapy, 2*, 110–114.

[66]de Young, *Sexual victimization*, p. 58.

[67]Pearlin, L., Lieberman, M., Menaghan, E., & Mullan, J. (1981). The stress process. *Journal of Health and Social Behavior, 22*, 337–356, p. 340.

[68]Caplan, G., & Killilea, M. (1976). *Support systems and mutual help: Multidisciplinary explorations.* New York: Grune & Stratton, p. 41.

[69]Cobb, S. (1976). Social support as a moderator of life stress. *Psychosomatic Medicine, 38*, 300–314.

[70]Forssman, H., & Thuwe, I. (1966). One hundred and twenty children born after application for therapeutic abortion refused. *Acta Psychiatrica Scandinavica, 42*, 71–88.

[71]Brenner, *Helping children cope*, p. 65.

[72]Melamed, B. G., & Siegel, L. J. (1975). Reduction of anxiety in children facing surgery by modeling. *Journal of Consulting and Clinical Psychology, 43*, 511–521.

[73]Medalie, J. H., & Goldbourt, U. (1976). Angina pectoris among 10,000 men: II. Psychosocial and other risk factors as evidenced by a multivariate analysis of a five year incidence study. *American Journal of Medicine, 60*, 910–921.

[74]Baekeland, F., & Lundwall, L. (1975). Dropping out of treatment: A critical review. *Psychological Bulletin, 82*, 738–783.

[75]Cobb, S. (1974). Physiological changes in men whose jobs were abolished. *Journal of Psychosomatic Research, 18*, 245–258.

[76]Turner, R. J. (1983). Direct, indirect, and moderating effects of social support on psychological distress and associated conditions. In H. B. Kaplan (Ed.), *Psychosocial stress: Trends in theory and research* (pp. 105–155). New York: Academic Press.

7

SOCIAL SOURCES OF STRESS: SOCIAL CHANGE, TECHNOLOGICAL CHANGE, AND LIFE-CHANGE

Our method of dealing with [social] dangers . . . is likely to be too slow and dangerous for the rate of change that exists today.

Aubrey Kagan

The years of 1968 through the early 1970s were exciting times for America's space program. Americans saw the first of several lunar landings. Public interest and involvement through the mass media were at an all-time high. Still, there were those who would not or could not be dragged into the space age no matter what kind of evidence they saw before their eyes. During one of the early lunar landings, an incident occurred that still stands out vividly. The checkout of the lunar module was taking some time, so the local station switched to the downtown shopping district for interviews with people on the street. The TV anchor asked several people a straightforward question: "What do you think of America's achievement in putting a man on the moon?" One person's reply was just as straightforward: "That's all a hoax. It's just the government tricking us. It can't be done. God didn't intend for us to be there and we'll never be there!"

In a lighter moment, one might suggest that this person was demonstrating the truth of the maxim that Ignorance Is Bliss. In fact, oblivion and denial do seem to bestow a type of protection against stress for some people in some situations.[1] It is equally possible that the person literally believed what he was saying and that he was ignorant of the technological power behind the space program. An alternative is that the person was employing a stress-reducing strategy to deal with a pace of change that was beyond him.

The coping strategies used in these situations include denial, defensive coping, and resistant coping or withdrawal. Whatever the term, the end result is likely to be the same. The closed-in, defensive person may end up, to paraphrase a biblical statement, living in society but not a part of society. Thus, change can exact heavy penalties from those unprepared or unwilling to meet the challenge of change.

◆ STRESS AND ILLNESS: ORIGINS OF A SOCIAL THEORY

For many years, sociologists, psychologists, and politicians expended tremendous effort and enormous sums of money to identify pressures imposed by social conditions. Studies conducted in the 1930s through the early 1960s suggested that crime, mental illness, and poor health increase in direct proportion to the degree of (1) financial stress, (2) urban crowding, and (3) lower socioeconomic status. Obviously, these three factors are highly related.

Many political action programs implemented during this time were apparently motivated by the belief that social conditions are primarily at fault in human misbehaviors. The logic was very simple and direct: Since social pressures are at the root of psychological stress and physical illness, simply correct the environment and get rid of stress and illness altogether.[2]

The Dodge–Martin Theory

Two social theorists, Dodge and Martin, were among the first to make an explicit statement about the relationship between social pressures and personal stress.[3] They based their theory on statistics of **death rate** in the population (mortality), but suggested that the theory could be considered appropriate for the **frequency of illness** (morbidity) as well.[4] In sum, their theory stated that both chronic (long-term) and acute (short-term) illnesses have social factors contributing, but the specific social factors differ for each type of illness.

Preventive Action or Delayed Reaction

Similar arguments relating social upheaval to stress and illness have been made by other authors. One life-change researcher, Aubrey Kagan, pointed to the dramatic increase in ill health associated with the Industrial Revolution, a period associated with a virtual explosion of technology and tremendous pressures on social structures. A similar analysis is appropriate in regard to the Great Depression. But Kagan saw a much greater danger:

> Our method of dealing with the dangers was, and still is, to recognize them usually after a large measure of damage has been done and to apply rational corrections. This method—sometimes called "planning from crisis to crisis"—is likely to be too slow and dangerous for the rate of change that exists today.[5]

Kagan's point makes plain the compelling motivation to understand the effects of social stressors in contemporary society.

Criticisms of Early Social Theory

Unfortunately, most early theories, whether of sociological or psychological origins, were one-sided. They looked for the cause of stress either in the social structure (sociogenic causes) *or* within the person (psychogenic causes). Social theories such as those just mentioned looked solely at the social structure and thereby failed to look at what individuals contribute to stress reactions. The idea of a *relational* analysis had simply not occurred yet.

Another glaring weakness is that these early theories failed to account for the many people raised in poverty and ghetto conditions who did not just survive, but seemed somehow immune to stress. The people who somehow escape the effects of stress probably are as important to study as those who succumb to stress. It is encouraging to note that the work of Kobasa and Maddi has taken positive steps in this direction.[6]

While the emphasis in this and the next chapters will be on society, life-changes, and environment, the separation of these topics from the discussion of personality and attitudes is for organizational convenience and thematic coherence only. *The conceptual focus is still on the relationship between environment and personal appraisal.*

◆ A SEARCH FOR SOCIAL STRESSORS

A review of the literature on stress suggests that we can confine our attention to a relatively few but very important sources of stress in our society. For example, a major governmental study entitled *Healthy People* identified four major sources contributing to stress and poor health. These were uprooting or the effects of dislocation and frequent relocations, dehumanizing of societal institutions by impersonal and mechanical delivery of services, the spread of technology, and obstacles to the efficient and effective delivery of human services.[7]

In more general terms, these major social stressors may be summarized as (1) rapid sociological and technological change, (2) dehumanizing and victimizing forces, and (3) environmental stressors including overcrowding, pollution, and so forth. The subject of rapid social change will provide the major theme for this chapter. Victimizing forces will be discussed in Chapter 8, and environmental stressors will be the subject of Chapter 9.

◆ STRESS AND SOCIAL CHANGE

Alvin Toffler has presented two separate analyses of major contemporary stressors, both revolving around the idea of rapid, continuous, and dramatic social change. The first was presented in his classic book *Future Shock,* the

second in *The Third Wave.* In *Future Shock,* Toffler talks about the information overload that comes from too much change in too short a period.[8] Future
shock is a disease most characteristic of highly developed technological societies. In short, future shock is the premature arrival of the future. It occurs
when the pace of change is so rapid that it exceeds our ability to integrate
change.

The pace of sociological and technological change is breathtaking. It is
clear that technological changes have dramatically affected the way in
which people work, learn, and spend their leisure time. Technology changes
the environment in which we live. Jobs change to keep pace with new technology. Education changes, and children ask us questions about problems
that did not even exist 30 years ago. Science has changed the amount and
range of information which is available to them. *It will change even faster in
the future.* Right now, nearly 7,000 scientific articles are written each day.
Scientific and technical information increases at the rate of 13% per year. At
this rate of production, the volume doubles every 5.5 years. Current projections are that the rate of growth will reach 40% in the very near future.[9] Yet
these technological changes only scratch the surface of what might lie ahead
in an exciting, challenging brave new world.

Social change is often reflected in life-style changes. Changes in the
family have challenged old values and religious traditions. Consensual marriage, gay liberation, abortion, and lesbian adoption of orphans have provoked families, communities, cities, and governments to heated exchanges.
Use of environmental resources has led to competition and often violent confrontation between special interest groups. Organized religion has abandoned traditions and revised its position on issues once thought fixed.
Another seemingly stable ground for personal values has shifted. The world
we thought we knew is somehow different from what it was before.

A Strange New Emerging World

Toffler's second work, *The Third Wave,* describes the end of the *second wave*
civilization, which was founded on industrialism, religious idealism, and a
representative but centralized democracy. Toffler viewed this second wave
as the society of the past 300 years, much of it the society of our immediate
past, and still part of a crumbling present. He suggested that the changes
now occurring are revolutionary not just in concept, but also in pace and
impact. The changes include a life-style

> based on diversified, renewable energy sources; on methods of production
> that make most factory assembly lines obsolete, on new, non-nuclear fam-
> ilies; on a novel institution that might be called the "electronic cottage";
> and on radically changed schools and corporations of the future.[10]

The implications of Toffler's analysis are clear. The old society with all
of its values and traditions is being torn down to make way for a new society.
The new society brings with it a whole new set of values and traditions,

which are even now being erected on the rubble of the old society. The transition to the new society will produce excitement for some, but despair for others.

For many people, personal change may come only after a heavy price is paid. This price will not likely be exacted in physical warfare, but in a more expensive psychological warfare fought rather privately at first in the domain of the human psyche as individuals struggle within themselves for the personal meaning of these new changes. Later, it may be fought in not-so-private arenas ripe for interpersonal conflict, such as marriage, the nuclear family, and the community.

Personal Stability and Social Change

The psychological impact of this revolution is highly visible. Confusion and anxiety tend to increase. Some authors have even referred to this time as the age of anxiety. Self-identity becomes less sure as many relationships that provided personal security seem to shift constantly. A sense of what Durkheim called *anomie* may increase. **Anomie** is a sense of aloneness and lostness in a huge, impersonal social structure that doesn't have room for individual differences.[11] An almost desperate quest for renewed stability appears. The quest itself may become laden with a spiritual fervor. The person may try even harder to hang onto the structures of the past or may be vulnerable to a variety of cults that appear to provide stability.

The appearance of a wide variety of cults and "isms" is enthusiastically and financially supported by a rapidly fragmenting populace. Cultural pluralism reaches out to encompass religious pluralism. Each of the churches has its own drive-up, tune-in, advice-column-length insights into human nature and cash-and-carry solutions. Each captures some part of the imagination of its followers by offering to restore sanity to a world that somehow has become unrecognizable.

Bernice Martin noted the myriad cults and religions that virtually exploded onto the American cultural scene in the 1960s and 1970s. She uses a term from Berger and Luckmann, *plausibility structures,* to describe the attraction of these cults, which seem to "prop up the subjective self" in a time of extreme cultural fluidity. As she said of the cults,

> they claim to be liberating while much of their real appeal lies in the latent function of providing firm and definitive conceptions of private individual identity which can be strongly internalized and which are usually backed up by psycho-social support structures.[12]

In human terms, though, it is the disparity between expectations and fulfillment, between the "American dream" and America's shame of poverty, unemployment, victimization, and institutionalized discrimination that yields frustration and quiet desperation. It is the discrepancy between one's reach and one's grasp, between goals and the capacity to achieve those goals that translates the social stressor into the personal stress.

As Robert Nisbet suggested in his discussion of family structure, social structure tends to be relatively stable and resistant to change, while people and processes may change rapidly, perhaps even explosively.[13] Immense pressure is exerted on the person when change appears to be out of personal control or imposed. The mere perception of lack of control and lack of predictability of events influencing our lives is frequently all that is necessary to produce intense stress. Future shock is part and parcel of the unpredictable, uncontrollable, imposed change.

Maladjustment can be seen at the personal level when technological developments (inventions), such as surrogate mothering and test-tube fertilization, confront individuals with new and radically different choices and decisions. In such cases, it is quite probable that family customs have left many people not only unprepared, but also in conflict with new technology. Personal beliefs and ethical philosophies, formed in the crucible of aging ideologies, may be incompatible with the philosophy implicit in the new and radical technology.

◆ PERSONAL CONFRONTATIONS WITH RAPID CHANGE

Toffler's analysis was confined to the shape of change itself. More recent research has provided some clues about the coping strategies people often choose under these circumstances.[14] Faced with rapid, incomprehensible change, people adopt a variety of defensive postures. Some strategies for coping with change are effective and promote personal growth. But others seem to be self-limiting if not self-defeating. Forced to make too many choices without time to integrate old standards and values, many people simply avoid making the choices altogether. One major negative outcome is **demoralization,** the psychological result when environmental demands exceed the person's capacity to meet them.[15]

◆ LIFE-CHANGE, STRESS, AND ILLNESS

Rapid social change appears to play a central part in the development of stress. Some of the effects of social change may exist as rather subtle, if not insidious, pressures on personal adaptive reserves. Other effects, however, appear to be much more direct and many times more serious. In the 1970s and 1980s, a number of empirical research programs were developed in an effort to pin down the relationship, if any, between life-change and illness. The details of this scientific pursuit and the conclusions that now stand with some degree of certainty will be the subject matter of the next few pages.

◆ LIFE-CHANGE UNITS: THE EMPIRICAL STORY

The most notable research on life-change and illness has been implemented by two separate teams of researchers. The first team was composed of Thomas Holmes from the University of Washington and Richard Rahe of the U.S. Navy Medical Neuropsychiatric Research Unit. The second was the wife-and-husband team of Barbara and Bruce Dohrenwend at Columbia University.[16] Since the work of the Dohrenwends built on the legacy of Holmes and Rahe, we will treat the two lines of inquiry as though they constitute a single program. Also, because this line of inquiry has been under attack recently for a number of reasons, a summary of some major criticisms will be presented later.

Holmes and Rahe set out to answer two of the most important questions in stress research. First, they wanted to know what life-change situations are viewed by people in our society as most stressful. Second, they wanted to know what physical problems, if any, were likely to occur as a result of life-changes that people view as stressful. Their reasoning was that risk for illness is determined by both constitutional variables and temporal factors in life experience. In the words of Richard Rahe:

> Constitutional endowment helps to explain an individual's susceptibilities to particular types of illnesses but does little to explain why an individual develops an illness at a particular point in time. . . . Recent life changes appear to act as "stressors" partially accounting for illness onset. Conversely, when subjects' lives are in a relatively steady state of psychosocial adjustment with few ongoing life changes, little or no illness tends to be reported.[17]

In regard to the first question, they set out to develop a scaling procedure to assess the degree of stress associated with commonly encountered life events. Taking a direct approach, they asked people what events were considered most stressful, and then assigned weights to the events based on ratings from a large group of people. They recognized that life events do not have to be extreme (such as war or pestilence) in order for stress to be present. Rather, they focused on naturally occurring stressors or life events such as marriage, divorce, childbirth, and death of a loved one.[18]

In regard to the second issue, the relationship between stress and illness, Holmes and Rahe were following the trail established by many laboratory investigators who had found that severe stress is often associated with a variety of physical ailments, including ulcers and death. If this laboratory finding was also true of people functioning in a natural environment, some important implications for detecting and preventing the sources of illness could emerge. But this is getting ahead of the story.

Holmes and Rahe began their research by asking a rather large number of clients (approximately 5,000) to indicate in an open-ended fashion what events they found to be most stressful. From this initial pool of responses, they put together a list of 43 events that were judged to require some adaptive struggle or *social readjustment* for effective dealing with the event. The events covered positive (for example, marriage), negative (such as being jailed), frequent (minor traffic violations, for example), and rare (such as death of spouse or child) happenings. Adaptive struggle might necessitate change in life-style or be indicated by psychological conflict and anxiety for a period of time.

In the next phase, 394 people were asked to rate the list of 43 events on the basis of their individual experiences with the stressors and in terms of the relative degree of disruption caused by each. **Social readjustment** was defined as "the intensity and length of time necessary to accommodate to a life event, *regardless of the desirability of this event*."[19] Marriage was assigned an arbitrary value of 500. Each person was asked to judge first whether each of the remaining events required more or less readjustment than marriage. Then they were to assign a value proportionate to the value of 500. For example, if death of spouse was judged to require twice as much readjustment effort as marriage, the person would assign it a value of 1000. After collecting responses to this questionnaire, Holmes and Rahe computed the average severity of life-change produced by the stressors and ranked the items from most intense to least intense.

◆ THE SOCIAL READJUSTMENT RATING SCALE

This resulted in the Social Readjustment Rating Scale (SRRS), shown in Table 7–1. Note that the first item, death of spouse, has a value of 100 assigned to it. The original rating was done with an arbitrary value of 500. When the final mean ratings were computed, the investigators assigned the most severe stressor the value of 100. All other means were then adjusted to this standard so that the relative intensity of each item was still reflected accurately. The value for each item was called a Life Change Unit (LCU). Now, presumably, the total amount of stress that a person went through in a given period could be measured by adding together all the LCUs for any items checked.

Note that the three items ranked as most stressful by this sample (death of spouse, divorce, and separation) involve life-changes in marital situation. In fact, eight of the top 10 stressors are either family or work related. Also, relatively few of the items are *high-severity* stressors, while a relatively large number are *low-to moderate-severity* stressors.

Also, it is worthy of note that a large number of events are obviously pleasant rather than negative. Most people would accept the fact that marriage, pregnancy, completion of school, change in line of work, outstanding personal achievement, vacation, and Christmas are positive events. It should be equally obvious, however, that these events do produce stress, some more than others. As the definition of stress proposed by Selye suggests, the body does not distinguish between positive and negative stressors.

Table 7–1. Rank of Life-change Events with Associated Life Change Units (LCU) as an Index of the Disruptiveness of the Stressor

Rank	Life Event	LCU
1.	Death of spouse	100
2.	Divorce	73
3.	Marital separation	65
4.	Jail term	63
5.	Death of close family member	63
6.	Personal injury or illness	53
7.	Marriage	50
8.	Fired at work	47
9.	Marital reconciliation	45
10.	Retirement	45
11.	Change in health of family member	44
12.	Pregnancy	40
13.	Sexual difficulties	39
14.	Gain of new family member	39
15.	Business readjustment	39
16.	Change in financial state	38
17.	Death of close friend	37
18.	Change to different lines of work	36
19.	Change in number of arguments with spouse	35
20.	Mortgage over $10,000	31
21.	Foreclosure of mortgage or loan	30
22.	Change in responsibilities at work	29
23.	Son or daughter leaving home	29
24.	Trouble with in-laws	29
25.	Outstanding personal achievement	28
26.	Wife begins or stops work	26
27.	Begin or end school	26
28.	Change in living conditions	25
29.	Revision of personal habits	24
30.	Trouble with boss	23
31.	Change in work hours or conditions	20
32.	Change in residence	20
33.	Change in schools	20
34.	Change in recreation	19
35.	Change in church activities	19
36.	Change in social activities	18
37.	Mortgage or loan less than $10,000	17
38.	Change in sleeping habits	16
39.	Change in number of family get-togethers	15
40.	Change in eating habits	13
41.	Vacation	13
42.	Christmas	12
43.	Minor violations of the law	11

Note. From "The Social Readjustment Rating Scale" by T. H. Holmes and R. H. Rahe, 1967, *Psychosomatic Medicine, 11.*

The excitement of marriage is almost as taxing as the grief suffered with the loss of a close member of the family.

Take a moment to respond to the scale before reading further. Circle the number on the left for any event that has occurred in the past six months. After you have done this, locate the score for the event on the right, circle it, and sum all of the scores. Information on interpretation will be provided in the text that follows.

◆ DO STRESSFUL LIFE EVENTS REALLY PRODUCE ILLNESS?

Having obtained these severity ratings, Holmes and Rahe tried to determine if life-changes impact on personal adjustment and health and, if so, in what ways. Previous research suggested that stressful life-changes could precipitate a variety of detrimental effects, including psychological disturbance and physical illness. Three lines of evidence contributed to the belief that stressful life-changes produce some deterioration in health, if not outright illness. One of these lines of evidence comes from a wide variety of laboratory and clinical research programs based on the work of Selye and others. A portion of this research has already been summarized in Chapters 2 and 3.

The second line of evidence comes from observations of the reactions of people to natural disasters, such as earthquakes and floods, and observations of individuals under conditions of abnormal stress, such as soldiers in combat. The term **posttraumatic stress syndrome** was coined to refer to the emotional–behavioral pattern that appears in extreme conditions. Information on stress reactions to catastrophic events will be presented in more detail in Chapter 9.

The third line of evidence represents the concerted effort of many investigators working over nearly two decades. Most have used the scaling techniques of Holmes and Rahe, while others have adapted the procedure or developed something similar. Always, however, the effort shared a common focus: to determine the relationship between the amount of stress and the amount of illness occurring in populations in the natural environment.

Physicians and Life Crises

Holmes and Rahe asked a group of 200 resident physicians to list all the "major health changes" they had experienced in the previous 10 years and to fill out the SRRS. Each of the responding physicians (88 total) was then given a score based on the sum of all LCU values. Of the 96 major health changes reported, 89 were associated with total LCU scores over 150. When the LCU score was under 150, the majority also reported good health in the succeeding year. But when the LCU score was over 300, over 70% of the physicians reported illness in the following year.[20] This value of 150 was then used for a preliminary definition of a *life crisis*.

Further analysis permitted Holmes and Rahe to establish more precise categories for life crises: 150–199 LCU defined a *mild* life crisis, 200–299 LCU defined a *moderate* life crisis, and over 300 LCU defined a *major* crisis.[21] (If you have already responded to the scale, you can compare your score against this standard.) The working assumption of most of this research now is that the more life crises that accumulate, the more likely the person will incur some illness within a short period following the crisis.

In an extensive review of studies aimed at testing this assumption, Holmes and Masuda found an impressive array of supporting evidence. Retrospective studies have found increased life-change associated with myocardial infarction, fractures, diabetes, tuberculosis, pregnancy, and leukemia.[22] One study in the academic environment showed that as life-change increased among college freshmen, their grade point averages went down. The findings have been repeated with groups from other countries including England, Wales, Norway, Sweden, Denmark, France, Belgium, Switzerland, Japan, Malaysia, Hawaii, El Salvador, and Peru. Also, confirming results have been found in children, identical twins, and college students. Among adults, the findings appear to be general regardless of occupational group.

Telephone Operators, Hungarian Refugees, and Carrier Pilots

Among the earliest evidence of this type was the work of Hinkle and his colleagues on a large group of female (1,327) and male (1,527) telephone company employees.[23] A random-sampling technique was used to get a smaller group of 226 employees who had 20 years or more of service with the company. A review of the medical histories of this group revealed a phenomenal difference in the amount of sickness. Some of the employees had had no sickness disability at all during the 20 years. Many had had no more than 5 days total absence due to sickness and only 1 or 2 episodes of illness-related leave each year. But company records on a third group of employees produced some startling facts. Many members of this group had missed up to a total of 1,000 work days during this 20-year period. Some had had nearly 100 episodes of disabling illness during the same 20-year period. All told, that is equivalent to missing a full 3 years of work, with roughly 5 illness-disability episodes per year.

The next step in the investigative process was even more revealing. Hinkle and his associates wanted to determine if a particular biological or psychosocial pattern might provide some explanation for the major differences between the healthy and the sick group. While they could not statistically rule out the possibility that the differences in distribution of illness were chance, there was strong evidence of a consistently different psychosocial pattern between the two groups. As the authors stated,

> the "healthy" telephone operators were women . . . who liked their work, found it easy and satisfying, liked their families and associates, and were generally content and comfortable with their lot in life. This was often not the case with the frequently ill telephone operators. . . . many of them were working at this job not because they liked it but from necessity. They often described it as confining or boring. For various reasons these women were unhappy with their lot in life, with their families, their associates, and their communities.[24]

Hinkle studied two other groups. One was a group of Chinese-born graduate students, technicians, and professional people living in New York

City. The other was a group of Hungarian refugees who had escaped to the United States following the 1956 Russian invasion of Hungary. Both groups had gone through severe dislocations, separation from families and long-standing social support groups, and extreme culture shock.

For the most part, the Chinese group showed little evidence of illness at all. At first, this result seemed to contradict the pattern observed in previous studies. But information from the Hungarian group provided a possible explanation for what was happening. The Hungarian group showed the same distribution of illness as the telephone operators *during the 10 years preceding their flight*. They described their time leading up to the confrontation with the Hungarian regime as one of insecurity and frustration. However, during the revolution and flight, and in spite of the severe disruption in their lives, they actually showed an improvement in overall health. It appeared that the general excitement and the anticipation of making a fresh start in a new country served as a type of inoculation against sickness. Hinkle concluded from these studies that the effect of dramatic social change on a person's health could not be determined solely from the nature of the change itself. Other factors must be important, including the psychological characteristics of the person.[25]

This conclusion has been confirmed by other investigators. For example, observations of enlisted sailors showed that a rather small proportion of the men accounted for a majority of the sick days. The men most frequently found to be ill were in the more routine and menial jobs, which required less skill. Also, the jobs were more frequently either hazardous or uncomfortable or both. In general, the men were described as immature and less capable than those who did not report illness.[26]

One of the most interesting studies conducted in a real-world environment was carried out on aircraft carrier pilot trainees. The type of situation encountered by these trainees appears similar in many respects to that arranged by Brady in his famous executive monkey study, which was reviewed earlier. And, as we shall see momentarily, the physical reaction observed was also very similar.[27] Here is how Rubin described the training situation and aircraft.

> The F-4B Phantom jet fighter-bomber is a two-man aircraft. The pilot in the front cockpit, has complete flight control. The radar intercept officer (RIO), in the rear cockpit, monitors the radar and other instruments but has no flight control. He does have excellent visibility. In an emergency both the pilot and the RIO can eject themselves from the aircraft, a procedure not without hazard. The RIO is aware of these hazards and the aircraft's position during the landing attempt, but he must rely completely on the pilot's skill for his own personal safety.[28]

In other words, the RIO is in exactly the same situation as the monkeys who could do nothing to control the delivery of shock. The cohorts could only put their safety in the hands of their pilot friend and hope.

Measurements of the physical responses of both the pilots and the co-pilots showed a very interesting pattern of reactivity. While the RIOs showed higher levels of subjective anxiety on all days tested, the pilots showed the type of stress reaction pattern observed in the laboratory animals. Again in the words of Rubin,

> these results indicate that aircraft carrier landing practice was considerably more stressful for the pilots than for their RIO's. In the context of the "executive" monkey paradigm, the "executive" naval aviator, who had to perform a highly complex task while avoiding serious potential harm to himself, his partner and his aircraft, showed an unequivocal adrenal cortical stress response. The passive partner, on the other hand, although completely aware of the risks involved, showed only a slight, statistically insignificant adrenal response.[29]

◆ THE CASE AGAINST LIFE-CHANGE CAUSING ILLNESS

Since the beginnings of this research, there has been a constant stream of criticism. Early prospective studies showed some expected but much less dramatic relationships and led to a skeptical attitude in the scientific community. As Dohrenwend and Dohrenwend suggested, "at present the belief that life stress causes illness is based on faith bolstered by some scientific evidence."[30]

Many criticisms are based on the methodological weakness of retrospective designs, which were used too frequently to establish the case for life stress and illness. Such designs have many difficulties including the fallibility of memory, subjective biases, and intervening distortions that may affect subjects' reports of what actually happened. Other criticisms center on the tendency for illness to be confounded with psychiatric and psychological problems, which makes it difficult to attribute the illness reliably to the life stress or life-change itself. In fact, it may well be that the psychiatric disability leads to a distorted perception of life stress or life-change itself. The life-change may be caused by psychological difficulties that also produce the illness. But life-change is not the cause of the illness. This is an important argument that cannot be easily discounted.

Another line of argument against the life-change–illness connection comes from studies designed to test in more subtle ways the actual or alleged connection. For example, David Schroeder and Paul Costa reported a prospective study that found no evidence for the connection. They employed physicians' records to determine the degree of illness in a broad population following a stress year. That is, a group of people were given a preliminary medical examination prior to a year designated as the target stress year. After the year, they were asked to report on life-change using a "56-item Homes–Rahe-style" checklist. An additional medical examination was used to ascertain the number of *new diseases not present on the prestress examination*. They found no correlation at all between the amount of life-change in the previous 12 months and the incidence of illness.[31]

Such disconfirming prospective studies must be weighed against the positive prospective studies. It may well be that moderator variables will turn out to resolve the discrepancy between the two contradictory outcomes. We have already pointed to one example of a moderator variable, personality, as it related to the illness of executives. Indeed, Sarason, Levine, and Sarason pointed to three broad classes of moderator variables that are probably closely related to whether life-change exerts the influence on illness that has been predicted by Holmes and Rahe. These three categories are relatively stable personal characteristics, such as locus of control and psychological hardiness; prior experiences that influence how a person responds to stress; and environmental factors, such as social support.[32]

◆ COPING WITH SOCIAL CHANGE

The very nature of the topic of social change precludes the possibility of giving the types of specific recommendations that might be made with more specific stresses. Social change is just too global, pervasive, insidious, and constant. It has become almost a cliché that the best way to prepare for the future is to understand the present.[33] Accepting the fact of change may be the first step. As several writers have suggested, change may well be the most constant part of our environment.

Preparation and self-education are probably the best ways of dealing with social change. The well-read, socially alert, and culturally conscious person will have the greatest likelihood of accepting new innovations, adapting to new technology, retraining to accept new jobs, and confronting new personal life-style choices with the least amount of stress. Ostrichlike responses to unwanted change will accomplish little. Naisbitt comments that the appropriate response to technology is "not to stop it, Luddite-like, but to accommodate it, respond to it, and shape it."[34]

Stress inoculation techniques, which will be described in Chapter 13, may also be of help. This approach focuses on imagining some of the very worst scenarios that might be expected to induce a high degree of personal stress. As an example, think of the type of social change that would produce the most difficulty for you. Do you have a great fear of computer banking, computer shopping, test-tube babies, genetic engineering, sperm banks, world government? Serious proposals have been made in regard to each of these. Consider one proposal (not necessarily one of these) as though someone were asking you to accept it as a part of your life-style. How would you respond to it? Consider what the advantages and disadvantages of this might be. Discuss it in your family and circle of friends. Try to anticipate how it might impact on your personal life-style.

The assumption of stress inoculation is that once you have worked through some of your worst possible anticipated fears, you will have an easier time dealing with the real choices when you actually face them. In addition, change will be easier to accept because you have come to grips with some of the more emotionally loaded changes even before they have actually occurred. Recognize that you do not have to be an advocate of a proposal in order to inquire about the merits of it. Also, in engaging in an exercise of this type, there is no intent that you actually change your mind, only that you consider it as thoroughly and fairly as possible.

Another approach is value clarification. This cognitive coping strategy enables the person to determine more clearly what specific values are producing the conflict or pressure. Once the values producing the problem have been identified, it seems to be much easier to respond to the information being presented in a more straightforward fashion. You may want to skip ahead to Chapter 13, which is about cognitive strategies and study some of these techniques.

The report on *Healthy People* suggested that the following factors are important in coping with social stress: belonging to a group, having acceptable substitute activities available, having ready access to advice, having someone to talk to about personal troubles, and having an education.[35] Belonging to a group is one of the most important means of obtaining social support. In this vein, a religious group can serve as a very important social support network.

◆ SUMMARY

In this chapter, we have traced briefly the concern for social stress and social stability in early research and theory. This work identified several primary conditions (such as poverty, overcrowding, and unemployment) thought to be the origins of frustration and stress in modern society. The idea that social stress may be linked to both mental and physical illness was also examined. The single most important source of stress is social change.

Change confronts us with many personal and social dilemmas. There are new decisions, new technologies, new jobs, new environments, new lifestyles. Many of these changes are imposed rather than under personal control. They confront us with a range of value conflicts that present difficulty, especially for the unprepared. Preparation through self-education, stress inoculation, and value clarification may be the best way to deal with social change. More specific elements of social stress related to environment and work will be dealt with in coming chapters with more specific suggestions for coping.

◆ NOTES

[1]Indeed, some research conducted on patients undergoing serious surgery suggests that they do fare much better without any knowledge of the seriousness of their situation. But this circumstance may be regarded as not comparable to that of the person who denies the existence of certain developments, as this person did.

[2]While there are many studies that could be cited, a few studies stand out as classics in this group: Faris, R., & Dunham, H. W. (1939). *Mental disorders in urban areas.* Chicago: University of Chicago Press; Hollingshead, A. B., & Redlich, F. C. (1958). *Social class and mental illness: A community study.* New York: Wiley; Srole, L., Langner, T. S., Michael, S. T., Opler, M. K., & Rennie, T. A. C. (1962). *Mental health in the metropolis.* New York: McGraw-Hill; Brenner, M. H. (1973). *Mental illness and the economy.* Cambridge, MA: Harvard University Press. The last reference presents a more up-to-date analysis of the issues involved, including a fairly cogent argument for the real effects of financial deprivation.

[3]Dodge, D. L., & Martin, W. T. (1970). *Social stress and chronic illness.* Notre Dame, IN: University of Notre Dame Press.

[4]*Mortality* refers to the proportion of deaths in a population in a given region in a given period. *Morbidity,* on the other hand, refers to the proportion or rate of disease in a given population. While extremely stressful conditions may produce death, the more common expectation is that stress will produce more or less severe deteriorations in health, including serious illnesses. The point, then, is that mortality data probably are not the most accurate index of the true relationship between stress and illness.

[5]Kagan, A. (1974). Psychosocial factors in disease: Hypotheses and future research. In E. K. E. Gunderson & R. H. Rahe (Eds.), *Life stress and illness.* Springfield, IL: Thomas, p. 42.

[6]Relevant information on this research was presented in Chapter 5, pp. 110–111.

[7]Institute of Medicine (United States). (1979). *Healthy people: The Surgeon General's report on health promotion and disease prevention.* (Government Document No. HE20.2:H34/5). Rockville, MD: U.S. Government Printing Office.

[8]Toffler, A. (1970). *Future shock.* New York: Bantam Books.

[9]Naisbitt, J. (1982). *Megatrends: Ten new directions transforming our lives.* New York: Warner Books, p. 24.

[10]Toffler, A. (1980). *The third wave.* New York: Bantam Books, p. 10.

[11]Durkheim, E. (1951). *Suicide.* New York: Free Press. (Original work published 1897)

[12]Martin, B. (1981). *A sociology of contemporary cultural change.* New York: St. Martin's Press, p. 222.

[13]Nisbet, R. A. (1970). *The social bond.* New York: Knopf.

[14]A variety of sources support the conclusions presented here, including: Lazarus, R. S. (1966). *Psychological stress and the coping process.* New York: McGraw-Hill; Gentry, W. D., Foster, S., and Harvey, T. (1972). Denial as a determinant of anxiety and perceived health status in the coronary care unit. *Psychosomatic Medicine, 34,* 39–44.

[15]The concept of demoralization is found in a number of sources, but two are cited, the first for its brevity and the second for its thoroughness: Wills, T. A., & Langner, T. S. (1980). Socioeconomic status and stress. In I. L. Kutash, L. B. Schlesinger, and associates (Eds.), *Handbook on stress and anxiety.* San Francisco: Jossey-Bass, Chapter 9, p. 165ff; Frank, J. D. (1973). *Persuasion and healing.* Baltimore: Johns Hopkins University Press.

[16]Holmes, T. H., & Masuda, M. (1974). Life change and illness susceptibility. In B. S. Dohrenwend & B. P. Dohrenwend (Eds.), *Stressful life events: Their nature and effect.* New York: Wiley; Holmes, T. H., & Rahe, R. H. (1967). The Social Readjustment Rating Scale. *Psychosomatic Medicine, 11,* 213–218; Dohrenwend, B. S., & Dohrenwend, B. P. (1982). Some issues in research on stressful life events. In T. Millon, C. Green, & R. Meagher (Eds.), *Handbook of clinical health psychology.* New York: Plenum Press.

[17]Rahe, R. (1974). Life change and subsequent illness reports. In Gunderson & Rahe, *Life stress and illness,* p. 58.

[18]Dohrenwend & Dohrenwend, Some issues in research, p. 1.

[19]Holmes & Masuda, Life change and illness susceptibility, p. 49.

[20]Rahe, Life change and subsequent illness reports, p. 62. The results reported for the physicians also appeared to hold quite well in a group of enlisted seamen who were observed for a period of 6 months prior to going on duty and for the following 6 months while on the high seas.

[21]Holmes & Masuda, Life change and illness susceptibility, p. 61.

[22]Rahe, R. H., & Arthur, R. J. (1978). Life change and illness studies: Past history and future directions. *Journal of Human Stress, 4,* 3–15. This survey presents a better overview of the literature on life-change and illness, whereas the Holmes and Masuda review puts the development of the scaling technique in perspective along with some of the major research findings. The reference to pregnancy requires some comment. After a disastrous coal avalanche in Wales killed 116 children and 28 adults in the community school, the birthrate increased by nearly 50%. This was true whether the parents had lost children in the disaster or not.

[23]Hinkle, L. E. (1974). The effect of exposure to culture change, social change, and changes in interpersonal relationships on health. In Dohrenwend & Dohrenwend, *Stressful life events.*

[24]Hinkle, The effect of exposure, p. 21.

[25]Hinkle, The effect of exposure, p. 41.

[26]Nelson, P. D. (1974). Comment. In Gunderson & Rahe, *Life stress and illness,* p. 80.

[27]Rubin, R. T. (1974). Biochemical and neuroendocrine responses to severe psychological stress. In Gunderson & Rahe, *Life stress and illness.*

[28]Rubin, Biochemical and neuroendocrine, p. 228.

[29]Rubin, Biochemical and neuroendocrine, pp. 231–232.

[30]Dohrenwend & Dohrenwend, Some issues in research, p. 91.

[31]Schroeder, D. H., & Costa, P. T. (1984, May). *Do stressful life events influence objectively-measured health? A prospective evaluation.* Paper presented at the Midwestern Psychological Association Annual Conference, Chicago.

[32]Sarason, I. G., Levine, H. M., & Sarason, B. R. (1982). Assessing the impact of life changes. In Millon, Green, & Meagher, *Handbook of clinical health psychology,* pp. 384, 385.

[33]Naisbitt echoed this familiar theme when he said that "the most reliable way to anticipate the future is by understanding the present." *Megatrends,* p. 2.

[34]Naisbitt, *Megatrends.*

[35]Institute of Medicine, *Healthy people,* p. 229.

8

COPING WITH VICTIMIZATION: FEAR, BRUTALIZATION, AND ISOLATION

There is no mathematical law of compensation. . . . Now it more than makes up for the evil, again there is no compensation at all. Much depends upon your attitude . . . and upon what energy you have to assimilate or transform the hurt.

Charles Horton Cooley

Tuesday, November 20, 1984, should have been just another school day for 17-year-old Ben Wilson, student and all-star basketball player at Simeon Vocational High School in Chicago. Instead, it would be his last day ever. Ben Wilson was shot to death by two 16-year-old students who became angry after he "bumped" into them on the sidewalk near the high school.[1] Ben was only one of the many victims on this particular day. His family and friends will continue to suffer the consequences of this senseless crime. As is true in so many cases like this, the effect reaches out to others and carries on for some time.

Crime creates literally millions of victims in our society each year. An estimated 650,000 aggravated assaults occur each year. Another 21,000 persons are murdered each year. One rape is committed every seven minutes.[2] Material loss from all types of robbery is estimated to approach $9.5 billion annually. Corporate and white-collar crime bilks untold millions through coercion, extortion, and fraud.[3] As great as the immediate physical and material loses are, the aftermath of crime produces even more sinister, pervasive, and debilitating effects. Call them "mind-rapes," if you will—the unwanted, continued forced entry into one's consciousness of all the memories, pain, and terror of the event. For many, this continued intrusion into the inner sanctum of the mind is the greater crime and the source of recurrent stress.

The psychological scars from being victimized range from confusion and insecurity to disillusionment, anger, and loss of self-esteem. A sense of futility and helplessness appears in the form of verbalized rage against the aggressor. Feelings of hopelessness are vented in frustration against an insensitive legal system, which is perceived as moving at a snail's pace to apprehend and punish, if ever it will.

◆ FEAR—THE VICTIM'S JAILER

The most pervasive effects, however, are those produced by fear. In fact, an assault or robbery does not even have to take place for fear to weave its web. Just the *threat* of being victimized is enough. William Berg and Robert Johnson spoke of the "fear of crime" syndrome and of "self-defined prisoners" who are left with "no havens of safety at all" when crime follows them into their homes.[4] Fear becomes the jailer, shutting off access to an outside world that still beckons but is too frightening to explore. The impact of fear is extensive, cutting across many thought and feeling processes. Personal freedom seems limited because victims generally feel compelled to alter patterns of social, market, and work behavior.[5] Constant vigilance is necessary to ensure that personal injury or loss does not occur again. Disillusionment about society in general and justice in particular become enduring attitudes. Mental energy is diverted from more creative pursuits. In effect, fear changes the victim's reality.

◆ VICTIMOLOGY: INVESTIGATING CRIMINAL–VICTIM RELATIONSHIPS

One group of researchers, called **criminologists,** investigates the relationships between social systems and criminal behavior. Another group, called **victimologists,** are working to discover the factors that contribute to becoming victims.[6] Among the many questions raised by these investigators, three are central to this chapter. One issue is *risk:* What are the factors that predispose some individuals to be more likely targets of crime? A second question has to do with *prevention:* What can be done to educate people to reduce their risk? Another is *coping:* What can be done to help victims put their work, social, family, and personal lives back together?

The Question of Risk: Who Are the Victims?

Victims of crime exist in virtually every segment of society, but some groups are more vulnerable than others. The term *vulnerable* is used to refer to groups of people with certain shared demographic or personal characteristics who are more or less susceptible to becoming victims through no fault of their own.[7] While many questions remain, a picture is emerging that provides some clues about the characteristics of high-risk groups. One research team, headed by Michael J. Hindelang, has supplied a wealth of information collected from a large eight-city sample.[8]

This research has identified four major demographic characteristics that seem to be important in distinguishing the victim from the nonvictim.[9] These are age, marital status, employment status, and sex. The relationship of each of these factors to vulnerability is summarized below.

Age. Younger persons have a higher likelihood of becoming victims than older persons. This is probably due to mobility and social behavior. In general, younger people are both more active and more mobile than older persons. Also, younger persons are generally more impulsive in behavior and emotional expressions. They may tend to be less discriminating, if not dangerously adventuresome, in frequenting places that increase the likelihood of conflict, confrontation, and assault. At the same time, the elderly experience much more anticipatory fear and are much more likely to feel the effects of victimization because of their relative powerlessness.[10] This may be because the elderly lose the sense of **active mastery,** the feeling that they are in control and can do something about their own fate.

Marital Status. An unmarried person has a greater risk of becoming a victim than a married person. Activity (seeking companionship), mobility (not having home responsibility), and socializing customs (being more likely to go out alone and frequent "hot spots") are probably the most likely explanations for this. On the other side, married persons generally spend more time at home or work than on the move.[11]

Employment Status. Unemployed people have a higher risk of becoming victims than employed people. There are a variety of factors involved here, not the least of which is the fact that the unemployed constitute one of the more destitute and highly frustrated groups in society. In general, this group lives in lower-income, high-risk areas and engages in more high-risk behaviors (frequenting bars, street hangouts, and so forth), which increases their likelihood of becoming victims.

Sex. Males are at higher risk than females. This finding is closely linked to the pattern already described: The most vulnerable person appears to be the youthful, unmarried, and unemployed male who may be in the wrong place at the right time. Females, however, report more fear of victimization.[12]

These risk factors were derived from frequency and primacy statistics observed in these groups. Race was not found to be significantly related, but regardless of race, risk decreased as income increased.

Hindelang and his colleagues also reported that the criminal offender is a stranger in 80% of the reports of personal crime. However, where the offender is related, injuries tend to be much more serious.[13] In fact, where homicide is concerned, a family member is more likely to be involved than a nonfamily member.[14] There may also be a victimization-prone personality much like the so-called accident-prone personality. This concept comes from observations that certain people seem repeatedly to become victims of crime.[15] While the information is too sketchy to draw any firm conclusions, the idea still bears watching.

Prevention: How to Avoid Becoming a Victim

Modern living entails certain risks, to be sure. But there are two very good reasons to be optimistic. First, the likelihood of serious loss or injury from personal crime is actually less than that from driving a car. Second, there are relatively few but simple steps that can be taken to reduce the risks of becoming a victim. In other words, *it does not require monumental changes in life-style to reduce risk.* Michael Hindelang concluded that "for most people, the behavioral effects of crime or the fear of crime appear more as subtle adjustments in behavior than as major shifts in what can be called behavioral policies."[16] This is *the single most important concept* of this entire discussion.

According to the research of Hindelang and his colleagues, life-styles are of great significance in personal crime in the first place because life-styles are related to being in places and situations with high *opportunities* for criminal victimization.[17] **Life-style** refers to routine daily activities, both vocational activities (work, school, keeping house, etc.) and leisure activities."[18] It encompasses the times and places we prefer to do things, the activities we most like to occupy our time with, and the people we like to be with.

Lifestyle Assessment

The goal of life-style assessment is to understand how personal behavior is related to environmental risks. The outcome of a thorough assessment should be a balance between feelings of personal security and an attitude of healthy caution. The extremes of obsessive fear on the one hand and feelings of invulnerability on the other hand are to be avoided.

Obsessive fear is not just self-limiting. It takes away the joy of daily living. At the same time, a feeling of invincibility may suppress good common sense, leading you to rush in where angels fear to tread. Healthy caution includes making a realistic appraisal of the dangers present in the environment, taking necessary steps to avoid those dangers, and thereby eliminating the necessity of undue worry or disabling fear.

A positive approach to personal security involves seizing control of the basic behavioral patterns that tend to place people in positions of risk. The first step is to identify your habits of shopping, socializing, and movement in your locale. Habits are by definition carried out automatically and with little or no conscious attention. Some habits could be dangerous but escape your notice because they are so automatic. Do you drive to work at the same time and over the same route? Do you shop at the same market at the same time each week? Do you go out alone, late at night, and so forth?

A life-style assessment can be done fairly quickly without any forms or predesigned scales. Just keep a log of activities over a one or two-week period. Record the activities you engage in, such as shopping, banking, or commuting to work, and the times at which you do them. Then cross-check your habits against the following information to determine if there are adjustments that should be considered.

Choose your time.   It should come as no surprise that nighttime carries the highest risk. In the eight-city study, the time frame between midnight and 6 A.M. yielded a higher rate of injury than any other time. Michael Hindelang's team observed that 91% of the victims said they felt safe being out alone during the day. But only 55% felt safe being out at night.[19]

There are some very good reasons for this. First, fewer bystanders are present to notice or intervene at night. Thus the offender has a much reduced risk of detection. Also, more alcohol is consumed at night, and alcohol is significantly related to criminal acts. Most importantly, *the contribution of alcohol to the risk of criminal assault comes as much from the victim as from the offender.*[20] Alcohol tends to affect decision processes and to lower some very important protective social inhibitions. Both behavior and attitudes are likely to change under the influence of alcohol. This seems to contribute to provoking criminal attacks and/or increasing the likelihood of injury.

The life-style adjustment suggested is relatively simple: Avoid very late activities such as late-night shopping or jogging. And be doubly cautious where alcohol is concerned. If you must drink, be a little more prepared to turn the other cheek. Being flip, argumentative, or belligerent could lead to assault and serious injury.

Know the high-risk places.

Two places are notably high-risk places: home and the street. However, the crimes occurring in these two arenas are dramatically different. Assaults in the home are most often crimes of passion started by a spouse, lover, or friend after some serious domestic strife. Criminal assaults on the street tend most often to be crimes of profit or power (territorial imperatives) precipitated by strangers experiencing personal frustrations.[21]

Street assaults can be avoided largely through adjusting time schedules and using modes of transportation that avoid prolonged contact on the street. Perhaps the best safety precaution is contained in the maxim There Is Safety in Numbers. This is true generally as long as the "numbers" are friends. Even a small group of two to four friends is usually enough to dissuade a would-be attacker from approaching. When the "numbers" are strangers, you will not be any more vulnerable, but you will be less likely to get help than if only a few people are around.[22]

Choose self-protection measures wisely.

After a crime has occurred, victims frequently replay the episode and second-guess their reactions to the event. Should I have done this or that differently? Should I have protected myself? What would have been the outcome if I had resisted more? Or less? The answer to all these questions is that it depends. First, in Hindelang's study, in four of five cases of theft there was no injury to the victim whatsoever.[23] Thus, where profit is the motive, you seem to have a better chance of avoiding personal injury by just letting the thief carry on without resisting.

Further, people who did take some form of self-protective action were more likely to be injured (29% versus 21% as reported in the Hindelang study) than those who did not. But this apparently depends on the *type* of self-protective measure taken.[24] The most successful measures for warding off attacks include verbal resistance in the form of threats of detection or of talking the offender out of carrying out the crime (20% were injured, 80% were not), evasive action (16% were injured, 84% were not), and simply yelling or screaming (36% were injured, 64% were not).

On the other side, physical counterattack tends to increase the risk of physical injury. The *Death Wish* vigilante mentality notwithstanding, use of physical force showed twice the injury rate overall (53% versus 25% not using it). The use of weapons of any kind for self-protection also tends to increase the likelihood of injury (30% injured when using weapons, 24% injured with no weapon).[25]

Serious injuries tend to occur more frequently in interactions with acquaintances than in those with strangers. In fact, statistics compiled by the FBI indicate that homicides are nearly twice as likely to involve family, friends, and acquaintances as strangers.[26] One of the critical reasons for this is that spouses, lovers, and friends are much more likely to engage in resistance to the assault. Not only that, they more frequently resist with violent counterattacks, which simply compounds the problem and increases the severity and extent of their own injury.[27] All of the information is thus consistent in suggesting that physical counterattack should probably be avoided and evasive or verbal actions should be the primary means of resisting. If a fight is brewing at home, the best course of action might be just to leave for a short period until things cool down and level-headed discussion can occur.

Finally, a person does not have to be capable of physically countering criminal attacks in order to achieve a sense of active mastery over the environment. The perception that this is the primary method of mastery may be a legacy of the frontier days. But modern society provides a variety of alternatives that have proven to be generally more effective and certainly less risky than aggressive counterattack. Active mastery and power can be achieved through the astute use of existing social and law enforcement agencies.

Adjust daily activities.   Only minor behavior adjustments seem necessary in most cases. For example, routine market behaviors (shopping for food, clothing) should be varied instead of maintained on a rigid schedule. This prevents potential thieves from establishing a pattern that can be exploited. Also, it is best to shop during the day or early evening hours. Job-related behaviors should also be adjusted so that hours of transit and mode of transit are optimal. Leave the office earlier if need be to take the metro when it is crowded, rather than later when you will be virtually alone.

Social activities (such as movies and dining out) can usually be carried on with reduced risks by going in small groups. In the Hindelang study, only a small proportion actually felt they had substantially decreased their social behavior because of crime. On some university and college campuses, late-night escort services have been initiated to enable people to move about with safety. If one exists, consider making use of it when appropriate.

Recreation behaviors also can be adjusted to include friends and optimal time arrangements. Overall, the interviews in the eight-city study show that it is not necessary to make major changes in *what* you do, only in the *way* in which you do them.[28]

◆ BARRIERS TO EFFECTIVE PREVENTION

On the surface, it would appear to be a rather simple and easy matter to implement most of these preventive measures. The information available is fairly clear, and the behavior changes suggested are relatively uncomplicated. But things are not always what they appear. There seem to be at least three psychological processes that can influence both the risks we take and the stress reactions we experience from victimization. These are cognitive appraisals, beliefs, and emotional reactions.

Cognitive appraisals, as defined earlier, are evaluations of the significance of various encounters with people, places, and things in our environment.[29] The encounters can be real, imagined, or anticipated. Appraisals with respect to crime include evaluating the risk of becoming victimized. Such evaluations weigh the past; influence our thoughts, feelings, and behaviors in the present; and anticipate the future. In regard to the past, we make attributions about the extent and causes of crimes. With respect to the present, we make inferences about imminent threats; we project our future safety.

Beliefs refer to our readiness to act based on the perception that the behavior will be beneficial in some respect. Problems arise when appraisals and beliefs operate to reduce vigilance and healthy caution. *Fear* is the emotional reaction of primary concern. Fear seems to be prominent and intense in the victim's reactions to criminal assault. The methods of dealing with fear will be discussed later.

Misattributions About Personal Crime

Three errors in attribution seem to play a crucial role in adaptive behaviors where crime is concerned. These are attributions about *local versus distant distribution* of crime, *local versus outside involvement,* and *self-blame* for cause of the crime.

Misattribution 1: Crime Is Worse Elsewhere. People tend to view crime as being more of a problem somewhere else rather than in their own community. This is true even where crime rates are high, such as in some urban inner-city districts.[30] People are also more likely to evaluate the threat in their own community as less than that in other communities, even within their own city. In the eight-city study, most of the people responding to the survey lived in large urban areas with relatively high crime rates. Yet they thought that crime had increased nationally more than in their own neighborhoods.[31] Hindelang suggested that higher-density exposure through the mass media to sensational crime reports from around the nation instead of news about crime in their own neighborhoods may account for this misattribution. The appraisal process may operate first to collect all of these highly visible "outside" crimes together. Then the crimes are attributed to a nebulous place, which is roughly "anyplace but here." Finally, that collection of crimes is compared to neighborhood crime but without regard to differences in the sizes of the populations at risk.[32] Through this means, threat may be perceptually diffused so that it will not be a constant burden.

Misattribution 2: The Outsiders Are Doing It. People tend to attribute crime in their area to people from outside their own neighborhood. In the eight-city study, people were asked to estimate the involvement of outsiders in neighborhood crime. In the final analysis, it did not make any difference whether the residents overestimated or underestimated the absolute involvement of outsiders. They still believed that outsiders were primarily the ones responsible for crimes in their community. Evidence presented by Schafer from a Florida sample suggests that this is a misattribution error. Contrary to most people's estimates, the victim is most likely to be assaulted by someone from the same neighborhood. In fact, in the Florida Sample 61.5% of the crimes were committed by offenders who lived in the same vicinity as their victims.[33]

Misattribution 3: I Am to Blame. The process whereby victims may accept blame for their misfortunes has been the subject of much research. While most of the work has been done by observing how other people assign blame to a victim, some suggestions may be helpful in understanding the cognitive processes of victims themselves. According to this line of thinking, there are at least two motives that affect the way in which people cope with serious accidents, injuries, or illness. The first, based on the work of Lerner, suggests that people need to maintain their belief in a "just world."[34] That is, people get what they deserve and deserve what they get. Misfortune cannot be simply random. Therefore, if something bad happens, the victim must have done something to deserve it. The second motive has do with the perception of control over the environment and is based on the work of Elaine Walster.[35] Walster suggested that most people attribute blame to a victim in order to reassure themselves that they are not likely to suffer the same misfortune. The basis of the reasoning is, again, that if the event is unpredictable or uncontrollable, it could happen to anybody at any time, including themselves. Therefore, the victim must have had something to do with the accident. Whether an individual will *personally accept blame* for a misfortune, however, seems to depend on whether the events were viewed as under personal control. If the victim had voluntary control over the circumstances leading up to an accident, the person is much more likely to assume responsibility. However, if other people were present, there is less tendency for the victim to accept blame. Another observed outcome is that the person evaluates the outcome as desirable, such as "God is testing me," "It really is a blessing in disguise," or "I know I will grow a lot because of this."[36]

The first attribution error, that crime is worse elsewhere, may contribute to reduced vigilance, thereby increasing risk of subsequent victimizations. Denial may be necessary to some extent to prevent people from experiencing overwhelming stress. However, recognizing the extent and nature of any local problems is a necessary first step to taking remedial action at both the personal and the community level.

The second attribution error, that crime is instigated by outsiders, may constitute another form of necessary denial while living in circumstances that seem unchangeable. Nonetheless, such denial may lead to self-limiting and self-defeating behaviors. Accepting the fact of local involvement might lead to active participation in community programs and projects that could lead to positive corrective action. This could have the benefit of improving the quality of life for everyone concerned, including the planners and developers. At the personal level, such participation usually has the positive effect of increasing self-esteem through demonstration of self-efficacy and active mastery of one's environment.

The third attribution error, that of self-blame, requires a careful and objective inspection of the chain of events leading up to the incident. Attributing personal blame adds a significant load to the coping process and may affect recovery from life-threatening assaults and illness. Blame should not be assigned or accepted lightly. Denial of blame may be a necessary defense for a while after a traumatic event. But continued denial may interfere with assessment and implementation of adaptive life-style changes that contributed to the risk in the first place. And it may further impair the healthy sense of caution needed to live safely and securely.

There may be a strong social element of scapegoating and collective defense of conscience in blaming victims. This may then take on a more insidious form of shaping a person or group of persons to accept the blame for a variety of misfortunes. Perhaps the most lucid illustrations of scapegoating come from the Vietnam War era. At Kent State University, for example, four young college students were killed and at least eight others were wounded by National Guard soldiers called in by the governor of the state.[37] Afterward, the injuries and deaths were blamed on the "dirty hippies" who were immoral and anti-American. Another example comes from the social blight of rape. Society on the one hand supports, if not encourages, male sexual aggressiveness, but then blames the woman.

The Victim Role

William Berg and Robert Johnson proposed a model that views the effects of victimization as a process of acquiring a role. Once a person has accepted a role, certain behaviors are expected consistent with that role. According to the Berg and Johnson model, certain groups in each society have relatively low power and status. Through a process of developmental learning occurring over several years, they come to express the values and attitudes of victims and engage in the behavior expected of victims.

> At a minimum, victims are expected to act like persons who have been vio-
> lated or compromised. Shock, confusion, impotent anger, or rage—even
> remorse and shame—are presumably appropriate sentiments. Victimiza-
> tion represents a concrete index of ... vulnerability... and depen-
> dence. . . . The prototypic victim is thus the person who acknowledges in
> the act and in his or her reactions to it, the inevitability and appropriate-
> ness of victimization and takes the experience to be a product of fate, how-
> ever unpleasant or unjust.[38]

This model might indeed explain why certain groups accept their fate and
even blame themselves for misfortune that has come on them through no
fault of their own. Johnson and Berg provided partially supporting evidence
for such a model among three groups they viewed as vulnerable: the elderly,
females, and blacks.

Beliefs That Affect Coping with Crime

In addition to these misattributions, the beliefs we hold about crime can be
important. **Beliefs** are predispositions to act in certain ways that are based
on positive and negative evaluations of people, places, and things. Developmental processes in operation from early childhood give rise to the form
and substance of our beliefs. For example, it is almost expected that you will
continue to drive your car regardless of the risk. In spite of the high rate of
injury from cars, people still believe that cars are necessary and act as
though they believe in the safety of the automobile. But people do not
believe that it is alright to be beaten, mugged, or burglarized. And even people who have never been victimized will go on believing that it is not safe to
open the door to a stranger or take a walk late at night alone.

Thus, beliefs enter into our perceptions of what we can safely do and not
do. They mold our views of the nature and severity of crime, and they influence our feelings of vulnerability. As a result, beliefs can increase or
decrease the likelihood of engaging in suitable preventive behaviors. They
can help or hurt coping efforts in the aftermath of crime. They can multiply
or minimize our stress load. Two beliefs seem to be most important in this
regard. These are beliefs in personal invulnerability and beliefs about the
seriousness of crime.

Belief in personal invulnerability. Beliefs about vulnerability may
affect behavior in one of two ways. First, the belief in constant vulnerability
may heighten fear and thus become disabling. Taken to the extreme this
belief approaches a paranoialike state, producing undesirable mental states
such as depression and disorientation while also placing unnecessary limits
on personal freedom. On the other hand, the person who believes that he or
she is virtually invincible has more of a tendency to take unnecessary risks.
Hindelang and his associates noted that even after controlling for personal
victimization, people were much more likely to view their own neighborhoods as safer than other metropolitan communities.[39] Such people are

likely to scorn suggestions they assess their life-style and to ignore most of the preventive actions suggested earlier.

Belief in seriousness of crime.   A related belief is that crime is only petty or trifling crime in the neighborhood. In general, people tend to believe that crime is much more serious the further the frame of reference is moved from the person.[40] Also, they tend to believe that local crime is less violent and threatening than crime that occurs somewhere else.[41] They believe that crime has a more negative impact on other people than on themselves.

◆ COPING WITH THE AFTERMATH OF CRIMINAL ASSAULT

The effects of a criminal attack can be displayed in a number of physical and psychological disturbances. Sleep disturbances, anxiety attacks, and changes in appetite may all occur. Compulsive lock checking, becoming housebound, and feelings of extreme terror may go on for weeks or months.[42] John Hepburn and Daniel Monti studied adaptive responses among a high-school population of victims and found that fear of crime was the single most significant variable explaining avoidance of groups and places.[43]

Managing Fear from Victimization

The most powerful emotion demonstrated by a person who has been victimized is fear. Fear is a complex response that includes thoughts, feelings, and bodily reactions. It also generalizes to encompass people who look similar to the offender, places that remind the victim of the original situation, and conditions that were present at the time. Eliminating fear thus requires techniques that deal with all three of these channels of involvement and that reduce the spread of effect.

The most successful method of treating specific fears in the past few years has been systematic desensitization. This technique requires three separate steps: learning deep muscular relaxation, developing a fear scale ordering imaginary events from low to high fear, and combining the events with relaxation in a step-by-step fashion until no fear is felt when imagining the most feared event. Instruction in deep muscular relaxation is provided beginning in Chapter 11. Details on how to conquer specific fears are provided in Chapter 13. The method for combining relaxation with a fear scale is also presented there.

Another technique that may help combat fear is rational emotive therapy, developed by Albert Ellis.[44] Rational emotive therapy assumes that there are some irrational thoughts bolstering the fear and underlying self-limiting behavior. The therapist attempts to point out the link between the person's emotions and thought processes. The goal is to disabuse the person of irrational thinking that stands in the way of healthy behavior. Unfortunately, this approach cannot generally be used without the assistance of an objective external observer. This is because we are all more or less blind to our own irrational thoughts, even though someone else can spot them fairly quickly.

Another technique is that of stress inoculation. This is actually a non-specific method combining several specific techniques. Stress inoculation attempts to get the individual to deal with small fears one at a time. A program can be structured so that success in dealing with little fears is almost a sure thing. As successes build up, the person acquires some resistance, so even the larger fears do not seem as overwhelming as before. As the process continues, even larger fears become more and more manageable until the person can deal successfully with the range of activities and people encountered in a well-balanced life. This technique will be discussed in more detail in Chapter 13.

One of the behavioral manifestations of fear is the avoidance of people, places, and things that are still associated with the original event. This has been described as anticipatory fear. Any behavior that leads to the reduction of anticipatory fear is more likely to be repeated. Avoiding people, places, and things associated with the original trauma tends to reduce such fear. This avoidance is generally unnecessary and thus constitutes one of the restrictions on personal freedom that need to be dealt with. Positive assertion, used to increase gradually the frequency and range of encounters with people and social situations previously avoided, is one of the approaches to dealing with behavioral avoidance.

Active Mastery: Keys to Coping with Victimization

The preceding material has reviewed several positive steps that can be taken to reduce stress and develop active coping skills. In this concluding section, social actions will be discussed that can increase one's sense of active mastery over the environment and contribute to the overall improvement of one's neighborhood.

Creating safe environments.   The theoretical orientation of this book views behavior as a transaction between the person and environment. One aspect of negotiating with the environment to move with safety and security is to focus on internal cognitions, attitudes, and beliefs, as we have just done. This does not necessarily blame the victim for the crime. The second aspect is to focus on the design (or undesigned) elements of environment that may contribute to increasing the risk of crime. This is not to suggest that crime can be eliminated solely by environmental design. Certain persons may become criminals or victims in virtually any environment. But some people may become criminals or victims because of a particular environment.

A great deal of attention has been devoted to the crime prevention through environmental design (CPTED) concept.[45] The concept involves three types of crime prevention. These are the punitive, mechanical, and corrective types. Punitive measures are not what you might think at first glance. They focus instead on designing environments that make it easy to detect and apprehend criminals, such as through the use of alarm and video systems. Mechanical methods focus on such things as barriers to unwanted entry and safe street design with proper lighting. Corrective measures involve the attempt to eliminate criminal motives, such as through social programming to provide meaningful activities of both a work and leisure variety.

Three problems are routinely encountered in trying to implement CPTED programs. First, there is often public resistance to such programs based on "selfish" economic concerns or lack of understanding of the potential benefit. One notable exception is the widespread acceptance of the 911 emergency assistance number. Another problem is the public's failure to support such programs. Perhaps the most discouraging problem is the lack of use of installed environmental design measures. For example, in buildings where well-thought-out barriers and alarms are provided, occupants have been observed to defeat the design features themselves merely for their own convenience.

The implications for personal conduct are clear. First, consider the long-range impact of proposed programs as much as the immediate impact on personal finances. Along with this, recognize that we are all generally influenced much more by concrete short-term rewards than by intangible long-term and delayed rewards. The impulse is to say no to the proposed project. But think again, carefully! Is it the short-term inconvenience or the long-term view that is influencing your decision? Also, be alert to the significance of proposed CPTED projects in your neighborhood and look for ways to become involved after evaluating the soundness of the project. Finally, consider the long-range implications when you defeat safety features because of personal inconvenience and frustration. The consequences could be deadly.

Obtaining restitution.   Actively seek information from local agencies on how you may obtain assistance to recover damages. A wide variety of restitution programs have been implemented nationwide to aid victims of criminal loss. These programs provide for both civil and criminal remedies against the offender. Compensation may be obtained from either local or state agencies though usually only within limits. One very novel program is the Victim–Offender Reconciliation Project (VORP) in Ontario, Canada. The goals of this program include an attempt to bring the victim and offender together, face-to-face, to reach reconciliation. Also, there is hope for a mutual agreement to provide restitution to the victim and possibly reduced sentencing for the offender.[46] Such programs can thus be as beneficial for the criminal as for the victim and add a welcome dimension not seen in the normal punitive program.

Utilizing human services. Actively seek the assistance of local agencies, especially to help through the period immediately following the victimizing event. Many local organizations can provide educational and counseling programs that speed recovery and help reduce future risks. It appears that people who ignore or avoid such assistance may be worse off in the long run. For example, one group of victims from 1974 decided not to participate in a prevention education/counseling program. In 1977, this same group had burglary rates almost three times greater than normal.[47]

◆ SUMMARY

This chapter has focused on the problem of stress caused by being victimized. Identification of risk factors, prevention of risk, and coping strategies to deal with the aftermath of crime were discussed. Information on risk factors indicates that the young, unmarried, and unemployed male is the most likely victim, although the impact of victimization is probably most keenly felt by women and the aged.

Prevention involves a life-style assessment to determine habitual behavior that may place the person at risk. In addition, misattribution of causes of crime and victimization must be inspected, along with faulty beliefs. Both misattributions and faulty beliefs tend to prevent effective coping behaviors. Guidelines to help examine problematic causal attributions and beliefs were also discussed.

Finally, coping strategies were presented that may be appropriate for dealing with fear. Fear can be reduced through desensitization and rational emotive therapy. Stress inoculation may be used to reduce the potential for overwhelming levels of stress. Positive assertion and social action are also helpful to eliminate the restrictive effects of fear. The key concept is to obtain active mastery of one's environment through personal and social actions designed to reduce risk.

◆ NOTES

[1] Berkow, I. The shooting of Ben Wilson. *The New York Times,* (1984, November 25). p. S-7.

[2] United States Federal Bureau of Investigation. (1982). *Uniform crime reports for the United States.* Washington, DC: U.S. Government Printing Office, pp. 6–34. The figures provided are all regarded as conservative estimates because of problems in reporting of crime statistics. Law enforcement agencies estimate that only 1 in 4 rapes is reported, while feminist groups believe that no more than 1 in 10 rapes is reported. Based on 77,763 rapes in 1982, the "true" number would be between 311,052 and 777,630. The argument for unreported rapes is presented by Smithyman, S. D. (1979). Characteristics of "undetected" rapists. In W. H. Parsonage (Ed.), *Perspectives on victimology* (pp. 99–120). Beverly Hills, CA: Sage Publications, p. 100.

[3]Meyer, P. B. (1981). Communities as victims of corporate crimes. In B. Galaway & J. Hudson (Eds.), *Perspective on crime victims* (pp. 33–44). St. Louis, Mosby.

[4]Berg, W. E., & Johnson, R. (1979). Assessing the impact of victimization: Acquisition of the victim role among elderly and female victims. In W. H. Parsonage, *Perspectives on victimology* (pp. 58–71), pp. 58, 59.

[5]Brooks, J. (1981). The fear of crime in the United States. In Galaway & Hudson, *Perspectives on crime victims* (pp. 90–92).

[6]More formally defined, **victimology** is the science that explores the role of the victim in crime. Early work was done by Hans von Hentig and B. Mendelsohn in the 1940s. An excellent historical survey of the field is provided by Schafer, S. (1977). *Victimology: The victim and his criminal*, Reston, VA: Reston. Schafer credits Mendelsohn with originating the term *victimology*. Von Hentig and Mendelsohn contended that attitudes, expressed desires, and personality factors contribute to the initiation of the criminal act. The most extreme statement of this position holds that the criminal is passive until triggered into action by some "misbehavior" of the victim. This stance has been roundly criticized and generally demonstrated to be in error. See Franklin, C., & Franklin, A. (1981). Victimology revisited: A critique and suggestions for future direction. In Galaway & Hudson, *Perspectives on crime victims*. (pp. 177–181).

[7]Galaway & Hudson, *Perspectives on crime victims*, p. 4.

[8]Hindelang, M. J., Gottfredson, M. R., & Garofalo, J. (1978). *Victims of personal crime: An empirical foundation for a theory of personal victimization*. Cambridge, MA: Ballinger. This project was supported by the Law Enforcement Assistance Administration (LEAA).

[9]Hindelang et al., *Victims*, p. 121.

[10]Berg & Johnson, Assessing the impact, p. 64.

[11]One study conducted by Schafer and based on a Florida sample presents information that disputes this general pattern. It suggests that both the number of criminals and the number of violent crimes is largest among married persons. The argument appears to be based on frequency statistics rather than proportional statistics, which casts doubt on the argument. However, the argument is qualified as pertaining to violent crime and not to all instances of victimization in general. Schafer, *Victimology*, p. 61.

[12]Hindelang et al., *Victims*, p. 201.

[13]Hindelang et al., *Victims*. See pp. 45–46 for information on the issue of the relationship of the offender to the victim and pp. 47–49 for information on severity of injuries.

[14]Schafer, *Victimology*, p. 61. This fact is also borne out by statistics presented by the United States FBI in the *Uniform crime report*.

[15]Hindelang et al., *Victims*, p. 130.

[16]Hindelang et al., *Victims*, p. 224.

[17]Hindelang et al., *Victims*, p. 121.

[18]Hindelang et al., *Victims*, p. 241.

[19]Hindelang et al., *Victims*, p. 176.

[20]Hindelang et al., *Victims*, p. 61.

[21]Schafer, *Victimology*, p. 69. The author notes that profit appears to be the dominant motive in criminal activity among those aged 30 or less, the group that is largely responsible for street crimes. Also, Schafer notes that it is the older group, over 30, whose emotions tend to play an increasing role in criminal acts.

[22]This rather paradoxical finding has been supported repeatedly by research on "bystander apathy," a line of research that was instituted by John Darley and Bibb Latané following the infamous case of the murder of Kitty Genovese. Latané, B., & Darley, J. M. (1970). *The unresponsive bystander: Why doesn't he help?* New York: Appleton-Century-Crofts.

[23]Hindelang et al., *Victims*, p. 83.

[24]Hindelang et al., *Victims*, p. 44.

[25]Hindelang et al., *Victims*, p. 43.

[26]United States Federal Bureau of Investigation, *Uniform Crime Report*, p. 11.

[27]Martin, D. Battered women: Scope of the problem. In Galaway & Hudson, *Perspectives on crime victims* (pp. 190–201). See also Hindelang et al., *Victims*, p. 60.

[28]Hindelang et al., *Victims*, p. 224.

[29]Lazarus, R. S., & Launier, R. (1978). Stress-related transactions between person and environment. In L. A. Pervin & M. Lewis (Eds.), *Perspectives in interactional psychology.* New York: Plenum Press.

[30]Hindelang et al., *Victims*, p. 168.

[31]Hindelang et al., *Victims*, p. 156.

[32]Hindelang et al., *Victims*, p. 157.

[33]Schafer, *Victimology*, p. 84.

[34]Lerner, M. J., & Matthews, G. (1967). Reactions to suffering of others under conditions of indirect responsibility. *Journal of Personality and Social Psychology, 5,* 319–325; Lerner, M. J., & Simmons, C. (1966). Observer's reaction to the "innocent victim": Compassion or rejection? *Journal of Personality and Social Psychology, 4,* 203–210.

[35]Walster, E. (1966). Assignment of responsibility for an accident. *Journal of Personality and Social Psychology, 3,* 73–79.

[36]Bulman, R. J., & Wortman, C. B. (1977). Attribution of blame and coping in the "real world": Severe accident victims react to their lot. *Journal of Personality and Social Psychology, 35,* 351–363.

[37]Kifner, J. 4 Kent State students killed by troops. *The New York Times.* (1970, May 5), pp. 1, 17.

[38]Berg & Johnson, Assessing the impact, pp. 60, 61.

[39]Hindelang et al., *Victims*, p. 168.

[40]Hindelang et al., *Victims*, p. 158.

[41]Hindelang et al., *Victims*, p. 158.

[42]Studies of crime victims indicate that the mental maelstrom following a personal assault or loss may last as long as three years. However, the duration is related to both the severity of the crime and the personal characteristics of the victim.

[43]Hepburn, J. R., & Monti, D. J. (1979). Victimization, fear of crime, and adaptive responses among high school students. In Parsonage, *Perspectives on victimology* (pp. 121–132), p. 129.

[44]Ellis, A. (1973). *Humanistic psychotherapy.* New York: McGraw-Hill.

[45]Pesce, E. J. (1981). Crime prevention through environmental design: The CPTED concept. In Galaway & Hudson, *Perspectives on crime victims* (pp. 347–348).

[46]McKnight (Edmonds), D. (1981). The victim-offender reconciliation project. In Galaway & Hudson, *Perspectives on crime victims* (pp. 292–299).

[47]Schneider, A. L., & Schneider, P. R. (1981). Victim assistance programs: An overview. In Galaway & Hudson, *Perspectives on crime victims* (pp. 364–373).

9

ENVIRONMENTAL STRESS: DISASTERS, POLLUTION, AND OVERCROWDING

*Man's attitude toward nature is today
critically important simply because we have
now acquired a fateful power to alter and
destroy nature.*

Rachel Carson

The night of December 2, 1984, began very much like any other night for the people of Bhopal, India. Before dawn came, though, a nightmare would leave over 2,500 of Bhopal's citizens dead and as many as 250,000 more scarred, blinded, disfigured, or disabled permanently. A combination of technical problems, mechanical failures, and human errors led to the leakage of deadly methyl isocyanate fumes from the Union Carbide plant—a plant that, until that night, had offered the hope of improved agricultural productivity to help feed India's 700 million people.

Natural catastrophes and technological disasters such as the one at Bhopal produce intense suffering for living victims, the survivors who must rebuild shattered lives and reconstruct dreams around a new reality. Less intense, though no less real, is the stress endured by the worried well, those who wait and wonder when and where and how the next disaster will occur. The more pervasive and important outcome may thus be the effect of such disasters on the perceptions people have of how safe and supportive their living habitat is.

In recent years we have come to recognize a wide variety of stressors that have resulted from the ways humans have altered, exploited, or literally dumped on their environment. Although all these alterations are done presumably to create progress, human tinkering has often brought as much disaster and destruction as safety and support. We now combat air and noise pollutions, chemical hazards poured into our streams and on the earth, toxins in our food, nuclear hazards, and urban crowding, to name only a few.

The study of environmental stress deals with both natural and human-created problems and it hopes to provide answers to a number of pressing questions. It is concerned with individual perceptions and thoughts that turn disaster into defeat for one but challenge for another. It seeks to understand environment–behavior interactions, especially those that seem to increase physical illness, emotional distress, and mental disturbance. Finally, the study of environmental stress may suggest useful applications. We may learn how to intervene in the environment without disrupting the habitat and destroying nature's balance.

We may also learn how to design self-control procedures so that people will be less wasteful of natural resources. This would have the positive effect of reducing strain on the environment while also reducing the psychological impact of environmental stressors. If, in the process, a healthier balance is established in human–environment relationships, that would be all the better.

The purpose of this chapter, then, is to provide a perspective on environmental stress by focusing on the most commonly encountered environmental stressors. Along the way, some of the more prominent theories of environmental stress will be presented. To begin, a few definitions are in order.

◆ ENVIRONMENT AND ECOLOGY

The terms most commonly encountered in environmental stress literature are *environment, ecology,* and *habitat*. **Environment** is used to refer to surroundings, the physical space we perceive and in which we behave. **Habitat** is the place where a particular animal is usually found. The natural habitat for trout is a lake; for deer, it is the forest.

But humans are normally gregarious creatures. That is, we tend to be fond of living together, sharing companionship and services among other things. For this reason, the town might be regarded as the closest thing to a natural human habitat that we can identify. However, humans are also endlessly adaptable. We are capable of surviving over a much wider range of climates and conditions than virtually any other animal.[1] Thus the notion of habitat may be less useful in the study of human–environment relations than in the study of animal–environment relations.

Ecology refers to a distinct branch of biology that studies the relationships between living organisms and their environment. The relationship between an organism and the environment is reciprocal. It is an exchange between the two that goes on over several cycles. For example, there was a time when hunters in the Southwest were given bounties for killing animals that were regarded as pests. As a result, coyotes and wildcats were depleted in and around the Kaibab forest of Arizona. This produced a rapid increase in the number of deer. They overgrazed the land, which destroyed ground cover and increased erosion over several years. Tragically, thousands of deer died because of the loss of their own food supply.

A great deal of concern for ecology has been generated since the 1960s because of our tendency to manipulate and operate drastically on our environment. We are not content just to build shelters for protection from the elements; we think we should also be able to harness and control the elements. The environment influences us through draughts, floods, earthquakes, volcanic eruptions, and sundry other forces. We in turn seed clouds, drill wells, drain swamps, build dams, design earthquake-proof buildings, and harness nuclear energy. Now we appear intent on farming the ocean and on exploiting space and anything else we can think of to try to control, if not master, nature.

As we change the environment, though, we change relationships between organisms, animals, or people, and their environmental niches. Some of these changes are beneficial, but some are not. Examples of injurious influences on the ecology of an area abound. The Aswan Dam—built to control floods along the Nile and provide hydroelectric power—had a devastating effect on fish and fishing all along the river's course. The same thing has happened with dams in other countries, including the Tennessee Valley Authority project. Acid rain, extinction of several species of animals by humans encroaching on natural habitats, and pollution of Love Canal furnish other examples. Viewed in this light, the disturbance of ecological relationships can produce powerful sources of stress for many organisms.

◆ THEORIES OF ENVIRONMENTAL STRESS

Over the years, a number of theories have been advanced to explain the basis of environmental stress. These include arousal theories (which exist in a number of different variations), learning theory, behavior constraint theory, ecological theory, and environmental stress theory. As will become apparent, environmental stress theory is an integration of two theories discussed earlier, the general adaptation syndrome proposed by Hans Selye and the cognitive–transactional theory proposed by Richard Lazarus.

Arousal and Stimulation Theories of Stress

One way of looking at the relationship between the environment and human behavior is in terms of the amount of stimulation provided by the environment. These *arousal theories* are a little more simplistic and restrictive than other environmental stress theories. However, there is some support for the notion that level of arousal is tied to stress. The team of Albert Mehrabian and James Russell, for example, tried to determine the dimensions that can best describe *any* environment. They found that this could be done with just three dimensions: pleasure, dominance, and arousal.[2]

The major idea common to arousal theories is that different degrees of stimulation will arouse people more or less. Very intense stimulation, such as a rock band rehearsing in the apartment just above you, will probably lead to too much arousal and thus to feelings of distress. On the other hand, very low levels of stimulation, such as the stimulus deprivation phenomenon reviewed in Chapter 4, can result in too little arousal and in feelings of boredom. This variation on the arousal theme is called a *stimulus load* theory.

Another approach is to look at environmental stimulation as a form of information and then to analyze human behavior in terms of an information-processing model. When too much information is provided, the person is "overloaded," attention is divided, tasks must be time-shared, and strain results. When too little information is provided, the person may not be able to make wise and appropriate decisions. One model of this type has been provided by Cohen.[3]

Another approach to stimulation theory is the *adaptation level* theory of Wohlwill.[4] Wohlwill assumed that each person has a preferred and optimal level of stimulation. This optimal level varies between people: Some people prefer more stimulation than others. Also, optimal levels vary within people over time: We prefer more stimulation at certain times than at other times. In addition, the current level of preferred stimulation is a result of adaptation: We adjust the value we place on certain types of stimulation because of continued exposure to a stimulus. What is understimulating and what is overstimulating depend on the current level of adaptation. For example, after spending a relatively intense time at an amusement park, you might view a comedy movie as relatively boring. Conversely, after being confined in a hospital for an extended time, you might view that same comedy movie as very entertaining. Or, after an exhilarating day at the office, you may be able to handle any amount of chaos at home without strain. But after a very trying day, even the slightest pressure from the family may be enough to trigger a strong negative reaction.

Conditioning and Environmental Stress

Learning models have been widely used to explain a variety of adaptive behaviors, including adaptation to the effects of stress. The classical conditioning model reviewed in Chapter 2 has been extended to the area of environmental stress by the research team of Byrne and Clore.[5] Their extension, though, includes a role for the conditioning of attitudes, which was not a part of the original theory. In general, Byrne and Clore have proposed that environmental stress is related to the conditioning of attitudes toward certain aspects of the environment. For example, a child goes to a doctor's office and receives a painful shot. The office and many other related signals (nurses, odors, and so forth) also become attached to the pain. Later on, whenever the child has to go to the office or even talks about the office, a strong negative emotional response occurs. The emotional response is also translated into a cognitive attitude of strong dislike: "I don't like that place."

In the Byrne and Clore model, pain from the shot is an unconditioned stimulus (UCS), while fear and avoidance are part of the unconditioned response (UCR). The office is the conditioned stimulus (CS), which was neutral prior to the shot. But afterwards it takes on the power of the UCS and produces fear and avoidance, the conditioned or learned response (CR), even when the doctor's office is only symbolically represented in conversation. Figure 9–1 shows the relationships suggested by Byrne and Clore, with additional examples.

The Behavior Constraint Model

On occasion, the environment can produce effects over which we have little or no control. Summer heat waves, hurricanes, or blizzards are forces that usually require a "ride-it-out" response. We may minimize the likelihood of personal damage by taking certain precautions. But no amount of effort will stop what has been set in motion.

Work situations may also take on some characteristics of this nature. For example, job security for many workers is tied to the success of companies that are competing in a volatile market. Computer hardware and software companies offer recent cases in point. Some companies offered excellent,

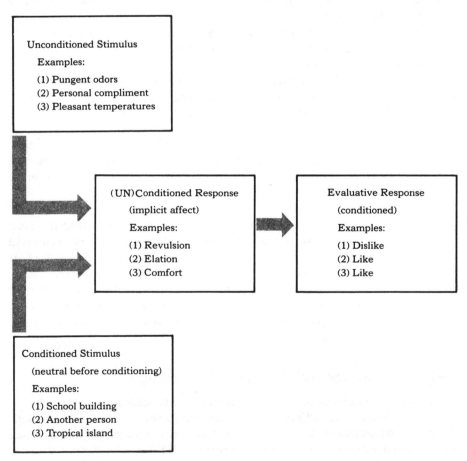

Figure 9–1.   The Byrne–Clore reinforcement–affect model, a conditioning model of environmental perception.

even superior, products. But the companies folded because they lacked market clout and advertising budgets or were competing against "name" companies. For the workers, the factors affecting their fates were largely out of their own control. It made no difference how hard they worked and how good their quality control was.

Under such conditions behavior is constrained or limited. We cannot do all the things we would like to do. We may even feel as though we cannot control our own destiny. According to the behavior constraint model, though, the limits imposed on our behavior do not have to be real. They can also be imaginary. If we merely *believe* that the situation is out of hand, our behavior will be just as limited as if the lack of control were a real fact. A number of people have discussed environmental stress in these terms.

Perhaps the most noteworthy example is the work of Judith Rodin and Andrew Baum.[6] According to their analysis, there are three steps leading to behavior constraint. The first is the perceived loss of control, as already described. The second is psychological reactance. The third step is a feeling of learned helplessness.[7]

Reactance is a concept that has been used to explain a variety of consumer behaviors.[8] Say that a salesperson comes to your door with a product that you really need, and this product is actually very good. But the salesperson makes you feel as though you are being manipulated or "sold." In general, people do not like the feeling of being out of control, so they take steps to regain control. You might even refuse to purchase the product solely to avoid being manipulated.

When people try to regain control but repeatedly fail to do so, they may develop learned helplessness. **Learned helplessness** is a condition in which the person can exert control but does not do so because of previous failures.

In emergency situations, such as natural and technological disasters, people may also give up because of the feeling that there is nothing they can do. The crash of a Japan Air Lines plane on August 12, 1985, offers an example of the positive effects of *not* giving up. It was reported that the four survivors invented things to do in their minds while waiting for rescue. Also, they refused to give up. They tried to hang on to whatever control they could, no matter how desperate the situation seemed. While the behavior constraint model has some interesting elements in it, it has seen relatively little use in environmental psychology.

Behavior Settings and Ecological Psychology

Roger Barker, of the University of Kansas, has advocated an ecological view of environmental stress.[9] The key concept in his theory is behavior settings. A **behavior setting** is a culturally determined physical milieu in which certain fixed patterns of behavior are expected. These behavior patterns are group behaviors, not just individual behaviors. For example, a church is a behavior setting that has a number of predictable behavior patterns. Schools and restaurants are other examples, as are business and faculty meetings. Knowing the setting enables one to predict with some certainty what the behavior will be. Change the setting and the behavior will change.

Related concepts in Barker's theory include under- and overmanning. For example, amusement parks can be "overmanned," in Barker's term, when more people are allowed in than the facilities can handle. In such circumstances, people may feel frustrated and stressed. In large universities and large classes, students may feel left out, uninvolved, and anonymous. On the other hand, in smaller universities and smaller classrooms, students feel more involved and worthwhile. Barker's model has been very useful in studying some of the stress processes that operate in businesses, mental institutions, schools, and churches. It has also been helpful in suggesting ways to engineer the environment to eliminate or reduce stressors.

Environmental Stress Theory

Environmental stress theory puts together the best of both Hans Selye's General Adaptation Syndrome theory and Richard Lazarus's cognitive transactional theory. An investigative team headed by Andrew Baum has analyzed a variety of environmental stressors, such as the Three Mile Island incident, in terms of these two theories.[10] This review indicated that the cognitive processes suggested by Lazarus and the physiological arousal proposed by Selye are consistently observed in a number of environmental stress situations, including catastrophic events, noise, and crowding. It appears, then, that a specialized theory of environmental stress does not add much, if anything, to understanding stress beyond what is provided by these two well-known and well-researched models. Figure 9–2 shows how the two theories have been integrated.[11]

◆ CATEGORIES OF ENVIRONMENTAL STRESS

Work on environmental stress has concentrated on several major stressors. There is, first, the short-term catastrophic disaster that affects relatively few people. The impact on the environment and people is usually severe, but such events tend to happen rather infrequently. Natural, technological, and social disasters[12] fit this category. Second, there are the ongoing or chronic stressors that affect many more people on a daily basis but in less severe ways, the effects sometimes not appearing for years. Fisher and his colleagues referred to these as *background stressors*.[13] Noise pollution, air pollution, chemical pollution, crowding, and commuting are examples of this type of environmental stress. For the remainder of this chapter, we will look at some of the most significant environmental stressors.

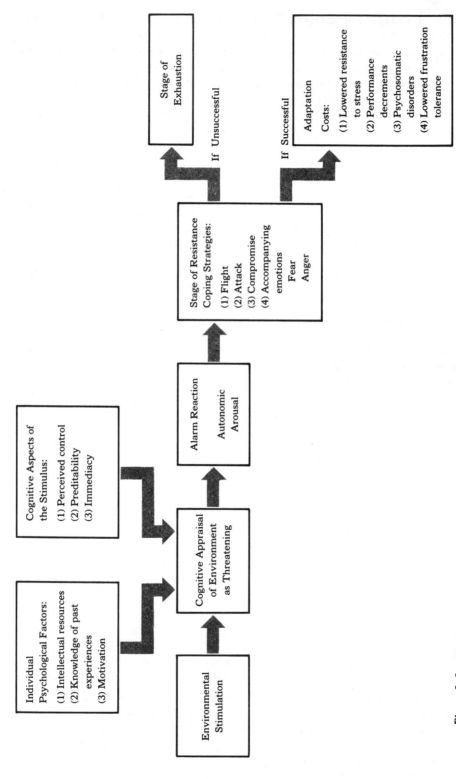

Figure 9–2.   The environmental stress model proposed by **Fisher, Bell,** and **Baum.**

◆ NATURAL DISASTERS

For those unfortunate enough to be in harm's way, natural disasters threaten people with physical destruction, psychological trauma, and family disorganization on a scale not encountered in most other type of stress. Hurricanes and tornados, floods and blizzards, volcanic eruptions and earthquakes are among the most catastrophic of the natural disasters.

The immediate impact of such events may be no more than a temporary panic until it is known that personal damage is minimal and all is well. The other extreme is the wholesale disruption of life-style. In such cases, a very comfortable existence is usually replaced, at least temporarily, by more or less discomfort, severe deprivation, and physical fatigue. Lengthy periods of clean-up, recovering personal effects from the devastation where possible, rebuilding, caring for the sick or injured, and arranging for the burial of deceased family members are among the activities that consume tremendous amounts of both physical and psychological energy. States of high anxiety based on uncertainty about the future and fear of a recurrence of the dread event erode decision-making ability and interfere with appropriate problem-solving behavior. The TV replay of scenes from Mexico City in the days following the 1985 earthquake vividly illustrated many of these reactions.

Natural disasters have several common characteristics. They are mostly unpredictable. Consider for example nature's lottery, the tornado. No matter how much weather reporting has advanced, a warning is all that is possible. Where and when one will actually hit is anybody's guess. Another common characteristic is that natural disasters are largely uncontrollable in any real sense. Thus people may feel that they are temporarily at the mercy of forces much more powerful than anything they could have imagined. Also, natural catastrophes require short-term and long-term coping responses from both the individual and the community.

Studies of natural disasters have noted a characteristic pattern of responding, which seems to occur in three stages. There is first a *shock stage,* in which victims appear to be stunned, dazed, and apathetic. Second, there is a *suggestible stage,* in which victims tend to be passive, suggestible, and willing to take directions from others. Finally, there is a *recovery stage,* in which individuals are tense and apprehensive. They often show a need to recount details of the catastrophic event over and over again at this time.[14]

Many psychological and physical symptoms have been observed in the wake of natural calamities. The psychological symptoms include initial panic, anxiety, phobic fear, vulnerability, guilt, isolation, withdrawal, depression (including some suicide attempts), anger, frustration, and interpersonal and marital problems.[15] Disorientation and a certain lack of attachment and security may occur for a while. Sleep and eating disturbances are common. Some people report that they relive the nightmare of the event over and over in their dreams, as though there will be no escape from the horror. The severity and duration of these effects seem to be dependent on the magnitude of the loss.

Destruction and despair in the wake of tornados at Sweetwater, Texas, April 20, 1986. *(AP/Wide World Photo)*

Physical symptoms include increased fatigue, headaches, colds and other illnesses, and weight loss from both sleep and eating disturbances. Overall, however, the amount of physical illness seems to be low—much less than what might be expected. It may be that the short-term, acute nature of disaster stress activates the body's natural self-defense mechanisms. But since the stress is over rather quickly, lowered resistance and exhaustion do not occur. This is also consistent with the observation that the severity and duration of both psychological and physical effects are tied to the magnitude of the loss produced by the disaster.

These symptoms appear to be nearly universal and have been observed in cultural groups around the world. The Sri Lanka cyclone of 1978, for example, provides one well-documented and confirming case study.[16]

◆ THE AFTERMATH OF MOUNT SAINT HELENS

One of the most widely publicized natural disasters of the recent past was the eruption of Mount Saint Helens of May 18, 1980. The 9,600-foot mountain, located in the southwestern part of the state of Washington, exploded with a force that lifted a cubic mile of debris from the peak. The force of the eruption hurled some of the ash as high as 50,000 feet into the atmosphere and covered several thousand square miles with volcanic ash.[17] Nearly 300 people were working, camping, or sightseeing in the vicinity of the volcano. More than 200 escaped or were rescued, although two of these died later. Another 60 persons died or were reported missing and presumed dead.[18]

Shortly after the volcano erupted, a team of investigators collected data from cities and towns in the main impact area.[19] What they found tended to confirm the findings from similar investigations. The data showed a pattern of initial short-term panic with little or no carry-over effect on a long-term basis. Within the first 24 hours of the explosion, phone lines were flooded with outgoing calls running a full 100% above normal levels. This level of activity subsided rather quickly, however.

Both physical symptoms and negative emotional moods were reported at a higher rate than in a normal population, but the level of reports varied with both proximity and temporal factors. When people were living in a dangerous area and still trying to deal with the day-to-day necessities of living, they tended to report *fewer* physical and emotional symptoms. They were also less willing to provide information to interviewers, which suggests that their anxiety levels were still high. The investigators concluded that these people still had not allowed themselves the time to work through their feelings about the disaster. As time went on, however, this pattern changed. Most residents showed minimal effects of the eruption in a follow-up nearly one year later.

Shirley Murphy also studied victims of the Mount Saint Helens eruption to determine how quickly and how completely people recover from the effects of a natural catastrophe.[20] Dr. Murphy classified victims into four categories. One group was composed of victims who had suffered the *presumed* loss of a relative or close friend. Another group was made up of people who had suffered the *confirmed* loss of a relative or close friend. The third and fourth groups had lost respectively permanent or vacation homes. A fifth group was studied that had suffered no loss at all.

Dr. Murphy found that bereaved victims reported overall higher levels of emotional stress and poorer mental health status. But they did not seem to suffer from any poorer physical health than the group that had experienced no loss. Those who had relatives or friends presumed dead appeared to show the most distress when interviewed. They talked about how "waiting was agony," how they went on "hoping, yet knowing they were dead," and that "it's hard to come to terms with no body."[21] People who lost permanent homes reported the same higher levels of stress as the bereaved group, but they reported no greater physical or emotional difficulties than the control group. These people also experienced greater amounts of anger, blame, and financial dissatisfaction with restoration efforts than any other group. Those who lost vacation homes did not seem to be affected on any of the measures. Most of the victims reported that they felt only partially recovered even 11 months after the disaster.

◆ TECHNOLOGICAL DISASTERS

Technological disasters share a number of characteristics in common with natural disasters. They tend to be unpredictable and uncontrollable. They can produce very intense physical suffering, psychological stress, and social disruption. In fact, one must look to the very worst of the natural disasters to find destruction on a par with the disasters of the bombings of Hiroshima and Nagasaki, the Vietnam War, or the Bhopal tragedy. Technological disasters are generally short-lived and thus they subject people to acute rather than chronic stressors. But some technological disasters produce stress effects over long periods. For example, Love Canal was a hazard for several years. The incident at Three Mile Island may have passed into memory for those living outside the region, but for those living in the immediate vicinity it continues to be a source of fear.

In other ways, though, technological disasters are very different from natural disasters. They usually result from human miscalculation, carelessness, avarice, or wholesale disregard for human values that hold life to be more important than the corporate balance sheet. They are, in a word, preventable. At least from the vantage point of hindsight it looks as though someone could have done something to prevent them from happening. From the standpoint of the victim, someone is to blame and that someone must be made to pay. The gas in Bhopal had not even settled when blame was being assigned. It is difficult to accuse a supreme being of malice when a tornado strikes, but sins of human error are not so easily forgiven.

There is, therefore, generally more anger and resentment following a technological disaster. Our sense of control is also more threatened by such events. The expectation is that what we create, we control. But after a technological disaster, it is painfully clear that what we created we could not and did not control.

◆ BUFFALO CREEK AND THREE MILE ISLAND

Of all the technological disasters, none have been more extensively studied than the Buffalo Creek flood of 1976 and the nuclear accident at Three Mile Island in 1979. Generally, the findings from these studies agree with the findings from studies of natural catastrophes. However, the effects of technological disasters appear to be more long-term than those of natural disasters.

The Buffalo Creek Flood

The Buffalo Mining Company built a dam out of coal slag to control flooding in the towns along the Buffalo Creek valley in West Virginia. In February of 1976, after rains had swollen the creek behind the dam, the dam collapsed. In 15 minutes of unbridled fury, the wall of water completely destroyed the town of Saunders along with several other settlements in the valley. Over 5,000 people were left homeless, and 125 would never come home again.

The physical and psychological effects of the flood were apparent as long as two to four years later. The physical and psychological scars that researchers found were

1. anxiety, grief and despair,
2. apathy and withdrawal,
3. depression,
4. stomach problems,
5. anger and rage,
6. regression in children,
7. nightmares and sleep disturbances, and
8. survival guilt.

Some combination of these symptoms was reported in roughly 80% of the adults and 90% of the children in the Buffalo Creek valley.

Many of the symptoms noted here were also observed in the aftermath of Bhopal. Although the reports were based on a less formal study, it was found that the citizens of Bhopal suffered from a generalized fear of additional gas leaks. In fact, there was a mass exodus from the city in the days following the accident. Other symptoms reported included nightmares, sleeplessness, depression, and anxiety.[22]

The Three Mile Island Nuclear Accident

Perhaps one of the most frightening types of disasters is a nuclear plant explosion or meltdown. Many movies have exploited the theme and graphically depicted a vision of the wholesale destruction that might take place. In spite of the assurances of safety from any number of sources, many people remain unconvinced. Thus, when Unit 2 at Three Mile Island was damaged and radioactive gases were let off into the atmosphere, the latent fears and suspicions quickly surfaced.

The crisis lasted several days, with evacuations and disruption of life in the immediate region. Even though the reactor was brought under control and the potential of severe danger was reduced rather quickly, the threat of radioactive leaks continued for some time. It was more than a year before contaminated water and gases were cleared from the building and the threat generally gone. Even today, the plant remains a focal point of contention. Suits have been filed that have prevented Three Mile Island from resuming operations even in units that were never damaged by the original accident. The long-term effects for the residents of the region may still be going on.

A number of studies done in the first two years following the accident report a variety of findings, including increased psychological distress, more physical complaints, and increased physiological arousal as indicated by levels of adrenaline in urine samples. Residents who had little or no social support network showed more evidence of stress than those who had good support.[23] This finding confirms the notion advanced by Cobb that social support operates as a buffer against the effects of stress (see Chapter 6).

Love Canal: The Silent Killer

In contrast to these dramatic disasters, Love Canal was a silent killer. Its onset was slow and insidious, since most people were not aware that anything was wrong. The total cost of Love Canal may not be known for years.

Love Canal was a 16-acre chemical dump site for Hooker Chemical Company located in Niagara Falls, New York. The abandoned canal was used for the disposal of nearly 20,000 tons of chemical wastes over a period of roughly 10 years ending in 1953. Hooker Chemical covered the canal and sold it to the local school district for $1.00. Homes were built during the next 20 years. But no one was told that the open field in their midst contained the seeds of deadly destruction. It was to be a beautiful park for the children.[24] Not until 1976 did the first real study of the problem begin and not until 1978 was any real action taken. At that time, 237 families were relocated from the lots next to the canal. However, 700 families were left on nearby streets to worry about their safety and fate.

Residents were generally frightened, frustrated with the lack of action by government offices, and angry at the type of cover-up that had occurred years before. The periods of most extreme frustration and anger took place when residents felt that they had no control over what was going on and when nothing was being done. Many residents reported feeling helpless and trapped.

But perhaps the most difficult problems were due to uncertainty and lack of information. Residents feared for their own safety and the safety of their young children, and feared that pregnant women would bear deformed children. Pregnant women and children under two were the only residents "officially" declared at risk in the area. Chromosome and ovum damage were known to be possibilities. Yet no one had any concrete answers to the many questions which residents asked.

As Lois Gibbs reported, many people threatened to take their own lives because of their inability to deal with the constant stress, and several succeeded. She also said that

> it [was not] uncommon to watch my neighbors, who before Love Canal were calm easygoing people, throw books at officials, use profanity in public, or threaten officials with physical harm at heated public meetings.[25]

The litany of problems the residents faced goes on, including disruption for children who had to relocate to different homes and schools as many as four times.

◆ COPING WITH THE EFFECTS OF DISASTER

While it is one thing to identify the problems resulting from natural and technological disasters, it is another thing to provide information on how to cope with disasters. At least one team of investigators attempted to address this issue, however. And one team found that survivors of a natural disaster may come out of the experience with much better coping skills than they had before the disaster.[26] The following information is based on one such analysis and on a composite of findings from the studies reported in the foregoing pages.

Following the Three Mile Island incident, an investigative team headed by Andrew Baum studied the coping strategies used by residents in the vicinity.[27] They asked a small sample of people to describe the type of coping strategies used over the months following the accident. The scale that was used[28] allowed them to determine the extent to which each person used an emotion control coping style as opposed to a problem control coping style. **Emotionally focused coping** was described as a strategy in which the person tries to control and release negative feelings (such as anger, frustration, and fear) provoked by the incident. **Problem focused coping** was described as a strategy in which the person tries to develop concrete plans of action and exerts as much direct control as possible.

Based on this initial assessment, each person was classified as high or low for emotionally focused coping and high or low for problem coping. Then the number of symptoms reported for each type of coping style was determined. The results were quite revealing. People who were *low* on emotionally focused coping reported nearly three times the number of symptoms as those who were high on this dimension. On the other side, people who were *high* on problem coping reported nearly three times the number of symptoms as those who were low on this dimension.

This suggests that in disaster situations, the most effective strategy is to focus first on getting rid of the negative emotions. Victims should seek ways of getting emotions out in the open and avoid keeping bad feelings bottled up inside. In addition, victims should probably be less concerned about trying to control through direct problem confrontation. This advice does not apply to all stress situations, though, for a specific reason. The investigative team reasoned that a disaster such as Three Mile Island confronts people with a situation that is inherently uncontrollable for anyone outside the technical team. Attempts to assert direct control, then, seem to add stress by increasing personal feelings of frustration at not being able to do anything about it. In other stressful situations, such as interpersonal conflict, a problem-solving approach may be the most effective means of managing the stress. But this represents a situation in which personal control is possible.

Information seeking is also a highly visible coping strategy in disaster situations. Recall that uncertainty seems to be one of the major causes of stress. Obtaining relevant and concrete information can help to reduce uncertainty. The problem is that information provided during and after disasters may be inaccurate, unclear, and confusing. This was the case with much of the information supplied during the Love Canal controversy. People often received mixed messages on health problems, relocation efforts, economic support, and so forth. In this situation, people who simply sat back and waited were often better off than those who were actively pressing for information. Therefore, officials charged with the responsibility of providing information should be careful to provide only information which is accurate and clear. Providing something just to provide it may contribute more to the problem than anything else.

◆ NOISE POLLUTION

The silence of forest and field is often sought out by urban dwellers as a vacation from the din of traffic, the clatter of jackhammers, and the roar of airplanes. The mere fact that many people try to escape noise, reduce noise, or engage in political battles to control noise suggests that the properties of noise are unpleasant. In some extreme cases, people even kill because of noise. Such was the case on a warm night early in the summer of 1985.

A normally quiet and responsible young man, Mike came home from his night shift job tired and looking for a peaceful night's sleep. He was soon disturbed by a loud party celebrating Kelly's 21st birthday. Mike asked the people at the party to quiet down. Heated words were exchanged, some shoving occurred, and Kelly led his friends in chasing Mike across the street. After an altercation at Mike's apartment, Kelly was shot to death. Noise does not usually produce such extreme outcomes, but it nonetheless is the source of stress for millions of people each day.

As this case illustrated, noise is a relative matter. One person's noise is another person's music. Noise is usually defined in terms of the effect it has on people. More formally, **noise** is unwanted sound. It is perceived as an unwarranted, offensive, and mostly uncontrollable intrusion on one's peace.

Three dimensions of sound are most closely related to whether sound is perceived as noise or not. These are intensity, predictability, and controllability. The intensity or volume of the sound is usually stated in decibels. The **decibel** (db) is a standard providing a physical reference for measuring and comparing sounds. Normal conversation is about 60 db; a rock band puts out about 120 db. Auditory pain begins to occur at about 100 db. Permanent damage can occur with sustained exposure to sounds above 100 db, such as are encountered in foundries. The United States Occupational Safety and Health Administration (OSHA) has set a 90-db ceiling for business and industry, but more than half the production workers in America are exposed to sound levels that can produce hearing loss.

Consumers commonly encounter the decibel in advertisements for stereo or television equipment and for cars. A stereo speaker that can only put out 85 db of sound at a standard level of input is inefficient relative to a speaker that can put out 105 db at the same input level. On the other hand, a car that has only 65 db of internal sound under normal driving conditions is quiet and desirable relative to one which has 85 db of internal sound. Table 9–1 shows some of the sounds commonly encountered in an urban environment.

In general, predictable noise is less disturbing than unpredictable noise. In fact, people can adapt to the effects of noise as long as it is consistent. For

Table 9–1. Decibel Levels for Common Sounds at Home and Work

Source	Decibel Level	Effect
Rocket engine	180	
	160	
Aircraft carrier deck	140	Intense pain
Emergency sirens at 100 feet		
Rock concert/discotheque	120	Moderate auditory pain
Automobile horn at 3 feet	110	
Off-road motorcycle		
Garbage truck	100	Beginning of pain
Subway station	90	Maximum OSHA Level
Lawn mower/outboard motor		Hearing damage begins
Noisy restaurant	80	
Freeway at 50 feet	70	Interference with use of phone
Washing machine		
Normal conversation	60	
Residential street noise	50	Quiet
Living room with TV on		
Refrigerator	40	
Library		
Whisper at 15 feet	30	Very quiet
	20	
Broadcasting studio	10	Barely audible
	0	Threshold of hearing

example, most people who have grown up in Chicago around the elevated trains can sleep through the night without great difficulty. They have adapted or habituated to the noise. But a person moving into Chicago from a rural area might have great difficulty sleeping at first, even though adaptation would probably come sooner or later.

The importance of predictability was dramatically illustrated one night. Police stations along the train route in Chicago were inundated with calls from curious residents who knew that something was wrong, but didn't know what. What had happened was very simple. A power outage had shut down the trains. People awoke because of the silence. In general, the more unpredictable and inconsistent the noise is, the more stressful it is. When it is predictable, we can adapt to it, anticipate it, and thus minimize its impact.

Finally, when we can control the noise, it is less aversive than when we cannot control it. Consider this example. The stereo is turned up rather loud and someone suggests looking for a different FM station. If someone else dials in a new station, you will probably react more negatively to noise between stations than if you do it yourself. In fact, muting switches are built into some stereo receivers to avoid this very problem, an example of engineering used to control the aversive properties of noise.

Noise has been shown to impair performance in schoolchildren.[29] It also may reduce production efficiency in factory and clerical workers. Noise may also increase certain types of illnesses. While the evidence linking noise to illness in general is rather weak, gastrointestinal disturbances (such as ulcers), vasoconstriction, higher blood pressure, and increased secretions of catecholamines (adrenaline and noradrenaline) occur consistently in association with high levels of noise.[30]

Even if noise is not strongly linked to health problems, it may have severe disrupting effects on social behavior. Noise apparently causes distortions in our perceptions of other people. It may thus affect our liking or disliking for another person.[31] In addition, a number of research projects have demonstrated that noise tends to increase the likelihood of aggression. But this may only occur when a person is already angry. Thus, noise may be a facilitator of aggression but not the instigator.[32] When Mike shot Kelly, it may well be that something happened during the day or at work that grated on Mike. The noise of the party may only have provided the excuse for ventilating anger. By the way, a jury later found Mike innocent of charges of murder.

Coping with Noise Pollution

A number of techniques are available for dealing with noise. In ecological terms, control techniques are called *noise abatement procedures*. Noise control techniques can be divided roughly into two broad categories. One approach is to control noise at the source. This would involve stricter laws and enforcement for mufflers on trucks, automobiles, and motorcycles. Quiet airplanes would have to be designed. Quiet office equipment would have to be built. Even then, all of the unpleasant sounds that are part of a modern industrial society could not be effectively eliminated.

The second general approach is to engage in better environmental design for work and living space that minimizes the potential for intrusion of unwanted sounds. Increased thickness of walls with attention to economically feasible soundproofing may go a long way to reducing the side effects of noise. In addition, thicker carpets, acoustic dampening on ceilings, sound-absorbing wall surfaces, curtains, and plants may all be used to reduce the spread or influx of sound. In addition, masking can be accomplished in some cases. Masking simply uses one sound to drown out another sound. Some masking may occur without design, such as the masking that occurs from heating and ventilating fans. Masking may also be done with design, as when music is piped in to an office or when music is kept at a background level at home to mask street sounds.

The Walkman Environment

One of the more interesting phenomena of recent years is the Walkman environment. People can be seen nearly anywhere running, driving, biking, or shopping, living in a world created by the Walkman stereo. Entire cities seem to be plugged in, turned on, but tuned out to whatever goes on outside the sphere of those two cushioned pads on the ears. It may be that the popularity of the Walkman is as much spawned by the control it gives people over noise as by the mere luxury of having portable music. In addition to providing a portable means for masking noise, these devices give virtually complete control over the type and volume of music. This makes the sound environment predictable. The Walkman may thus be one of the most effective means available for people to minimize noise pollution while on the move. At the same time, a new danger—hearing loss—may have been created for those who play their Walkman stereos at high levels for long periods.

◆ AIR POLLUTION

The Taj Mahal is one of the greatest architectural achievements in the world. The design of the building alone took 7 years, and the construction took nearly 22 years. More than 20,000 workers were employed year-round during the course of the project. It was finished in exquisite detail with precious and semiprecious stones inlaid in marble. And now a massive effort is underway to restore, preserve, and save the Taj Mahal from destruction. It is slowly being eaten away by corrosive air pollutants from a nearby power plant.

While air pollution does not seem to cause the psychological distress that disasters, crowding, and noise do, it is nonetheless important. At least three specific harmful effects are related to air pollution. First, it is a direct threat to human and animal health. Second, air pollution can have sweeping effects on the environment through a variety of atmospheric and climatic changes, including depletion of ozone, smog, and acid rain. Third, air pollution has the potential for harm and destruction to buildings through corrosive effects, as illustrated by the case of the Taj Mahal.

One of the problems with air pollution is that it is not always detectable to the senses. The most apparent sign of air pollution is smog, the haze that can be observed by looking at the horizon. We may be able to smell many air pollutants, such as gases from automobiles, smoke from processing plants, and odors from smoking tobacco. But many pollutants, such as carbon monoxide and radon gas, are undetectable to either the eye or the nose. This is well illustrated in the case of airtight homes. The air inside some of these homes was found to be more polluted than the air outside, yet the owners were not conscious of this.[33]

The Air Pollution Syndrome

The health hazards of air pollution are fairly well known. At the extreme end of the spectrum, it is now thought that as much as 50–90% of cancer cases result from air pollution. In the United States alone, it is estimated that

140,000 deaths result from air pollution each year. In Mexico City, with a population of 18 million people and dense industrialization, 100,000 people die each year from air pollution, 30,000 of whom are children. It has been reported that one breath of air in an average city contains 70,000 dust and dirt particles; just breathing in New York City is equivalent to smoking 38 cigarettes a day.[34]

Doctors have identified an air pollution syndrome (APS).[35] The syndome includes headaches, fatigue, insomnia, depression, irritability, eye irritation, and stomach problems. Fisher and his colleagues have provided a short but detailed summary of some other health hazards of air pollution.[36] Long-term exposure to carbon monoxide poisoning, for example, can result in headaches, epilepsy, memory disturbances, visual and auditory impairments, Parkinsonism, and physical fatigue. In addition, carbon monoxide deprives body tissue of oxygen, producing a condition known as hypoxia. Particulates such as those coming from smokestacks, exhausts, and other sources include lead, mercury, and asbestos. These pollutants can cause cancer, anemia, and respiratory and neural problems. Psychiatric problems also seem to be aggravated by air pollution, as indicated by increased hospital admissions.

There are other effects of air pollution. Human performance tends to suffer as pollutants increase. Deficits in reaction time, attention, and perceptual–motor coordination occur. It is possible that such effects contribute to the frequency of automobile accidents in heavily congested cities. Air pollution may also change some forms of social behaviors, including increasing aggression.

The Issue of Smoking

One of the more divisive issues in recent years is the rights of nonsmokers. A number of research studies have shown that the smoke inhaled from someone else's cigarette can have detrimental health effects. In general, breathing rate and heart rate increase, and blood pressure goes up. Improved ventilation systems and air purifiers provide direct means of reducing the impact. Many states have adopted legislation restricting smokers to certain areas of public buildings, and similar rules have been in effect for most public transportation systems. While segregation may be a step in the direction of reducing the irritation and anxiety that nonsmokers report feeling in the presence of smoking, it does not provide a fully effective means of eliminating the harm.

◆ STRESS AND OVERCROWDING

Stress is frequently related to management or mismanagement of space. Perhaps the most important issue in this context is that of overcrowding. Researchers use two terms, *density* and *crowding,* when talking about overcrowding.[37] **Density** is the physical condition of overpopulation. **Crowding,** on the other hand, has been defined as "a psychological state characterized by stress and having motivational properties (e.g., it elicits attempts to reduce discomfort)."[38]

To illustrate what is meant by density, consider the fact that in a city the size of San Francisco, one can encounter 300,000 people in a 15-minute walk. In Calcutta, India, the inner city is one of the most densely populated in the world with nearly 35,000 people per square kilometer. Relative to an American city, this is the equivalent of 35,000 people in the space of five square blocks. That is density. Even when there is a very dense population, some people may not feel crowded. Without doubt, a complex web of psychological factors probably combine to produce the subjective feeling.

The effects of overcrowding on human behavior can be summarized as follows.

1. Negative moods are frequently associated with high density. This is true for men only, as women appear to have negative moods more frequently in low-density conditions. This suggests a *socialization* process, which is assumed to differ for males and females.[39]

2. Physiological arousal—as measured by higher blood pressure and increased skin conductance, sweating, and cortisol and epinephrine output—occurs in a variety of laboratory and natural settings under conditions of crowding. One study of commuters noted that the extent of arousal, however, was dependent on the degree of control that commuters had in choosing their space on the train.[40] This suggests that the effect of crowding is dependent on how the person appraises the *controllability* of the situation.

3. Illness tends to increase as density increases, as indicated by studies of prison inmates, college students, and naval crews. The types of illnesses reported are not serious, but the frequency seems to be increased.

4. Overcrowding may also increase both withdrawal and aggression. Withdrawal responses include lower levels of eye contact and maintenance of greater interpersonal distance.[41] If aggression increases at all, it does so only in males. The findings are somewhat weak and inconsistent on the latter issue.

Most of the negative outcomes of overcrowding are consistent with the cognitive–transactional model based on the idea of loss of control. As Baum and Valins noted, overcrowding generally leads to an increase in unwanted interactions, which itself is a basic loss in controlling the range and type of interactions felt desirable.[42] Fisher and his colleagues also saw stimulus overload and behavior constraint as potentially contributing factors, but these are still consistent with the cognitive model.[43] Loss of control might increase physiological arousal, activate the sympathetic nervous system, and increase the risk of illness.

Coping with Crowding

At least two different means of coping with overcrowding have been suggested. The first focuses on environmental design aimed at reducing the feeling of crowding. Bright colors, wall decorations, higher ceilings, and rectangular rooms can all increase the perception of space and reduce the feeling of crowding.

The second approach focuses on the feelings of anxiety or apprehension felt by people in situations of crowding. One study used three different techniques to reduce anxiety in commuters.[44] The three techniques were the relaxation approach (discussed in Chapters 11 and 12), cognitive reappraisal, and imagery (both discussed in Chapter 13). The results suggest that all of the techniques provided some help but that cognitive reappraisal produced the most positive results.

Commuting in Urban Environments

Commuting may well be one of the more stressful experiences for urban workers living in the suburbs. Above and beyond the time and expense of commuting, there are traffic jams, accidents, rude if not hostile drivers, and competition for right of way, position at stop lights, access to on and off ramps and parking. Research shows that commuting stress increases with the volume of traffic and changes in the weather, and on two-lane or curving roads.[45] The effects of commuting are affected by a number of factors, including personality and the degree of control that the person can exert in crowded conditions.

◆ SUMMARY

This chapter has reviewed the status of research on stress and health related to environmental factors such as disasters, pollution, and crowding. While disasters produce more intense but acute stress, pollution and crowding produce less intense but chronic stress. Negative health effects are generally mild, including short-term disturbances in eating and sleeping and physical fatigue, with some increase in the frequency of normal illnesses. Severe effects, short of death from disaster, have been observed only in the case of long-term environmental hazards.

Explanations of these effects can be encompassed in a cognitive–transactional model through a number of cognitive mediators such as perception of loss of control. Reduction of the effects of these stressors can be accomplished through environmental design and personal interventions aimed at reducing anxiety, ventilating negative emotions, and increasing the perception of personal control. A number of stress management techniques to be discussed in later chapters may be useful in this regard.

◆ NOTES

[1]Moran, E. F. (1981). Human adaptation to arctic zones. *Annual Review of Anthropology, 10,* 1–25.

[2]Mehrabian, A., & Russell, J. A. (1974). *An approach to environmental psychology.* Cambridge, MA: M.I.T. Press.

[3]Cohen, S. (1978). Environmental load and the allocation of attention. In A. Baum, J. E. Singer, & S. Valins (Eds.), *Advances in environmental psychology* (Vol. 1). Hillsdale, NJ: Erlbaum.

[4]Wohlwill, J. F. (1974). Human adaptation to levels of environmental stimulation. *Human Ecology, 2,* 127–147.

[5]Byrne, D., & Clore, G. L. (1970). A reinforcement model of evaluative responses. *Personality: An International Journal, 1,* 103–128.

[6]Rodin, J., & Baum, A. (1978). Crowding and helplessness: Potential consequences of density and loss of control. In A. Baum & Y. Epstein (Eds.), *Human response to crowding.* Hillsdale, NJ: Erlbaum.

[7]Seligman, M. E. P. (1975). *Helplessness.* San Francisco: Freeman.

[8]Brehm, S. S., & Brehm, J. W. (1981). *Psychological reactance: A theory of freedom and control.* New York: Academic Press.

[9]Barker, R. G. (1968). *Ecological psychology: Concepts and methods for studying the environment of human behavior.* Stanford, CA: Stanford University Press.

[10]Baum, A., Singer, J. E., & Baum, C. S. (1981). Stress and the environment. *Journal of Social Issues, 37,* 4–35.

[11]Fisher, J. D., Bell, P. A., & Baum, A. (1984). *Environmental psychology* (2nd ed.). New York: Holt, Rinehart & Winston, p. 79.

[12]The term *social disaster* is one of the author's own choosing to encompass those events that do not readily fit the natural and technological categories but nonetheless share common elements of unpredictability and lack of control and produce a powerful impact on the lives of people. The McDonald's massacre of the summer of 1984 and the Jonestown suicides may be considered in this category.

[13]Fisher et al., *Environmental psychology,* p. 86.

[14]Coleman, J. C., Butcher, J. N.,& Carson, R. C. (1980). *Abnormal psychology and modern life* (6th ed.). Glenview, IL: Scott, Foresman.

[15]McLeod, B. (1984). In the wake of disaster. *Psychology Today, 18,* 54–57.

[16]Patrick, V., & Patrick, W. K. (1981). Cyclone '78 in Sri Lanka—The mental health trail. *British Journal of Psychiatry, 138,* 210–216.

[17]To get some sense of what a cubic mile of earth means in volume, consider this. A cubic mile of earth is equal to 5.5 billion cubic yards. Most standard sand and gravel trucks are twin-axle vehicles that can carry approximately 14 cubic yards of dirt. If you could line up enough trucks to haul away all the debris that came off of Mount Saint Helens, it would take a string of 390,741,623 trucks. If you could fill one truck every 10 minutes working 24 hours a day, it would still take 2,713,483.49 days. In other words, it would take you a total of 7,434 years to accomplish what Mount Saint Helens accomplished in a matter of a few minutes.

[18]Murphy, S. A. (1984). Stress levels and health status of victims of a natural disaster. *Research in Nursing and Health, 7,* 205–215.

[19]Pennebaker, J. W., & Newtson, D. (1983). Observation of a unique event: The psychological impact of the Mount Saint Helens volcano. *New Directions for Methodology of Social and Behavioral Sciences, 15,* 93–109.

[20]Murphy, Stress levels.

[21]Murphy, Stress levels, p. 212.

[22]Bales, J. (1985). Fear is residue of Bhopal tragedy. *APA Monitor, 16,* 15.

[23]Fleming, R., Baum, A., Gisriel, M. M., & Gatchel, R. J. (1982). Mediating influences of social support on stress at Three Mile Island. *Journal of Human Stress, 8,* 14–22.

[24]Gibbs, L. M. (1983). Community response to an emergency situation: Psychological destruction and the Love Canal. *American Journal of Community Psychology, 11,* 116–125.

[25]Gibbs, Community response, pp. 123–124.

[26]Quarantelli, E. L., & Dynes, R. R. (1977). *Response to social crisis and disaster.* Palo Alto, CA: Annual Reviews of Sociology, pp. 23–49.

[27]Baum, A., Fleming, R., & Singer, J. (1983). Coping with victimization by technological disaster. *Journal of Social Issues, 39,* 117–138.

[28]Folkman, S., & Lazarus, R. S. (1980). An analysis of coping in a middle-aged community sample. *Journal of Health and Social Behavior, 21,* 219–239. This study provided the Ways of Coping Inventory that Baum and his associates used in the Three Mile Island study.

[29]Bronzaft, A. L., & McCarthy, D. P. (1975). The effects of elevated train noise on reading ability. *Environment and Behavior, 7,* 517–527.

[30]Cohen, S., Evans, G. W., Krantz, D. S., & Stokols, D. (1980). Physiological, motivational, and cognitive effects of aircraft noise on children: Moving from the laboratory to the field. *American Psychologist, 35,* 231–243.

[31]Siegel, J. M., & Steele, C. M. (1980). Environmental distraction and interpersonal judgments. *British Journal of Social and Clinical Psychology, 19,* 23–32.

[32]Konecni, V. J., Libuser, L., Morton, H., & Ebbesen, E. B. (1975). Effects of a violation of personal space on escape and helping responses. *Journal of Experimental Social Psychology, 11,* 288–299.

[33]Guenther, R. (1982, August 4). Ways are found to minimize pollutants in airtight houses. *Wall Street Journal,* p. 25.

[34]As reported by Fisher et al., *Environmental psychology,* p. 243.

[35]Hart, R. H. (1970). The concept of APS: Air pollution syndrome(s). *Journal of the South Carolina Medical Association, 66,* 71–73.

[36]Fisher et al., *Environmental psychology,* pp. 144–145.

[37]Baron, R. M., & Needel, S. P. (1980). Toward an understanding of the differences in the responses of humans and other animals to density. *Psychological Review, 87,* 320–326.

[38]Fisher et al., *Environmental psychology,* p. 216. It should be noted, however, that some researchers take exception to this definition.

[39]Freedman, J. L. (1975). *Crowding and behavior.* San Francisco: Freeman.

[40]Lundberg, U. (1976). Urban commuting: Crowdedness and catecholamine excretion. *Journal of Human Stress, 2,* 26–32.

[41]Baum, A., & Koman, S. (1976). Differential response to anticipated crowding: Psychological effects of social and spatial density. *Journal of Personality and Social Psychology, 34,* 526–536.

[42]Baum, A., & Valins, S. (1979). Architectural mediation of residential density and control: Crowding and the regulation of social contact. In L. Berkowitz (Ed.), *Advances in experimental social psychology* (Vol. 12). New York: Academic Press.

[43]Fisher et al., *Environmental psychology,* p. 216.

[44]Karlin, R. A., Katz, S., Epstein, Y., & Woolfolk, R. (1979). The use of therapeutic interventions to reduce crowding-related arousal: A preliminary investigation. *Environmental Psychology and Nonverbal Behavior, 3,* 219–227.

[45]Stokols, D., & Novaco, R. (1981). Transportation and well-being: An ecological perspective. In I. Altman, J. F. Wohlwill, & P. B. Everett (Eds.), *Transportation and behavior.* New York: Plenum Press.

10

JOB STRESS: DISSATISFACTION, BURNOUT, AND OBSOLESCENCE

> *Many . . . have reached the top of the*
> *success ladder but are beginning to suspect*
> *it may be leaning against the wrong wall.*
>
> *Sam Keen*

---◇---

Sunday, May 19, 1985: Headlines in the *New York Times* business section read "Warren Anderson: A Public Crisis, a Personal Ordeal."[1] Using several hours of interviewing, Stuart Diamond tried to uncover the inside story of a corporation and its chief officer struggling to deal with a tragedy of immense proportions. For both company and chairman, it was a period of intense, unyielding stress. One half of the story was the public, legal, and corporate pressure on Union Carbide Corporation in the months following the Bhopal tragedy. The accident tarnished the image of Union Carbide worldwide, contributed to plummeting stock, slowed the pace of company expansion, and produced multibillion-dollar lawsuits.

The other half of the story was more intimate and personal. It was the story of the dramatic changes in life-style for Warren Anderson, Chairman of Union Carbide. While Anderson was not directly involved in the events contributing to the spilling of toxic gases, he alone had to accept ultimate responsibility as chief officer of the company. Immediately after the immensity of the tragedy was known, he assembled a team of technical and medical experts to fly to Bhopal with him. In Bombay, he met two Indian officials from Union Carbide of India. Upon arrival in Bhopal, all three were arrested and jailed. Anderson was held for several hours before flying to New Delhi, while his Indian colleagues were held for nine days. For his wife Lillian, those few days while he was in India were filled with more terror than she had known for most of her life.

When Anderson returned to his Danbury, Connecticut office, he devoted his attention solely to matters related to the Bhopal accident. The day-to-day operation of the company was left to his junior officers. Anderson said that he felt "like I'm taking tests all the time. You know there is going to be a grade on everything you do and say."

Meanwhile, Lillian kept a doctor on call for fear that her husband might collapse from the stress. All the while, she kept secret her own worries to avoid adding any more to the load she knew he carried. The Andersons felt that they had become trapped by the Bhopal incident, a private jail they carried anywhere they went. Reading the paper, watching the news, or going out for an evening dinner might bring unwelcome reminders of what had happened. Always regarded as a low-profile type of couple, they became almost reclusive. They lay down at night with lumps in their chests and both experienced difficulty sleeping.

◆ DIMENSIONS OF JOB STRESS

This case study highlights important aspects of job stress. First, work stress generally involves both the organization and its employees. Job stress is not a private matter for the employee to deal with alone and in isolation. Admittedly, employees may transport some personal and family problems to the job. But work problems also spill over to the home.[2]

Second, work stress produces negative effects for both the company and the employee. For the organization, the results are disorganization, disruption in normal operations, lowered productivity, and lower overall margins of profit. For the employee, the effects are seen in increased physical health problems, psychological distress, and behavioral changes. Problems with health are not so much related to the onset of a specific disease as to the quiet and gradual loss of health. Psychological distress usually goes along with loss of job satisfaction and a variety of related negative emotions. The changes in behavior tend to affect productivity within the company and life-style outside the confines of the job.

Third, work stress requires both organizational and personal solutions. No matter how well-intentioned, employee assistance programs that focus solely on the employee only perpetuate the myth that job stress is the worker's fault. In many cases, removing job stress requires some type of intervention in the organization. It must change in order to eliminate or reduce job stress. Unless and until this is done, personal coping strategies may be little more than bandages that help the employee survive from one crisis to the next. A number of organizational and personal intervention strategies will be described later in the chapter.

◆ DEFINING JOB STRESS

One definition suggests that job stress results from "characteristics of the job *environment* which pose a threat to the individual."[3] The threat may be due either to excessive demands of the job or to insufficient supplies to meet the worker's needs. The first has to do with the kind of job stress usually described as job overload, when too much work is expected in too short a period of time. The second has to do with things the worker expects from the job, such as adequate salary, job satisfaction, and promotion or growth in the job.

After reviewing a number of definitions, Terry Beehr and John Newman defined job stress as the interaction of work conditions with worker characteristics that changes normal psychological and/or physiological functions.[4] They make room in their definition, however, for stress that improves performance—what Selye called eustress.

In this chapter, **job stress** will be defined as work demands that exceed the worker's ability to cope. This definition is also consistent with the cognitive–transactional concept presented earlier.

◆ THE COSTS OF WORK STRESS

One of the major reasons for concern about work stress and work environments is the great amount of economic loss suffered because of job stress and unsafe conditions on the job. The cost of work stress has to be calculated across a spreading network of accounts ranging from personal, to family, to business, to society.

The federal government has made estimates, based on studies of many occupations, that 100,000 workers die each year from job-related diseases, while another 390,000 develop some type of job-related illness. In addition, 14,000 workers die each year from accidents on the job. Another 2.2 million suffer some type of disabling injury.[5]

Using data from a 1976 survey by the Bureau of Labor Statistics, Robert Veninga and James Spradley reported that Americans lose 3.5% of their work hours through absenteeism. They estimated that one out of three workers on any particular day has called in sick because of stress-related problems.[6] As a result, job stress costs millions of dollars each year in unpaid wages.

At the business level, lost productivity accounts for over $32.8 billion in losses each year. According to an analysis by James Greenwood, stress on the job adds up to billions of dollars in direct and indirect costs every year. Greenwood calculated the direct costs of *executive* stress alone at $19.7 billion per year. The indirect costs are difficult to calculate but may be as large as or larger than the direct costs.[7] Loss from training an employee who subsequently must be let go or quits because of job dissatisfaction can cost the company $5,000 or more for blue-collar laborers and support staff. For executives, the loss to the company may be in excess of $100,000.[8]

◆ SYMPTOMS OF WORK STRESS

A mere monetary computation of losses overlooks some of the most important results of work stress. Adults spend roughly half their waking lives on the job. Because more wage earners are working overtime or are employed at two jobs, that figure may be an underestimate. Because of the amount of time people spend working, conditions at work contribute significantly to life-style and health and thus spread the effect, either positive or negative, to all facets of life beyond the job.

Terry Beehr and John Newman reviewed a number of studies of work stress and concluded that there are three types of negative personal outcomes due to work stress.[9] These are psychological health symptoms, physical health symptoms, and behavioral symptoms. The following is a compilation of the symptoms that reveal the onset of work stress. The list will probably change in the coming years as more is discovered about what work stress does, but it is the best guide available at this time.

Psychological Symptoms of Work Stress

This list of psychological symptoms is representative of the findings from job stress research without being either exhaustive or overly condensed. These symptoms have been observed in a number of occupational settings.

1. Anxiety, tension, confusion and irritability
2. Feelings of frustration, anger and resentment
3. Emotional hypersensitivity and hyperreactivity
4. Suppression of feelings
5. Reduced effectiveness in communication
6. Withdrawal and depression
7. Feelings of isolation and alienation
8. Boredom and job dissatisfaction
9. Mental fatigue and lower intellectual functioning
10. Loss of concentration
11. Loss of spontaneity and creativity
12. Lowered self-esteem

Perhaps the most predictable psychological consequence of job stress is job dissatisfaction. When this occurs, the person feels little or no motivation for going to work, for doing a good job while at work, or for continuing on the job. The other symptoms occur at different stages on the road to job dissatisfaction and vary from one person to another.

Anxiety, tension, anger and resentment are among the more commonly reported symptoms. Some people find the job pressure so great that they psychologically withdraw more and more from the job and gradually get more and more depressed. This may occur after the employee has tried and failed to correct the stress situation. If this occurs often enough, the outcome may be a form of learned helplessness that prevents the employee from making corrections even when it is within his or her power to do so. On the other hand, some employees probably never try because they bring a load of learned helplessness to the job.

Physical Health Symptoms of Work Stress

The major physical symptoms of work stress are listed here. There is adequate research to verify the effects of work stress on the cardiovascular and gastrointestinal systems. Physical fatigue, bodily injuries, and sleep disturbances are also fairly well established. The remaining disorders, however, are not as reliably established.

1. Increased heart rate and blood pressure
2. Cardiovascular disease
3. Increased secretions of adrenaline and noradrenaline
4. Gastrointestinal disorders such as ulcers
5. Respiratory problems
6. Increased sweating
7. Skin disorders
8. Headaches
9. Cancer
10. Bodily injuries
11. Physical fatigue
12. Muscular tension
13. Sleep disturbances
14. Death

One problem in making the work–stress–health connection is that some employees bring some physical health problems to the job. These may be related to high-risk behaviors in the social environment. Work conditions may intensify the health problem, though, making it more visible. But the job gets the blame for the health problem.

In addition, job conditions may simply be unsafe. Poor lighting, unclean shop areas that create hazards, high-intensity noise levels, and inadequate ventilation may contribute to a variety of physical health problems. Eyestrain can contribute to headaches and increase errors, and thus lower productivity. Shop hazards can contribute to personal injuries, including loss of limb and life. Unsafe noise levels can lead to impairment or loss of hearing. Inadequate ventilation can lead to respiratory problems and strain on the cardiovascular system.

The most obvious examples of unsafe work environments are plants where toxic chemicals or materials are produced through unsafe methods that expose employees to risks above and beyond those normally encountered. Kenneth Pelletier, in his book *Healthy People in Unhealthy Places*, summarized the results of studies by several federal agencies linking hazardous chemicals to on-the-job diseases.[10] Included in his list are asbestos, which is known to cause white lung disease and cancer; benzene, which causes leukemia and aplastic anemia; coal dust, which causes black lung disease; radiation, which causes cancer, leukemia, and genetic damage; and lead, which causes kidney disorders, anemia, central nervous system damage, sterility, and birth defects. The National Institute for Occupational Safety and Health (NIOSH) has estimated that 1 million of the 16 million working women of child-bearing years are in jobs with the potential for exposure to hazards that can produce birth defects or miscarriages.[11]

Behavioral Symptoms of Work Stress

A large number of behavioral consequences are observed as a result of job stress. These include the following.

1. Procrastination and avoidance of work
2. Lowered overall performance and productivity
3. Increased alcohol and drug use and abuse
4. Outright sabotage on the job
5. Increased visits to the dispensary
6. Overeating as an escape leading to obesity
7. Undereating as a withdrawal, probably combined with signs of depression
8. Loss of appetite and sudden weight loss
9. Increased risk-taking behavior, including driving and gambling
10. Aggression, vandalism, and stealing
11. Deteriorating relationships with family and friends
12. Suicide or attempted suicide

Procrastination is sometimes disguised as busywork. The oft-heard comment "just getting organized" may be a mere cover-up for keeping busy in order to avoid doing something that is more bothersome. Work stress is also frequently combined with other problems, such as alcoholism and drug abuse.

Behavioral Symptoms with Organizational Impact

Just as work stress is revealed in certain behaviors with a major impact on the worker, work stress is revealed in behaviors that have an impact on the organization. Randall Schuler, of The Ohio State University, identified the following behaviors that affect the organization negatively.

1. Quantitatively and qualitatively low performance
2. Low job involvement
3. Loss of a sense of responsibility to the job
4. Lack of concern for the organization
5. Lack of concern for colleagues
6. Absenteeism
7. Leaving the job
8. Accident proneness[12]

◆ SOURCES OF WORK STRESS

Attempts to identify the sources of stress on the job have turned up many culprits. It should be noted that how individuals perceive the conditions of work relative to their own skills is more critical to a determination of whether stress will occur than the actual conditions of work. Thus, the list of sources of job stress provided here does not imply that these sources alone are responsible for job stress. Rather, they add to the potential for stress and combine with worker traits to produce stress.

While many different categorization schemes have been proposed, the most comprehensive yet concise list has been provided by Cary Cooper. He listed these six sources of work stress:

1. job-specific stress,
2. role stress,
3. interpersonal stress,
4. career development,
5. organizational structure and development, and
6. home–work interface.[13]

Before you read on, it may be instructive to fill out the Work Stress Profile in Self-Study Exercise 10–1.

Self-Study Exercise 10–1. Work Stress Profile

This scale provides some information on work stress. Instructions for scoring and interpreting the scale appear at the end.

The following statements describe work conditions, job environments, or personal feelings that workers encounter in their jobs. After reading each statement, circle the answer that best reflects the working conditions at your place of employment. If the statement is about a personal feeling, indicate the extent to which you have that feeling about your job. The scale markers ask you to judge the approximate percentage of time the condition or feeling is true to the best of your knowledge.

NEVER = not at all true of your work conditions or feelings
RARELY = the condition or feeling exists about 25% of the time
SOMETIMES = the condition or feeling exists about 50% of the time
OFTEN = the condition or feeling exists about 75% of the time
MOST TIMES = the condition or feeling is virtually always present

	NEVER	RARELY	SOME-TIMES	OFTEN	MOST TIMES
1. Support personnel are incompetent or inefficient.	1	2	3	4	5
2. My job is not very well defined.	1	2	3	4	5
3. I am not sure about what is expected of me.	1	2	3	4	5
4. I am not sure what will be expected of me in the future.	1	2	3	4	5
5. I cannot seem to satisfy my superiors.	1	2	3	4	5

6. I seem to be able to talk with my superiors.

| 5 | 4 | 3 | 2 | 1 |

7. My superiors strike me as incompetent, yet I have to take orders from them.

| 1 | 2 | 3 | 4 | 5 |

8. My superiors seem to care about me as a person.

| 5 | 4 | 3 | 2 | 1 |

9. There is a feeling of trust, respect, and friendliness between myself and my superiors.

| 5 | 4 | 3 | 2 | 1 |

10. There seems to be tension between administrative personnel and staff personnel.

| 1 | 2 | 3 | 4 | 5 |

11. I have autonomy in carrying out my job duties.

| 5 | 4 | 3 | 2 | 1 |

12. I feel as though I can shape my own destiny in this job.

| 5 | 4 | 3 | 2 | 1 |

13. There are too many bosses in my area.

| 1 | 2 | 3 | 4 | 5 |

14. It appears that my boss has "retired on the job."

| 1 | 2 | 3 | 4 | 5 |

15. My superiors give me adequate feedback about my job performance.

| 5 | 4 | 3 | 2 | 1 |

16. My abilities are not appreciated by my superiors.

| 1 | 2 | 3 | 4 | 5 |

17. There is little prospect of personal or professional growth in this job.

| 1 | 2 | 3 | 4 | 5 |

18. The level of participation in planning and decision making at my place of work is satisfactory.

| 5 | 4 | 3 | 2 | 1 |

19. I feel that I am overeducated for my job.

| 1 | 2 | 3 | 4 | 5 |

20. I feel that my educational background is just right for this job.

| 5 | 4 | 3 | 2 | 1 |

21. I fear that I will be laid off or fired.

| 1 | 2 | 3 | 4 | 5 |

22. In-service training for my job is inadequate.

| 1 | 2 | 3 | 4 | 5 |

23. Most of my colleagues are unfriendly or seem uninterested in me as a person.   [1] [2] [3] [4] [5]

24. I feel uneasy about going to work.   [1] [2] [3] [4] [5]

25. There is no release time for personal affairs or business.   [1] [2] [3] [4] [5]

26. There is obvious sex/race/age discrimination in this job.   [1] [2] [3] [4] [5]

NOTE: Complete the entire questionnaire first! Then add up all the values circled for questions 1–26 and enter here.   →   [   ]

Total 1–26

---

27. The physical work environment is crowded, noisy, or dreary.   [1] [2] [3] [4] [5]

28. Physical demands of the job are unreasonable (heavy lifting, extraordinary periods of concentration required, etc.).   [1] [2] [3] [4] [5]

29. My work load is never-ending.   [1] [2] [3] [4] [5]

30. The pace of work is too fast.   [1] [2] [3] [4] [5]

31. My job seems to consist of responding to emergencies.   [1] [2] [3] [4] [5]

32. There is no time for relaxation, coffee breaks, or lunch breaks on the job.   [1] [2] [3] [4] [5]

33. Job deadlines are constant and unreasonable.   [1] [2] [3] [4] [5]

34. Job requirements are beyond the range of my ability.   [1] [2] [3] [4] [5]

35. At the end of the day, I am physically exhausted from work.   [1] [2] [3] [4] [5]

36. I can't even enjoy my leisure because of the toll my job takes on my energy.   [1] [2] [3] [4] [5]

37. I have to take work home to keep up.   [1] [2] [3] [4] [5]

38. I have responsibility for too many people.   [1] [2] [3] [4] [5]

39. Support personnel are too few.
    [1] [2] [3] [4] [5]

40. Support personnel are incompetent or inefficient.
    [1] [2] [3] [4] [5]

41. I am not sure about what is expected of me.
    [1] [2] [3] [4] [5]

42. I am not sure what will be expected of me in the future.
    [1] [2] [3] [4] [5]

43. I leave work feeling burned out.
    [1] [2] [3] [4] [5]

44. There is little prospect for personal or professional growth in this job.
    [1] [2] [3] [4] [5]

45. In-service training for my job is inadequate.
    [1] [2] [3] [4] [5]

46. There is little contact with colleagues on the job.
    [1] [2] [3] [4] [5]

47. Most of my colleagues are unfriendly or seem uninterested in me as a person.
    [1] [2] [3] [4] [5]

48. I feel uneasy about going to work.
    [1] [2] [3] [4] [5]

NOTE: Complete the entire questionnaire first! Then add up all the values circled for questions 27–48 and enter here. → [   ]   Total 27–48

---

49. The complexity of my job is enough to keep me interested.
    [5] [4] [3] [2] [1]

50. My job is very exciting.
    [5] [4] [3] [2] [1]

51. My job is varied enough to prevent boredom.
    [5] [4] [3] [2] [1]

52. I seem to have lost interest in my work.
    [1] [2] [3] [4] [5]

53. I feel as though I can shape my own destiny in this job.
    [5] [4] [3] [2] [1]

54. I leave work feeling burned out.
    [1] [2] [3] [4] [5]

55. I would continue to work at my job even if I did not need the money.
    [5] [4] [3] [2] [1]

56. I am trapped in this job.
    [1] [2] [3] [4] [5]

57. If I had it to do all over again, I
would still choose this job.   [5]   [4]   [3]   [2]   [1]

NOTE: Now go back and add up the values for
questions 1–26. Do the same for questions
27–48. Enter the values where indicated.
Then add up all the values circled for
questions 49–57.

[ ] Total 49–57

Last, enter those sums for each of the following
groups of questions and add them all together to get a
cumulative total.

QUESTIONS:	1–26 Inter- personal	27–48 Physical Conditions	49–57 Job Interest	TOTAL 1–57
TOTALS:	[ ] +	[ ] +	[ ] =	[ ]

The first scale measures stress due to problems in interpersonal relationships and job satisfaction or dissatisfaction, as the case may be. The second scale measures the physical demands of work that wear on the person
daily. The third scale measures job interest and involvement. For each of the
scales, you can gain some sense of how much job stress you live with relative
to the original test group by locating your scores on the scale provided below.
On each scale, a high score means more job-related stress. If you are high in
one of the areas, say interpersonal stress, it could be of some help to pay
attention to the interpersonal aspects of your job.

	Low ← Stress →		← Normal Stress →		High ← Stress →
Interpersonal	.. 39 .... 43 46	.... 51 .... 54 57	 62	.... 68 .... 75..
Physical	.. 35 .... 40 44	.... 48 .... 52 55	 58	.... 62 .... 67..
Interest	.. 13 .... 15 17	.... 18 .... 19 21	 23	.... 25 .... 27..
Total	.. 91 ... 101 ... 111	... 117 ... 123 ... 134	... 141	... 151 ... 167..
Percentile	.. 10 .... 20 30	.... 40 .... 50 60	 70	.... 80 .... 90..

The work stress profile has been tested in a sample of 275 school psychologists. The three scales are virtually identical to those identified in other
work stress scales. The reliability of this scale is quite high. For the total
scale, the reliability is .921. Reliabilities for the three subscales are .898,

.883, and .816, respectively. A reliability of 1.00 indicates perfect reliability. The high reliability shown by this scale may be due in part to the fact that it was tested on a single occupational group. Additional studies with other occupational groups will be needed to determine if the scales are stable across a variety of occupations.

Stress Related to Job Conditions

The specific conditions contributing to stress include such things as job complexity, work overload or underload, unsafe physical conditions, and shift work. **Job complexity** is the inherent difficulty of the work to be done. It is usually related to such things as the amount and sophistication of information required to function in the job, the expansion or addition of methods for performing the job, or the introduction of contingency plans for completing a job.[14]

Work overload. Work overload is customarily divided into quantitative and qualitative overload. **Quantitative overload** occurs when the physical demands of the job exceed the worker's capacity. This happens when too much work is required in too short a period, as when unreasonably high quotas are set. The job may require physical strength beyond the worker's capacity. The assembly line may keep moving no matter how strained or fatigued the worker is. The day may be so heavily scheduled that there is no "down" time to catch one's breath. Or the travel schedule may place constant demands on the employee.

Qualitative overload is work that is too complex or difficult to do. In this case, either the technical or the mental skills of the worker have been taxed beyond capacity.

Assembly line hysteria. On the other side, **work underload** means that the job is not challenging or fails to maintain the interest and attention of the worker in any meaningful way. George Everly and Daniel Girdano used the term *deprivational stress* for this work condition. They suggested that understimulation is most frequently found in assembly line workers and in the large bureaucracy.[15] NIOSH has described a so-called *assembly line hysteria,* which consists of nausea, muscle weakness, severe headaches, and blurred vision. In spite of the physical symptoms, there is no physical basis for the symptoms. Rather, they appear to be part of the psychological response to a job that is seen as boring, repetitive, lacking in social interaction, and low in job satisfaction.

Decision making, responsibility, and stress. One situation in which qualitative overload can occur happens when a manager or supervisor is responsible for making decisions that affect the company's production and the employee's future. Managers may have to plan production schedules, procure materials, evaluate staff, and make recommendations on hiring, firing, and layoffs. As long as the decisions involve only *things* as opposed to *people,* managers may function fairly well. However, the more the manager's decision involves responsibility for other people, the more likely that stress will occur.

In general, as the manager assumes more responsibility for the decision, the more stressful it is to make the decision. When the decision is spread out, as in governance by committee, stress is reduced. Also, a decision that has to be made by some deadline can be highly stressful. Indeed, some people try to avoid making decisions under such conditions. But, in many jobs time is not available. People who work in life-and-death situations, such as emergency service workers, cannot take their ideas to a boardroom or request a computer simulation showing the likelihood of success for one plan relative to another. Presidents, military leaders, and pilots of stricken aircraft also fit in this category.

Physical danger.   Physical danger is a potential source of job stress when the worker has to confront the actual threat of injury while carrying out the duties of the job. People who work in emergency service jobs, such as police, mine workers, firefighters, soldiers, and bomb disposal squad members, confront this type of stress. How well they cope with stress from their jobs is very closely related to one critical factor: whether or not they feel they are adequately trained to handle the emergencies that come their way. This is consistent with the cognitive view of stress, which sees stress resulting from situations where demands exceed capacity.

Shift work.   Shift work requires workers to change their schedules on a rotating basis. This can produce disturbances in normal patterns of sleep, neurophysiological rhythms, metabolic rate, and mental efficiency. All of these reactions are commonly encountered when the *circadian rhythm,* a type of internal body clock, is upset. Jet lag is one example of the kind of problem that can develop when this clock is upset.

A number of body processes seem to be related to the body clock. For example, secretions of the stress hormones adrenaline and noradrenaline are low in the morning but increase as the day progresses. Also, some people describe themselves as morning people. That is, they feel the most alert and work most efficiently in the morning. They more or less fizzle out by late afternoon. Other people are night owls. They never really seem to get going until midday and do not hit their full stride until even later. They may work late into the night but struggle to get out of bed in the morning.

One circadian rhythm is the 24-hour sleep–waking cycle with the norm of nighttime for sleep and daytime for work. Work and business often force people out of this cycle. An extreme example is the so-called graveyard shift. The body's clock can be upset, at least temporarily, when shifted to this work schedule. The physical and psychological effects referred to earlier may be triggered in this case. The person may feel out of sync mentally and physically. Irritability may increase, and social patterns in the family are often disrupted.

There is evidence that the 24-hour cycle may not be the best for everyone. In fact, some people would be better off on a 23-hour cycle, while others would work best on a 26-hour cycle. But time-based societies such as ours do not take circadian rhythms into account when work schedules are set. So it is the worker who suffers while adjusting the best way possible. There is evidence that people can adjust to shift work, but it is not easy. The fast adapters adjust in about one week, the slower ones in around three weeks. But some people feel they never really do adjust at all. If the swing-shift rotates on a monthly basis, the body may never make a complete adjustment before another change occurs.

Role Ambiguity: What Am I Doing Here?

Role ambiguity as a source of work stress is one of the more frequently cited problems, especially in very large and/or ill-structured organizations. The term *role* refers to the expectations placed on you by reason of your being in a certain position. Thus **role ambiguity** is quite simply what you experience when you do not know what is expected of you and what your job is supposed to accomplish. The *1977 Quality of Employment Survey*[16] showed 52% of the workers reported conflicting demands on them. Role conflict is central to the midcareer crisis. In a midcareer crisis, the employee feels stress from such conditions as overpromotion, underpromotion, lack of job security, and thwarted ambition.

The effects of role ambiguity include low performance and low job satisfaction, high anxiety, tension, and motivation to leave the company.[17] French and his colleagues showed that women tend to perceive more role ambiguity than men do. In the same sample, they also observed that women had higher levels of life stress than males did.[18] There are many reasons that may account for this finding, including social factors having to do with sex-role stereotypes and with dual-career families, which place more stress on the woman.

Interpersonal Stress: Does Anyone Care?

Personal relationships on the job are very important to job satisfaction. The broader the network of social support the better. The presence of social support from other workers, management, family, and friends tends to relieve strain. This is consistent with Cobb's findings (discussed in Chapter 6) that social support serves as a buffer against stress. Social support on the job appears to temper physiological stress reactions by reducing the amount of cortisone, lowering blood pressure, holding down the number of cigarettes smoked, and promoting complete cessation of smoking.

The *1977 Quality of Employment Survey* mentioned earlier revealed that 30% of the workers were unsure whether their supervisors were concerned about their welfare. This type of concern is often found to be related to the personal characteristics of leaders and to the way in which leader processes are structured in the organization. The style of management, what the manager believes about the employee, is also critical.

Career Development: Where Am I Going?

Job stress is affected significantly by the way in which the employee's career develops. According to one national study of work stress, people bring several specific hopes to a job. This includes the hope for rapid or at least steady advancement, hope for some freedom in the job, hope for increased earning power, the desire to learn new things and work at doing new jobs, and the desire to find solutions to certain work problems.[19]

When hopes are dashed and dreams only faintly remembered, the employee often loses the sense of accomplishment and self-esteem that is important to job satisfaction. In the process, little irritants which, when the dream was fresh, would have been brushed aside now irritate and build up inside. The psychological sore becomes a spreading infection rather than a minor scrape to be ignored. When the promotion does not come or when the job that looked so secure is threatened with elimination, the employee tends to respond to most facets of the job in ways that reveal building stress. The factors most related to stress in career development have been identified as underpromotion and overpromotion (also called the Peter principle), lack of job security, and frustrated ambitions. It has been noted that job insecurity, rather than increasing productivity as some managers believe, actually increases stress and generally lowers productivity.

Organizational Structure: What Are They Doing Up There?

The way in which a business is organized can also produce stress for employees. The most frequent complaints have to do with rigid structure, inter- or intraoffice political squabbles, lack of effective supervision from management, lack of involvement in decision making, and restrictions on employee behavior, including lack of support for individual initiative and creativity.

The Home–Work Connection: Sanctuaries and Spillover

The fact that work and home are related in ways that are mutually beneficial or mutually detrimental has already been noted. When things are going well on the job, pressure at home tends to be relieved and vice versa. Most people think of home as a sanctuary, a retreat that allows personal rebuilding and regrouping of inner strengths to meet outside demands. But when this sanctuary is disturbed, whether by upsets at work or by conflict at home, the effects of stress at work tend to be magnified.

Denise Rousseau has provided evidence that work and nonwork are related in a fashion that has been termed *spillover*.[20] The spillover model suggests that work experiences are positively related to nonwork experiences. That is, if a person has a job that tends to diminish self-esteem and produce low overall satisfaction, the person will have similar experiences in social life. Spillover has been observed in a number of occupations including logging, manufacturing, and professional work.

One example of stress that is due to the home–work connection is *dual-career stress*. Cary Cooper reported on statistics compiled by the U.S. Department of Labor showing that the "typical American family" with a working husband, a homemaker wife, and two children now makes up only 7% of the nation's families. Nearly 45% of all married women are now working outside the home. Even of those with children under the age of 6, 37% of the women are working. These figures show substantial increases from the 1960 figures, which were 31% and 19%, respectively.[21]

◆ ARE BOREDOM AND MONOTONY REALLY STRESSORS?

For some time now, the popular conception of job stress has included the idea that monotonous and repetitive jobs, such as those encountered in assembly line work and a number of other industrial jobs, are stressful. It has been noted in support of this notion that blue-collar workers tend to be high on job boredom while professionals tend to be low on boredom.[22] In most discussions of this issue, three terms seem to be used interchangeably: *boredom, monotony,* and *repetition*. It may be more accurate to say that repetitive and low-complexity jobs are perceived as monotonous and lead to a psychological state of boredom. In this way, the characteristics of the job are kept distinct from subjective feelings of the employee.

Boredom does seem to have some bad side effects. For example, monotonous jobs appear to be associated with low self-esteem, job dissatisfaction, and also low satisfaction with life in general.[23] However, whether a monotonous job leads to physiological arousal as predicted by stress theory seems to depend on other factors, such as the complexity and/or risks involved in the job itself. Boredom does not appear to be capable of producing stress itself.

Indeed, Richard Thackray directly disputed the idea that boredom is a stressor, basing his argument on his review of laboratory and field studies.[24] Thackray defined boredom and monotony in terms of job conditions that seldom change or are highly repetitive. Lack of change produces a desire for change or variety in the employee. But laboratory studies of repetitive work show lowered levels of physiological arousal rather than heightened arousal.

On the other side, a field study of highly mechanized logging work in Sweden showed that certain groups of employees were more vulnerable to disturbances such as sleep disorders, gastrointestinal disorders, headaches, and nervous tension. Following up on these observations, one research team from the University of Stockholm looked at differences in physiological and psychological measures between a high-risk group and a low-risk control group.[25] Higher levels of urinary adrenaline were observed in the high-risk group, which also reported stronger feelings of subjective tension and negative mood relative to the control group. Physical symptoms of illness were also higher in the high-risk group, but this difference was not statistically significant.

In looking at the jobs in the high-risk group, the research team noted several important characteristics that might account for the results. The high-risk workers were in positions requiring complex judgments and constant attention. Most importantly, they worked under a more or less forced work tempo. That is because the rate of their production was the bottleneck in the plant's flow of production. All employees worked on a piece-rate system. What these men produced determined what all the other men earned further down the line. The high-risk group thus had a great weight of responsibility. It made no difference how mechanized and repetitive the job was because they worked and lived with a psychosocial pressure that radically changed the meaning of the job from "monotonous" to the "livelihood" of their fellow workers.

◆ TECHNOSTRESS: THE CHANGING FACES OF JOBS

One of the major problems confronting workers in a modern technological society is job obsolescence. This requires many workers to find new work perhaps several times within the space of their short careers. It is now estimated that the average turnover for most jobs is approximately 10–15 years. That is, a job that existed at one point in time will be redefined in such a way as to require essentially different skills in roughly 10–15 years. Assuming an average career of 40–45 years, each worker may find it necessary to retrain in some fashion or find a new job three to four times during the course of the adult working life. Nowhere is this more evident than in those areas of the work environment subject to rapid technological changes.

Craig Brod defined **technostress** as "a condition resulting from the inability of an individual or organization to adapt to the introduction and operation of new technology."[26] Thus the term *technostress* refers to the strain felt by workers when either they are faced with the necessity of changing their own skills in order to keep up with the changing face of their jobs or their jobs are in jeopardy of being phased out because of new technology.

Gavriel Salvendy of the Human Factors Program at Purdue University wrote that approximately 10 million people are now working on computers in their jobs—where none existed just a few years ago.[27] Further, this number is likely to increase to nearly 25 million by 1990. By the year 2000, according to Salvendy's projections, jobs in computer-related fields will have expanded at a rate faster than that of any other job area, and blue-collar workers will account for only a fraction of the total work force.

Technostress is frequently compounded by employee's efforts to stay as comfortable as possible and resist any change that requires adaptive effort. They also tend to view the required new skills as a threat to their self-esteem instead of a positive road to personal growth and advancement. Employees will probably only come to grips with technostress when the potential benefits are communicated in a clear and convincing fashion and the threats of new technology defused.

Brod suggested that technostress can be managed through education, rehearsal, and self-assessments. The educational phase is aimed at understanding technostress and the human response to it. The rehearsal phase requires that the employee apply a variety of stress management techniques to technostress itself, such as cognitive reappraisal and stress inoculation. Self-assessments can be carried out to determine the extent to which negative thoughts and attitudes still stand in the way of acceptance of technology.

◆ JOB BURNOUT: THE END OF WORK STRESS

If the buzzword of the stress-prone personality is *Type A*, the buzzword of work stress is *job burnout*. A great deal has been written about burnout. *Job burnout is not a symptom of work stress, it is the end of unmanaged work stress.* One of the most detailed studies of job burnout was carried out by Robert Veninga and James Spradley. They defined burnout as "a debilitating psychological condition brought about by unrelieved work stress, which results in:

1. depleted energy reserves
2. lowered resistance to illness
3. increased dissatisfaction and pessimism
4. increased absenteeism and inefficiency at work"[28]

When the symptoms appear in more severe form, it is time to take more serious steps to intervene before stress becomes burnout.

According to the analysis of Veninga and Spradley, there are five stages leading to burnout. In the *honeymoon stage*, the new employee is motivated by youthful ideals, has loads of energy, and bubbles over with enthusiasm. Job satisfaction is evident and the person may be able to continue with energy and satisfaction if any early problems are dealt with in a constructive way. In the second *fuel shortage stage*, the actual signs of burnout begin to appear and intensify as time goes on. In the third *chronic stage*, the symptoms of exhaustion, illness, anger, and depression are evident on a continuous basis. When the *crisis stage* is reached, symptoms are so severe that the person feels as though life is falling apart or that he or she is barely hanging on by a thumbnail. In the final stage, *hitting the wall,* the person can no longer function and signs of deterioration are evident.[29]

There is a tendency to equate workaholism with job burnout. While the association is not perfect, there is some evidence that the more hours you work per week, the more likely you are to burn out. Many workaholics work up to 80 hours per week or more. Some people have physical systems that allow them to work longer and run on less sleep than others. But for most people, such long hours add a load to the physical system that sooner or later weighs them down with fatigue.

The hard-working, hard-driving person was once looked at as an almost superhuman individual. But that has changed. Businesses now consider the workaholic a high-risk liability rather than an asset. Workaholics may be driven by a fear of failure, which is a negative, stifling motivation rather than a positive and enhancing motivation. While they work hard, they are not necessarily productive and imaginative. In fact, workaholics may work long hours because they are unable to concentrate all their energies efficiently on one thing at a time and thus need more time to complete their work.

◆ WORK STRESS IN SPECIAL GROUPS

Certain groups of people and certain occupational groups are apparently subject to more stress than others. Time does not permit a lengthy discussion of all of the groups facing unusual levels of stress, but a few bear at least some comment.

Working Women and Job Stress

Women as a group still face a number of blatant discriminatory practices that add stress to their working conditions. On average, women are still locked into a variety of dead-end, lower-paying, and less respectable jobs than their male counterparts. In spite of federal and state legislation to protect women against such practices, evidence has revealed that the earning gap between women and men is actually widening rather than narrowing. For example, in 1965, white women earned about 60% of the salary of white men. In 1975, after 10 years of effort and legislative work, women's economic value had declined to 58% of what white males earn. Barbara Pletcher noted in 1978 that if a woman was making more than $15,000 a year she was earning more than about 99% of all working women.[30]

A study published by the Census Bureau in 1983 reported that a bachelor's degree was worth $329,000 to a male worker relative to his high-school educated counterpart. The same bachelor's degree will provide the woman with $142,000 advantage relative to her high-school educated counterpart. While the man would earn $1,190,000 in his lifetime, the woman would earn only $523,000.[31]

When women work, they often do so in the context of a dual-career home. Unless the home has been organized on an egalitarian basis, the woman often ends up working two jobs—one on the outside, the other as a housewife at home. Thus the woman must carry a double load of work in order to break into the work force. The factors supporting this type of discriminatory practice are largely rooted in the social and economic values of society. As a result, the position of women in the work force and the stress they must bear on a routine basis are not likely to change dramatically unless and until the social attitudes underlying the overt discriminatory behaviors toward women are changed.

Sexual Harassment: Women's Hazardous Duty

Perhaps the most oppressive form of stress for women comes through sexual harassment on the job. Whether the harassment is a part of some misguided male's games to prop up his own ego or a part of a power game designed to keep woman in her place, the effect on the woman is the same: exploitation and oppression in the work force combined with more personal conflict and higher levels of stress. Barbara Pletcher said that "sexual harassment is a weapon used against women in the pervasive power game. The intention . . . is to put you in your place. . . . Harassment is not flattering: it is an insult."[32]

More active efforts may be needed to weed out the sexual harasser from the workplace. Women have available a number of legal remedies, which are still somewhat difficult to implement. Nonetheless, filing a legal suit against a supervisor or colleague may be a necessary act of courage both to protect a highly valued professional career and to advance the position of women in general. Women should be aware of the agencies in their own organization and community that provide assistance in the event of discrimination in pay, position, and promotion. They should also be aware of agencies that can help in the event of sexual harassment on the job.

One of the strategies recommended by Barbara Pletcher is to keep a careful log of contacts, dates, times, incidents, words, and so forth.[33] This may include instances of sexual innuendo, sexual jokes of an offensive nature, and, of course, actual instances of pressure, coercion, or job blackmail. Periodically, the notes from this log should be put in an envelope and sent by registered mail to yourself or a trusted friend. The envelope should not be opened unless and until some legal action is taken. Such documents are generally admissible in court and can serve to prevent a defense attorney's attack on memory and fabrication, which may occur in the actual trial in the absence of such documents.

Finally, even though there is an argument for fighting the battle for equality from within the ranks of women, there may be times when the men are valuable and perhaps even necessary allies. First, more men are coming to recognize that men who engage in sexual harassment are an embarrassment to men. Many more men are now ready and willing to help in imposing sanctions or ridding the company of the offender. Second, the source of the problem is largely rooted in the psyche of men and the social conditions that support the macho mentality and dual standards of sexuality. Until men as a group refuse to reinforce and play a part in these games, most actions will be largely bandages applied after the hurts have already occurred.

Stress in Air Traffic Controllers

A great deal of attention has been focused on air traffic controllers (ATCs) following some celebrated air traffic accidents. In many of the more congested airports around the world, airplanes take off or land every 30–45 seconds. ATCs bear the burden of responsibility for the safety of thousands of people each day and for the protection of the airlines' multimillion dollar investments. Maintaining strained attention, as is necessary during long hours of peering into their radar monitors, puts extreme pressure on many ATCs. Early studies of ATCs showed the expected stress effects, including hypertension, peptic ulcers, diabetes, headaches, indigestion, chest pain, and burnout. One study revealed, however, that these effects do not occur outside of the most densely populated airports and further, that these physical symptoms do not occur until after three years of service.[34]

The results of many studies now show that this job must be considered on a site-by-site basis. Not all ATCs experience the pressures of an O'Hare or Kennedy airport. For example, in one study of ATCs in low-density airports, none of the stress effects found in earlier studies were found.[35] In one extensive review of research on ATCs, John Crump concluded that "the stress of ATC work is no greater than could be expected in 'normal' populations."[36] It is the workload that ultimately determines stress for ATCs, not the job itself. An interesting sidelight comes from a study of ATCs in Europe's largest airport—Frankfurt, West Germany. There, ATCs indicated that the major sources of dissatisfaction were the administration, pay, and working conditions, not the stress of managing the airplanes.[37]

◆ TELECOMMUTING OR THE ELECTRONIC SWEATSHOP?

One of the more interesting though controversial developments in the work place is a result of the personal computer revolution. In 1976, a University of Southern California futurist, Jack Nilles, coined the term *telecommuting* for the situation of people who work at home on jobs that in some fashion depend on computers, especially in the information industry, or who communicate the results of their work to their employers via computers.[38]

The first signs of the telecommuting work force appeared several years ago, but only in relatively large and specialized industries. IBM and a dozen other Fortune 500 companies sponsored a study of telecommuting. They found that about 100,000 people already are telecommuting at least part time. Further, even at the current level of computer technology, up to 7 million people could work under similar conditions.[39]

The expectation is that telecommuting will serve to reduce many of the pressures that people feel when working in a traditional work place. In contrast to the centralized shop where the means of production are supervised directly, telecommuting seems to offer solutions to a number of management–employee problems. In addition to decentralizing work and reducing energy waste from commuting to the job, telecommuting offers flex scheduling, sharing work between spouses or friends, individual control over the actual flow of production, released time for personal business, and elimination of many problems having to do with child care services required for centralized work. In addition, telecommuting obviously removes the worker from the arena of office politics and assembly line conflicts. There is also the economic argument of lower business overhead and higher productivity.

Some people feel, however, that these promises will ultimately lure workers into electronic sweatshops. The most vocal opposition to telecommuting has come from union leaders who see an erosion of their control and influence in the work force. They see telecommuting as a computer-age excuse for exploitation and suggest that the electronic cottage industry is the contemporary equivalent of the sweatshop of yesteryear. Nonetheless, telecommuting may become a means for workers to obtain a higher degree of personal participation in and individual structuring of the conditions of their own work. The positive effects of this type of situation for reducing stress should be examined carefully before being rejected out of hand.

◆ COPING WITH JOB STRESS AND BURNOUT

As noted above, dealing with job stress requires intervention at both organizational and personal levels. In the next few pages, the approaches that have been found to be helpful in dealing with job stress will be summarized. The actual techniques will be developed in later chapters.

Personal Strategies for Relieving Job Stress

Managing work stress may involve attempts to deal with perceptions and thought patterns, reduce levels of physical arousal, ventilate negative emotions, and engage in active problem solving to change negative aspects of the work environment related to organizational characteristics.

Cognitive techniques generally focus on perceptions and thoughts contributing to stress patterns. By focusing on what we believe about our bosses, work conditions, personal relationships, and personal involvement in the job, we may be able to see mental stumbling blocks or irrational thought patterns that need to be removed. Veninga and Spradley suggested that the employee faced with burnout must give up the myth that something outside is always responsible. While it may seem reasonable on the surface, blaming does nothing to correct the situation. In addition, this approach tends to abandon personal control instead of encouraging one to believe that personal actions can be effective in changing the conditions of stress.

Many techniques have been reported in the literature based both on experimental models of stress management in industry and on active employee assistance programs being run in major businesses. One such program used a combination of rational emotive and cognitive reappraisal techniques to deal with the thoughts and emotions associated with job stress.[40] It also used relaxation training to deal with job-related tension and excess physiological arousal. The study reported success in helping participants reduce physiological arousal as measured by epinephrine levels and in reducing feelings of depression. While the study was successful in a statistical sense, the authors were quick to point out that personal stress management programs may be little more than cover-ups for poor job conditions within the organization itself.

Physical exercise is too often overlooked as a coping tool for job stress. There are many reasons why physical exercise is a good coping technique above and beyond the fact that it helps to maintain good health. Physical exercise is an excellent change of pace from the job, especially for those workers who are in desk-bound jobs. It provides a release for emotional and mental tension. It allows you to ventilate negative feelings toward others or the workplace. In this way, physical exercise provides relief from frustration and allows displacement of anger or aggression, which might be self-destructive on the job.

Another effective technique for coping with job stress is to find some way of *changing gears* from work speed. This can be done by getting involved in some interesting hobby, being active in some creative pursuit such as painting or woodworking, or finding some other form of distraction. Both exercise and changing gears help to reduce physiological arousal from stress and to restore a natural body balance. Hobbies may be connected to your job if they are truly relaxing. But some hobby that keeps you active physically, mentally, and spiritually is important to maintaining a sense of perspective.

Jere Yates listed eight general rules for dealing with job stress.[41] These are paraphrased here; some extending comments will be provided later.

1. Maintain good physical health.
2. Accept yourself as you are with all your strengths, weaknesses, successes and failures.
3. Keep a confidante, a close personal friend to whom you can talk with complete candor.
4. Take positive, constructive action to deal with the sources of stress in your job.
5. Maintain a social life apart from the people with whom you work.

    6. Engage in creative activities outside the work place.

    7. Engage in meaningful work.

    8. Apply an analytic (scientific) method to personal stress problems.

Accepting yourself as you are may be one of the most important rules to keep for living in general. Self-acceptance helps to reduce the discrepancy between expectations and fulfillment, between reach and grasp. But self-acceptance must also be related to accurate self-appraisal or self-perception. This topic was discussed in Chapter 4.

In some cases, the problem of a mismatch between job requirements and job skills occurs because the employee did not properly evaluate his or her skills relative to the demands of the job. Too many promotion decisions are still based on subjective assessments of performance in a lower-level job that is not directly comparable to the higher-level job. Then, when the promotion occurs, the person is caught in a job that demands more than the employee can possibly give. The job that looked attractive in prospect may in fact threaten the employees future with the company.

This situation has been popularly described in *The Peter Principle,* which refers to the promotion of individuals to their highest level of incompetency.[42] When this occurs, the company and the employee are often viewed with derision and disdain. The more sympathetic may simply suggest that "poor Ed didn't know what he was getting himself into." But the fault is frequently laid at the door steps of the organization. What is often forgotten is that for every person the organization promoted to a level of incompetency, there was a person with an unrealistic perception of self who was willing to be promoted. If more attention were devoted to accurate self-appraisal in the early stages of career development, perhaps more people would be content to find their niche in business and occupy it with pride instead of pressing to get into positions that will ultimately tax their skills to the breaking point. Employee assistance programs should incorporate this element along with other skill-development services.

Having a friend to talk things over with is more than just a high-schooler's dream. Friends provide the closeness of lovers without the threat of rejection. Someone has said that lovers are easier to come by than friends, but friends last longer. In spite of the slightly cynical tone of that opinion, there is much truth in it. Perhaps the most important thing a friend provides is a source of support. "Talking it out" provides some useful psychological balms, including the chance to ventilate feelings of frustration and anger or the sense of futility and alienation. In addition to the catharsis afforded by talking to a friend, you may also gain insights into the situations and people that distress you. If you find it difficult to talk to someone, a useful area for change would be to work on openness.

In general, the more actively you work to manage stress, the more skill you develop and the greater sense of mastery you will have. On the other side, the more passive you are, the more likely you are to perpetuate a type of learned helplessness, the more frustration and anger are likely to build in the job, and the more likely you are to experience job dissatisfaction if not job burnout.

Too many times, people work all day with the same set of people they socialize with at night. This tends to transport problems from the job to the home. Relaxation is disturbed because reminders of work intrude. Social events are compromised because issues from work are brought up. When you are at work, the rule should be: Work! But when you are at play, the same rule should apply: Play!

If your job is not meaningful to you, you will find it difficult to maintain interest, enthusiasm, and energy in the discharge of your duties. If you feel extraordinary fatigue and can find no physical reason and no specific sources of stress on the job, look carefully at your most private thoughts about your job. If you have been harboring negative thoughts about your job, you need to get them out in the open. You may be able to construct a positive plan to deal with the problem of a less-meaningful job, but not if you keep the ideas bottled up inside. Evaluate your priorities for the job as well. If you find yourself tempted by a job that has more money and more prestige associated with it, ask yourself what the job means beyond these things before committing to the position. If the job is basically devoid of real meaning relative to your values, you would be better off turning the job down. While intrinsic motivation may not put meat on the table, it is essential to a sense of psychological satisfaction.

Using the scientific or analytic approach to dealing with personal stress means forming hypotheses about what may be the source of the problem. Collect as much data as possible from relevant sources, including your friends and colleagues. Then evaluate the hypotheses in light of the data. The information may be used to intervene or plan some constructive course of action to prevent the problem from recurring. In this sense, the scientific method is not used for theory building, but for application to the real world.

Perhaps the most important point is to work on developing ways of becoming more aware of the stressors that are unique to your position. Use an inventory, a diary, or some other type of daily log. Use a resource person who has objectivity. Also, cultivate the art of listening to your body. Your body is probably the most important watchdog you have. It can sound the alarm in the early stages and thus enable you to prevent the appearance of stress, but only if you are prepared to listen. One way or the other, try to study what is happening on the job so that you can set about changing it.

Coping by Taking Legal Action

Employees should be aware of the legal remedies at their disposal. These remedies may be used to redress personal grievances or bring about wholesale organizational reform when the condition affects a large group of the employees. For example, employees have the right to file a complaint with OSHA about unsafe and hazardous work conditions. Federal agencies are required to conduct inspections and evaluations of site conditions and may levy fines or recommend other sanctions against companies that do not correct the conditions.

Organizational Strategies for Relieving Job Stress

As noted several times in this chapter, participation in the design of the work environment and in setting of job conditions goes a long way to addressing many of the problems and dissatisfactions which employees confront. For example, Veninga and Spradley reported on a group of keypunchers who redesigned their jobs. Absenteeism dropped by 24%. Mistakes on the job dropped 35%. Productivity went up 40%. Supervisory positions were eliminated, which brought total savings for the company to $64,305 per year.[43] If employee participation is absent or weak, efforts to gain such may be very helpful.

Employee Assistance Programs

Perhaps the most positive sign of organizations taking an active role in dealing with employee stress is the formation of employee assistance programs. In the 1970s, fewer than 300 firms offered such programs. Today, over 2,400 firms offer employee assistance programs—including some of the most prestigious Fortune 500 companies.

An employee assistance program offers a variety of services to deal with many different facets of worker adjustments to the conditions of work. Most of these programs extend to areas beyond the job and include assistance for problems that may have developed outside the job but are affecting the worker's performance on the job. The services include personal counseling, classes on stress management and coping, job retraining, and career counseling among others. Some programs may include a fully professional staff retained by the company solely to work with employees. Beyond this, corporations are developing a broad range of services to help employees keep the enthusiasm and freshness of a new employee. Child care programs, complete health gyms, and exercise and nutrition programs are becoming more common. These programs address some important needs but do not always directly deal with the issue of reform of the organization itself.

◆ SUMMARY

In this chapter, an overview of job stress and burnout has been presented. We have seen that job stress costs employers and employees many millions of dollars each year. The symptoms of job stress include a wide range of physical, psychological, and behavioral disturbances. Sources of stress include physical conditions of the job, role ambiguity, interpersonal relationships on the job, career development, organizational structure, and the home–work connection. Certain occupational groups, such as women and emergency service providers, are more subject to stress because of outright discrimination or the dangerous nature of their jobs.

With early recognition of the onset of stress, effective interventions including cognitive appraisal, relaxation training, and physical exercise may be applied to reduce if not eliminate the effects of stress. Personal coping skills must be combined with corporate interventions to bring about the long-term elimination of work stress.

◆ NOTES

[1]Diamond, S. 1985, May 19. Warren Anderson: A public crisis, a personal ordeal. *The New York Times,* Section 3, pp. 1F, 8F.

[2]Rousseau, D. M. (1978). Relationship of work to nonwork. *Journal of Applied Psychology, 63,* 513–517, p. 517.

[3]Caplan, R. D., Cobb, S., French, J. R. P., Jr., Van Harrison, R., & Pinneau, S. R. (1975). *Job demands and worker health: Main effects and occupational differences.* Washington, DC: U.S. Government Printing Office, p. 3.

[4]Beehr, T. A., & Newman, J. E. (1978). Job stress, employee health, and organizational effectiveness: A facet analysis, model, and literature review. *Personnel Psychology, 31,* 665–699.

[5]Institute of Medicine (United States). (1979). *Healthy people: The Surgeon General's report on health promotion and disease prevention: Background papers* (Government Document No. HE20.2:H34/5). Rockville, MD: U.S. Government Printing Office, p. 389.

[6]Veninga, R. L., & Spradley, J. P. (1981). *The work stress connection.* Boston: Little, Brown, p. 10.

[7]As cited by Everly, G. S., Jr., & Girdano, D. A. (1980). *The stress mess solution.* Bowie, MD: Brady, p. 4.

[8]Adams, J. D. (1981). Health, stress, and the manager's life style. *Group and Organization Studies, 6,* 291–301.

[9]Beehr & Newman, Job stress.

[10]Pelletier, K. R. (1984). *Healthy people in unhealthy places.* New York: Delacorte Press, p. 90.

[11]Institute of Medicine, *Healthy people: Background papers,* p. 393.

[12]Schuler, R. S. (1980). Definition and conceptualization of stress in organizations. *Organizational Behavior and Human Performance, 25,* 184–215.

[13]Cooper, C. L. (1983). Identifying stressors at work: Recent research developments. *Journal of Psychosomatic Research, 27,* 369–376.

[14]Everly & Girdano, *Stress mess,* p. 34.

[15]Everly & Girdano, *Stress mess,* p. 40.

[16]Quinn, R. P., & Staines, G. L. (1979). *The 1977 quality of employment survey.* Ann Arbor: Survey Research Center, University of Michigan, pp. 218–219.

[17]Moch, M. K., Bartunek, J., & Brass, D. J. (1979). Structure, task characteristics, and experienced role stress in organizations employing complex technology. *Organizational Behavior and Human Performance, 24,* 258–268.

[18]French, J. R. P., Caplan, R. D., & Van Harrison, R. (1982). *The mechanisms of job stress and strain.* New York: Wiley, p. 111.

[19]Veninga & Spradley, *Work stress connection,* p. 204.

[20]Rousseau, Relationship of work, p. 517.

[21]Cooper, Identifying stressors, p. 374.

[22]French et al., *Mechanisms of job stress,* p. 102.

[23]Johansson, G., Aronsson, G., & Lindstrom, B. O. (1976). *Social psychological and neuroendocrine stress reactions in highly mechanized work.* Report No. 488 of the Department of Psychology, University of Stockholm. This research team provides a brief review of some of the studies supporting the idea of boredom and stress and produced evidence of their own on the issue.

[24]Thackray, R. I. (1981). The stress of boredom and monotony: A consideration of the evidence. *Psychosomatic Medicine, 43,* 165–176.

[25]Johansson et al, *Social psychological.*

[26]Brod, C. (1982). Managing technostress: Optimizing the use of computer technology. *Personnel Journal, 61,* 753–757.

[27]Salvendy, G. (1982). Human-computer communications with special reference to technological developments, occupational stress and educational needs. *Ergonomics, 25,* 435–447.

[28]Veninga, R. L., & Spradley, J. P. (1981). *The work stress connection.* Boston: Little, Brown, pp. 6–7.

[29]Veninga & Spradley, *Work stress connection,* pp. 56ff.

[30]Pletcher, B. A. (1978). *Saleswoman: A guide to career success.* Homewood, IL: Dow Jones–Irwin.

[31]U.S. Bureau of the Census. (1983). *Lifetime earnings estimates for men and women in the United States: 1979* (Current Population Reports, Series P-60, No. 139). Washington, DC: U.S. Government Printing Office, pp. 2–3.

[32]Pletcher, *Saleswoman,* p. 93.

[33]Pletcher, *Saleswoman,* p. 95.

[34]Crump, J. H. (1979). Review of stress in air traffic control: Its measurement and effects. *Aviation, Space, and Environmental Medicine, 50,* 243–248.

[35]Federal Aviation Administration, U.S. Department of Transportation. 1977, September. *Stress in air traffic personnel: Low-density towers and flight service stations* (FAA-AM-77-23, Microfiche TD 4.210:77-23). Washington, DC: U.S. Government Printing Office.

[36]Crump, Review of stress, p. 244.

[37]Singer, R., & Rutenfranz, J. (1971). Attitudes of air traffic controllers at Frankfurt airport towards work and the working environment. *Ergonomics, 14,* 633–639.

[38]Nilles, J. M., Carlson, F. R., Jr., Gray, P., & Honneman, G. J. (1976). *The telecommunications–transportation tradeoff.* New York: Wiley, p. 4.

[39]Porter, M. (1985). Home work increasing despite union opposition. *PC Magazine, 4*, 42.

[40]Ganster, D. C., Mayes, B. T., Sime, W. E., & Tharp, G. D. (1982). Managing organizational stress: a field experiment. *Journal of Applied Psychology, 67*, 533–542.

[41]Yates, J. (1979). *Managing stress: A businessperson's guide*. New York: AMACOM: Division of American Management Association, pp. 99–102.

[42]Peter, L. J. (1969). *The Peter principle*. New York: Morrow.

[43]Veninga & Spradley, *Work stress connection*, p. 175.

Part 5

RELAXATION, DESENSITIZATION, AND STRESS INOCULATION

11

PROGRESSIVE MUSCLE RELAXATION: PROMISES, PREMISES, AND PREPARATION

> *Abandoning attachments to the fruits of action,*
> *Constantly content, independent,*
> *Even when he sets out upon action,*
> *He yet does (in effect) nothing whatsoever.*
>
> *The Bhagavad Gita*

The preceding chapters provided many of the basic principles and theories of stress and health. This information should enable you to identify the sources of stress in family, social, and work environments. You should also be better able to identify the attitudes, beliefs, behavioral patterns, and high-risk behaviors that can add stress to each person's load. And you should now understand how these sources of stress are translated into real physical effects that can damage the body.

These concepts form the foundation of any informed and focused stress-management program, whether that program is professionally built and monitored or personally constructed and managed. They also provide a sound support base for implementing a personal health program. In this chapter, we begin the actual task of learning stress-management skills that can be used in your personal and professional life.

◆ RELAXATION: A FAMILY OF TECHNIQUES

The next six chapters cover techniques that will either enable you to deal with stress or help you in designing your personal health programs. If it helps to attach a label, the first cluster of techniques will deal with skills most often referred to as *stress-management skills*. The other cluster of skills will deal with *personal health programming skills*.

This section deals primarily with the relaxation technique called *progressive muscle relaxation*. There are a number of techniques that build on this skill, including cue-controlled relaxation, differential relaxation, and desensitization. Relaxation is very useful in dealing with a variety of tensions, and it is one of the most widely used and generally applicable stress-management techniques.

In addition to relaxation, a variety of procedures including autogenics, stress inoculation, meditation, and biofeedback will be covered in Chapters 13 and 14. Chapter 15 will describe time-management techniques and Chapter 16 will discuss nutrition, diet, and exercise. Chapter 16 also includes principles of behavior analysis that should enable you to design self-management programs for other areas of concern. The intent is that you become able to deal with high-risk behaviors you want to eliminate—whether smoking, drug abuse, lack of proper physical exercise, overeating, or lack of sleep.

These techniques were chosen to provide comprehensive coverage without being exhaustive of all the techniques. This means that some popular but esoteric practices (such as hypnosis) are not covered.

◆ PROGRESSIVE MUSCLE RELAXATION: THE PROMISE

Few techniques have proven as powerful and generally applicable as the relaxation technique. It has withstood the test of time as well as very stiff competition from the new kid on the block—*biofeedback*. The advantages of the relaxation technique are many. Relaxation can be used in the privacy of one's home or exported to the office. It can infiltrate the boardroom or the courtroom. You can take it on the road during rush-hour traffic or settle jittery nerves at 30,000 feet. Without fanfare and public recognition, it has appeared at Wimbledon restoring smoothness to tense muscles and accuracy to a champion's service. It also got a novice skier down a terrifying ski slope in Utah. Relaxation procedures have been used successfully to treat migrain, hypertension, insomnia, tension headaches, test anxiety, performance anxiety, flight phobias, and Raynaud's disease.[1] Indeed, it sometimes seems there is no end to the applications for deep muscle relaxation.

Relaxation training has been marketed in a variety of ways and under a number of different names. The particular technique described here is called progressive muscle relaxation (PMR), progressive relaxation, or deep muscular relaxation. It has grown steadily in popularity since its founder, Edmund Jacobson, first wrote about it in 1938.[2] Its use is now supported by a wealth of clinical studies and research data.

Because of the care Jacobson took in developing progressive relaxation and because of the extensive use by many clinicians who have added to and refined the practice, it is now possible to provide fairly clear, step-by-step instructions on how it is practiced and how it may be applied. Thus, conveying the skill does not require a face-to-face encounter or high-cost therapy. This means that many people who could not afford a private therapist nonetheless have access to both the rationale and the technique. And, given the proper adherence to procedure and appropriate practice, most can begin to practice the skill in a relatively short time.

Several variants of the relaxation procedure have become popular among different groups and have been suggested for use in stress management. These include the relaxation response, transcendental meditation, autogenic training, and hypnosis. The relaxation response (not to be confused with PMR) was developed by Herbert Benson and is based on his research on Transcendental Meditation, a Westernized version of the ancient and venerable system of Mantra Yoga.[3] Benson's procedure will be described in Chapter 14.

Autogenic training was developed by Johannes Schultz in Germany during the early 1950s. It is more imagery-based than deep muscular relaxation. Autogenics is currently the most popular relaxation procedure in Europe even as progressive relaxation seems to be the most popular in the United States. Instructions for developing skill in autogenics will be given later. Hypnosis can only be loosely regarded as a relaxation technique, but it has been used in this sense by a number of clinicians.

These variants of progressive relaxation have been noted to make one very important point: *The particular form of the skill you develop is practically unimportant.* While it may seem odd for an author to make such a statement, there is a very good reason for it. That is, research has demonstrated that no one of the particular techniques has any special advantage over any of the others. They will all do very much the same thing for you in enabling you to cope with stress. The only important issue is that you develop one skill of this type to some degree of practical proficiency.

Also, note that any given coping technique may work well for one person but be of little value to another. Do not be unduly alarmed, therefore, or consider yourself a failure if you find that one of the procedures described here does not seem to suit you.

If you are already highly accomplished in meditation, self-hypnosis, or autogenic training, you may be better off continuing with that skill and looking primarily for applications in this material. You may benefit greatly from the practice of relaxation by developing the skill of tuning in to your body signals of stress. This is most important in being able to deal with tensions effectively.

◆ FROM PROMISE TO PREMISE

Relaxation training is based on a very simple premise: You cannot be both relaxed and tense at the same time. In spite of the apparent simplicity of this statement, there is much more to it than that. Tension and relaxation are two body states that correspond to two very important parts of our nervous system, the sympathetic and the parasympathetic. The operation of these two components of the autonomic nervous system was described in Chapter 3. Only the essential elements that pertain to the relaxation technique will be reviewed here.

Recall that when we are in a charged-up state, as when threatened, afraid, angry, or excited, the sympathetic nervous system is in control. It is called the *fight-or-flight* system or the emergency system. Blood is pulled out of the center digestive tract and delivered to important muscle groups, such as the arms and legs. Heart rate speeds up and blood pressure usually goes up as well. Breathing rate increases and sweating may occur in conjunction with the increased rate with which energy is being expended. During a charged-up state, the body burns energy at a tremendous rate. Sympathetic arousal is thus recognized as the tearing down process of the body.

In this state of sympathetic arousal, *muscle tension increases dramatically.* But do not think of this in all-or-none terms. Depending on the type of stress, only certain muscle groups may tense. Which group tenses usually depends upon factors unique to your body and its way of dealing with stress. In other words, every person expresses stress to some extent in an individual way with tension in muscles that go unaffected in someone else. Some have the tension in the back, some in the forehead, some in the neck, and so forth. Depending on the degree of stress, muscle tension varies on a continuum from very slight to extreme tension. To repeat, stress tends to drive the sympathetic nervous system into operation and with it comes some muscle tension.

Conversely, when we are in a quiet, contemplative mood, happy and contented, or asleep, the parasympathetic system is in control. Blood is delivered to the center of the body for the important processes of digestion and energy storage. Muscle tension decreases and a general feeling of muscular heaviness or relaxation is generally reported. It is the building up, the repairing or constructive process of the body. Heart rate slows, blood pressure normally goes down, and breathing is slow and easy.

Notice that the processes talked about in relationship to the parasympathetic nervous system are generally opposite of those talked about in relationship to the sympathetic nervous system. In technical terms, these two systems are said to be reciprocally inhibitory. That is, they inhibit each other on an alternating basis. In less technical terms, it means that when one system is talking, the other system must be quiet. When one is dominant, the other must be subordinate. Both systems cannot be highly actively at the same time. Stated in behavioral terms again, you cannot be both tense and relaxed at the same time.

This relationship seems intuitively obvious, even simple. Jacobson recognized this but took it a step further. His progressive relaxation program was built on the premise that a person can directly control the balance in the autonomic nervous system. But this placed him in conflict with established scientific theory, which regarded the autonomic nervous systems as the *involuntary* system. Presumably, we have no control over what happens in that system. On the surface of it, the logic seems acceptable. This is the system that has to do with virtually all of the life-support systems of the body. Control in this system was assumed to be involuntary because all the processes continue whether we are asleep or awake.

However, a long history of observations and research began to expose the fallacy of the label. For example, we have known for a long while that the Yogis of India are able to produce rather startling changes in their body processes—being buried alive for days and surviving through heart and respiratory control, regulating temperature to be able to withstand freezing temperatures with scant clothing, altering brain waves while inducing trancelike states. Joint American and Indian research teams studied these remarkable men and came to the conclusion that the Yogis' ability to control these so-called involuntary responses was legitimate.[4]

The dilemma was clear: What should be done with the theory of the involuntary nervous system? True to the scientific spirit, more laboratory-based research confirmed that indeed these responses are susceptible to voluntary control, and therefore the theory has been revised.[5] It was Jacobson who put two and two together in the relaxation-training program. Very simply stated, *relaxation is a voluntary behavioral method of controlling the alternating relationship between the excited and calm sides of your autonomic nervous system.* If you are tense, you can get the parasympathetic nervous system back in control by inducing relaxation. It is as though you have behavioral control over the switch that turns off the charged-up state and turns on the toned-down state. Think of it like this: When the sympathetic system is talking too loud—your stomach is tied in knots, your muscles are tense, or a headache is pounding so loud you think your head is a drum—you can tell it to quiet down behaviorally. You can turn on the parasympathetic system instead and let it talk to you with its own messages of calmness.

◆ FROM PREMISE TO PREPARATION

There are four very important items that must be attended to before you begin to practice deep muscular relaxation. These are *setting, mood, preparation,* and *medical precautions.* In effect, what follows are the dos and don'ts for your practice of relaxation.

Setting

Where you practice relaxation can be very important for success and persistence. First, you should *select a room in your home that is comfortable and quiet and can be shut off from the rest of the family for a short period.* The room should be properly ventilated in the summer so it is not stuffy and properly heated in the winter so it is not too cool.

Even if you are used to living in a house with a lower-than-average thermostat setting, you should not try to shiver through your relaxation sessions in a cold room. The primary problem is that being cold will generally increase the likelihood of muscular tension associated with distribution of blood to the periphery of the body. You not only are trying to get rid of muscular tension that is due to stress, but also muscular tension that is due to coldness. Later on, after you have developed the technique, you may be able to use it virtually anywhere, even under downright abominable conditions. But it is better to start off as far ahead as possible.

Use a comfortable chair that provides as much support for the entire body as possible. A recliner is ideal for most people, but you should not use the recliner as though it were a bed. Your body should be supported in a semireclined position, not a fully reclined position. In fact, some clinicians insist on a hard and straight-backed chair for initial training. The reason for this is that *you should practice relaxation for the first few weeks with an optimal level of self-awareness and observation.* It is crucial to your later extended use of the technique that you come to recognize the difference between tension and relaxation in your muscle systems. That level of self-awareness cannot come if you are nearly asleep. The tendency when fully reclining is to become groggy and possibly even to fall off to sleep. It may seem desirable for this to occur, especially if you are suffering from insomnia. Indeed, the relaxation technique is frequently used for the treatment of sleep disturbances. But for now, resist the temptation. Select a chair for support, not for sleep.

Also, the room should be quiet and as free from distractions as possible. The most frequent sources of interruptions are the phone and members of your family. If you have a phone in the room, disconnect it if at all possible. If that is not possible, ask some member of the family to answer the phone for you immediately, and muffle the phone in your room with a pillow or turn off the ringer. If no one else is home, you can simply take the phone off the hook.

If you struggle with the idea of missing calls, examine what is going on in your own mental life that makes being there for all calls so important. Permit me a brief anecdote. While on a social visit to a friend's home one evening, I watched as one, then two phone calls came and went without the host or hostess so much as stirring a finger to answer. I and a few of the other guests were becoming uneasy because this is indeed not customary behavior. Perhaps we are slaves to the phone more than we are willing to admit. After a few minutes, I asked my friend about his apparent lack of concern for the phone calls. His response was simple and direct: "We don't answer the phone unless we choose to. This is our night off with our friends. If the call is important they will get back to us later." In the same way, you can try not to worry if one or two callers tried to get you during your half hour for yourself. You have a right to privacy and a right to have time for yourself. You can choose not to have that privacy invaded and to simplify your life in the process.

The same things cannot be said so easily in regard to family. Probably the best solution is to appeal to their understanding by explaining what it is you are about and why it is important to you. Enlisting family support can be very helpful in keeping many other chance interruptions from occurring as well. This may work well in the case of older children, but not as well where younger children are involved. Perhaps a simple matter of timing will suffice. Try to practice during their naps or after they have gone to bed in the evening.

A relatively important condition for success, at least early in your practice, is consistency. *Practice your relaxation exercises twice daily at roughly the same time each day for the first three to four weeks.* This will increase the likelihood of success and speed your development of the skill. The rule is not meant to be applied compulsively, but within some limits. Once per day may be adequate, especially if you have had some training before. But twice daily is preferable. Some books recommend even more daily practice, up to four times per day. Experience suggests that such a recommendation is not likely to be followed because of its sheer impracticality; also, no evidence suggests that you will get substantially further faster by the use of three or four practice sessions per day. For some people, the morning and the evening work best. For others, a noon period and a late evening are preferred. It is not so important *what* the particular schedule is, only *that* you have a schedule. But once you have hit on a convenient arrangement, try to maintain as much consistency as possible, at least through the early stages of training.

Finally, *use background music for your practice if you wish.* It can foster a sense of tranquility and facilitate relaxation, but only if the right type of music is chosen. Quiet classical or easy listening music is probably preferable. One very nice type of composition is "nature" music that uses sounds of the wind and the seashore, including calls of whales and porpoises. The music is among the most relaxing available and is similar to that used in clinics. Whatever you choose, play it at a low level so you will not be attending to the music more than to the relaxation exercise itself.

Mood

Approaching your daily sessions in the right frame of mind is extremely important to both objective success and the subjective sense of satisfaction you have with the technique. Here are some of the most important rules that should guide your approach to relaxation training.

Cultivate a sense of passive attention. In order to learn relaxation well, you must have a balance between attention and quiescence. The key to doing relaxation in the privacy of your home as well as to applying the skill successfully to your real world is to be able to read tension in your muscles. Muscular tension is the *red-light warning system* of your body telling you that you are under stress. Especially in the early stages of practice, the sequence of instructions is geared precisely to serve this educational function. Being able to *read* tension both as it clamors and as it whispers requires attention but of a passive variety. It cannot be a strained attention, or everything else in your life becomes secondary. Also, if it is strained, you will probably be putting more tension into the system than you are removing.

The attending you need to develop should be like listening with an inner or third ear, something that just goes on with no conscious thought. It should become second nature to you so that after you have practiced for a while, you do not even think about attending. Yet the slightest knotting of the stomach, cramping of the neck, or labored breathing is immediately recognized.

Do not try to make relaxation happen.   This is not a task like learning to type, in which you must strain and practice to get over hurdles until you master the task. It is not a technique you can force or beat into submission. Rather, it is a technique that comes upon you quietly and gently. Just let it happen and enjoy.

Do not rush.   Relaxation is not like calisthenics, to be run through at a frenzied pace with much energy expended. It is more like prayer and meditation, or lying on a beach soaking up rays, or peacefully reclining in a boat listening to the lapping of gentle waves. At these moments, time is the least important condition of existence. Time can even stand still. And when time is up, you may wish that the experience could go on forever and regret that tranquility must be abandoned for the clamor of the real world. Getting through relaxation exercises is not what is important. Experiencing the moment and enjoying it is.

Do not use any drugs.   While drugs may help you relax, drugs will interfere with the primary goal of relaxation training: learning to recognize muscular tension that is signaling stress. Mere relaxation is not enough. You want ultimately to be able to deal with stress in your life. For that you need to know when stress is occurring so you can do something about it. Using drugs will not help you in that regard. In general, relaxing or tranquilizing drugs serve more as depressants of normal brain function. The normal connections made by the brain between some signal and its meaning will be clouded; some signals may even get totally lost in the maze of signals that are solely drug-dependent. Thus is may be more difficult to recognize the *real signals* of body tension as opposed to the *noise* generated by the drugs. The end result is that developing a sensitivity to body signals will be made harder, not easier.

Train first; apply later.   One of the biggest mistakes people make in developing any technique of this nature is trying to use it for the big jobs too quickly. If, for whatever reason, you take on an extreme stress problem right away and it doesn't work, the natural tendency is to blame the failure on the technique itself. The technique may be abandoned, and you may feel not only frustrated, but even more helpless and hopeless than before.

If you already find yourself wanting to tackle the central issues in your stress life, resist! Get the technique and its extensions firmly in hand before moving on. It is much better to work from a strong base of graduated successes than to fight against the negative influence of premature failure.

The sequence of exercises presented next is calculated to help you work up to the big issues. By the time you get there, you should not only have developed the skill to the required level, but you should also know that you are ready to take on the major stress problems. In addition, you should know by that time how to analyze the critical components of the stress situation and which variant of the relaxation technique is best suited to the problem.

Do not be afraid of different feelings.   Engaging in the practice of relaxation can produce some feelings or sensations you might not have experienced before. For example, the experience of very deep relaxation can produce a feeling of loss of control for some people. This feeling is interpreted in a fashion that induces stronger feelings of fear. In fact, it is the thought of losing control that is so frightening to these people. We do not know how to explain *why* people feel this way, only *that* some do. The feeling generally passes rather quickly, however, once the benefits of the technique are realized. Relaxation may not be the method of choice where a past history of extreme anxiety reactions is present.[6]

Another feeling some clients report is that of not being able to come back. The sensation of deep relaxation is interpreted almost as a hypnotic trance with no one around to bring the person back out of the trance. In reality, coming back out of a relaxation state is no more dangerous and no more aversive than waking up from a nice nap. In many ways, the heavy feeling of the body and the pleasant tranquil state of the mind are very similar to what people report feeling when just passing into a nap state. So even though the sensations you feel are different from body sensations you have had before, do not fear. You may soon come to welcome and enjoy these sensations.

Preparation

At least for the first few weeks, go over the mechanics of what you are to do just before each relaxation session. Review the instructions for the proper sequence of relaxing muscle groups and make the final arrangements you prefer in regard to phone, music, lighting, and so on. If you are using taped relaxation instructions make sure the recorder is adjusted for proper volume (a little on the soft side is preferable) and set at the right place to begin. Attention to these little details can make for a much smoother and easier relaxation period. Obviously, as you progress in your practice, more and more of these details will become second nature to you. Then relaxation will have become a useful tool requiring little effort for its use.

Medical Precautions

Persons with certain physical conditions should be cautious about the practice of relaxation. If you have had any severe back injuries, recent muscle strains, or broken bones you should *determine from your physician that it is permissible to engage in an exercise that will place a moderate strain on bones and muscles.* In the case of strains or broken bones, it may simply be a matter of waiting a proper length of time for complete healing before commencing your practice. In the case of severe back injuries, alternate procedures for stress control may need to be considered. For example, the autogenic exercises provided in Chapter 13 may be suitable.

Another option is to develop Benson's relaxation response using instructions provided in Chapter 14 or his own instruction.[7] Benson derived his technique from the practice of meditation. It is thus more passive and intuitive, and it eliminates the muscle tension practice used in PMR. For the medical conditions of concern, there is no other work more highly recommended. But its primary strength is also its limitation. Benson's book is solely devoted to the practice of relaxation. It does not provide exercises and extending guides for use in stress management. Also, it does not delve into basic issues of how to spot stress and how to deal with personal health issues.

Persons with a history of heart difficulty should also seek the advice of their attending physician before commencing the practice of relaxation. The most acute problem normally occurs where there is a history of heart difficulty that is currently overlaid with a severe cold, especially a cold coupled with chest congestion. In this case, the deep breathing exercises could be painful and produce anxiety, which itself could aggravate a heart condition.

Finally, many people have asked about beginning relaxation training when they are physically run down. Usually, this question comes from people who have just had a severe bout with the flu or a bad cold. Most are either still on or have been taking some form of medication for relief. If you are in this situation, wait a short while, especially if you are still taking medication, until most of the residual effects of the illness are past. Waiting another week or two will probably put you in better shape for getting off on the right foot and help ensure quicker success when you do start.

◆ GETTING STARTED WITH RELAXATION

The following instructions are for the first few relaxation sessions. Subsequently, the instructions are abbreviated and shortcuts taken to produce relaxation faster. These techniques will be discussed in the next chapter. To begin, *read through the instructions entirely once before trying to actually relax*. The instructions for self-direction are written in indented blocks. Some comments are interspersed that will enable you to understand why you are being asked to do certain things.

During the first reading, you may try some of the tension–relaxation cycles just to get a feel for what it is like. But do not count your first run through as a relaxation session! After reading through once, get in your chair, turn the lights down low, put on your background music—whatever you have decided on for your setting and preparation—and actually go through the procedure to relax. You will soon find that there is a logic to the progression, which will come in handy for further sessions. Further instructions for timing and other matters will be provided as needed.

You may want to record the instructions on tape in your own voice. This will allow you to concentrate on relaxing instead of worrying about what the next instruction is. Should you decide to do this, just read the instructions given and elaborate or extend where necessary as you are putting it on tape. You may paraphrase the instructions to some extent. Pronouns can be changed and sequences extended for the number of repetitions required. As long as the sense is the same, the words used do not make a difference. (More will be said about ways to handle the instructions at the end of the chapter.)

◆ INSTRUCTIONS FOR RELAXATION

What you are going to do for the next few minutes is study the difference between tension and relaxation in a number of your muscles. In the process you should begin to feel more and more relaxed. At the end, you should experience a comfortable heaviness in your body and have a feeling of easy peacefulness.

Remove any tight-fitting clothes first. Loosen ties, belts or any other articles of clothing that are tight. Take off your shoes. Also remove any tight-fitting jewelry such as watches, rings, or necklaces. Get comfortably situated in your chair. Put your arms on the arms of the chair with your palms down and hands open over the end of the chair's arms. Sit back in the chair and let your head fall gently onto your chest. Close your eyes. Let your legs lie comfortably apart on a stool or the leg support of your recliner. Do not cross your legs regardless of the type of chair you are using. If your chair is not a recliner and you do not have a footstool available, place your feet a few inches apart on the floor and let your arms lie across your thighs with your hands in your lap. (For self-guided or self-taped instructions, begin here. Use only those sections that are indented and elaborate or extend them as necessary.)

> Now, take a few deep breaths, hold each breath for a few seconds, and then let each breath out fully and completely. As you breathe in, you will notice some tension in your chest and diaphragm. As you breathe out, you will notice a sense of relaxing, almost of going limp. Relaxing feels good and comfortable and it would be nice if the feeling could be kept. But as you breathe in deeply again you feel the same tension as before, especially as you hold it for a moment. Let the breath out again, completely, and feel the pleasant relaxing sensation of letting go. Try it one more time. Dwell for just a moment on the sense of relaxation as you let the breath out.

> Try to maintain that sense of relaxation in your chest and diaphragm for a moment. As you breathe from now on, just breathe easily and naturally, almost as though you were napping.

> Concentrate for a moment on your right arm (left arm if you are left-handed). Now flex your biceps as though you were showing off your muscles. Notice how it feels.

It may be easiest to do this by just pushing your elbow into the arm of the chair. Also, by doing it this way, you do not actually have to raise your arm from the chair.

> Flex it as tight as you can and hold it (about 10 seconds). As you hold, study the sensation of tension. Notice how unpleasant it can be. Now let it go all at once. Let your arm go completely limp. Relax! And study the contrast. Notice how different it is from tension. Store the contrast in your mind even as you are studying it. One more time. Tense your bicep and hold it. Observe the feeling of tightness. Tune in to the signal of tension in your muscle. Then let it go. Completely relaxed. If someone picked your arm up and turned it loose, it would simply drop to your side. There is no tension at all. It feels so good. One more time. *Tense; hold; observe; relax; and observe.*

We are going to repeat this same sequence now for several other muscle groups. You will notice a general progression from the head down with the exception of this first arm–hand sequence. The arm–hand sequence is done first because it is easy to experience the difference between tension and relaxation in these muscle groups. Also, note the pattern for each muscle group: Tense; hold; observe; relax; and observe. The cycles will be *approximately 10–15 seconds for the tension segments and 15–20 seconds for the relaxation segments or roughly 30 seconds per cycle with just slightly longer devoted to the relaxation than to the tension.* In normal practice, especially in the early stages, you should *do about three repetitions for each muscle group.* Later on, it will not be necessary to do as many. But hold fairly strictly to the time limits and repetitions for now.

> Breathe deeply for a moment, hold, let it out. Relax. Your arm is relaxed also. Now, do the other arm. Tense your bicep. Recognize the presence of tension in your arm even as the rest of your body is mostly relaxed. Hold and then release. Tune in to the pleasant sensation of relaxation. Repeat again. *Tense; hold; observe; relax; and observe.* And once more. Now both of your arms are relaxed and you continue to breathe in a calm and easy fashion.

Note that I said "Repeat again" and gave the abbreviated sequence. If you are putting these instructions on a tape, this is your signal to extend or elaborate the instructions to cover additional repetitions.

While the arms may not be frequently involved in tension patterns, your fingers and your palms often indicate the presence of stress. Your palms can sweat, your fingers can start to lock up, or your fists may clench during stress. The palms have long been recognized as indicators of emotionality, and this fact is capitalized on in the so-called lie-detector test. Athletes frequently try a variety of measures to relieve their hands of tension in order to be able to perform better.

> Breathe deeply again. As you breathe out say to yourself "Relax." And let it go all at once. Your arms are still relaxed. Clench

your right fist (left if you are left-handed). Hold it for a moment and observe the tightness. Notice the sensation of tension. Put that sensation in your memory. Now let your fist go completely loose, relaxed. Your fingers could not hold anything even if you tried. Once more, notice the difference in the sensations. Observe the pleasant heaviness of the hand when all the tension is gone. Clench your fist again, tight, very tight. Hold it for just a few seconds and study the sensation. Then let it go. All at once and completely. Study the contrast. Feel how good the relaxation is. Once more. *Tense; hold; observe; relax; observe.*

From this point on, I will give you the muscle group, some abbreviated instructions, and any special things to look for. But I will not repeat the extended instructions for each of the repetitions. Instead, you will see a bracketed statement that is some variation on the theme such as this: [Repeat the tension–relaxation cycle twice more]. This tells you where to repeat the instructions. To emphasize, *for each muscle group, repeat the tension–relaxation cycle three times.* Carry out the study and observation for each segment of tension and relaxation with diligence. It is through this means that you begin to feel the difference between relaxed and tense muscles. It is the beginning of being able to hear your muscles telling you that tension is present.

The next set of muscles is the shoulder muscle group. These muscles very frequently tense under stress, such as during driving or intense periods of concentration. They may roll up in a knot or just ache as though they have been overworked. But they will hurt. Shoulder muscle tension, if not relieved quickly, may also spread to the neck and back and additionally contribute to a headache.

Take a deep breathe now and hold it for a moment. Then say to yourself "Relax" as you let the air out of your lungs completely. Now tighten up the shoulder muscle as tight as you can get it.

You may have to experiment with different ways of doing this. A slight rolling forward and upward of the shoulder may work best.

Hold the tension for a moment and study the feeling. Then let your shoulder simply slump. Let all the tension go out of it. Study the difference and enjoy the feeling of relaxation. [Repeat this with the same shoulder two more times.] Next, do the other shoulder in the same way. At all times take care to notice the difference between relaxation and tension. [Repeat this with the alternate shoulder two more times.]

Continue to keep all the parts of the body relaxed that you have relaxed to this point—the arms, the hands, the shoulders. Take another deep breath and hold it for a moment. Again release it as you are saying to yourself "Relax." Enjoy the feeling of relaxation as it settles more and more over your whole body.

Now you are going to relax the neck muscles. They may become tense apart from the shoulder muscles, which you just relaxed. More often than not, neck muscles are tense when mental pressures are high. Neck muscle tension is also associated with severe forms of headache. Later on you will want to make mental connections to any experiences of neck muscle tension from the past. This will help you to spot conditions in your environment that are putting pressure on you. To tense your neck muscle:

> Flex your head backward, as though you were pulling down on the back of your skull with your neck. (You may even feel a slight amount of pain right at the base of the skull if you pull hard enough. Do not pull so hard that you strain something!) As you tense the neck muscles, again study the feeling of tightness. Hold it for about 10 seconds. Now release all the tension. Let your head fall gently back onto your chest and enjoy the feeling of relief from letting the tension go. Just enjoy relaxing for a few seconds, and observe the difference. [Repeat the neck tension and relaxation cycle two more times.] Continue at all times to breathe easily and naturally. When you are done, scan the rest of your body to see if any parts seem tense. Do not do anything about it right now; just make a mental note of it. But *if any part of the body that you have relaxed before has become tense again, go back quickly and relax that part again.*

It may take you a little while to feel comfortable with this request—that is, trying to keep the rest of the body relaxed while you are concentrating on one part of the body and tensing it. But you will get used to it after a while. Also, it is important to start developing a sense of what it means to scan the body. Perhaps an analogy will help.

Many people have a type of CB radio that is only a receiver, but a special type of receiver. The radio actually scans up to 40 channels used by police, fire chiefs, sheriffs, ambulances, and people who are just into CB radio. The scanner electronically runs through all 40 channels as fast as it can in some systematic fashion. When it is done scanning channels, it does it all over again. It is actually looking for action, a radio signal, some sign that someone somewhere is talking. You need to develop a sense of scanning your body in the same way. It should become an internal sixth sense that automatically scans the muscle groups from one to the other and then *locks in* on any muscle group when a signal, tension, is found. It may be the most important talking your body does.

Now, concentrate on the forehead muscles. These muscles are referred to in medicine as the frontalis muscles. They wrinkle when you frown. They tighten when you are under pressure. Some clinicians believe that tension in the frontalis muscle group is associated with one form of headache, the tension headache. One high-tech solution to this problem is biofeedback.

Biofeedback in the treatment of tension headaches teaches how to relax the frontalis muscles. Over all, the clinical tests that have pitted biofeedback against relaxation find that the gains in symptomatic relief are largely a result of the relaxation itself. But some people experience difficulty trying to learn relaxation through the PMR procedure. They seem to need the visual picture that electronic feedback provides in order to learn how to relax. Biofeedback serves as an ally helping people learn how to relax and how to "read" body signals of tension. It makes little difference, practically speaking, whether you learn to relax through PMR or through biofeedback. The outcome is the same. Once the skill of reading body tension has been developed, the person can use this body information to help with a variety of coping procedures.

If you suffer from tension headaches, pay attention to this muscle group and learn how to relax it, through PMR or through biofeedback. If your headaches are of a different variety (vascular pressure instead of muscular tension), they may not respond to relaxation training as readily as to other types of training, including biofeedback. For now just concentrate on the contrast between tension and relief in this muscle group.

> Wrinkle up your forehead. Squint your eyes if you wish. It can help you feel the tension. You will feel your scalp tighten at the same time. Do not worry about any of those other tensions. Just treat them all as though they belong to one group. Hold the tension. Look at the tension. Turn your mind's eye up and look at it. Then let it go. Completely relaxed. Forehead, scalp, and eyes—all are relaxed. Study the difference. Enjoy the feeling of relaxation. [Repeat the cycle two more times, each time paying attention to the difference in the feelings.]

Now we will move to the jaws and tongue. Both of these muscles can be treated independently. I prefer to work only with the jaw muscles for a variety of reasons. If you find yourself having any difficulty achieving complete relaxation of the face, you may want to give the tongue special attention. This is usually done by rolling the tongue up to about the middle of the roof of the mouth. Then, just like doing an isometric exercise, you can push against the roof of the mouth and feel the tightness come into the tongue. Relaxing is merely letting the tongue fall back to its natural resting place in the mouth.

The jaw muscles are frequently involved when stress is occurring. For example, during anger many people clench their jaws. In a slender-cheeked person, one can see the ropelike muscle stand out on the side of the cheek when the jaw is clenched. In some cases of chronic stress, certain people will develop a **tic**, a condition in which a particular muscle group (usually in the jaw or cheek area) twitches convulsively. Tension may be relieved in these muscle groups through the use of relaxation training.

> Again, take a deep breath. Hold it. Let it out, saying "Relax" at the same time. Clench your jaws by biting down just as though you were chewing on a stick. Hold it for a moment. Study the sensations, the tightness going all the way up to the ears, the cheeks swelling out as the muscles tighten. Now let it go. Quickly, completely, let the jaw relax. You do not have to open your mouth for the

jaws to relax. Just let all the tension go. Observe the difference again between this comfortable easy feeling and the tightness you felt before. [Repeat the tension–relaxation cycle twice more.]

Continue relaxing. Enjoy the feeling. Now, take a very deep breath and hold it for a few seconds. Notice the tightness in your chest and diaphragm. Try not to tighten your stomach as you are breathing in. Now, say "Relax" to yourself as you let your breath go. Your whole body just seems to go into relaxation with the release. Try it once more. Breathe deeply. *Tense; hold; observe; relax; observe.* And once more. Breathe deeply; hold; study; relax; and study. Just let the relaxation take hold. You really do not have to do much to relax. It just comes when you let tension go.

Go on breathing easily and naturally for a few moments. While you are coasting, quickly scan your body. Do you notice any muscle tension anywhere? Are your arms still relaxed? Your hands? Your neck and shoulder muscles? Your forehead, eyes, and jaws? If not, quickly relax them again. All of your body is sinking into a pleasant state of heaviness, as though you couldn't lift a finger if you wanted to. Continue to scan and relax and drift and enjoy for a moment longer.

Now, it is time to turn attention to your stomach. Try to pull your stomach in to itself; shrink it by pulling in the muscles around it. It feels somewhat like it does when you have a *knot* in it. It is not all that comfortable. Hold the tightness for a moment and notice the sensations that occur. Try to link up to times when your stomach has been literally tied in knots and see how similar it is. Now, let it go. Let all the tightness, all the tension out. Observe . . . feel . . . enjoy for a moment. [Repeat the cycle twice.]

Few problems are as distressing as lower back pain. When the pain is of a chronic variety, going on and on without end, it becomes almost unbearable. A variety of conditions may produce or relate to lower back pain. Some people seem to be more prone to express the results of stress through tension in the lower back than in other parts of their body. For this reason, it is a good idea to include the lower back as a specific part of your relaxation exercises.

One word of caution is in order. Be very careful if you have had any history of back disorders or have had back surgery. It would be wise to obtain clearance from your physician before engaging in any strenuous back tensing. If permission has been given to proceed or you feel comfortable in going ahead on your own, at the least move into the back tension exercises somewhat gingerly until you are confident that you are not going to produce undue strain.

It is sometimes difficult to get a very good feeling of the pull in the lower back muscles from the prescribed means of producing tension. The instructions given here suggest arching the back—in other words, bending forward, pulling the shoulders slightly in, and making the small of your back stick out relative to the rest of the back. If you find that you are not getting any strong sensation from this technique, you may want to try some alternative approaches. One is to try to roll the lower back muscles toward each other just as you might roll your shoulders back and toward each other to produce tension there. One problem with this technique is that rolling the muscles may put tension into the stomach at the same time you are putting tension into the back. The arched back approach tends to put less tension in the stomach and more pure pull into the back muscles. This is something you will need to experiment with until you find what is right for you.

Concentrate now on your lower back. Arch your back and feel the pull of the muscles along the spine. Hold this tension for a few seconds. Notice the feeling. Try not to tense the stomach area, if at all possible, while tensing the back muscles. Now let yourself settle back, release the arch in your back and notice the feeling of relaxation settling into your back. Enjoy the pleasant feeling for a few seconds, and once again arch your back, study the sensations of tightness, and release. [Repeat one more time.] Each time you let go, try to get a picture in your mind of the muscles letting go and relaxing.

Continue to breathe calmly and easily. Keep your head resting gently on your chest. And squeeze your buttocks together, just as though you were trying to shut off your sphincter muscle. You may feel your hips and sphincter all tighten up together. That's all right. Hold for a few seconds while you tune in to the signals of tightness. Now let the muscle tension go. Relax and observe. Pay attention to the difference. [And repeat the cycle twice.]

Now concentrate on your legs, starting with the thighs. Do just your right thigh first (left if you prefer). Tighten the large muscles on the back of your legs. Think of it as though you were pushing against something, as though you were climbing a mountain or a set of steps. Pull your upper leg muscles as tight as you can without tightening your calves, feet, and toes. And study the feeling. Hold it for a few seconds. Now let go. Study the contrast, how pleasant the relief is. Feel the difference. [Then repeat the cycle two more times. Then do the same thing three times with your left thigh, or right if you started with the left.]

Now, attend to the calves and feet. Again, just concentrate on your right leg (left if preferred). Pull your foot toward your body, tightening your calf muscle as you do. Be careful not to pull so hard that you start a cramp in the muscle. Hold it for a moment and notice how it feels. Then let the tension go. Just let it loose all at once. And notice the difference. For a moment, let the relaxation settle on you and enjoy the comfortable heaviness throughout your body and in your leg. [Tense and relax two more times for the right leg. Then tense and relax three times for the left leg.]

Every part of your body is relaxed. Breathe easily, peacefully. And feel how good it feels when the body is completely relaxed. Without stirring or changing positions, scan your entire body. Tune in to any signs of tension anywhere. If any parts have tension, relax them again. Take a deep breath and hold it for a short while. Then let it go and say to yourself "Relax." Drift for a moment and feel the pleasant sensation of having all the tension drained out of your body. Take some time (about 1 or 2 minutes) to experience this feeling of relaxing.

Now, I am going to count backward from three to one. On the count of one, I want you to open your eyes slowly, raise your head, and just as though you were waking up from a nap, reach your arms over your head and stretch. Three, two, one. And you are done with your first relaxation session.

◆ RELAXATION IN REVIEW

Before going any further, a quick review of the sequence and some added details are in order. Table 11–1 provides a summary of the essential details. First, the tension–relaxation cycles should be about 30 seconds each, with slightly more time given to the relaxation phase than to the tension phase. It should take you approximately 45–75 minutes the first three or four times you do this. After you become familiar with the procedure and use the technique for a short while, you should find the time required to achieve relaxation shortening by as much as half. Experienced practitioners can achieve complete body relaxation in about 5–15 minutes. You should not expect to relax this quickly, though, until you have practiced for several weeks. In addition, cutting down on the time usually requires some shortcut tech-

Table 11–1.   Sequence and Timing for Engaging in Self-directed Progressive Muscular Relaxation

---

Sequence Guide for Relaxation Practice

---

 1. Preferred arm
 2. Alternate arm
 3. Preferred hand
 4. Alternate hand
 5. Shoulder muscles
     a. Preferred hand side
     b. Alternate side
 6. Neck muscles
 7. Forehead, eyes, scalp
 8. Jaws and mouth (tongue, optional as extra step)
 9. Breathing—chest and trunk
10. Stomach
11. Lower back
12. Buttocks
13. Preferred thigh
14. Alternate thigh
15. Preferred foot and calf
16. Alternate foot and calf

Additional Reminders:

Two sessions per day, same time, same place
Three repetitions for each muscle set
10–15 seconds for tension sets
15–20 seconds for relaxation sets
45–75 minutes for the first few sessions

Sessions will be greatly reduced in length after the first few sessions.

---

niques, which will be introduced in the next chapter. For now, do not rush! Especially the first few times you relax, it is better to take a little more time than to try to get through too quickly and not experience the full benefit of the practice.

Second, it is of paramount importance to spend the allotted time studying the difference between tension and relaxation. It may seem that I have belabored this point. But it is for a very good reason.

All too often, people report they feel something is wrong, but they can not figure out what it is. They feel they are under pressure, but they do not know why. Sometimes they do not even seem to know where the pressure is coming from. Most often, it turns out that these same people do not hear what their body is telling them. It is as though their scanners are turned off. Some people, even when they hear the body signals, do not understand the connection between the body's distress cries and what is going on in their environment.

As noted earlier in the discussion of drugs, relaxation training involves more than just learning how to relax. It includes learning how to spot the signs of stress in mind and body and how to connect these signs to the conditions present in your environment. Ultimately, it also includes learning how to apply the skill selectively to a variety of situations and individual muscle groups.

The differences in muscle sensations you have been asked to focus on during relaxation training are exaggerated examples of what goes on in your body during stress. Once you begin to distinguish the difference between tension and relaxation, and can especially feel what relaxation is like at its most pleasant level, you will be better able to detect the more subtle indicators of tension that occur in your body as you move through your daily activities.

When you acquire the ability to detect the more subtle changes in muscular tension, you are then ready to look for the connections to your environment, connections that might have escaped your notice before. Body tension sounds the alarm that stress of some type is occurring. When the alarm sounds, the natural response should be, What triggered the alarm? Who is present? Is it a family member? My boss? A friend? What is the situation? Is it work, social, family, an intimate situation? What is the topic or theme of the conversation or behavior that triggered this tension? Money? Sex? Control? How am I responding to it? Defensively, aggressively, angrily? Has this same cycle occurred before? If it is the first time you noticed the connection, take special care to record the incident and be on the lookout for any recurrence of the same situation.

◆ A TENSION-SCANNING EXERCISE

It is generally helpful to carry out a simple exercise to go along with relaxation training. A good rule is to practice relaxation for about one week before undertaking this exercise. Pick a period of time, preferably one full week beginning on a Sunday or a Monday. Make a mental note to yourself each day of this week that you have one personal project to carry out, namely to *tune in* to signs of muscular tension. During this week, observe your body tension reactions all day long, not just during relaxation. Carry a small notebook with you, such as a schedule book, with blank pages to allow ample writing space. *Whenever you spot signs of muscular tension, make a brief note of the time, place, and people involved as soon after the tension has appeared as possible.*

You do not have to make the record immediately, unless you can do so conveniently. Just do it as quickly as you can without disrupting your normal routine. For example, if you are a nurse attending to a troublesome patient, you obviously do not want to stop and record that you are having shoulder tension before completing your attention to the patient's needs. As soon as you are back at the nurse's station, though, and have completed the patient's chart, you might be able to make a record of the event.

Or you may be a school principal who has just had an unpleasant encounter with irate parents. You may notice that your stomach is tied in knots but you are already late for a staff meeting. Go on to your staff meeting, but try to make a notice of the stomach tension as soon as possible.

The tension event may be very loud and long or very quiet and short. It may involve many of the muscle groups in your body or only one isolated muscle. But it will usually result in noticeable change somewhere in the body. The most frequently occurring signs of tension are neck muscles cramping, shoulder muscles knotting up, lower back muscles tightening, stomach contracting (aside from hunger pangs), forehead muscles tensing, jaws clenching, teeth grinding, fist doubling, breathing increasing, and heart pounding. These are all signals from the body's red-light warning system. The objective of this exercise is for you to learn now to identify these signals in the normal course of your working world, before you get distressed or physically sick. For the time being, do not worry about whether you are catching all the signals or not. Just do the best you can.

◆ MOVING ON: WHEN CAN I DO SOMETHING WITH IT?

One of the great dangers in developing a skill of this nature is trying to do too much too fast. Recall the earlier comment that if you find yourself wanting to tackle the central issues in your stress life right away, you should resist. The practical problem, then, is "When can I move on?" First, *give yourself a minimum of two weeks of practice.* You should have worked through the observation exercise described herein for one week before you even consider the possibility of moving on with the other techniques introduced in the next chapters.

Second, *try to scale subjectively the depth of the relaxation and the satisfaction you get from relaxing.* Some clinicians take this to the extreme with formalized scales to assess relaxation. This seems unnecessary, and it also gives the illusion of an objectivity that is highly unlikely. At any rate, make regular attempts to gauge the depth and satisfaction. You should find changes in the direction of increasing depth and greater personal satisfaction. At the same time, you will come to recognize the days or times when you did not get as much as you wanted from the session.

Another gauge of your success is the amount of time it takes you to induce relaxation. Do not be concerned with time for the first few days. You may take from 45 minutes to 75 minutes for the first few sessions. This will begin to drop very rapidly into the 25–35 minute range. Additional practice and some extending instructions will be required before you get much more reduction in the time required. Once you have reached these criteria, you should be able to move on to the techniques discussed in the next chapters.

To repeat: Practice for at least two full weeks including a one-week observation exercise before moving on. Amount of time to induce relaxation should have dropped approximately by half what it was when you first started. And, finally, assure yourself through your subjective evaluation that both depth of relaxation and satisfaction with the feeling of relaxing are substantially improved from your first attempts at relaxation. Then go on to Chapter 12. It will give more information on how to gauge your progress and how to take the appropriate steps for extending your skills.

◆ WHY SHOULD I SAY RELAX?

You may have wondered on several occasions about one instruction that was repeated several times. That is, "Breathe out and say 'Relax' at the same time." This instruction has an important relationship to a technique that will be introduced later called cue-controlled relaxation. Practice the *breathe out—say relax* sequence as indicated throughout, and when you are ready to move on you will be that much further ahead.

For the sake of simplicity, I have used the generic word *relax*. You should note that the particular word, however, is relatively unimportant. Select a word that is of significance to you. It may be better to actually use some other word than *relax* because of the frequency with which that word is used in everyday communication. Your personal cue word can be very secret, very unique. Whatever you select as that word, however, use it consistently. Simply substitute it in the instructions anytime you read "Relax."

◆ PREPARING YOUR OWN RELAXATION INSTRUCTIONS

In general, there are four basic methods of presenting the instructions. First, you could try to recall the gist of the instructions and *think* yourself through the entire relaxation exercise without any external prompts. In some ways, this is the preferred technique because then you can take relaxation with you to the office or on the road wherever you are. You want the technique to be something very private, even in public. You want to be able to relax in the board meeting, on the plane, or at the church bazaar. But you do not want anyone to know that you are relaxing. If you have the procedure as an internally controlled routine, this is possible. Try to persevere with this internal control procedure through the first week or two. You should find the routine becoming virtually habitual. You may even come to *see* with the mind's eye your muscles relaxing in the prescribed sequence. That is, you will be able to relax without thinking specifically about each and every muscle, without having to tell yourself verbally each and every instructional set. This is the ideal, the goal to which you should aspire. Any of the other techniques suggested in the following should be regarded as intermediate steps to be used only in the early stages and abandoned as soon as possible.

As a second alternative, you can have someone read the instructions for you the first few times. This will relieve you of the need to concentrate on both the sequence and the relaxing. It would free you to tune in to the differing sensations of relaxation and tension. You will probably acquire an incidental feel for the sequence and the logic of the procedure just by being guided through it by spouse or friend. In a short time, you will probably sense that the external prompts are no longer necessary and you will very naturally move to the optimal situation described in the first option.

The third approach is to tape the instructions in your own voice on a cassette recorder. Once you have put the instructions on tape, you are free to concentrate on the relaxation exercises without undue worry about what should come next. In addition, should you decide to have a friend handle the instructions initially, your friend may not always be available. The taped instructions provide you with a backup. Also, you might use relaxation for a period of time and then let it go for awhile. When you return to use it, you might feel rusty. A taped set of instructions can help you get back into the routine very quickly and efficiently.

Fourth, you can buy a commercially prepared tape that gives the complete instructional sequence. Several publishing companies offer tapes of this variety, some of which are quite expensive.

◆ NOTES

[1]Pinkerton, S. S., Hughes, H., & Wenrich, W. W. (1982). *Behavior medicine: Clinical applications.* New York: Wiley.

[2]Jacobson, E. (1938). *Progressive relaxation* (2nd ed.). Chicago: University of Chicago Press.

[3]Benson, H. (1975). *The relaxation response.* New York: Avon Books.

[4]Bagchi, B. K., & Wenger, M. A. (1957). Electrophysiological correlates of some Yogi exercises. *EEG and Clinical Neurophysiology* (Suppl. 7), 132–149. Also note: Anand, B. K., Chhina, G., & Singh, B. (1961). Some aspects of electroencephalographic studies in Yogis. *EEG and Clinical Neurophysiology, 13,* 452–456.

[5]Several important references stand out here, including the work of Joe Kamiya at McGill University in Canada, Neal Miller and colleagues, and Charles Tart, whose edited books make many of these works readily accessible. Kamiya, J. (1969). Operant control of the EEG alpha rhythm and some of its reported effects on consciousness. In C. T. Tart (Ed.), *Altered states of consciousness*. New York: Wiley; Miller, N. E. (1969). Learning of visceral and glandular responses. *Science, 163,* 434–445.

[6]Heide, F. J., & Borkovec, T. D. (1983). Relaxation-induced anxiety: Paradoxical anxiety enhancement due to relaxation training. *Journal of Consulting and Clinical Psychology, 51,* 171–182.

[7]Benson, *Relaxation response.*

12

CUE-CONTROLLED AND GRADUATED RELAXATION: TAKING IT WITH YOU

The real task is to succeed in setting man free by making him master of himself.

Antoine de Saint-Exupéry

In the process of teaching off-campus courses in stress management and personal health, I have encountered a number of interesting and unusual cases for which relaxation has provided a remedy. One of these involved a woman I'll call Elaine. She suffered from a condition known in medical circles as chostochondritis or sometimes Tietze's syndrome.[1] It is an affliction that leaves the front walls of the chest inflamed and very irritated. The effects of the inflammation can be very powerful and extensive. People afflicted with chostochondritis may think that they are the victims of a heart problem or a serious stomach disease. It is suffered more frequently by women. The condition may be intensified by tension and overwork.

When I first met her, Elaine had been suffering from the condition for nearly a year. Medical diagnosis and treatment had been obtained during the year. X ray examination of the chest, stress tests, electrocardiograms and other exams all revealed no evidence of a physical cause. The attending physician diagnosed the condition as chostochondritis and recommended that Elaine use a heating pad whenever possible and take three aspirins four times daily. After complying with this medical regimen for awhile, Elaine reported that "the chest pains continued. It was as if I were having a heart attack many times a day, although I was relieved to know this wasn't my problem."[2] Further tests for stomach and colon disease were also negative, and a stronger drug was prescribed. However, nothing seemed to work.

At the beginning of the stress management class Elaine had registered for, I assigned each student the task of researching a stress situation or personal health problem of current concern. Then each student was to design a program that would attempt to change the condition in order to reduce stress and/or improve health. In the meantime, training had commenced on the relaxation response.

In the course of class discussions, we were able to piece together some vital bits of information about the times and places when Elaine's chest pain seemed most likely to strike. She worked as a real estate appraiser and reported that stresses, both mental and physical, occurred frequently. Almost always, the most severe inflammation occurred during these periods of severe work stress. Because of this, the condition seemed to occur much more regularly than not. The recognition that stress was somehow related either to the onset, or at least to the intensification, of the condition suggested that it might respond to a stress management technique such as progressive relaxation.

With this in mind, a structured approach was taken to introduce the relaxation response in relation to the condition. First, Elaine practiced the relaxation response, using techniques described later, until she could induce relaxation very rapidly. Simultaneously, she monitored the frequency, intensity, and duration of the attacks. Finally, Elaine was instructed to implement the relaxation response as soon as possible upon recognition of the presence of stress during the day. Over a period of approximately five weeks, she reported that the frequency of attacks decreased to virtually zero. Even when an occasional attack occurred, it was much less intense and was over much quicker than prior to the training. This outcome is nearly as important as the decrease in frequency of attacks. Overall, it was rather convincing evidence for the effectiveness of the relaxation technique. It had eliminated a very painful physical condition that had lasted for nearly a year. And it had done so in a period of approximately seven weeks.

◆ GETTING RELAXED THE FAST WAY

If you had to spend nearly an hour every time to get relaxed, you might wonder how useful the technique could really be. If you had to have a nice recliner, music, taped instructions, and complete quietness with no interruptions, you might say, "That's fine, but what about when I need it right now! What do I do then?" As you will see, you can still reduce the tension through relaxation, but you can learn to do it quickly. And you can do it quietly through a combination of techniques that are part of the whole package of relaxation training.

First, you will learn how to reduce the amount of time it takes to get relaxed by relaxing whole groups of muscles at once. Then you will learn how to obtain quick partial relaxation through cue-controlled relaxation. A single word, or cue, that you have learned to associate with relaxing becomes your password to immediate relief. Later on, you will learn how to relax one muscle group by itself through the technique of differential and graduated relaxation.

Before starting these procedures, cross-check your progress to this point. Have you met the following criteria: *Have you had at least two weeks of practice, as suggested? Do you feel comfortable with the procedure? Can you feel the relaxation as it gets deeper? Are you able to achieve relaxation in approximately 25–35 minutes or less?* If you feel that you have met all of these criteria, then by all means proceed. If you are short on any of them, it would be best to wait a while before trying the following procedures.

◆ RELAXING A GROUP OF MUSCLES

The procedure described in the previous chapter required you to work through 16 steps to achieve relaxation. Each muscle was treated as through it was distinct from any other muscle. It is possible, however, to treat certain groups of muscles as though they belong together. Instead of relaxing each one separately, you relax some together.

Except for grouping muscles together, the overall procedure will be exactly the same as before. First, take care to maintain the same setting for these relaxation exercises as you did for the beginning exercises. You will be changing enough that you don't want the additional burden of changing the place you are practicing as well. Second, continue to observe the critical mood factors for awhile. Make sure that your mental attitude is right as you begin each session. Review the guidelines for this in the previous chapter if you need. Finally, take care of all the preparations before beginning your relaxation exercises so that you know where you are headed. You should *try one dry run through each new procedure before actually trying to obtain full and deep relaxation with the procedure.* This will help take some of the pressure off during the first attempt at a new relaxation exercise.

There are five stages required to reduce the number of steps for relaxation. Several of the steps are devoted to reducing the amount of muscle tension you induce in the tension phase. The first stage cuts the number of steps in half.

From Sixteen to Eight Steps

For the first few days, relax (1) both arms together, (2) both hands together, (3) both the shoulder and neck muscles, (4) the forehead with the scalp and jaws and mouth all together, (5) the chest and stomach muscles, (6) the lower back and buttocks together, (7) both thighs, and (8) both calves and feet together. The 16-step procedure has been cut in half to 8 steps. Table 12–1 will help to track the steps you need to take over a few days. Later in this section, more will be said about how long this might take you. For now, we need to review how the specific instructions will change for this procedure.

You should have a good working knowledge of the basic instructions and sequence for relaxing. In fact, you may have already weaned yourself from whatever instructional prompts, such as tapes or a friend, you were using early in your practice. If so, all you need for this new step is to *read* the instructions with the very slight modifications suggested here. If you are still dependent on a tape or friend to give the instructions to you, then you may

Table 12–1. Guide for Reduction Steps in Relaxation Practice

First Reduction Set	Second Reduction Set
1. Both arms	1. Both arms and hands
2. Both hands	
3. Shoulder and neck	2. Shoulders, neck, and head
4. All head muscles	
5. Chest and stomach	3. Chest, stomach, lower back, and
6. Lower back and buttocks	buttocks
7. Both thighs	4. Thighs, feet, and calves
8. Both feet and calves	

Additional Reminders:

Two sessions per day, same time, same place
Three repetitions for each muscle group
10–15 seconds for tension sets
15–20 seconds for relaxation sets
25–35 minutes for the first few sessions

Sessions will be further reduced in length after the first few times.

Reduce tension about 25% after the main criterion has been reached and before going on to the second reduction set. Reduce tension about 25% more at the end of the second reduction set.

Reduce tension about another 25% and practice to criterion. Go on to cue-controlled relaxation.

want to set up an alternate tape or provide your friend with a new listing of the instructions following the suggested modifications. Remember that each session starts with the deep breathing exercise before going into the first tension–relaxation cycle.

Now, I want you to take a few deep breaths, hold each breath for a few seconds, and then let each breath out fully and completely. As you breathe in, you will notice some tension in your chest and diaphragm. As you breathe out, you will notice a sense of relaxing, almost going limp. Relaxing feels good and comfortable and it would be nice if the feeling could be kept. But as you breathe in deeply again you feel the same tension as before, especially as you hold it for a moment. Let the breath out again, completely, and feel the pleasant relaxing sensation of letting go. Try it one more time. Dwell for just a moment on the sense of relaxation as you let this breath out.

Try to maintain the relaxation in your chest and diaphragm. As you breathe from now on, breathe easily and naturally, almost as though you were napping.

Concentrate for a moment on both your arms. How do they feel? Flex the biceps on both your arms as though you were showing off your muscles.

Flex them as tight as you can and hold [for about 10 seconds]. As you keep both biceps flexed, notice the sensation of tension. Notice how unpleasant it can be. Now let it go all at once. Let your arms go completely limp. Relax! And study the contrast. Notice how different it is from tension. Store the contrast in your mind even as you are studying it. One more time. Tense your biceps and hold the tension. Observe the feeling of tightness. Tune in to the signal of tension in your muscles. Then let it go. Become completely relaxed. If someone picked your arms up and let them loose, they would simply drop to your side. There is no tension at all. It feels so good. One more time: tense; hold; observe; relax; and observe.

Notice what has changed in the instructions. Instead of telling yourself to relax only the preferred arm, you tell yourself to relax both arms. This grouping of muscles can be done all the way through the instructions you have learned. For each of the eight steps listed in the chart, simply modify the instructions accordingly. Otherwise, the instructions remain the same, as will be shown. Continue the same pattern: tense, hold, observe, relax, and observe.

During the first sessions, you may experience difficulty with the tension–relaxation contrasts. The arms, hands, and legs will probably be the easiest for you to work on. When you tense and alternately relax the arms, as you did at the beginning of your first relaxation session, remember to study the contrasts in tension and relaxation. The only difference is that you are feeling tension in two arms at the same time. And when you let the tension go, you are feeling it in both arms simultaneously. You may need to try this a few more than the usual three repetitions until you are sure that you feel the tension and relaxation as deeply for both arms together as you did when treating them separately. If you are able to accomplish this in your arms with some degree of ease, move on to your hands and proceed as indicated by the steps in the chart.

Some people encounter difficulty with the group of muscles for the head. A large number of muscles of very different types have been grouped together. If you feel that this set is too much for you the first time, then just treat them as separate muscles as you did at the beginning of training. You can practice with the other combined muscle groups until you have achieved success with them. Then come back later and try to get the group of head muscles relaxed as one group.

It is difficult to recommend an absolute number of days for this first step in the reduction phase. In general, you should not expect to get full proficiency with this technique in fewer than about 5 days. It is possible, however, that some very adept people may make rapid progress in as few as 3 days or so. Even if you are still struggling with this step through about 7–10 days, though, do not fight with yourself. Remember, this is not a competitive sport. Speed is not the measure of success. A personally satisfying level of deep relaxation is the only measure of success. *When* you attain success is unimportant. *That* you can achieve it is all that matters.

Now Softer on the Tension Also

Work on the first phase of this reduction training until you feel that you are getting as much relaxation with the grouped muscles as you were before.

When you have reached this criterion, there is another very important step to take before going on to the second reduction phase. *Try to reduce the intensity of the tension phase of your tension–relaxation cycle.* That is, instead of tensing your biceps very tightly, just tense them a moderate amount. When you tense the forehead muscle, tense it a little bit less than before. For all of the muscle groups, lower the overall amount of tension without reducing the amount of time devoted to the tension cycle itself. Do not change the relaxation cycle in any fashion.

It may be easier if you can imagine muscle tension on a 100-point scale. The high end of the scale occurs when you are putting the most effort into tensing your muscles. The bottom end occurs when your muscles are relaxed as deeply as you can imagine. For the first softer tension level, try to imagine what your muscles would feel like at the 75-point mark on the scale, or at about 25% less tension. Try to tense only to that 75% level. But do not be concerned about absolutes. The scale is very subjective and personal. So is your feeling of where the 75% point is. Knowing that the tension is at a lower level than your most strained efforts is all that is important. Later on, you will reduce this tension even further.

This instruction may seem paradoxical but there is a good reason for it. Ultimately, you should be able to sense natural tension whenever and wherever it occurs. That is the main reason for working through these tension–relaxation cycles in the first place. But you need to be able to sense subtle tension as well as nagging tension. Sometimes the tension that occurs with stress is very quiet. Until you can spot the whispers of stress as well as the screams, you will not be able to get the most out of this training. Beginning to reduce the level of tension in the muscles will help you develop the skill you need to get the maximum benefit from relaxation.

But there is another important reason for this instruction. In the very near future, you should be able to go directly into relaxation without having to go through these tension–relaxation cycles. In fact, all of the later variants of this procedure, which are designed to make relaxation training portable, depend upon your ability to go directly into relaxation. By the time you have finished reducing the muscle groups to the bare minimum, you should have also phased out the intense muscle-tightening routine. From that point on, you will return to the muscle tension cycle only if you need a kind of booster for your skill.

Finally, note that when I talk about reducing muscle tension at this point, I am only talking about the voluntarily induced tension that has been a part of the instructional sequence. I am not talking about any reduction in tension that may occur later on because you are more effectively managing stress. Now for the second step.

From Eight Muscle Groups to Four

The second reduction set is also shown in Table 12–1. The procedure is exactly the same as was detailed before. Try to relax all the muscles in a group at the same time. Again, if you have any initial difficulty with a particular group of muscles, go back to the earlier step for that muscle group. Once you have gotten the overall reduction mastered, then you can concentrate on the problem group.

The general idea is to be flexible. The rules for these groupings are not carved in stone. If you have to work with nine groups in the first reduction phase (for example, treating the head muscles in two separate groups), do not worry about it. If you have to work with five muscle groups initially in the second reduction phase (such as keeping the head group and the neck and shoulder group separate at the beginning), that is fine. Your timing is your own. Allow yourself the freedom to read your own body, and adjust the groupings as it feels right for you.

You should probably take at least another five to seven days for this reduction phase. In fact, if it takes a slight bit longer even than the first reduction, do not be surprised. You are accomplishing a great amount of economy with this second step. Expending some additional effort may be required, but it will also be worth the effort later.

And Softer Still

At the end of your first reduction phase, you were asked to reduce the amount of tension voluntarily induced in the tension–relaxation cycle to about 75% of maximum. Now you should reduce the voluntarily produced level of tension even further. Try to imagine how your muscles would feel tensed to a point corresponding to about 50% on the original scale. Throughout your practice from now on use this 50% norm for the level of tension you voluntarily produce in your muscles. It is important, however, that you do not try this step until you have successfully achieved the reduction to the 4-step procedure described in the last section. That is, you should be able to relax as quickly and as deeply with the 4-step procedure as you did with either the 16- or the 8-step procedures taught earlier.

If you feel comfortable with your level of proficiency using the criteria of attaining quick and fairly deep relaxation, feel free to proceed to this muscle–tension–reducing phase. Remember that you should spend the same amount of time tensing as you did before. It is only the level of tension that is reduced. Also, you should keep the relaxation periods exactly the same as before, with the obvious difference that you are relaxing large groups of muscles all at the same time.

To review the steps, over approximately two weeks progressively reduce the number of steps to achieve relaxation by grouping muscles together. Also, reduce the amount of artificially induced muscle tension. An outline of the process follows.

1. Reduce from 16 muscle sets to 8 muscle groups over a five-to-seven-day period. When you reach the criterion of being able to relax as quickly and almost as deeply as you did before, take step 2.

2. Reduce the amount of artificially induced muscle tension to roughly 75% of the original level, and practice until you achieve the same criterion as indicated in step 1. Then move to step 3.
3. Reduce from 8 muscle groups to 4 muscle groups over five to seven days. Practice until you can relax as quickly and deeply as before and then take step 4.
4. Reduce the amount of artificially induced muscle tension to roughly 50% of the original level. Again, practice until you achieve the criterion before moving on.

And Now Ever So Softly

You have just one more step to take to reach the desired level before moving on to the major techniques of cue-controlled and differential relaxation. This is to reduce the level of induced muscle tension to roughly 25% of the original level. The procedure is exactly the same as described earlier. Try to imagine the 25% level on the scale of muscle tension. Then when instructing yourself for the tension cycle, tense to a level that is just about at the 25% point. This may take another three to five days to get right. Once again, you should make sure that you are getting a fairly deep feeling of relaxation and that you are getting there as quickly as before. If you are short on either of these criteria, practice at least a little longer before going on. By this point you should be able to induce relaxation very quickly and much more directly than you did at the beginning. In fact, you may find at this point that you can get deep relaxation in anywhere from 5 to 15 minutes. If you have experienced that, you may congratulate yourself and feel well rewarded for your efforts. It may have seemed like a long road at times, but the dividends are just beginning.

◆ TERRIFYING SLOPES: RELAXATION TO THE RESCUE

Life can have its terrifying moments, even when you are supposed to be having fun. Such was the case when I was combining a business trip with some skiing pleasure on the slopes at Park City, Utah. The morning went splendidly with no untoward incidents, even though I had only been on skis once before in my life.

After lunch I somehow got on a slope that simply disappeared from view. It was also contoured with those beautiful moguls—many, many moguls tightly packed and small. For me it was too much too soon. The end of the slope was an ignominious slide on my posterior with skis in hand while all the supportive souls riding the lift right over me found their afternoon much lightened by this comic sight. But the real terror was yet to come, on the way out and down.

A quick search on the trail map revealed a green-marked trail, the beginner's route down the mountain. I settled back, relieved that I would have a nice cruise to the bottom where I could count my ego losses, reconstruct my self-image, and prepare for a frontal assault on the mountains another day. And at first the trail looked like a gentle slope and slowly winding descent down the mountain. Of course it wasn't really the easy way down. It was only the easiest from that part of the mountain.

We skied past a rope tied with red flags and signs warning of danger. Off to the left, over the rope and flags, was a sheer ice-packed slope that looked like it went straight down. It was obviously intended to convey any object in a straight line the shortest distance between the two points of top and bottom and with the maximum aid of gravity. Only later did I learn that it was the downhill race course. But that sheer cliff was there, and here where I was skiing that nice trail still stretched out gently in front of me. Its disappearance around a cluster of trees ahead could only mean one thing—the *real* trail must continue somewhere beyond and to the side of this ice sled. But disappearing wasn't the half of it. Sure the trail wound around those trees and disappeared—right onto the top of that downhill course. And there was no way back, around, or down . . . except!

My terror was complete. I had never seen anything like this. My partner gave a brief reassuring smile and a "See you at the bottom" salute. He pointed his skis straight down and was gracefully rounding a ridge beyond the bottom of the slope before I could even consider what I was going to do. If only I could be off this mountain that fast.

But my problem was with my body and my mind. And both had to be dealt with before I could get down that hill. My mind was a jumble of thoughts. My body felt like a system of muscular pretzels. Every inch of me was in knots except for the knees, which wouldn't stand still for anything.

I went through two processes to get down off that mountain: thought stopping and muscular relaxation. The mental process was really a combination of rational problem solving and an emotional control process to get the frightening, self-defeating thoughts out of my head. The relaxation process was to get my body under control. If you have watched professional skiers at all, you realize how fluid and loose they look. In fact, muscular tension is the enemy of the athlete.

Because I had practiced the technique before, it took only a few minutes to get relaxation even on this mountain slope. I concentrated on the major body systems that were tied up—my stomach, shoulders, and legs. Finally, I carefully planned a path down the mountain that included a lot of traversing. This helped mentally as well because I recognized that I could control my speed down the mountain with this technique. I must have spent several minutes transfixed in the middle of that course thinking and relaxing. But the trip down went smoothly. So smoothly, in fact, that when I hit the bottom I turned briefly to give a defiant salute to the mountain and congratulated myself on a victory over both the physical elements and the fear that only moments ago had been my oppressor.

These are obviously not the conditions in which you should practice relaxation for the first time. But once you have developed the skill, you may be surprised at the places you will take relaxation. This incident is an example of one situation in which portions of the relaxation technique may be used. In fact, it combined parts of both the cue-controlled relaxation procedure and the differential relaxation procedure. In the next few pages, we will look at these two techniques to see how they might operate in the overall process of stress management.

◆ RELAXING WITH A WORD

As part of your relaxation practice, you have carried out a routine breathing exercise. Each time you breathed out, you were asked to say to yourself "Relax" (or some other word of your choice). You did this several times during each relaxation session. Even though you did not know it at the time, you were really building a base for cue-controlled relaxation.

The secret of the technique is simply this: The repeated connection between a cue and a response makes it possible for the cue to produce the response more or less automatically. A familiar example may help to illustrate what is meant.

When you were born, many cues, such as words, did not have any real power to control or change your behavior in and of themselves. But through a long process of learning, certain words become connected to important events in such a way that the words can now change or control your behavior just as directly as the events themselves did.

For example, a mother's command to "Stop!" or the ubiquitous parental directive "No!" has no special meaning to a child early in the child's development. But along the way, there will be many connections made for the child between such commands and something the child is doing that might be dangerous. To illustrate further, the first time a child touches a hot stove, a powerful incentive to withdraw the hand, burning pain, will be produced. Pain usually leads to very quick and permanent learning—in this case, not to touch hot things.

If luck should have it that the parent is around, the child may hear a loud "No, no!" just before touching the stove. In this case, a very quick yet permanent connection may be built between the command and the dangerous event. Over the course of time, many repeated connections between the cue (parent's warning words) and some dangerous event (running into a heavily traveled street) will occur. The child's ability to control its behavior will increase as it internalizes more and more examples of cue–response connections. This may not happen on the very first try, but it will come with time. In fact, you may have seen an additional step in the development of personal control after an incident of this type.

The child approaches the stove again, and actually reaches toward the stove. But the child stops, looks at the parent, and says "No" aloud to itself.

The word has been internalized as a controlling cue that can be used voluntarily. There is no need to be burned or hit repeatedly in order to avoid hot stoves and onrushing cars. In summary, the word or cue *No* is associated over time with the stimulus of the hot stove. The response, avoiding touching the hot stove, may then be controlled by either hearing or saying to oneself the cue word.

In general, the process of getting some word to control relaxation behavior is very much the same. Relaxation is a response that we would like to control directly with some cue. The word relax serves as the cue to produce the response of relaxation. The cue word may have only a general meaning based on our past experience with it. But once it has been associated with the process of relaxation, we should be able to use it as a cue to induce relaxation directly. This is analogous to the child saying "No" to itself to control its own behavior. In principle, we will have internalized a controlling cue that will be able to produce the response almost automatically. Instead of having to go through the lengthy process of relaxing each time, we can simply say "Relax" to ourselves, and relax!

What's the Word?

Throughout the instructions, the word *relax* has been consistently used as the cue word. However, it was suggested that you can use any word as long as it is used consistently. There is certainly no magic in this particular word. In fact, there may be a good reason to use another word, one less likely to occur on a routine basis. Some people use words like *peace, quiet, easy,* or *warm.* Some select a word that is similar to a **mantra,** a sacred, privileged, and secret word. Whatever the word you elect to use, make sure that you use it, *and only it,* when you are breathing out.

Beginning Cue-Controlled Relaxation

This procedure should be somewhat easier than the other steps you have taken to learn relaxation. There is nothing special that you really have to do except practice without going through the entire relaxation process itself. To begin this phase, we will assume that you

1. are still relaxing twice daily,
2. have met the criteria for reducing the number of steps needed to get relaxed, and
3. are now able to induce relaxation in approximately 5–15 minutes.

At the beginning of each relaxation session, before trying to get relaxed through the tension–relaxation cycles, follow the next set of instructions.

Breathe in deeply. Hold the breath for approximately 10 seconds. Then let the breath out completely as you are saying your personal cue word. Also, as you say the cue word, let your entire body go limp. Go immediately into a state of deep relaxation. It may help to form a mental image of your whole body going limp, as though you are seeing yourself at the end of one of your regular relaxation sessions. Take a moment to evaluate subjectively how good and deep the feeling of relaxation is.

Do this about 15–20 times, but no more. Now for the important part: At any time during the 15 or more cycles, should you feel that your relaxation is even 50–75% as good and deep as you have been getting through the tension–relaxation cycles, congratulate yourself and count the session a success. Complete the minimum of 15 cycles and go on relaxing for your normal length of time.

If you are not able to get relaxed to the 50–75% level, stop after the 20th cycle. Then *wait until the next relaxation period to try the deep breathing–cue-word–relaxation cycle again by itself*. But before you quit, go back to the usual tension–relaxation cycle and get the fullest depth of relaxation possible. Then enjoy your normal period of relaxing. Remember that you should always use the breathing–cue-word cycles a few times in your tension–relaxation cycles as you have been taught from the beginning.

Repeat this sequence for approximately one week. That is, start each relaxation period with 15–20 breathing–cue-word–relaxation cycles. Complete each period by getting relaxed with the tension–relaxation cycles if necessary. Always take time to enjoy the period of relaxation itself. When you are able to achieve a state of relaxation anywhere in the 50–75% range of what you expect to achieve using the tension–relaxation cycle, you can move on to the next step.

In general, you should not expect to be able to achieve the same deep level of relaxation that you get from the tension–relaxation cycles. You may be able to get close, and if you do you can count yourself among the more fortunate and adept practitioners. But do not worry if you feel that you are not getting much more than the 50% level of relaxation. The most practical uses of this technique do not demand complete relaxation. In fact, complete relaxation would be detrimental to its everyday use, as you will see in a moment.

Using Cue-Controlled Relaxation

In order to use cue-controlled relaxation to ward off the slings and arrows of everyday stress, you need two things: You need to know how to do it, and you need to know where and when to do it. We have already discussed the first part. The second part is a little more problematic. Here are the guidelines for how to proceed.

Some time ago, you were asked to start a daily log noting the times you experienced tension. You should also have identified the places and people involved. If you carried out this self-observation with consistency, you should have some very useful information by now, such as particular people who get on your nerves or situations that seem to put you on edge. You may even have noticed certain themes in conversations that can set you off. Assuming that you have some of this information in hand, you have the basic information to tell you where and when to practice cue-controlled relaxation.

In order to make the use of cue-controlled relaxation as easy as possible, categorize the incidents of stress you logged in your diary on two dimensions. Take a single sheet of paper divided into quarters or use Table 12–2. Label the top Home for the left half of the page and Work (if you are employed outside the home) for the right side of the page. On the side, label the top half High Tension and the bottom half Low Tension. Then go through the daily log and consider the times you noted tension. The correct classification for home or work should be automatic. The correct classification for level of tension may be a little bit tougher. There is no way that I can tell you

Table 12–2.   Work Sheet for Home and Work Stressors

Home	Work
High Tension	
Low Tension	

which of the stress situations or people should go where. You are the sole judge of how intense the tension was.

Perhaps the easiest way is first to pick out the time you had the most intense muscle tension and the time you had the least intense muscle tension. Then use these two extremes to scale or evaluate the remaining events. Once this is done, you are ready to proceed to your first assignment: applying cue-controlled relaxation to a situation that is in process.

Select one of the situations in the Low-tension–Home category. It is best to pick a situation that seems to happen fairly regularly (so you can get in more practice and sooner) but is among the lowest in tension. The first time you recognize that the event is in process, prompt yourself to try cue-controlled relaxation. Take a deep breath, hold it for a moment, and let it go completely while you say to yourself your personal cue word. Nobody has to know that you are doing it. In fact, it is probably best to not let the other people around know what you are doing. Especially in the middle of an intense exchange, it might serve to irritate others more than to relieve them.

You should notice a decrease in your overall level of arousal. Most people report a *rush* of relaxation and with it a reduction in the level of anxiety. The positive effects, however, should be even more pronounced in your interpersonal relationships and problem-solving ability. In the midst of interpersonal conflict and crisis situations, extreme arousal and tension tend to reduce ability to think clearly, to respond sensitively, and to read the nuances of meaning in the messages being sent, both verbal and nonverbal, from the other parties to the conflict. We get defensive, responding to protect our own egos and our own needs rather than listening to the needs that are being expressed by others. What happens then is fairly predictable. We miss alternative solutions to the problem or overlook the important clues to what the other person is saying. Thus we tend to feed more tension into the situation, rather than helping to reduce it.

The decrease in tension produced by cue-controlled relaxation should help prevent defensive posturing and garbled communication. It should enable you to be at your best, thinking more clearly, seeing alternative interpretations for the words and behaviors of the other party to the conflict, and finding mutually satisfactory solutions to the problem.

It should also be obvious now why complete relaxation is not the goal of cue-controlled relaxation. Complete relaxation would not be constructive in the middle of interpersonal conflict or a crisis situation. Can you hear your teenager telling her friends "Every time I ask Dad if I can go on a date with Bob, he has to go relax for 15 minutes."? All we want is to bring tension back to a more desirable level. Moderate arousal is usually preferred. Hyperarousal is detrimental. Cue-controlled relaxation is intended to replace hyperarousal with moderate arousal.

When you have gained success with one of your home stressors, add more of the situations for practice. Make sure that they all come from the same low-tension category, however. Remember: Do not tackle the major problems until you have achieved some success with the minor problems.

◆ CUE-CONTROLLED RELAXING AT WORK

After you have successfully tried cue-controlled relaxation at home a few times, you are ready to take it to work with you. Once again, go back to your chart. Look only in the section labeled Low-tension. Identify one or two situations that seem to occur with some regularity at work. The principle is the same as before: Find a situation that will allow you to practice cue-controlled relaxation with a fairly high degree of frequency yet will not be too difficult to handle.

When you have identified one or two situations, remind yourself to be prepared for them to occur. When you recognize that one is developing, try cue-controlled relaxation. Go through exactly the same procedure as you did at home: Take a deep breath; hold momentarily; let the breath go; say your personal cue word to yourself; and relax. If necessary, repeat the cycle again. Do so discretely, however. It is not necessary to take such deep breaths that it sounds as though you are gasping for air.

Make a mental note of the effect. If you were successful, continue to work with this situation until you feel that you can control your tension whenever necessary. Also, go on to work with other situations in this same category. If you do not seem to get as much relaxation as you feel you should, do not fight it or try to force it. You may repeat the breathing–cue-word cycle a few times. but if you find you are concentrating more on the relaxing than on the situation, it might be best just to back off on the relaxation for this time.

If you did not get a sense of moderate relaxation and some feeling of relief in the midst of the situation, reexamine it. Determine if either the situation was generally more stressful than you originally thought or if just this particular episode got a little more stressful than normal. If the former, reassign the situation to the high-tension category and pick another stress situation to work with. Come back to this one later. If it just got a little more stressful than usual, continue with it, especially if you attained at least some degree of relaxation.

Once you have obtained success with both home and work low-tension stress situations, move on to the high-tension stressors. It may be helpful to reexamine the situations originally put in the high-tension categories. First, determine if you can make any finer distinctions among situations in this category. Using the experience you have now had trying to apply cue-controlled relaxation, you might see some differences that did not appear earlier. If so, try to subdivide these high-tension stressors into two categories, such as moderate stressors and the real tough ones. Take one or two of the moderate stressors at home and deal with them in the same way as indicated before.

When you have achieved success here, go on to the moderate stressors at work. Next, take one of the toughest home stressors and work on it. Try to make sure that at each step you have at least three to five successes before taking the next step. Finally, pick one of the toughest stressors from your work list. Once you have achieved success with one of your toughest stressors, be it of the home or work variety, you should be a long way down the road to having a useful stress-management technique in hand. From here on you can pick any of the stressors, old or new, easy or hard, and feel fairly confident that you can bring it under control using cue-controlled relaxation.

A last word of caution is in order. Cue-controlled relaxation is not a panacea. It will not make up for lack of training in areas of technical–professional expertise on the job. It will not solve the problem of insensitivity, lack of impulse control, or incompetence in other people. No matter how reasonable, calm, and in control you are, it will not necessarily make other people more reasonable, calm, and in control.

What it may do is help you assess better when circumstances are out of your control. Then instead of dumping more pressure on yourself, you may recognize that long-term and group-established goals will have to be set in order to change the way things have been working, at home or at work. It may also help you see when you need to go outside of yourself for help with the situation. And it is important for you to recognize that admitting you need outside help on occasion is not the same as admitting defeat. It is more properly recognizing the limits of your abilities, an important part of realistic self-appraisal. A popular saying expresses the message very well: "God grant me the courage to change the things I can, the ability to accept the things I can't, and the wisdom to know the difference."

◆ DIFFERENTIAL AND GRADUATED RELAXATION

The last section of this chapter deals with one of the more finely tuned aspects of relaxation training. It can also work for you in a variety of situations, private or public, to help reduce tension and physical fatigue that is due to stress. The technique is referred to as *differential and graduated relaxation*. It depends upon two essential skills: the ability to scan your muscles mentally to determine which muscle group is tense at the moment and the ability to relax that muscle group by itself to whatever level is both necessary and appropriate for the situation. While this may seem like a tall order, you will see that you already have done some of the work.

Mental Scanning for Tension

Scanning your body for tension should be almost second nature by now. As described before, mental scanning is like a CB scanner, quietly but automatically scanning all of the body channels until it finds a signal. Once it has found a signal, it should lock in and sound the alert so that you become aware something is amiss. Then you can respond with more focus but also more control.

You have practiced attending to muscle tension in all parts of your body for the entire time you have practiced relaxation. You have made note of muscle tension in both home and work stress situations. You have used muscle tension as a warning system to tell you when stress was building in these situations. You then took another step and actually tried to reduce tension by applying cue-controlled relaxation when the situation warranted. This practiced sensitivity to the signs of stress was the building block of the mental scanning technique.

Relaxing One Muscle Group

Perhaps an example will help. When driving in heavy traffic and pushing a deadline, I sometimes find my right shoulder muscle getting very tight. For a while I just tried to ignore it. But gradually I came to realize that tension had been there for a long time before I actually admitted it. Also, I came to recognize that the tension was making me much more tired and was interfering with concentration on the job at hand. It was also taking some of the joy out of driving.

This is an example of the kind of situation in which differential relaxation might be used. We do not want to reduce the overall level of arousal as with cue-controlled relaxation. We just want to reduce the tension in one muscle group and only that muscle group. And most importantly, we want to be able to control the depth of the relaxation. Obviously, too much relaxation while driving can be dangerous. In many situations, we still want to maintain some muscle tension, but we want fluid tension, such as when playing tennis or basketball. This is the basis for designating the procedure as differential and graduated relaxation.

To develop this skill to its fullest, proceed as follows. First, look back through your log of tension situations and determine if there are any muscle groups that seem to be more regularly involved than others. Some people report that the neck muscles always seem to tighten. For others, it is the shoulder muscles. Some notice a tightening of the muscles in the front of the neck under the chin. At any rate, see if you can detect a pattern.

Assuming that you do, take some time in your relaxation periods to practice with that muscle group alone. Tense the muscle by itself and then relax. Try to make sure that you are working only on that muscle and do not worry about the rest of your body. When you are able to obtain fairly deep relaxation in that muscle, work on graduated levels of relaxation. Try to scale tension–relaxation as you did before and reduce tension about 25%. Practice with this approach until you feel you can fairly readily produce any degree of relaxation desirable in the muscle.

It is not necessary to be able to produce the deepest relaxation that you would get with full body relaxation. In fact, most clinical studies suggest that you will not be able to do that. Even if you can get somewhere in the 50% level of relaxation, you are probably doing very well. Also, that level of reduction in muscle tension will usually suffice for the practical application of the technique.

There are two other techniques that can be combined with relaxation in order to achieve better control. One is to attach a cue word to your relaxation of the particular muscle group. If you are usually only concerned with one muscle group, this can be a very effective technique. Just be sure to select a different cue word from the one you use for general relaxation. Combine deep breathing and the word with relaxing that muscle group alone. With enough practice sessions of this nature, you may be able to reduce tension in the particular muscle in the same way you reduce general muscle tension—with a word. You should be able to regulate the depth of relaxation by the number of repetitions of breathing and cueing you go through.

A second technique is to use a form of visual imagery. Try to form a mental picture of something unique—for example, seeing yourself with that shoulder muscle in a whirlpool bath with warm jets of water pulsing the muscle. Or see yourself receiving a massage of the tense muscle. This principle is similar to autogenics, which makes extensive use of visual imagery.

The important part is how you sequence it in your practice. If you voluntarily tense the muscle during practice, the image should not be present. Just as you relax, call up the image and get it as strong as possible while you continue to relax. You can even prepare slides or cut pictures from a magazine to pin up on the wall. Close your eyes during the tension phase. Open your eyes and look at the picture during the relaxation phase. Try to get the picture locked in your mind so it can be called up very quickly and vividly. If you already know that you are very good at imagery, this technique may be right for you. If you have always had some difficulty forming mental images, it might be better to stick with the cue-word technique.

Once you have practiced this for a while at home, the next step is to apply it on the go. Go back to the daily log or chart. Are there situations you still have not dealt with that would be suitable for this technique? Maybe you play bridge regularly and find that you get tension in the neck muscles during keen competition (or because your partner does not always play well). Here is a social situation that might be a suitable candidate for differential relaxation.

There are a number of potentially appropriate situations for differential relaxation. As noted earlier, this technique is finding widespread acceptance among professional athletes, who need to maintain fluid muscle control even in the midst of intense competition. It can be used while driving, flying, or skydiving. It has even been used by mountain climbers. You might find it more useful on the tennis court, in a staff meeting, or some other setting relevant to your life-style.

The list of applications may be endless. Wherever and however you seek to apply it, stick to these few basic rules:

1. Develop the mental scanning skill first.
2. Practice regulating depth secondly.

3. Attach cue-word or imagery control for better control.
4. Practice in the neutral setting of your home for some time before taking it on the road.
5. Ensure that your application is situationally appropriate.

The last point bears some elaboration because we have developed three different techniques in this chapter. You certainly would not want to try to go into a deep state of relaxation while driving. But after a long, pressure-packed day at the office, deep relaxation may be most useful. Alternately, differential relaxation may not be desirable in a staff meeting if general anxiety is the problem. Cue-controlled relaxation would be better. By the same token, an intense cramp in the neck muscle occurring when you are taking a licensing exam might call for differential relaxation.

The next chapter will take you into extensions of the imagery technique and teach you the application of the relaxation technique to situation-specific fears. In the meantime, you have developed a varied and relatively powerful group of skills that can help you deal with tension in the private, social, and professional arenas of your life.

◆ NOTES

[1]The term *Tietze's syndrome* is technically reserved for the condition in which local swelling occurs, which does not occur in chostochondritis.

[2]Personal statement supplied by the patient. Permission granted for use of information in anonymity.

13

COGNITIVE AND IMAGERY TECHNIQUES: AUTOGENICS, DESENSITIZATION, AND STRESS INOCULATION

All our interior world is reality—and that perhaps more so than our apparent world.

Marc Chagall

———————————◇———————————

Tom was a 28-year-old male who had suffered several years with severe colitis.[1] For nearly seven years, he had been from one doctor to another seeking a physical remedy for the ailment. He had even checked into a prominent medical facility for a lengthy series of tests. Still the answer seemed to elude him and the abdominal pain and diarrhea kept on crippling him. The first time he called, it was to seek help for the colitis. But in a short time it became obvious that Tom's colitis was just one branch in a maze of symptoms, a complex set of anxieties and fears that prevented him from enjoying life to the fullest.

In addition to colitis, Tom had a phobic fear of meeting customers in the store where he worked. The most debilitating fear, though, was his obsessive fear that he would be stricken by a heart attack while he was out with friends. This fear was based on an earlier social engagement, when he was attracted to a young woman. The intensity of his arousal frightened him. But this was not the worst of it. He felt guilty because of his desire, and he also was extremely fearful that he would be rejected. The result was a terrifying panic attack with hyperventilation. He thought that his heart was quite literally going to stop. Unfortunately, he gave the worst possible interpretation to the symptoms—that he had a serious heart problem and thus could not ask anyone to share his life. As a result, at 28 years of age, he had become a virtual recluse with little or no social life.

But the symptoms did not stop there. Tom had extreme difficulty getting to sleep and he could not relax at all. He had a pervasive pattern of obsessional thinking, which influenced all of his activities. At home, he was obsessed with the thought that he had left his gas range turned on or the windows open during rain. He was convinced that the landlord would find out and that he would be evicted from his apartment. At work, he was obsessed with the thought that he would do something wrong and lose his job. He would go home at night and worry that he had left some machine on at work, which would destroy the store or get him in trouble with the manager. At times, these thoughts so overwhelmed him that he felt compelled to leave his apartment in the wee hours of the morning, walk nearly a mile to the store, and reassure himself that the machine was off.

Dealing with pervasive anxiety, deep-seated fears, and panic requires more than just relaxation. It requires some way of coming to grips with the irrational thoughts and attitudes that prompt self-defeating and self-restricting behaviors. In this chapter, a variation of the relaxation technique, *autogenics,* will be introduced. Also, a method called *desensitization* will be described that uses deep muscular relaxation to deal with specific fears and obsessional thought patterns. Finally, the principles and practice of *stress inoculation* will be discussed. This approach prepares you to deal with stress in advance.

◆ IMAGERY: THE CORE OF RELAXATION

In many clinical studies of relaxation techniques, including meditation, investigators have tried to find out what clients are doing internally, what they are thinking or saying to themselves to bring on the deep, quieting, and satisfying states of relaxation. One of the common threads running through client reports was that they were using mental pictures or images. For example, one person might get a picture of a sunlit beach, hearing the lapping of waves and gentle cries of sea gulls. Another might imagine being on top of a mountain peak looking out over a vast, unspoiled wilderness while listening to the wind murmur through the spruce. Still another might imagine the face of a friend or lover.

Eastern meditators use a variety of imagery techniques in the process of gaining control over mind and body. During their religious ecstasies, they produce a brain wave called **alpha**, a slow (12–14 hertz) wave form that is between the alert waking state and the first stages of sleep. Joe Kamiya, pioneer biofeedback researcher, showed that people can learn to control alpha rhythms through the use of *biofeedback.* In the course of his studies, though, Kamiya noted that many of his subjects were using some form of visualization to keep alpha turned on.[2] It may have been the images used, more than the specific biofeedback procedure, that allowed them to control alpha. Runners and other athletes also report that visualization helps in both training and competition.

◆ AUTOGENICS:
IMAGERY-BASED RELAXATION

Autogenic therapy (*autogenic* means "self-produced") is a relaxation technique that emphasizes imagery and self-suggestion. It has become the relaxation method of choice in Europe, where it was first introduced in 1932 by the German psychiatrist Johannes Schultz. According to Schultz and his protégé Wolfgang Luthe, **autogenics** is a means of maintaining the internal psychophysiological balance of the body.[3] Further, it allows a person to plumb the depths of the unconscious. Its major appeal, though, is that autogenics can be rather simple for beginners wanting to learn a basic tension-reducing method. But it is complex enough to permit the more adept users to go on to more esoteric practices that presumably tap the recesses of the psyche. A cautionary note is important: Advanced autogenics may require professional guidance for safe and effective use.

The training procedure for autogenics bears a certain resemblance to the procedure for deep muscular relaxation. As the following pages show, there are certain points of difference, however. These differences are apparent both in practice and in application.

Relaxation training is a very active muscle exercise procedure that teaches the person to recognize the difference between tension and relief. In autogenics, the goal is to develop an association between a verbal (thought) cue and the desired body state of calm. There are no active physical exercises. Thus, while autogenics focuses on body posture, imagery, and self-instructions, the body remains more or less passive.

Preparing for Autogenic Training

Just as there are certain things that you should do in preparing for relaxation, there are several conditions that Schultz and Luthe recommended for successful autogenic training. These are

1. A high degree of motivation and willingness to follow the instructions explicitly.
2. An adequate degree of self-direction and self-control.
3. Use and maintenance of correct body posture.
4. Reduction of external stimuli and mental focusing on internal physical and mental states.
5. Use of monotonous, repetitive input to the various senses.
6. Concentration on somatic processes in order to bring about an inward focused consciousness as opposed to an outward focused consciousness.

If these conditions are met, there will presumably be a feeling of passivity, an almost vegetative state of mental activity that melts into an altered state of consciousness.

7. The emergence of an overpowering, reflexive psychic reorganization.
8. The occurrence of disassociative and autonomous mental processes leading to an alteration of ego functioning and dissolution of ego boundaries.[4]

These last two conditions are actually more the end results of autogenic training than the preparation. They are signs of success when the instructions are adhered to faithfully. But you must be prepared to accept the altered state of awareness, look for it, perhaps even long for it. Otherwise, its appearance can be regarded as a stranger, something to be feared and rejected rather than welcomed. This could interfere with continued progress in autogenic training or lead to abandoning the technique altogether.

Luthe discussed a type of reflex motor tremor that occurs during early training called the *autogenic discharge*. Also, crying spells may occur during training. This is viewed as a type of emotional catharsis related to the release of pent-up mental tension. The similarity to relaxation—the strange sensations some people report—is apparent.

Maintaining passive concentration during the exercise is important to continued progress in training. Therefore, if and when any of these foreign sensations occur, do not try to fight them. Rather, let them pass as part of the process—as signs of progress, not failure.

All of the other preparations that were discussed in Chapter 11 also pertain here: Choose the time and place for comfort and isolation. Reduce external distractions by removing the phone or having calls intercepted. Remove tight-fitting clothes or jewelry, and prepare your mood for passive attention to the exercises.

Autogenic Body Postures

In relaxation training, the recommendation was to use an easy chair, even a recliner in a partial (never full) stage of reclining. In autogenic training, three body positions are allowed, none of which is the same as the relaxation procedure. These are (1) lying down, (2) seated with back support, and (3) seated without back support.

In the first position, you lie down on the floor with pillows or blankets to cushion the head and knees. If you use a pillow under your head, make sure that you do not throw your head up and forward onto your chest. A shallow pillow which cushions without misaligning your head and body is preferred. Arms should be at your side with hands near your thighs and palms turned up. Your legs may be slightly apart with toes pointed away from the body. In general, you should not lie down on a bed, as there is more of a tendency to pass off into sleep.

The second position requires a chair with a high, straight back. A chair with arms is all right but not necessary. Position yourself back in the chair so that support is provided for both your back and your head. Keep your head aligned straight over your neck and back. Resist the temptation to let it fall off to either side, as correct alignment with the body axis is important to success. Arms can be supported on the arms of the chair or in your lap if you do not use an armchair.

The third position uses a stool or low-backed chair. With either type of seat, sit forward on the stool or chair. Your arms are supported on the thighs and the hands dangle loosely over your knees. Your head may come forward over your chest but may not touch the chest. Keep your feet shoulder-width apart and just slightly forward of the knees.

The image suggested by Schultz and Luthe may help you to visualize this position. Imagine that you are a big rag doll with a string attached to the top of your head. The string is attached to the ceiling and you are pulled up in the chair. Because you are a rag doll, you will be completely limp, legs and arms dangling without a bit of tension. Then imagine that you are let down, the string is cut, and you flop back onto the chair. What would happen to the doll? The head, neck, and shoulders would collapse forward. This is the posture you want. However, take care that your head and chest do not roll so far forward that breathing is restricted.

You will not get as much muscular relaxation with either of the seated positions as in reclining because of the support for the body that your muscles must maintain. However, you can still obtain an adequate degree of relaxation if you focus on the proper body position. Whichever position you choose, stick with that position in the early stages of training until you have seen the results. The only exception to this is that some exercises specify a particular position. Later on, you will be able to switch from one position to another. In the meantime, if you find yourself tensing your muscles to support yourself in one of the seated positions, check to be sure that your alignment is correct.

Learning autogenics consists of two different segments each with six different exercises. The basic exercises focus on body sensations in order to establish a balance and rhythm in the autonomic system. The imagery exercises focus on the mental capacity to form, hold, and manipulate mental images of external objects. Do not rush to get through and do not move on to the second set until you have achieved the criterion for completing the basic exercises. This criterion is given at the end of the first set.

The Six Primary Exercises of Autogenics

At the beginning of autogenic training, there are six stages that focus attention on different parts of the body or different sensations. Here are the basic exercises and instructions that will enable you to begin to practice autogenic relaxation.

Stage 1: Arm and Leg Heaviness.   Focus your attention first on the arm that is your most active arm. If you are right-handed, start with the right arm. Repeat these instructions (silently) to yourself as you concentrate on the arm:

"**My right (left) arm is heavy.**"

Do this about three to six times in a 30–60-second period. Close your eyes if you wish. At the end of this period, shake yourself out of any lethargy and open your eyes before you move on to the other arm. This is referred to as *cancellation*. Repeat the same instruction for the other arm using the rule of three to six repetitions in each 30–60-second interval. Then do each of the legs using the same instruction:

"My right (left) leg is heavy."

Finally, do the limbs together using the sequence indicated in these instructions:

"Both my arms are heavy."
"Both my legs are heavy."
"My arms and legs are heavy."

Remember to do the cancellation after each of the sequences before moving on to the next exercise.

Stage 2: Arm and Leg Warmth.   In the second stage of the exercise, focus on the sensation of warmth. It is not unusual for people to experience feelings of warmth during the earlier exercise for heaviness. But here the specific focus is on warmth, which should be experienced as a spreading sensation of warmth throughout the body. The same general procedure is repeated as in stage 1, but with the instructions modified to suit the desired outcome as follows:

"My right (left) arm is warm."
"My right (left) leg is warm."
"Both my arms are warm."
"Both my legs are warm."
"My arms and legs are warm."

If it helps to use a mental image, think of the warm sun as you recline on a beach or imagine that you are in a soothing tub of hot water.

With each of these exercises, it may take some time for you to experience the comfortable and pleasant sensations of warmth and heaviness. You may need anywhere from four to eight weeks to learn to produce warmth in the limbs.[5] Several months may be required before you produce the entire range of experiences with ease and speed. Do not become concerned, then, if you feel that you are not moving as fast as you would like.

Also, keep in mind that the speed with which you develop the skill depends on how consistently you practice. In autogenic training, regular practice is anywhere from one to six sessions *per day*, with each session lasting 10–45 minutes. The norm is two to three sessions. If you have time for more sessions per day, by all means do them. You will make faster progress. For the most part, however, you will be able to gain a great deal by being able to practice twice a day. Expect early sessions to take 40–45 minutes. Later on, you may experience the full benefits in as few as 10–15 minutes.

Stage 3: Heaviness and Warmth in the Heart.   In the third stage, extend the heaviness and warmth exercises to the area of the heart. The instruction to repeat to yourself is:

> "My heartbeat is regular and calm."

Do this for two to three minutes, repeating the instruction at regular intervals during this time. You may want to hold your hand over your heart so that you can feel the changes occurring. Also, you may find it easiest to use the reclining position for this exercise. Remember, always use a cancellation between each instruction and stage.

Stage 4: Paced Respiration.   After focusing on heaviness and warmth in the heart region, the exercises move on to measured or paced respiration. Paced breathing can have a very calming effect on the mind. It takes on a rhythmic, trancelike quality when attended to deeply. Breathing has been used for a long time and by a large number of groups as a means to enhance muscular relaxation and mental tranquility. The self-instruction to be used can alternate between the two listed here:

> "It breathes me."
> "My breathing is calm and relaxed."

Repeat these instructions four to five times in roughly a 90–150 second period. Mental visualization of some image may also help. For example, you might visualize waves rolling in on the beach and pace your breathing to each wave that breaks. With this exercise, you may notice significant gains in anywhere from one to five weeks.

Stage 5: Abdominal (Solar Plexus) Warmth.   In the fifth exercise, you attempt to induce warmth in the abdominal region. The actual focus of attention is the solar plexus, the upper abdomen just above the stomach but below the heart. The same instruction used for the heart can be used here with just the minor modification:

> "My solar plexus is warm."

It is important to note that you are trying not to warm the surface of the skin but rather to produce a warmth deep inside the upper abdominal cavity. Warming the solar plexus is known to have a soothing effect on the activity of the central nervous system. It will also enhance muscular relaxation and it may cause drowsiness.

These effects may be related to action of the parasympathetic nervous system. Imagining warmth in the abdomen may induce increased blood flow to the center of the body through the parasympathetic system. Since the parasympathetic is the calm, tranquilizing side of the autonomic nervous system, most of the other effects associated with its operation (as were introduced earlier in the study of relaxation) may be expected to occur, such as muscular relaxation. Thus the verbal cues of autogenics may accomplish a behavioral switching of the autonomic system from sympathetic arousal to parasympathetic calmness.

Stage 6: A Cool Forehead.   The last basic exercise is to practice cooling the forehead. The instruction is:

"My forehead is cool."

Although all of the other exercises have focused on warmth or heaviness, this one tries to induce a feeling of coolness on the forehead. Also, this exercise may require the prone posture rather than the seated postures. If you try to work at this exercise too quickly, you might experience some dizziness or fainting. It is advised, then, that you start slowly with no more than two or three repetitions over about 20–30 seconds. Later, you can build up to four or five repetitions lasting two to four minutes.

Sometime during the first year, most people reach a point where they can go through the entire six exercises in less than five minutes. As noted earlier, you should not expect this to occur sooner than about two months. Some exercises may not feel right until much later, while others, such as breathing, may feel right much sooner. When you reach this point of proficiency, though, you should stay in the state of autogenic meditation for from 30 minutes to an hour.

Beginning Autogenic Visualization

Although only a little visualization is used in the basic exercises, imagery is an integral part of advanced autogenics. According to Schultz and Luthe, the purpose of visualization exercises is to be able to hold on to images for a period of time while determining their effects on consciousness itself. You should not attempt to move into this stage until you are confident that the prior six exercises have been mastered, as indicated by the criterion of being able to enter autogenic meditation in less than five minutes and hold on to the autogenic state for 30–60 minutes.

It is important to note that some people feel the assistance of an autogenic therapist is necessary at the beginning of this sequence. Even though autogenic exercises can be much more complex than what is described here, it may be difficult to proceed without professional assistance. If you feel unsure of yourself and find progress less than satisfactory, consider locating an autogenic therapist.

If you choose to proceed, remember to use the cancellation exercise (described earlier) between each visualization exercise. Also, if you encounter any distorted, unpleasant, or disturbing images, use the cancellation procedure before resuming visualization.

Looking at your forehead.   The first exercise is to roll your eyeballs upward. Imagine that you are trying to look at a spot just above and between the eyebrows on the inside of your forehead. This eye position has been commonly used by many people using a wide variety of meditative practices. It tends to increase brain alpha and enhances a trancelike state.

Immersing the mind in color.   The second exercise is to pick a favorite color and try to "see" that color. Imagine that you are in a room that has no form or dimension and that the entire room is swathed in your favorite color. It fills your entire visual field. Let your mind be immersed in that color. After mastering this exercise, you are ready to move on to more complex images.

Autogenic therapists suggest that different colors have different effects. For example, purples, reds, yellows, and oranges are apparently associated with warmth. Blue and green, on the other hand, are more frequently connected with coolness. Try different colors so you will know which ones have the most beneficial effect for you. If you find that certain colors are "warm" colors, some are "heavy," and others are "cool," use those colors to reinforce your autogenic meditation.

From this point on, you can begin to visualize more complex shapes and colors. For example, visualize bright white clouds against a blue sky. Visualize those clouds moving. Then try simple geometric forms such as squares, triangles, circles, and so forth. Fill those forms with color and change them. Zoom in so that they fill your entire mental frame, and then draw back so that you see them from a distance. The intent is to become familiar with the ability of the mind to manipulate images of form and color.

Focusing on objects.   For this exercise, pick some object and try to visualize it against a dark void. You might pick a vase or Greek theater masks. The choice of object is yours, but at first keep the object relatively simple. If an object spontaneously comes to your mind as you are reading this, stop and make a note of that object immediately. It may be an object of special significance and thus easy to use for practice. Training at this stage can take more time than in the previous stages. Induce the autogenic state as quickly as you can, and then spend 40–60 minutes in object-imagery practice.

Transforming abstractions.   This exercise concentrates on some abstract idea, such as truth, love, justice, or freedom. The intent is to obtain a mental picture of these ideas, transforming concepts into concrete symbols. You may hear a word, such as *love,* being repeated in your mind, or see a symbol that represents unity better than any dictionary can. This is the meaning of transforming abstractions. You will need roughly two to six weeks for this imagery exercise.

Transcending feelings.   The previous exercises involved some form of visual or auditory imagery. This exercise requires that you focus on a feeling, an emotion that wells up inside you. You want to feel it just as though it had been started by something outside. Imagery is still used and is important to reaching the goal of this exercise. But imagery is only a tool. It is the feeling that is important. Practice in this stage should also go on for 30–60 minutes per session. You may use some of the mental images already described for certain emotions. For example, seeing yourself on top of a mountain peak overlooking a vast wilderness may be associated with joy, contentment, or ecstasy. Erotic fantasies may also occur and be experienced as though you are a part of the scene.

The intent of this practice is to explore the role that you play in transactions filled with emotionality. When you are able to place yourself in these dreamlike roles and recognize the times when you switch from reality (so caught up in the dream that it seems real) to fantasy (standing outside of it and treating it as fantasy), you may be in a position to begin to plumb the depths of your own psyche, to gain insights into conflicts and tensions that are of your own doing. When this happens, you may indeed be able to manage most effectively the things that are stressful and be able to maintain the physiological balance most conducive to good health.

Visualizing others.   In the last stage of imagery practice, the task is to visualize other people. At first, focus on rather innocuous people with some personal distance from you. Then visualize people much closer to you—peers, colleagues, and family members, for example. As you progress, these significant others may include those with whom you have been in conflict at some time. Try to visualize some transaction you have had with the person. As you get a more and more vivid image of the person and the setting, let the emotions you felt toward the person also be experienced again. This type of training may provide you with valuable insights into your feelings toward others, help alter your attitudes towards others, and thus help alter your perceptions of them.

In sum, the exercises proposed in autogenic training are intended to provide a means of self-regulation and self-study. Through the powers of imagery, a balance can be obtained between the arousing influence of the sympathetic system and the calming influence of the parasympathetic system. One line of speculation suggests that this is because the right side of the brain, which controls the autonomic nervous system, is also the creative, holistic, image-processing side of the brain. Thus, we may have a means whereby we can tell the autonomic system at what speed or in what gear we want the body to run. The exercises may also provide a way of bringing tension-laden feelings closer to the surface so we can neutralize, if not eliminate, the festering germs of conflict that tend to keep the body in a charged-up state.

Autogenics for Coping and Wellness

Autogenic exercise has been found useful for a wide variety of health problems. However, a note of caution must be sounded before any more is said of its successes and failures. Many psychotherapeutic techniques have been introduced over the years that seemed to hold some bright hope for helping people resolve personal dilemmas. All too often there has been a broad sweep of "research" touching on all kinds of physical and mental ailments, accompanied by reports of great success. Then the technique is "marketed" with great fanfare, and people jump on the bandwagon. After some years of careful and dispassionate observation, the practice is found to be far less than the panacea originally claimed. Yet it has a special niche it can fill with some success. Unfortunately, great expectations followed by a negative press and gradually eroding confidence can destroy the credibility of the practice even for that special niche.

An example of the success of autogenics is provided by Luthe, who summarized the treatment outcomes for 78 patients who had been treated in eight weekly group-training sessions.[6] The clients presented a number of complaints, including anxiety, phobic, and hysterical disorders. Out of the 78 patients, 10 (12%) showed very good improvement and 20 (26%) showed little or no change. The remaining 48 clients showed good improvement. Luthe and Blumberger summarized a number of other conditions for which autogenics has been used.[7]

In looking at the research on autogenics, one cannot help but be impressed by the success it has enjoyed over the years. But also one cannot help being disconcerted by the quality of the claims for autogenics. It has been studied for everything from rehabilitation of the neurologically impaired to curing cancer,[8] from treatment of epilepsy and alcoholism to treatment of tension headaches[9] and hypertension,[10] and from reducing smoking to curing sexual dysfunction. Recently, a more healthy degree of skepticism has emerged in regard to some of the less restrained claims. But this should not lead to the wholesale dismissal of autogenics. Whatever the failures it has had with certain types of disorders, autogenics is still a valuable coping technique.

◆ MANAGING SPECIFIC FEARS

Although relaxation and autogenics can be used for a large number of stress and health problems, another group of stress problems requires alternate approaches. This is especially true when extreme anxiety and specific fears are concerned, as the case of Tom illustrated. For these people, it is more than just being anxious or fearful. It is knowing that anxiety and fear are always there, keeping them captive with invisible bars. It is knowing that no matter how silly or irrational the thoughts may be, they cannot be driven from consciousness. It is wrestling with the mental distress, behavioral restrictions, and social confinement that fear brings.

Fear of any kind produces (1) behavioral changes, (2) physical reactions, and (3) altered thought processes. Behavior motivated by fear is usually some type of escape or avoidance behavior whereby you seek to get away from the feared object or event. Physical reactions range from cold sweat and light-headedness to chest pains, nausea, and fainting. Thought processes include recurring images of the feared scene, feelings of unworthiness and being out of control, and fear of going crazy.

There are different types of fears. First, **simple fear** is defined as alarm or fright of some real or imaginary danger. The most severe fear is a **phobia**, the irrational but persistent fear of some specific object or situation. **Anxiety** is the feeling of impending doom without knowing when, where, and how the doom will occur. When it is severe, anxiety can render a person incapable of speech, movement, or coherent thought.[11] **Panic attacks** are the most severe anxiety reactions. During a panic attack, the person experiences a sudden onset of terror or apprehension of doom. In addition, physical changes occur, including sweating, faintness or dizziness, shaking, nausea, rapid pulse, shallow breathing, and hyperventilation.

The most common phobia is **agoraphobia**. The word is from *agora,* which is Greek for marketplace. It is fear of the marketplace or open, public places. The effect is to make the individual more or less housebound. Social phobias involve an irrational fear of situations that subjects the individual to public observation and possible embarrassment. One of the most common social phobias is fear of speaking or performing in public. Another common social phobia afflicts men who are afraid to use public urinals. Simple phobias include fear of animals, such as dogs or snakes; fear of closed spaces, such as elevators and tunnels; and fear of heights, such as being on tall buildings and flying. But, as C. B. Scrignar pointed out, simple fears are not really simple. They can interfere with travel, personal relationships, vocations, and even recreation.[12]

Anxiety also seems to be the core of obsessive–compulsive disorders. The obsessive–compulsive disorder is characterized by a recurrent and persistent thought pattern (the obsession) that cannot be voluntarily stopped and a repetitive behavior pattern (the compulsion) that seems to go on almost automatically, no matter what the person may try to do to stop it.

Tom had the obsessive thought that he had not shut off the gas stove. Several times he walked to work only to be overcome by his fear that the stove was still on. Then he would walk all the way home, check again, and return to work late. His solution was to get up nearly one hour earlier each morning so he would have time to check the stove to his satisfaction—sometimes 15 or 20 checks—and still get to work on time.

◆ MANAGING SPECIFIC FEARS WITH DESENSITIZATION

In recent years, desensitization has proven to be a very effective means of dealing with ongoing anxiety. The procedure was developed in the 1950s by Joseph Wolpe, a South African psychiatrist. Wolpe worked for several years with phobic and obsessive–compulsive clients, using traditional psychoanalytic therapy. But he became more and more disturbed at the low rate of success in curing his patients. This same lack of success was reported at the same time by many other clinicians.

After reading a wide range of experimental literature, Wolpe became convinced that these two disorders could be treated using recently developed behavioral theories. In the behavioral model, phobic and compulsive disorders are viewed as learned disorders that can be unlearned. The procedure Wolpe pioneered was first detailed in his now-classic book *Psychotherapy by Reciprocal Inhibition*.[13] The meaning of **reciprocal inhibition,** as discussed earlier, is that the two branches of the autonomic nervous system stop each other in turn. When the sympathetic system is aroused, the parasympathetic is quiet, and vice versa.

Wolpe accepted the idea that relaxation can be used as a behavioral switch to turn sympathetic arousal off, but he went far beyond this. He reasoned that when a feared object or event is presented at low levels through mental imagery, its power to produce fear can be controlled. If the person is relaxing while imagining the object, it will become associated with relaxation rather than fear. Gradually more intense representations of the feared object can be presented until the person is able to stay relaxed while imagining the most feared object. The meaning of the term **desensitization**, then, is the removal of sensitizing power of a feared object. In this way, fear is counterconditioned or unlearned.

◆ THE THREE KEYS TO DESENSITIZATION

Desensitization requires three elements: training in deep muscular relaxation, construction of a hierarchy of feared objects or events, and imagining the feared objects while in a state of relaxation. The previous chapters have explained relaxation training and provided guidance for becoming skilled in its use. The next few pages will explain the remaining two keys to the technique.

Constructing a Ladder of Fear

The second step in desensitization is to build a stimulus hierarchy, a type of ladder of feared objects, in which low rungs are for less feared objects while the highest rungs are occupied by the most feared objects. The rationale for building this hierarchy can be explained as follows.

Fear of objects can be controlled by maintaining physical distance. If you are afraid of heights, the solution is to stay off of tall buildings. If you are afraid of snakes, stay away from any area that is known to have snakes, including reptile gardens at the zoo. Restrict the amount of time spent in elevators if you are afraid of closed-in spaces.

Psychologically, fear decreases as objects or events become less and less similar to the original. For example, suppose someone is deathly afraid of rats or mice. The person might keep a physical distance from rodents by having frequent visits from the local exterminator and staying away from pet shops or laboratories experimenting with rats and mice. Now assume that this person goes to a theater to see a movie. The action takes the characters into a dark basement where rats run across their feet, much to the dismay of the viewer. The moving picture of the rats may be too realistic, and, as a result, it produces some tension. But suppose I showed this person a rather abstract representation of a rat (Figure 13–1). In all likelihood, the person would experience very little anxiety because the artwork is so different from the real thing.

In more formal terms, this is the principle of *stimulus generalization*. Simply put, **stimulus generalization** occurs when the same response is given to similar objects. The more similar the objects, the more likely the same response is to occur. Rats, mice, and possibly gerbils may all produce the same fear response. Rabbits and guinea pigs probably would not because there are major differences in appearance and meaning. The abstract rat is even less likely to produce the fear.

Thus, whether or not a similar response will occur to similar objects is not an all-or-none affair. It is related to a **stimulus generalization gradient**, a scale describing objects in terms of degree of similarity. One fear gradient of generalization is shown in Figure 13–2. Objects at one end of the scale, rats and mice, are very similar. At the other extreme are objects that are much less similar. On the vertical scale is the strength of the fear response. As objects become less and less like rats and mice, the fear response is less and less likely to occur.

Building a ladder of fear, a *stimulus hierarchy* in technical terms, is building a stimulus generalization gradient. Objects are placed on all rungs of the ladder in order of increasing fear, with the real thing at the top of the ladder. Examples of fear ladders for flying and public speaking are shown in Figure 13–3. By starting at the lowest level, you can control fear, keeping it at a distance, as it were, so that calm will prevail instead of tension.

Generally, though, we cannot use the real objects or events. This is where visualization comes in. The mind is capable of replaying images of feared objects, as we know very well. These are the mental videotapes of anticipated encounters that contain threat and arouse fear as though the

Figure 13–1.   An abstract rat.

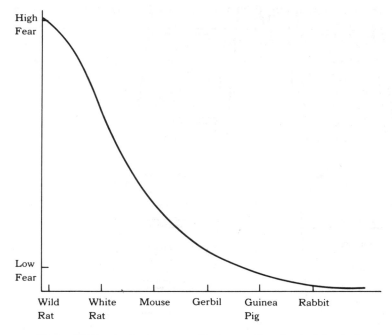

Figure 13–2.   A stimulus generalization gradient for the feared stimulus of rats.

object were there. In fact, research cited earlier shows that the brain does not distinguish between a real and an imagined event.[14] This is also why the process of imagining a feared event can produce the positive effects observed in this procedure. Desensitization uses a controlled voluntary replay of images to maintain psychological distance from the object and thus keep fear at manageable levels.

When we imagine the object on the lowest rung of the fear ladder while staying relaxed, the stimulus generalization process also works in our favor. The association between calmness and the first object spreads to the second rung on the ladder, so the second object arouses less fear than it did before. As we climb the ladder, we can handle more greatly feared items because each one has been desensitized by the spread of relaxation from the lower rungs. Finally, we are able to handle the object that was originally the most feared. At this point, the object has been desensitized and fear will no longer occur when it is present.

Here are some rules of thumb for building a hierarchy or fear ladder. First, keep the length of the ladder at 15 rungs, give or take a few. You may want to brainstorm until you have about 20 or 25 objects at first because you may find it necessary to drop some objects later on. Second, put the most feared object or event at the top of the ladder. Third, try to think of an object far enough away from the top that it will produce very little tension. This will be the bottom rung of the fear ladder. It is important, though, that the object bear some similarity to the most feared object. You cannot just select any

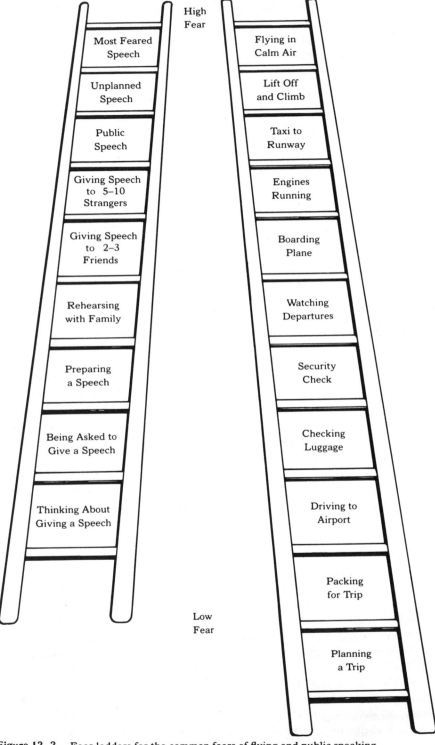

Figure 13–3.   Fear ladders for the common fears of flying and public speaking.

object to fill this bottom rung. Finally, select objects to fill the rungs in between the top (most feared) and the bottom (least feared).

After the ladder is built, go through the objects—from bottom to top—as you have placed them on the ladder and try to visualize each object or event as vividly as possible. Note the amount of tension you feel and decide if you have placed all the items in the right order. If you find any pair where the lower object produces more tension than the next higher one, reverse the order or find a new one to fill that rung.

If you want to be really precise, assign the lowest rung on the ladder a scale value of 1 and the top rung a value of 100. Then assign values to all the other objects reflecting the relative increase in fear you feel when going from low to high. For example, you may feel that the distance from the first to the second deserves a scale value of 5 units because of a very small jump in fear. But the next one might deserve a scale value of 15 because there is a relatively larger jump in tension. You can experiment with these values until you have all the rungs rated within the 1–100 scale, but each rung should be spaced about the same distance apart on the fear scale. A scale of fear constructed in this fashion is called a *subjective units of distress scale.*

If you find that some pairs of items are too close to each other on this scale, go back to the large pool of objects set up at the beginning. The objective is to have about 15 items with equal distances between each object in terms of the amount of fear produced. Just as climbing a ladder takes basically the same effort for each rung because the rungs are equally spaced, your subjective distress should change by the same amount as you climb the fear ladder.

Fear of dogs can be represented on a continuum from seeing a dog at some distance to petting a dog. Fear of leaving home can be represented in terms of distance from home in blocks or miles, amount of time away from home in minutes or hours, and number of supportive family members present or being alone away from home. Claustrophobia can be scaled in terms of the size of the room and the amount of time spent in the room. These are examples of the more common fear ladders that are constructed.

Before you take the third and final step, a few comments are necessary on how to present the items to yourself. As noted before, you do not typically work with the real objects of your fear. There are approaches that do, and Wolpe's technique can be modified to do so if necessary. When desensitization is done with the real object, it is called *contact desensitization* or *in vivo desensitization.* The latter means desensitization done in the natural environment.

The two methods most often used for presenting the fear ladder are emotive imagery and pictorial representation. Which is better for you probably depends most on how visual or how concrete you are. If you have very good powers of visual imagery, you should start with emotive imagery. If you need more concrete stimuli and do not consider yourself to be good at visualizing, the pictorial method may be best. You may also use the autogenic exercises to increase your ability to visualize. Either way, the method should not affect the outcome. It is mostly a matter of personal choice.

Emotive imagery.   The technique of emotive imagery is the old standby for desensitization. A feared scene or object on the ladder is presented to the mind as though you are drawing a verbal picture of it or playing a mental videotape. A conscious effort is made to get the scene to appear as vividly as possible. The scene usually has some emotion that goes along with it. You should be rather passive in this regard. In other words, you should not try to force a feeling into the moment nor should you try to block a feeling that wells up.

In the clinical setting, it is the clinician's job to prompt you with verbal phrases that help make the mental image more vivid. This luxury is not available in the privacy of your home. Some people find that a verbal cue for each rung of the ladder written on a sheet of paper is all that is necessary. Others put prompts on a tape recorder so that they can have a stand-in for the clinician. Whatever the method, know what objects or scenes are going to be used prior to beginning relaxation. Since you need no more than 3 or 4 objects from the fear ladder in any given session, it is fairly easy to do this.

Pictorial representation.   The pictorial method uses drawings, pictures, or slides to represent the feared scenes. It is possible to mix drawings and pictures. In fact, drawings make it very easy to obtain some remote symbols of feared objects. Some years ago, a student of mine was quite distraught about a rodent phobia she had had since about 6 years of age. She used a self-conducted desensitization program based on my instruction, beginning with line drawings and pictures. She first used line drawings like the abstract rat and cartoons of rats and mice for the lower rungs of her fear ladder. Blurred and dark pictures of rats were just below the middle of the ladder. More vivid color pictures were placed just above the middle. Pictures of people holding rats were near the top. Scenes of this nature can be presented by slides also, though I do not recommend mixing pictures and slides in the same fear ladder.

Pairing Relaxation and Fear

At this point you are ready to take the third and final step in desensitization. This is to practice relaxation while imagining the objects on the fear ladder. To proceed, first prepare your quiet retreat just as though you were going to engage in a regular relaxation session. If you used quiet background music during daily relaxation, omit it for these desensitization sessions. Then decide on the three or four prompts to be used for the session. Next, induce a deep level of relaxation and maintain it for a short period.

When you are comfortably relaxed, stir yourself enough to imagine the first item on the fear ladder. Concentrate on the image so it becomes as vivid as possible. While you passively try to remain relaxed, scan your body to spot any rise of tension. Hold the image for approximately one minute. If after this time you find no disturbance in the level of relaxation, stop the image and continue to relax for a few seconds. Repeat the imagery of the first rung one or two more times and then go on to the second rung of the fear ladder. Repeat the process through the set of objects selected for the session.

At any point that you experience a disruption in relaxation while imagining an object, *stop the imagery immediately!* Reinstate the deepest possible relaxation and enjoy it for a short time, a minute or two. Then step back down the ladder one rung to the previous object. Imagine the scene again while relaxing, and start back up the ladder. Sometimes you have to back down the ladder two steps, but usually you will be able to manage these setbacks by going back just one step.

Do not worry about these slight regressions. They are part of the process, and they only suggest that you either moved up the ladder too quickly or that you were trying to take a much bigger emotive step than you thought. After two or three tries, if you are still hung up at the same level on the ladder, you may need to insert one or two more rungs from your first pool of items.

Each session should work with no more than three or four scenes and present each image two to three times. In most cases, it takes about three weeks to desensitize all the objects on the hierarchy fully. This depends, though, on the nature and intensity of the fear. Some hierarchies might be done in a little as one week while others might take six weeks or more.

When you have finished the procedure, you may want to test yourself in the real world. It is advisable, though, to *proceed slowly.* To the extent possible, try lower rungs of the hierarchy in the real world first. Once you have tested yourself at this level, test yourself with one or more items from the upper range before finally trying the most feared thing. This is tantamount to doing in vivo desensitization. It is necessary to do this is some cases of severe phobias. But in most cases the process of desensitizing through emotive imagery is enough to eliminate fear of the real object or event.

◆ STRESS INOCULATION: PREPARING FOR STRESS

Medical research, faced with the problem of disease of epidemic proportions, developed inoculation procedures. Vaccines are injected into the body in controlled amounts. The body, through the autoimmune system, reacts to the presence of the germ cells by developing antigens to fight the disease. In other words, the body acquires immunity to the disease so that any future exposure will not be as likely to make the person sick.

Stress inoculation, the brainchild of Donald Meichenbaum, is based on the same idea, but the "germ" is psychological stress and the "vaccine" is exposure to low doses of stress in controlled conditions.[15] If people are exposed to low levels of psychosocial threat and then given ideas and skills to deal with that threat, they develop a resistance to the effects of stress. Later, when exposed to threat, they may seem to have an immunity. Psychosocial stress does not appear to affect them.

This procedure has been used successfully in a wide variety of stress situations including surgery in adult patients, childbirth, and preparing for painful medical tests. People with phobias, test anxiety, social shyness, speech anxiety, depression, anger, and chronic pain have been treated in the same way.[16] It appears to help those who are in conflict after making difficult career decisions and those who have decided to file for divorce. It may also be helpful in dealing with problems of recidivism in dieting and nutrition, smoking, and alcohol consumption.[17]

Stress inoculation involves three distinct phases. These are education, rehearsal of coping skills, and graded exposure to stressors combined with practice of coping skills.[18] The goal of the educational phase is to provide some understanding of the nature of the stress response and normal stress reactions. This information must be specific to the major current or anticipated stressor.

For example, people facing surgery or the death of a loved one are provided with information on what to expect and the kind of emotional and physical reactions that are likely to occur. Surgical patients seem better able to endure disruptive emotional and physical effects, whether anticipated or real, when information is provided on what to expect and what kinds of sensations and pains are likely to follow.[19] Reassurances are also provided to remove feelings of helplessness and hopelessness and to increase a feeling of self-efficacy. Because of this, stress inoculation may change the extent to which a person feels in control of a threatening situation.[20]

In the second phase, specific techniques are provided to deal with particular situations. The techniques may include relaxation, cognitive rehearsal, thought stopping, and self-instructions, among others. Meichenbaum listed a variety of self-instructions that can be used in a number of situations. For example, in getting ready for some type of provocation, the person might mentally rehearse such statements as "This is going to upset me, but I know how to deal with it" or "Try not to take this too seriously." When the situation is one of confrontation, an appropriate self-instruction might be "If I get mad, I'll just be banging my head against the wall. So I might as well just relax."[21] Cognitive rehearsals are very effective for changing perceptions and attitudes that serve to initiate and perpetuate stress interpretations.

The third phase involves applying the new coping skills to a graded series of imaginary and real stress situations. Seymour Epstein was one of the first to emphasize self-pacing and exposure to small doses of threat while developing coping skills in men who were engaged in dangerous activities, such as parachuting and combat flying. For example, assume that a manager has had difficulty providing candid periodic evaluations of employees. The manager might prepare for an upcoming meeting by imagining an evaluation session in process. Aspects of the situation that produce fear might be desensitized while tense interactions might be met with cue-controlled relaxation. Self-instructions might be mentally rehearsed, directed to aspects of the interactions that seem most often to undermine the integrity of the process. In this way, when the real sessions take place, the manager is much more likely to be able to handle them in a calm and professional fashion.

Perhaps the clearest example of stress inoculation is found in the work of Donald Meichenbaum's associate, R. W. Novaco. Novaco suggested that the flames of anger are fanned and kept burning by self-statements made in tense situations. For example, police dealing with rioters or involved in crowd control are under a lot of pressure. Anger can be aroused very quickly. One impulsive move, prompted by frustration, can lead to counterattack and to many disastrous consequences. The Chicago riots of 1968 during the Democratic Convention amply illustrate this point.

In Novaco's educational scheme, anger is conceptualized in terms of a sequence of events involving cognitive appraisal and physical arousal. When physical arousal occurs, the brain will probably interpret it as a result of real danger or threat. When this happens, there is a tendency to label the opponent in a negative, perhaps even demeaning, way. Then anger–attack schemata are played out in the mind, which drives the physical system to even higher levels of arousal. The higher the level of arousal, the more likely that some trigger will set off the mental anger–attack schema so that it is played out in physical attack.

For the second phase, relaxation training and self-instructional rehearsal are taught. The person, in this case the police officer, is taught how to self-prompt with statements about the sequence of events that will occur and with thought-stopping statements to interrupt the labeling process and the upward arousal spiral. Finally, in the third phase, the person is asked to imagine various anger-arousing situations. Then he or she cognitively rehearses coping with such provocations through relaxation, deep breathing, and self-statements.[22]

In a sense, much of the information provided in the first half of this book was related to the first inoculation phase, education about the internal processes, and situations that lead to stress interpretations and reactions. Information on techniques, which forms the second part of this book, is provided so you will have the skills necessary to be able to cope with a variety of stress situations. The third phase, graded exposure, is something you have to do on your own.

Think of stress inoculation as a type of broad-based desensitization before the fact. If you are aware of some troublesome social, personal, or professional situations you would like to manage more effectively, consider applying the principles of stress inoculation. You may be pleasantly surprised at the results.

◆ SUMMARY

In this chapter, three techniques were presented that use imagery and cognitive representations of stress situations. Autogenics, a variation of deep muscular relaxation, is more passive and incorporates explicit imagery exercises. The development of imagery skills can be very helpful in applying autogenics to a number of anxiety and stress problems; it can also enhance the practice of other stress-management skills, such as desensitization and stress inoculation, that have significant imagery components included.

Desensitization is best used for anxiety, fear, and mild panic disturbances. It can be tailored to individual situations and fears, is carried out in the privacy of one's home, and requires no more equipment than the capacity to use mental visualization. It is a natural extension of relaxation training to deal with specific fears.

Stress inoculation is the preventive branch of stress management. The primary purpose is to bring about a type of immunity to stress by teaching people how to anticipate stress transactions and defuse the potential for stress by rehearsing statements and behaviors that can be carried out in the real situation. By building up the dosage of mentally rehearsed stress conditions, the individual can more effectively deal with a wide variety and intensity of stress-arousing situations.

◆ NOTES

[1]Tom is a pseudonym used to protect the identity of the real person.

[2]Kamiya, J. (1969). Operant control of the EEG alpha rhythm and some of its reported effects on consciousness. In C. T. Tart (Ed.), *Altered states of consciousness* (pp. 519–529). Garden City, NY: Anchor Books.

[3]Schultz, J., & Luthe, W. (1959). *Autogenic training: A psychophysiological approach to psychotherapy.* New York: Grune & Stratton.

[4]Pelletier, K. R. (1977). *Mind as healer, mind as slayer.* New York: Dell, p. 232.

[5]Pelletier, *Mind as healer*, p. 240.

[6]Luthe, W. (1969). *Autogenic therapy.* New York: Grune & Stratton, pp. 66–70.

[7]Luthe, W., & Blumberger, S. R. (1977). Autogenic therapy. In E. D. Wittkower & H. Warnes (Eds.), *Psychosomatic medicine: Its clinical applications* (pp. 146–165). New York: Harper & Row.

[8]Simonton, O. C., & Simonton, S. (1975). Belief systems and management of the emotional aspects of malignancy. *Journal of Transpersonal Psychology, 7,* 29–48.

[9]Anderson, N. B., Lawrence, P. S., & Olson, T. W. (1981). Within-subject analysis of autogenic training and cognitive coping training in the treatment of tension headache pain. *Journal of Behavior Therapy and Experimental Psychiatry, 12,* 219–223.

[10]Charlesworth, E. A., & Nathan, R. G. (1982). *Stress management: A comprehensive guide to wellness.* Houston: Biobehavioral Press.

[11]Scrignar, C. B. (1983). *Stress strategies: The treatment of the anxiety disorders.* New York: Karger, p. 1.

[12]Scrignar, *Stress strategies,* p. 165.

[13]Wolpe, J. (1958). *Psychotherapy by reciprocal inhibition*. Stanford, CA: Stanford University Press.

[14]John, E. R. (1967). *Mechanisms of memory*. New York: Academic Press.

[15]Meichenbaum, D. (1977). *Cognitive-behavior modification: An integrative approach*. New York: Plenum.

[16]Janis, I. L. (1982). *Stress, attitudes. and decisions*. New York: Praeger, p. 267.

[17]Janis, *Stress, attitudes, and decisions*, p. 264.

[18]Meichenbaum, *Cognitive-behavior modification*, p. 150.

[19]Janis, *Stress, attitudes, and decisions*, p. 262.

[20]Janis, *Stress, attitudes, and decisions*, p. 278.

[21]Meichenbaum, *Cognitive-behavior modification*, pp. 166–167.

[22]Novaco, R. W. (1977). A stress inoculation approach to anger management in the training of law enforcement officers. *American Journal of Community Psychology, 5,* 327–346.

14

THE CONCENTRATION TECHNIQUES: MEDITATION AND BIOFEEDBACK

One night . . . being kept awake by pain, I availed myself of the stoical means of concentration upon some different object of thought. . . . in this way I found it possible to divert my attention, so that pain was soon dulled.

Immanuel Kant

The systematic approaches to relaxing and treating anxiety described earlier are mostly the products of modern technological culture. They mesh well with the Western penchant for scientific study and treatment of mental and physical health problems. But there is a long tradition of altering and controlling internal body states that reaches back to the dawn of recorded history. While there are many different representatives of this tradition spanning a variety of cultures and times, probably the most prominent is the Yoga tradition of deep meditation, which has its roots in ancient Hindu society. The sequence of events that led from the Western "discovery" of Eastern Yoga to practical coping methods cannot be detailed at length. But even the most cursory historical sleuthing reveals a fascinating story with intriguing vignettes and often startling insights.

◆ THE MYSTERIOUS GOD-MEN OF INDIA

From the time the British landed in India to current times, reports have filtered out of India about Yogis who could control their bodies to a degree never before believed attainable. Since the 1950s Western scientists have been observing these mysterious *god-men*[1] of India. What they have seen and examined with scientific methods has led to some modifications in conceptions of how the mind and body communicate.

For example, there were sensational reports of gurus who could reduce their heart rate to the point of total cessation. In a type of suspended animation, they could be literally buried alive for days.[2] The mystery of what they were doing to their hearts is now partially solved, but having it

302

explained does not detract from the sheer wonder that they were able to do it at all.[3] Other reports told of Yogis who could control the blood flow to their bodies so that they could withstand relatively severe temperatures.

What is the secret behind these Yoga practices? And what can we learn, if anything, that is useful for modern living? To answer the first question, we must look at the primary Yoga practice, meditation. In the process, we will study meditation as it has been imported into Western culture in Transcendental Meditation. In addition, Herbert Benson's secular meditation will be described.

To answer the second question, we must look at how the West has placed meditation under the scientific microscope. One outcome of this laboratory close-up is biofeedback, once touted as a high-tech alternative to years of religious discipline. The last section of this chapter will describe the more common biofeedback procedures and offer some suggestions on how these procedures can be used to complement the coping techniques described in Chapters 11–16.

◆ THE HIGH ROAD OF MEDITATION

It is apparent from ancient Hindu literature that meditation was viewed as the high road to spiritual enlightenment. In fact, meditation often occupied a position on a par with sacrifice and prayer. It was a means to an end, a concentrative practice that would allow one to withdraw from the world of illusion, escape the cycle of rebirths, and obtain union with the oversoul.

The Yoga System of Meditation

One such world view was the system of Yoga, which literally means *union*. The first systematic record of the Yoga way of life is contained in the *Yoga Sutras,* a manual written by Patanjali about 200 B.C.[4] The *Yoga Sutras* reveal a moral philosophy with rather strict ethical and moral codes of conduct. It prescribes an ascetic life-style and teaches a set of rigorous physical and mental exercises.

The practice of Yoga is an eightfold pathway beginning with ethical teachings to (1) restrain antisocial and selfish behavior and to (2) ensure positive conduct.[5] Then the student learns (3) postures, (4) control of breathing, and (5) withdrawal of the senses.[6] The physical path of postures and strenuous exercises has become associated with Hatha Yoga. Breathing exercises consist of learning how to inhale properly, hold the breath, and exhale with control.[7] All of these exercises were designed to enable a person to gain control of the body so that the mind can also be controlled. Control of the mind, though, is the province of (6) meditation, (7) contemplation, and (8) isolation.[8] The result in this life is supposed to be a reconditioning of the mind to release creative energy while freeing the person from chains of unconscious impulses and bondage to the senses.

A Yogi sitting in the lotus position.

Science Tunes In to Meditation

While philosophers had written about the Yoga system for years, most of the claims for altering heart rate, changing temperature, fire walking, needle penetration without bleeding, and altering consciousness were largely ignored if not discounted by the Western scientific community. Beginning in the 1950s, though, several investigative teams set out to substantiate some of the claims. Their efforts were presaged by the work of a French cardiologist, Therese Brosse, who traveled through India during 1935. She carried a portable electrocardiograph, which she used to measure Yogis as they tried to control their heart activity. One of her published records showed heart potentials approaching zero. Her work served to give some credibility to the scientific investigation of such claims and had a major impact on the next team to make a similar trip, nearly 20 years later.

The team of Wenger and Bagchi traveled in India for five months during the early part of 1957. The purpose of their trip was to test "various claims of voluntary control of autonomic functions and [record] physiological changes during Yogic meditation."[9] In observations of 45 Yogis, they observed temperature control, voluntary regurgitation, heart control, increased systolic blood pressure, and lowered skin resistance. They concluded that the Yogis were controlling heart processes through muscular control and breathing but not through any direct control. This conclusion was later confirmed through study of a Yogi at the Menninger Clinic in Topeka, Kansas.[10]

Wenger and Bagchi also attempted to measure arousal in the sympathetic nervous system in beginning and advanced students of Yoga. The Yoga school had claimed for centuries that the practice of meditation is beneficial to both the mental and the physical life of the practitioner. If this claim is true, Wenger and Bagchi reasoned, there ought to be some correlate in lowered activity of the sympathetic system. After making their observations, they made comparisons to an American control group. The results were somewhat surprising. On 7 of the 11 measures, the Yoga group showed *higher* sympathetic activity than the American control group. If meditation was serving to aid in coping with stress, it was not apparent in these observations. Still, Wenger and Bagchi recognized the limitations of their method and urged that more research be devoted to understanding the nature of the changes associated with meditation.

The West has probably been most fascinated with *alpha*, a brain wave consistently produced by Yogis during periods of meditation. Increased alpha has also been observed in Zen monks who practice a form of meditation derived from the Indian Buddhist tradition.[11] More will be said about alpha later.

◆ TRANSCENDENTAL MEDITATION: A WESTERN MANTRA YOGA?

During the 1960s, political, social, and religious activism were at a fever pitch. It was the decade of hippies, communes, resistance to the war effort in Vietnam, and Transcendental Meditation (TM). TM may be viewed as an adaptation of Mantra Yoga to conform to Western sensibilities. The Maharishi Mahesh Yogi, TM's founding father, pared out what he considered to be nonessential elements of traditional Yoga practices. He also stripped it of theological significance so it could be marketed as a secular practice. Efforts were made to ensure that TM was not associated with hypnosis, autosuggestion, or any of the then-popular encounter groups.[12] TM attracted between 500,000 and 1 million followers at one time and had a university with its own curriculum.

The practice of TM is remarkably simple, although the formal initiation ceremonies make it seem more mysterious and complex. The normal format of instruction includes three sessions; an opening information session; a second, more detailed instructional session, at which a commitment to practice TM is made; and a third initiation ceremony, in which a secret mantra is chosen. TM uses a secret word or mantra that is not to be divulged to anyone else. The word is presumably chosen by an experienced guide especially for the novice. But from that point on, the person basically practices TM alone.

The guidelines for practicing TM are relatively few. It is practiced for about 20–30 minutes per day, twice a day. The preferred times for practice are just before breakfast and just before the evening meal. During meditation, the person takes a seated position on a bed or on a floor cushion. The lotus position, the posture of "physical centeredness," is preferred. This position has been found to be the most relaxed of any seated position.[13] Eyes are usually closed and the room should be free of any other possible distractions. During meditation, the personal mantra is repeated over and over. This mental focusing prevents the appearance of thoughts of object attachment or concern with mundane matters. The use of the mantra, thus, is similar to the practice of visual focusing used in other circles. Zen monks concentrate on a koan, an unsolvable riddle, to help focus the mind but also drive the mind beyond itself.[14]

TM Under the Microscope

Shortly after TM was introduced to America, the team of Robert Wallace and Herbert Benson put TM under the scientific microscope.[15] Observations were made using instruments to allow for continuous recording of blood pressure, heart rate, temperature, skin resistance, and brain waves. Oxygen consumption and carbon dioxide elimination were also measured. Another measure, blood lactate level, was of special interest because it was believed to be related to anxiety.

The observations were carried out on 36 subjects with experience in the practice of TM ranging from one month to nine years. After a brief period to adapt to the laboratory situation, each person was observed for three 20–30 minute periods prior to, during, and following meditation. The results showed reduced oxygen use, a marked decrease in blood lactate, increased skin resistance, and intensification of the alpha wave. These results basically duplicated those obtained in the earlier field studies of Yoga and Zen monks.

Based on their observations, Wallace and Benson suggested that TM can be viewed as a fourth state of consciousness, which they called a "wakeful, hypometabolic" state. It is different from any of the three primary states of consciousness—waking, sleeping, or dreaming—although it shares some similarities with each. It is called *hypometabolic* because overall energy expenditure is reduced. Because several physiological indicators related to stress and anxiety are lowered during meditation, Wallace and Benson argued that TM could be used to ensure better mental and physical health.

After a number of initial glowing reports were published, TM was widely touted as the new mental wonder cure of the 1970s. It was supposed to help reduce drug dependency, cure smoking, even increase IQ, improve emotional stability by controlling depression and reducing anxiety, and facilitate self-actualization.[16] One of the best-selling books of the day was *TM: Discovering Inner Energy and Overcoming Stress,* which extolled the virtures of TM and went so far as to suggest that a fulfilled society could be produced if only everyone would practice TM.[17]

However, subsequent research led to skepticism about many of the claims for TM, including the notion that meditation produces a unique state of consciousness. One study showed that meditators actually spend a great deal of time in sleep stages as well as in alpha.[18] Another study failed to find any reduction in the physiological indicators of anxiety during a stress test.[19] TM was tested head to head against self-relaxation, PMR combined with cognitive coping skills, and a waiting-list control group. TM clients actually had a higher cardiovascular stress response following treatment than before and were worse than the waiting list group! Both of the relaxation groups showed significant decreases in their cardiovascular stress responses.[20] Thus, if TM has any positive effects at all, they apparently cannot be attributed to any unique ingredient. Rather, the benefits are more likely the result of some nonspecific general element that is shared with other relaxation procedures.

Be that as it may, the ease with which TM can be practiced is an asset, and the results may be as good as can be expected from any general relaxation procedure.[21] Therefore, if you find it appealing, there is no reason not to use TM. Indeed, an exercise that has some intrinsic appeal to you may be very useful for getting you into the habit of relaxing. The only word of caution offered is that you do not expect it to be a panacea. As with any other technique, it cannot be all things to all people for all situations. In addition, TM does not have the clinical track record of PMR, especially when PMR is combined with cue-controlled relaxation and desensitization.

◆ THE RELAXATION RESPONSE: SECULAR MEDITATION

After studying TM for some period of time, Herbert Benson also became convinced that the major active agent in TM is the general state of relaxation. On this basis, he reasoned that relaxation should be attainable without the physical tensing and relaxing exercises of PMR or the initiation rites of TM. The outcome was the development of a secular meditation procedure described in his book *The Relaxation Response*.[22]

In brief, Benson felt that four basic ingredients are necessary to prompt the appearance of the relaxation response. These elements are unprejudiced by any cultural, religious, or philosophical content. This is why it is called a *secular* meditation and why it may be practiced by anyone regardless of creed or religious beliefs. The four elements are

1. a quiet environment,
2. an object to focus on mentally,
3. a passive attitude, and
4. a comfortable position.[23]

A quick inspection shows similarities to both progressive muscle relaxation and autogenics. A controllable, quiet environment is essential for any of the relaxation–concentration exercises described earlier. Getting into a comfortable position is also important, although the actual position does not seem to be important. In PMR it is a semireclined seated position. In autogenics it could be any one of three positions. In Benson's view a sitting position is preferred, but other positions may be used including the lotus position. Any position that is conducive to sleep should be avoided, however.

Mental focusing is accomplished in TM with the **mantra,** the sacred word. The word is repeated over and over again silently, never aloud. Focusing can be accomplished in many other ways as well. In autogenics it is through color and form. In PMR it is through alternating states of tension and relaxation. Symbols may be especially good choices for mental focusing. The mandala, or circle, a universal religious symbol, is often used. The Eastern symbol of unity might serve just as well. Another ancient practice is to focus on the naval, the forehead, or some other body part. Arthur Deikman used a blue vase in his work.[24] You may pick virtually any word, sound, symbol, or object and achieve the same relaxing result. Benson recommended a rhythmic breathing cadence with the word *one* repeated every time you breath out.[25]

If you find difficulty with intrusive thoughts during the first sessions of meditation, Benson recommended use of a thought-stopping technique. Repeat for a short time the word *no* each time the intrusive thought occurs. After awhile, you should be able to eliminate unwanted thoughts easily and return to focused concentration. If the cue word has been well-established, you may be able to eliminate the intrusive thought by going through a short cycle of breathing while saying the cue word each time you breathe out.

All of the relaxation procedures emphasize a passive attitude. In fact, attitude seems to be the most important thing in producing alpha during meditation.[26] Attempts to make relaxation happen will only destroy the effort. Simply allow it to happen. Even if you do not find relaxation to be as deep as you think it should be at first, do not fight it and especially do not fret about it. Go on in the state of quiet contemplation until the time period is up. Deeper states of relaxation will eventually come.

Benson's secular method may produce many of the positive benefits that have been claimed for PMR, autogenics, and TM. Benson said that the relaxation response "can act as a built-in method of counteracting the stresses of everyday living which bring forth the fight-or-flight response."[27]

While secular meditation has not been tested in the range of settings that PMR has, it may be possible to extend the procedure somewhat. For example, Benson's procedure recommends the use of a cue word in association with breathing, much like progressive relaxation. This cue word is the backbone of cue-controlled relaxation, the ability to relax anywhere. Intuitively, it seems there is no reason why secular meditation could not be applied in the same way and thus cover the same range of stressful situations. It must be emphasized, however, that the effective ingredient of cue-controlled as well as of differential relaxation is not known. In addition, this type of application has not been clinically tested with secular meditation.

How far secular meditation can be taken is really a matter of guesswork at this point and any extensions must be tried on a solely experimental basis.

◆ BIOFEEDBACK: ELECTRONIC EUPHORIA OR PRACTICAL TOOL?

Even as meditation was being subjected to critical analysis in field and laboratory investigations, other researchers were looking at new ways of producing altered states of consciousness. The reasoning seemed to be twofold. First, if the physiological and brain-wave changes produced through meditation are real and stable effects, then science ought to do its best to understand and explain the conditions of such changes. Second, there ought to be some way to speed up the process without going through 20 years of asceticism. But how could this be done? In essence, a number of investigators thought that they had found the answer in biofeedback.

Putting Information Back into the System

Biofeedback has its historical roots in the field of *cybernetics*, or communication and control science. The mathematician Norbert Weiner defined **feedback** as regulating a system by putting back into the system information about its past performance.[28] Biofeedback uses a special type of information—information about the performance of the biological system. Whenever we obtain information about how our body is working by making internal signals externally visible, we are engaged in biofeedback. George Fuller defined **biofeedback** in a more formal sense as "the use of instrumentation to mirror psychophysiological processes of which the individual is not normally aware and which may be brought under voluntary control."[29]

An Overview of Biofeedback Procedures

In actual practice, biofeedback has very few components. A decision is first made on the physiological system to be altered. A body signal produced by that system is identified. A system is selected to amplify and display the body signal. The display is adjusted from time to time so that larger and larger changes in the body response are required for positive feedback. When the desired state is reached (for example, elimination of headaches or reliable production of alpha), the feedback system is faded out and an attempt is made to transfer control of the body response to cognitive and/or behavioral cues.

Body signals can be displayed with lights or meters, with sounds or strip charts. In fact, any method that tells a person when the desired internal state is present is acceptable. Some very novel displays of body messages have been devised. In one case, feedback was provided by a model train that ran when alpha was present and stopped when alpha disappeared. One team

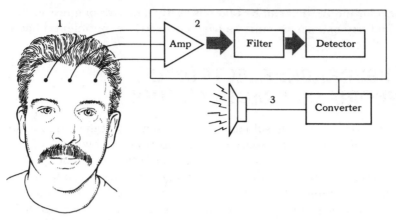

Figure 14–1. A biofeedback system usually includes (1) a sensing device that reads body signals, such as electrodes; (2) a filter–amplifier system to select the right signals and convert the body signal into some type of electrical signal; and (3) a display device to make the signal visible to the person.

working with children who were polio victims used muscle signals to light up a clown's face.[30] No matter how the body signals are displayed, the idea is to enable the person to make some connection to a behavior, a thought, an image that made the internal change happen. By engaging in the same behavior later, it may be possible to produce the internal state voluntarily.

◆ LISTENING TO YOUR BODY

A wide range of biofeedback techniques have been developed to make many internal responses visible. The procedures most often used are electromyography, electroencephalography, and feedback from skin temperature, skin resistance, blood pressure, and heart rate.

Listening to Muscle Tension

As muscles contract, they give off an electrical signal that can be detected through small electrodes. Electromyographic (EMG) feedback amplifies this signal and provides information on the amount of muscle tension. Visual feedback is most often a meter somewhat like an ammeter, which shows when a battery is charging (high tension) or discharging (low tension). Auditory feedback is commonly provided in one of two ways. In the first method, a single tone goes on when muscle tension is too high and off when it drops to an acceptable level. In the second method, a tone goes on when muscle tension exceeds a certain level and increases in loudness as muscle tension goes up. As muscle tension drops, so does the loudness of the tone until it turns off when muscle tension is under the desired level again. This method is very effective when used to aid relaxation training.

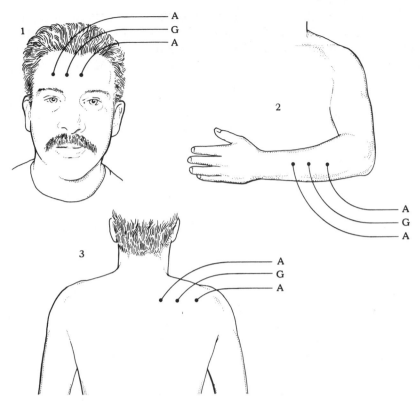

Figure 14–2.   Location of measuring electrodes for EMG biofeedback in muscle tension at (1) the frontalis muscle, (2) forearm, and (3) the trapezius. The labels on the electrodes indicate the active (A) and ground (G) electrodes.

Where the electrodes are placed depends on the physiological response to be altered. (See Figure 14–2.) If the intent is to aid general relaxation, either the trapezius muscles of the shoulder or the forearm site is appropriate. If the intent is to reduce tension headaches, then the frontalis muscle location on the forehead is preferred. EMG biofeedback has proven most useful in the treatment of tension headaches and lower back pain and in the neuromuscular rehabilitation of stroke victims.

EEG Feedback: The Alpha Wave Revisited

The brain emits tiny electrical discharges, just as muscles do. In 1928, Hans Berger showed that these minute currents could be amplified and displayed in graphic form on a machine of his invention, the electroencephalograph (EEG). The process is still somewhat troublesome because of the care that must be taken to get accurate recordings.

In most clinical settings, EEGs are taken from electrodes placed on the surface of the skull. This means that the electrodes pick up the combined activity of thousands, if not millions, of cells located just below the electrodes. Uniquely different brain waves, alpha, beta, theta, and delta, are related to different states of consciousness. Alpha is associated with a relaxed, meditative state and beta is present during alert waking stages. Theta is related to states such as daydreaming or a hypnogogic state and delta is related to deep sleep.

Sensing devices can be "tuned" to see a certain brain wave. For example, if the intent is to feed back information on alpha, the instrument is set so that it filters out any brainwave that is below 8 hertz and above 12 hertz. When the filter detects a brain wave within this window, the wave can be amplified and used to turn on a tone or a light. For EEG feedback, an auditory signal is most frequently used.

EEG recording is difficult to carry out at home. A great deal of care has to be taken in placement of electrodes and a special electrolytic gel is generally required to get good readings. While new techniques have been developed to make the process easier and more reliable in the clinic, they are not likely to filter down to the home market for some time to come.

Most importantly, EEG biofeedback has proven to have few clinical applications. It may be useful in the treatment of insomnia and epilepsy, and some studies have also shown improvements in concentration, attention, and shifting awareness. But the potential for self-management seems even more limited than the clinical applications. Even the hope for an electronic euphoria, equivalent to the Eastern mystical trance, did not materialize.

Temperature Biofeedback: Keeping Cool

In general, temperature control is obtained by changing the amount of blood in the extremities. Surface blood vessels expand or contract in response to environmental conditions and internal demands. When the vessels relax, they permit more blood to flow, thus raising body temperature. When the vessels contract, they restrict the volume of blood, thus lowering body temperature.

The Yogis of India were reported to have very fine control of blood flow. One Yogi was reported to be able to raise the temperature in the right earlobe by several degrees and simultaneously drop the temperature in the left earlobe by an equal amount. Clinical applications usually focus on finger temperature. This method is usually prescribed in the case of migraine headaches and a rare disorder called Raynaud's disease.[31]

In temperature biofeedback, a small electrode called a thermistor is used to measure finger temperature. Feedback may be visual or auditory or a combination. Displays that change to yellow and red as the temperature goes up seem to be very effective. Electrodes are moved from finger to finger and from hand to hand as learning takes place. This is to ensure that the individual learns a global, whole-hand warming response. Huge changes may be possible in a single finger. But unless the entire hand is warmed, the change will not be enough to alter the main symptom that needs to be controlled, such as migraine.

Producing skin temperature change is usually aided by visual imagery such as the type used in autogenics. In fact, the Menninger Clinic reported using autogenics in combination with biofeedback. They have suggested that the cognitive aspects of autogenics can be guided by biofeedback, while biofeedback aids in producing the desired physical change more rapidly.[32]

The Telltale Skin

When a person has an emotional reaction, a subtle but telltale change occurs in the skin. The skin's resistance goes down so that it conducts an electric current more readily. This is the principle behind the lie detector test. The galvanic skin response (GSR) may actually measure several different underlying processes. It may be related to increased moisture, or sympathetic activity, or some other process.

Few biofeedback procedures depend on the GSR. Mostly it is used to help people become sensitive to internal changes they did not recognize were occurring. It may also be helpful for sorting items in a desensitization hierarchy.

Changing Cardiovascular Activity

Obtaining a reliable measure of cardiovascular activity is in some ways even more difficult than getting reliable brain-wave measures. Attempts have been made to teach people how to control blood pressure and heart rate. These techniques seemed to have a wide range of applications for people with hypertension, cardiac arrhythmias, and other heart problems. Unfortunately, the instrumentation is still complicated and expensive. Also, some of the gains obtained with biofeedback, such as reducing blood pressure, may be obtained through relaxation and/or EMG biofeedback.[33] It thus seems that useful cardiovascular biofeedback is still a few years away from practical realization, and then may not be necessary anyway.

◆ BUT IS IT GOOD FOR ANYTHING?

While many questions have been raised about the promise of biofeedback, three questions are of central importance to this discussion. The first is whether biofeedback can be used to teach a person how to alter a specific internal process. The answer seems to be an unqualified yes. The second question is whether biofeedback is useful for treating a variety of stress and health problems. The answer seems to be a qualified maybe. The third question is whether the positive outcomes are a result of some unique property of biofeedback not present in other procedures. The answer is mostly no. In fact, the more biofeedback is studied, the more it appears to share common elements with both relaxation and cognitive stress-managment procedures. The following is a brief summary of its major successes and failures.

Biofeedback for High Blood Pressure

Attempts have been made to treat high blood pressure with biofeedback. In general, subjects are able to reduce both systolic and diastolic blood pressure to a degree that is not due to chance factors. But the results are often not clinically meaningful because the amount of change is so small and/or the training does not have a long-term effect. Where large changes do occur, they are usually due to extremely high blood pressure at the outset. In addition, the blood pressure levels reached at the end of training are generally still above safe levels. Biofeedback may help subjects reduce blood pressure more than relaxation itself, but both procedures do lead to lower levels.[34] There is still disagreement among professionals on both the issue of permanence and the issue of superiority, though. Some studies show that biofeedback and relaxation are equally effective and that both can maintain lowered blood pressure up to a full year after treatment.[35]

Excedrin Headache #27 or EMG Headache #1?

The use of biofeedback for treatment of headaches has been quite popular. Most frequently, the targets are either tension headaches or migraine headaches. Tension headaches are thought to be the result of prolonged muscle contractions, which in turn are a result of some form of stress. Migraine headaches are most often attributed to vasoconstriction.[36] EMG biofeedback is used for tension headaches while skin temperature feedback is used for migraine headaches.[37] In an extensive study of three headache groups (migraine, tension, and combined migraine with tension), relaxation alone led to significant improvement in all three groups, but biofeedback led to significant added gains. Overall, 73% of the tension headache group were greatly improved, as were 52% of the migraine group.[38]

In spite of some of these successes, there is still reason to doubt that biofeedback is necessary. For example, a study by Theodor Knapp showed that both biofeedback and cognitive coping skills were capable of reducing frequency, duration, and intensity of migraines.[39] In addition, the patients were able to use less medication after treatment, regardless of type of treatment. The Colorado group headed by Thomas Budzynski concluded one report by noting that "EMG training [for tension headaches] alone is not effective in all cases."[40] Robert Stern and William Ray suggested that the real benefit of biofeedback in the treatment of tension headaches may be to teach people to recognize signs of tension in body muscles and to begin relaxing immediately.[41] Biofeedback is probably not essential for control of headaches, but it seems to be an important element in education. Another research team summed up the situation even more bluntly. They stated that where biofeedback has been compared to other procedures, there is no consistent advantage to any one form of treatment.[42]

A Cure for Cold Hands and Feet?

Raynaud's disease is a condition in which peripheral blood volume is restricted to such an extent that the person feels uncomfortably or painfully cold. Usually the hands and/or feet are affected, but the face and tongue may also feel cold at times. Both cold outside temperatures and emotional stress can trigger attacks.[43] As the attack progresses, the affected area may change color from whitish to cyanotic blue to bright red.

Raynaud's disease has been treated with temperature biofeedback. In one study, finger temperature biofeedback was compared to frontalis EMG biofeedback or autogenic training.[44] The patients treated with finger temperature biofeedback had a significant reduction (92.5%) in symptoms compared to the other two groups (32.6% and 17%, respectively). This difference was still significant one year later at follow-up. After a thorough review of the literature, however, David Holmes concluded that "there is no consistent scientific support for the effectiveness of biofeedback for treating patients with migraine headaches, Raynaud's disease, or hypertension."[45]

While biofeedback has been used for a wide variety of other ailments and medical conditions, it is beyond the scope of this book to review these various uses. A very easy to read yet comprehensive review of biofeedback research is available in the work cited earlier by Stern and Ray.

◆ BIOFEEDBACK: THE FINAL SCORE

In spite of the attention and the great expectations, biofeedback has not lived up to its promise as a treatment technique or as a coping procedure. Independent reviews of biofeedback have provided similar rather sobering conclusions. One such review concluded that biofeedback has no demonstrated superiority over other procedures such as relaxing or cognitive coping skills training, which can be carried out with much less cost and effort than biofeedback.[46] In addition, the authors pointed out that many of their biofeedback clients reported using many cognitive controls and instructional sets in the process of obtaining a successful outcome.

Thomas Burish looked at EMG biofeedback specifically for stress-related disorders. His conclusion was that biofeedback has not been proven effective in reducing either internal or behavioral reactions to stress. As he stated,

> It may be naive to think not only that a biofeedback procedure aimed at changing the EMG level of a specific muscle group will produce a general (i.e., multisystem) relaxation effect, but also that any type of relaxation strategy will *by itself* produce and maintain a permanent change in stress-related symptoms if the nature and intensity of the stressor is not modified.[47]

Lawrence Simkins asked the rhetorical question, Is "biofeedback clinically valid or oversold?"[48] He pointed out that many studies are designed with internal flaws and fail to eliminate alternative explanations, especially the placebo effect. In addition, many studies use small samples and lack adequate controls. In conclusion, Simkins pointed out that we are probably expecting too much from biofeedback. Effective stress management and personal health maintenance must incorporate cognitive, attitudinal, and life-style change as well.[49]

It is important to note there is no question that biofeedback can play an important part in teaching people how to read the signals of their body, including signals of tension. When used as an educational procedure, biofeedback can be a very important ally. There is also no dispute that biofeedback *can* produce some positive outcomes. The point is that *it is not absolutely necessary to use biofeedback to produce these results.* If we could shift focus from biofeedback as a primary treatment or coping strategy and focus instead on the information gained from biofeedback that can be used in other ways, then this procedure should find an honored and rightful place along with the other techniques described here.

◆ SHOULD I TRY BIOFEEDBACK?

Whether you should try biofeedback or not depends on a number of factors such as (1) the intended use, (2) the nature and severity of the symptom to be treated, (3) prior treatment history, if any, and (4) the demonstrated usefulness for treating the target symptom. Obviously, if you only want to explore biofeedback because you are curious about how it works, there is little to argue against it. If you want more objective ratings of anxiety to help in putting together a fear ladder for desensitization, use it. And should you want to improve your ability to tune in to body signals for self-education, biofeedback can be quite valuable. But if the intent is to alter a symptom that has medical implications, exercise a fair degree of caution. The more serious the symptom, the more cautious you should be. Also, if you have never been treated for the symptom, seek a medical examination first.

If you feel that you might have a situation for which biofeedback is appropriate, consider these additional guidelines before beginning. First, seek information to show that biofeedback is reasonably successful for the symptom you want to change. In the absence of this evidence, stop! Look for a treatment suited specifically to the symptom.

If positive evidence is available, locate the necessary instrumentation to carry out the program. As with relaxation, strive for one or more sessions per day and practice on a daily basis. Keep very careful records of both positive and negative changes. If negative changes occur, stop immediately. If the practice is successful, later on work to transfer the gains to alternative procedures, such as relaxation or autogenics.

Finally, a few practical dos and don'ts are in order. Set realistic goals for what you expect to achieve. Do not expect to achieve global changes in health problems, and do not expect to achieve anything overnight. Do not expect biofeedback to cure everything, and especially do not expect biofeedback to cure anything by itself. As suggested before, you generally need to combine biofeedback with life-style change and cognitive coping strategies in order to obtain satisfactory long-term results.

◆ SUMMARY

This chapter reviewed the status of some popular methods for coping with stress and improving health. These included Yoga meditation, the Western version of Mantra Yoga called Transcendental Meditation, and Herbert Benson's variation of TM called secular meditation. The claims for meditation were examined in historical and scientific perspective. Meditation seems to be capable of producing certain altered mental and physical states that are desirable. However, these changes are not unique to the practice of meditation. Other procedures, such as deep muscle relaxation and autogenics, are capable of the same positive results. In addition, extensive applications and backup research have not been provided with meditation, so it seems more limited at this time in comparison to the previously mentioned procedures. Because of the ease of learning for Benson's meditation, guidelines to begin practicing were provided.

The high-tech solution, biofeedback, was also reviewed. In general, biofeedback is most commonly done with EMG, EEG, GSR, or some form of cardiovascular feedback. The stress symptoms most frequently treated with biofeedback include migraine and tension headaches, hypertension, and chronic pain. While biofeedback is capable of producing some positive results, the overall score for the procedure is no longer as positive as it once was. This is because biofeedback does not always result in clinically meaningful change, the results do not always last, other cheaper and easier techniques are as successful, and other techniques often must be added to obtain satisfactory results anyway. Biofeedback may still be valuable for education and symptomatic relief if certain precautions are taken.

◆ NOTES

[1]This term comes from the work of Peter Brent, who spent three years following the Yogis of India and wrote of his experiences. Brent, P. L. (1972). *The god-men of India.* London: Allen Lane.

[2]Hoenig, J. (1968). Medical research on Yoga. *Confinia Psychiatrica* (Basel), *11,* 69–89.

[3]Anand, B. K., Chhina, G. S., & Singh, B. (1961). Studies on Shri Ramananda Yogi during his stay in an air-tight box. *Indian Journal of Medical Research, 49,* 82–89.

[4]There is a controversy among scholars of the East on the exact time frame of Patan-jali's life and the date of the *Yoga sutras*. The dates range from the third century B.C. to the fourth century A.D. Selection of this date is based on Dasgupta, S. (1957). *A history of Indian philosophy.* Cambridge: The University Press.

[5]The negative ethical code was referred to as *yamas* and the positive ethical code was called *niyamas*. These were the first two steps in Yoga practice.

[6]The postures are called *asanas*, breathing rituals are called *pranayamas*, and with-drawal is called *pratyahara*.

[7]Behanan, K. T. (1964). *Yoga: A scientific evaluation.* New York: Dover, p. 202.

[8]Meditation is called *dharana* and contemplation is *dhyana*. Isolation is the final release, called *samadhi*.

[9]Wenger, M. A., & Bagchi, B. K. (1961). Studies of autonomic function in practition-ers of Yoga in India. *Behavioral Science, 6,* 312–323.

[10]Green, E., Green, A., & Walters, D. (1972). Biofeedback for mind-body self-regu-lation: Healing and creativity. *Fields Within Fields . . . Within Fields, 5,* 131–144.

[11]Kasamatsu, A., & Hirai, T. (1963). Science of zazen. *Psychologia, 6,* 86–91.

[12]These comments are based on a presentation made by a TM instructor at the first of three sessions to introduce and initiate a group of people into TM. I was in attendance at the meeting to observe and consider whether I myself would learn TM.

[13]Shapiro, D. H., & Zifferblatt, S. M. (1976, July). Zen meditation and behavioral self-control: Similarities, differences, and clinical applications. *American Psy-chologist,* pp. 519–532. The authors reported on studies of the lotus position.

[14]Kapleau, P. (Ed.) (1965). *The three pillars of Zen.* New York: Weatherhill.

[15]Wallace, R. K., & Benson, H. (1972). The physiology of meditation. *Scientific Amer-ican, 226,* 84–90.

[16]Dillbeck, M. C., Aron, A. P., & Dillbeck, S. L. (1979, November). The Transcen-dental Meditation program as an educational technology: Research and appli-cations. *Educational Technology,* pp. 7–13.

[17]Bloomfield, H. H., Cain, M. P., Jaffe, D. T., & Kory, R. B. (1975). *TM: Discovering inner energy and overcoming stress.* New York: Dell.

[18]Pagano, R. R., Rose, R. M., Stivers, R.M., & Warrenburg, S. (1976). Sleep during Transcendental Meditation. *Science, 191,* 308–309.

[19]Lintel, A. G. (1980). Physiological anxiety responses in transcendental meditators and nonmeditators. *Perceptual and Motor Skills, 50,* 295–300.

[20]Puente, A. E., & Beiman, I. (1980). The effects of behavior therapy, self-relaxation, and Transcendental Meditation on cardiovascular stress response. *Journal of Clinical Psychology, 36,* 291–295.

[21]Throll, D. A. (1982). Transcendental Meditation and progressive relaxation: Their physiological effects. *Journal of Clinical Psychology, 38,* 522–530.

[22]Benson, H. (1975). *The relaxation response.* New York: Morrow.

[23]Benson, *Relaxation response,* pp. 78, 79.

[24]Deikman, A. (1969). Experimental meditation. In C. Tart (Ed.), *Altered states of consciousness* (pp. 203–223). New York: Wiley.

[25]Benson, *Relaxation response*, p. 114.

[26]Shapiro & Zifferblatt, Zen meditation.

[27]Benson, *Relaxation response*, p. 111.

[28]Weiner, N. (1954). *The human use of human beings: Cybernetics and society.* Garden City, NY: Doubleday/Anchor.

[29]Fuller, G. D. (1977). *Biofeedback: Methods and procedures in clinical practice.* San Francisco: Biofeedback Press, p. 3.

[30]As reported by Robert M. Stern and William J. Ray (1977) in their very useful review volume entitled *Biofeedback: Potential and limits.* Lincoln: University of Nebraska Press.

[31]Blanchard, E. B., & Haynes, M. R. (1975). Biofeedback treatment of a case of Raynaud's disease. *Journal of Behavior Therapy and Experimental Psychiatry, 6,* 230–234.

[32]Green, E. E., Green, A. M., Walter, E. D., Sargent, J. D., & Meyer, R. G. (1973, May 10). *Autogenic feedback training.* Topeka, KS: The Menninger Foundation.

[33]Lustman, P. J., & Sowa, C. J. (1983). Comparative efficacy of biofeedback and stress inoculation for stress reduction. *Journal of Clinical Psychology, 39,* 191–197.

[34]Engel, B. T., Glasgow, M. S., & Gaarder, K. R. (1983). Behavioral treatment of high blood pressure: III. Follow-up results and treatment recommendations. *Psychosomatic Medicine, 45,* 23–29.

[35]Walsh, P., Dale, A., & Anderson, D. E. (1977). Comparison of biofeedback, pulse wave velocity and progressive relaxation in essential hypertensives. *Perceptual and Motor Skills, 44,* 839–843.

[36]Cohen, R. A., et al. (1983). Psychophysiological response patterns in vascular and muscle-contraction headaches. *Journal of Behavioral Medicine, 6,* 93–107.

[37]Budzynski, T., Stoyva, J., & Adler, C. (1970). Feedback-induced muscle relaxation: Application to tension headache. *Journal of Behavior Therapy and Experimental Psychiatry, 1,* 205–211.

[38]Blanchard, E. B., et al. (1982). Biofeedback and relaxation training with three kinds of headache: Treatment effects and their prediction. *Journal of Consulting and Clinical Psychology, 50,* 562–575.

[39]Knapp, T. W. (1982). Treating migraine by training in temporal artery vasoconstriction and/or cognitive behavioral coping: A one-year follow-up. *Journal of Psychosomatic Research, 26,* 551–557.

[40]Budzynski, T. H., Stoyva, J. M., Adler, C. S., & Mullaney, D. J. (1973). EMG biofeedback and tension headache: A controlled outcome study. *Psychosomatic Medicine, 35,* 484–496.

[41]Stern & Ray, *Biofeedback.*

[42]Silver, B. V., & Blanchard, E. B. (1978). Biofeedback and relaxation training in the treatment of psychophysiological disorders: Or are the machines really necessary? *Journal of Behavioral Medicine, 2,* 217–239.

[43]Pinkerton, S. S., Hughes, H., & Wenrich, W. W. (1982). *Behavioral medicine: Clinical applications.* New York: Wiley.

[44]Freedman, R. R., Ianni, P., & Wenig, P. (1983). Behavioral treatment of Raynaud's disease. *Journal of Consulting and Clinical Psychology, 51,* 539–549.

[45]Holmes, D. S. (1981). The use of biofeedback for treating patients with migraine headaches, Raynaud's disease, and hypertension: A critical evaluation. In C. K. Prokop & L. A. Bradley (Eds.), *Medical psychology: Contributions to behavioral medicine.* (pp. 423–437). New York: Academic Press.

[46]Turk, D. C., Meichenbaum, D. H., & Berman, W. H. (1979). Application of biofeedback for the regulation of pain: A critical review. *Psychological Bulletin, 86,* 1322–1338.

[47]Burish, T. G. (1981). EMG biofeedback in the treatment of stress-related disorders. In Prokop & Bradley, *Medical psychology* (pp. 395–421), p. 418.

[48]Simkins, L. (1982). Biofeedback: Clinically valid or oversold? *Psychological Record, 32,* 3–17.

[49]Simkins, Biofeedback, p. 14.

Part 6

TIME MANAGEMENT AND BEHAVIORAL HEALTH STRATEGIES

15

MANAGING TIME-RELATED STRESS

Finding better ways of doing what you're doing isn't worthwhile when what you're doing isn't worth doing anyway.

Anonymous manager

Remember those childhood days when time passed without a care? Remember how all of those childhood activities, playing house or going fishing, were seldom calculated in terms of time? True, our parents were constantly reminding us of time: "Be home for supper"; "You have to have your homework done by 6:00 or you can't watch TV." No matter. When we were engrossed in pursuits of the imagination, time did not seem to matter.

If anything, time hung heavy. School days could wear on and on. Waiting to become an adult seemed to be a trip down the long road of eternity itself. And being an adult meant being on your own and being able do with your time what you wanted.

How times change! Now time passes too quickly. Now there is never enough time. If only we could have a 36-hour day! But time is one commodity that is fixed. It is not how much time we have but how we use it that makes the difference. And, perhaps most crucial, it is not so much the absolute standard of time that pushes us, but how we think about time that pressures us.

◆ WHY STUDY TIME MANAGEMENT?

According to Jack Ferner, **time management** is "efficient use of our resources, including time, in such a way that we are effective in achieving important personal goals."[1] There are several reasons why it is also central to the problem of stress and health. First, using some rather simple time-management techniques can improve personal productivity. The net effect is to provide more discretionary time for social pursuits, exercise, recreation, and hobbies. Lack of time for personal pursuits tends to be one of the most frequently cited stressors. Providing time for self and family usually has the desirable effect of reducing levels of subjective stress.

Second, it has become almost a truism that modern society is time-driven if not time-obsessed. The Type A behavior pattern is presumably the epitome, the extreme expression of that all-consuming sense of time urgency. It may also be a statement of much that is wrong with the way value is calculated. All too often it is calculated in terms of money, power, and position, which generally require high productivity to attain. And being productive usually means working hard and long hours. The study of time management may help us rethink some of our attitudes toward time and reduce the sense of time urgency.

But time management should never become a goal in and of itself. Time management is a tool to be used for a short while to reset priorities and recast inefficient work habits. But then it should be put on the back shelf until needed again. It should never become a chore that must be done every day. Time management should help you use time more efficiently. But time management should never manage you. If it does, throw it out!

In the same vein, a number of time management books seem, if anything, to reinforce the Type A pattern. The bottom line is productivity and the score card is the dollar. The ethic is more work in less time, ever onward and upward to that next promotion. If there is any concern with those basic human values of caring and sharing, they are not evident. We each need to take time to give expression to all facets of our personality, to appreciate the creative and artistic expressions of others. If time management does not free us for these pursuits, it is a misplaced effort.

◆ TIME IS IN THE EYE OF THE BEHOLDER

Attitudes toward time have changed greatly over the years. They also vary among different cultures and among people in the same society. How we think about time is a critical determinant of whether time is viewed as pressure or not. Here are some of the most common attitudes towards time.

Sociocultural Context of Time

Even a casual inspection of history suggests that ancient cultures show an almost timeless quality. It is not that they were "nontimed," but that precise time keeping was not central to their existence. Presumably all this changed with the appearance of clocks in medieval Europe. From that point on, keeping track of time seemed to be an important pursuit in its own right. If anything, the industrial revolution added to this concern because precise time keeping was viewed as crucial to meeting urgent survival needs.

Another legacy began with Sir Isaac Newton, who viewed each time interval as unique but equal. This view presumably encourages continuous but short-range activity and may obscure long-range goals and futuristic planning. It also seems to foster guilt when nothing that passes as valued activity is observed during an interval.

The importance of time in modern society is further emphasized in research on people who have a high need for achievement. Such people feel annoyed when their watches stop running. For them, a watch is not a luxury but a necessity that keeps them functioning properly. They often feel anxious when they are not certain about the time and wonder how people can get along without watches.[2]

Metaphors and Myths of Time

In contemporary society, there are a number of verbal statements, such as Time Is Money, that seem to capture the essence of our attitudes toward time. Metaphors for time or maybe myths, they reflect the implicit, often untested values that focus efforts and guide behavior.

Edwin Bliss told a wonderful anecdote of a first-grader who observed his father bringing home a briefcase full of work every night. Puzzled over this ongoing state of affairs, the little boy asked his mother why it had to be that way. The mother gave a very adult response: "Daddy has so much to do he can't finish at the office and has to work nights." The child's response was simple and uncluttered with the value-laden adult explanation: "Well, then, why don't they just put him in a slower group?"[3]

The behavior of the parents reflects their untested assumptions: Daddy's behavior is normal and necessary; the solution to work problems is to work longer and harder. Several attitudes seem most prominently taught or espoused in modern society:

1. Time is money.
2. Time is a resource.
3. Wasting time is sinful.
4. An idle mind is the devil's playground.
5. I have all the time in the world.

The first is the number-one cliché. The second may come closest to representing a valid argument for wise use of time. The third and fourth have their roots in the industrial revolution as much as in theology. All four are meant to increase personal commitment to use time wisely. The last one is an attitude that works in the opposite direction. Each is, in some sense, a mental trap, a set or perceptual bias that needs to be examined.

Time is money. The central value expressed in this metaphor is obvious, yet is too widely and readily accepted as a creed to live by. Problems arise when the same value interferes with home and social life. Calculating time at home, time with the spouse, with children, for yourself, for exercise, cannot be calculated in terms of money. If the family is not on an equal footing with work, something is wrong. Counselors have found families torn apart by pressures from an absentee wage earner who thought that providing material comforts was all-important. In the midst of counseling, revelations made by a neglected spouse and lonely children suggested that they would have gladly done with much less in order to have more time together.

Even in business, time is paramount only in certain occupations. Speculative professions (such as stocks and commodities brokerage or land development) tend to put time on a pedestal. Fortunes may turn on a matter of the minutes or seconds it takes to make a decision to buy or sell or contract. For many businesses, however, creativity and quality are as important as speed. If time is money, it is so only in a limited arena or to those who prize money above all else.

Time is a resource.   The notion that time is a resource is somewhat reminiscent of a famous statement made by the witty Will Rogers about land: Buy it. It is one thing they're not making any more. Unlike land, we can not buy, sell, or save time. But, like land, time cannot be manufactured. each come into the world with exactly the same amount of time, 24 hours per day, 8,736 hours per year. But if time is conceived as a resource, then the proper way to get the most out of it is through wise management. The cliché is Work Smart, Not Hard.

Idle minds.   The assumption behind this metaphor is that a mind not filled with purposeful thought (directed to productive activity, income deriving, or serving some pressing social need) must certainly be filled with ideas of a baser variety. Concentration on work and service came to be synonymous with the active mind. But some of the most creative and brilliant insights have occurred during the most idle of moments, during flights of fantasy, while daydreaming, or during dreaming itself. In addition, it now appears that some mental idling serves a useful purpose by providing an outlet for pent-up emotions.

Wasting time is sinful.   The hidden trap in this metaphor is the term *wasting*. But what is wasteful? It may be well be that you could buy a good rocker or cradle at your favorite store for a very reasonable price, much less than it would cost you for the lumber and time to build one yourself. But the time spent building one may prove to be valuable to you in many intangible ways. Getting your mind off of job pressures, changing gears mentally, and taking time for yourself all may result from engaging in this type of activity. If the activity is spent with family, teaching a daughter or son some useful skill or hobby, the expenditure of time cannot and should not be calculated in terms of money. If you find yourself saying "I am wasting time," ask yourself this question: "Based on what value?"

All the time in the world.   For the most part, this is an illusion of youth. Youth is often filled with perceptions of invulnerability and agelessness.

Such perceptions frequently lead to procrastination, which eats up valuable time and results in aimless action. While time obsessions should be avoided, very little that is worthwhile in life can be accomplished if time is ignored or treated as though it counts for nothing. The goal of effective time management is to find the harmony or balance in use of time that serves productive, wage-earning needs but still meets personal needs of caring, sharing, and growing.

◆ SEVEN DEADLY SINS OF TIME MISMANAGEMENT

Before talking about how to manage time, it may prove useful to consider how time is mismanaged. Indeed, the start of any time-management program should be a personal inventory of how time is being used. Through this means, you gain a sense of what needs to be changed and what should stay the same. More details will be given later on how to do this. For now, consider the following sins of time mismanagement, the acts of omission and commission that drain this resource. The most common are confusion, indecision, diffusion, procrastination, avoidance, interruptions, and perfectionism.

Confusion: Where Am I Going?

When someone complains they are wasting too much time but are not sure where their time is actually going, you can be fairly sure it is because they do not know where they are going. Lewis Carroll's *Alice's Adventures in Wonderland* has an interaction between Alice and the Cheshire Cat that aptly captures this problem in time management. Alice has come to a fork in the road, obviously confused about what to do. Spying the Cheshire Cat in the tree, she asks:

> "Would you tell me, please, which way I ought to go from here?"
> "That depends a good deal on where you want to get to," said the Cat.
> "I don't much care where—"said Alice.
> "Then it doesn't matter which way you go," said the Cat.[4]

As one time management specialist pointed out, time management does not make a lot of sense unless you know where you want to go.[5] Failing to plot a course for the next few months and years may be the single biggest error in time management.

Indecision: What Should I Do?

The second major error in time management is indecision, or failing to make a decision that needs to be made. It is similar to the approach taken by the ostrich, ignoring whatever does not seem pleasant. It has been noted that there is no such thing as indecision; there is only the decision not to decide. In any case, indecision is the hidden foe of effective time management.

Indecision means that we often end up handling tasks several times instead of once. It also tends to increase confusion and tension in ourselves. Further, the more we are in a position of leadership and management, the more it compounds confusion and tension in those around us. Rather than being restricted to the realm of personal outcomes, then, the effects of indecision add to team inefficiency as well.

Indecision increases confusion and tension because the decision is easily put off but not so easily put away. The decision is still there, waiting to be made, playing on the backroads of the mind even while other tasks are pressing. It robs of the freedom to focus, to relax, to create. Also, inability to make decisions may be behind other problems in time management such as procrastination, creating and allowing interruptions, and avoidance of duties.

Indecision may come from many psychological factors. Stress may intrude from some other area of life and erode decision-making capabilities. Or it may be due to lack of interest in the task, a failure of motivation. Indecision may result from a deep-seated fear of making the wrong decision. Finally, it may result from lack of the information necessary to make a good decision. But in this case, indecision may be acceptable and wise.

Diffusion: Mental and Physical Overload

Diffusion is trying to do far more than is necessary, perhaps even more than is possible. It is having too many irons in the fire. Mental diffusion produces ineffective problem solving, lack of concentration, and poor motivation for even the simpler tasks. Trying to keep up with all the duties then takes its toll on the body in physical fatigue. This has a tendency to put further strain on the mental system.

Diffusion results from not knowing the limits of your own capabilities. It also results from not knowing when and how to say no to the requests from your friends and colleagues to become involved. In some cases, the two may be related. That is, the inability to say no may be due to not knowing your own limits.

Charles Kozoll described the *battered mind syndrome,* which is quite typical of the effects of diffusion. This syndrome is widely reported among educators, both teachers and/or administrators. The major characteristics of the syndrome include (1) many thoughts at once, (2) pervasive worry about what remains to be done, and (3) loss of focus on what can and should be done as pressures continue to mount. In addition, (4) the battered educator seems to operate on the assumption that interruptions will occur often and therefore involvement in immediate tasks is very shallow.[6]

Procrastination: That Will Keep for Another Day

Procrastination is the cardinal sin of time mismanagement. **Procrastination** has been defined as putting off until tomorrow what you should do today. Merrill and Donna Douglass have identified three types of procrastination: putting off unpleasant things, putting off things that are difficult, and putting off things that involve tough decisions.[7]

Robert Rutherford talked about two excuses that keep people from going to work: "I wish" and "I just can't get started."[8] The "I wish" excuse is usually on the order of wishing not to have to do the work or wishing for some type of miracle to do the job. In essence, it removes the responsibility of making something happen. The second wish is a type of self-fulfilling prophecy. It turns self-deceit into reality, which in the end is a self-defeat.

Eliminating habitual procrastination requires some remedial action. For a while you should make note of the tasks that you keep putting off. Then look for a common pattern in these tasks. Jim Davidson suggested that you try to find out why you do not like the job. Then, if possible, you could delegate the job to someone else. Otherwise, you might break the job down into smaller units or change the job in some way so that it is easier to finish.[9]

One rather simple rule is to do the things you do not like first. With the unpleasant tasks out of the way, you should feel freer to concentrate on the jobs you do like. Otherwise, you have the set-aside job hanging over your head, which may distract and reduce your effectiveness for the job you like. Some people find it helpful to make a contract with themselves. They may reward themselves for finishing the less desirable tasks by taking a short extra break or earning some clothing or a record from money that has been set aside for this purpose.

Avoidance: Escape to Fantasyland

People find many ways of avoiding doing work. They stretch coffee breaks. They wander the hallways looking for someone to talk to, presumably on business. They read books or sections of the newspaper that really do not need to be read. They get off on trivial aspects of organizing their work. The person who is constantly cleaning the desk or files may really be engaged in escape behavior. Another common escape is daydreaming. Managers do work that could, and probably should, be delegated to someone else while they attend to more important developmental matters. People write and rewrite letters or memos in the name of perfection. In fact they are probably avoiding some other task they do not want to do. If you catch yourself frequently saying that you are a perfectionist, consider whether you are also avoiding by overdoing.

Interruptions: Getting Started Is the Hard Part

One of the most frustrating time-killers is the unscheduled interruption. People who work in walk-in businesses are victims of constant interruptions. But many other offices and businesses have their share of interruptions. Phone calls, the boss dropping in for a chat, colleagues stopping by to say hello, and emergencies all represent disruptions to the normal flow of work.

According to one study, the average manager is interrupted an average of once every eight minutes.[10] Another writer suggested that even if the manager is not interrupted at least once every half hour, the manager will arrange for an interruption. This points to the fact that interruptions are not completely uncontrollable. A number of the interruptions that occur could be prevented by decisive action on our own part. As will become evident later on, even the uncontrolled interruptions can be reduced and made predictable.

Interruptions are perhaps most damaging in complex projects in which larger blocks of time are important to the flow of thought or in the development of some sequential idea. Computer programming and creative writing are two examples of such projects. Such jobs involve a warm-up period for getting into a rhythm. Frequent interruptions require additional time for reorienting and warming up again.

If anything is unscheduled, it is the emergency. While some organizations are structured to respond to emergencies, most are not. A survey of managers showed that fully 12% of their work day was devoted to emergencies. Only 44% of the work day was devoted to planned activities! Another 14% was devoted to customer-initiated activities.[11]

Charles Hummel said that there is a tension between the urgent and the important. Important tasks virtually never have to be done right away, today, or even this week. On the other hand, urgent tasks and crises require instant action.[12] The problem is that the crisis diverts attention from what is important. It takes time away from planned activities and thus disrupts the schedule. But the crisis also becomes an excuse. Work, important work, is not done. It's all right, though, because there was an emergency!

Perfectionism: I Was Raised a Perfectionist

You have probably heard it many times: "I'm a perfectionist." Perfectionism may have a place in life. But perfectionism for the sake of perfection is about as useful as rewaxing the whole car because a tiny spot was missed the first time. This type of perfectionism is really little more than compulsive overdoing.

The problem is to draw the line between the necessary and the excessive, between quality that will return dividends and meticulousness that will never be noticed and will not bring any gain. It is the law of diminished returns. Up to a point, the extra effort will be worthwhile. But after that point, no amount of extra effort will produce any gain.

◆ GETTING READY FOR TIME MANAGEMENT

It is one thing to identify time traps. It is another thing to weed them out of one's personal and professional habits. Many people talk about time management, but few are prepared to become involved in the primary task of identifying how real time is spent. If you feel that you are already managing your time efficiently, there may be little point in doing a time study. On the other hand, if you feel that some improvement is in order, be prepared to make a commitment for a short time at least. As noted before, though, do not think of it as a life-long task.

To begin with a time-management program, you need to know what needs to be changed. You can find this out through a time inventory, which is taking stock of how and where you spend your time. This may be done through many formal means. If you wish, you can purchase books solely devoted to time management with tailored worksheets to help you study your use of time. But in actuality you can carry out a time study with a few pennies worth of paper, a pencil, and a few days of attention.

◆ TIME STUDY: FINDING YOUR TIME-MANAGEMENT WEAKNESSES

If you find yourself at the end of the day wondering where the time went, you may benefit from a time study. A time study seeks answers to three basic questions: What do you do? When do you do it? How much time does it take?

A simple way to get this information is to keep a daily log in which time periods are listed down the left side of the page and days across the top. Use periods as short as 15 minutes or as long as one hour depending on the type of work. A 30-minute period will probably work for most purposes.

If your concern is for time spent at work, then chart only the primary working days. If you are concerned about both personal and professional time, use the entire week. Divide each day into two columns, one for the type of activity, the other for the people present. Jot down a short-hand reminder of the activity you carried out for each period and note the people present. If the activity continues for more than one period, you may either fill successive periods with dittos or leave them blank until the activity changes.

After you have collected at least one week of information, begin the search for patterns. First, set out all nonjob blocks of time, including commuting to and from the job. Then identify time that is discretionary—that is, time under your own control. Finally, label all the nondiscretionary time—time determined by supervisors or requirements of the job or related to family function.

Peter Drucker, one of the first to talk about time management, believed that managers have only about 25% controllable time, while the remaining 75% of their time is uncontrollable.[13] After you have set aside the nondiscretionary time, look at the discretionary time to see where improvements or wastes are occurring. But do not label time as nondiscretionary just to be rid of the responsibility of managing it more effectively.

If you see blocks of discretionary time being broken up by interruptions, identify the people (yourself included) or events responsible for those interruptions. You may see a simple plan of action to correct the situation that was not obvious before. If you find that a great deal of time is nonproductive commuting, you may be able to transform it into productive time.

◆ POSITIVE TIME MANAGEMENT

Previously the most common errors of time management were identified. This section and the following provide some positive steps to eliminate the errors.

Priorities: The Solution to Confusion

"You have to have your priorities straight!" The cliché is overworked but nonetheless true. The best solution for confusion is to set goals and reevaluate those goals periodically. There are a few basic guidelines for setting goals. First, establish clear and achievable goals. Second, assign priorities to each of your goals. Third, identify small tasks related to your goals that can be carried out in short work periods. Fourth, set target dates for completion of the smaller tasks. Finally, reevaluate your goals periodically. Even if you have a personal five-year plan, you may still need to reevaluate it each year.

Goals should be clear and achievable. While dreams may be the stuff of progress, unrealistic dreams generally only produce disillusionment and lowered resolve. Set your goals for three distinct time frames: long-term, medium-range, and short-term goals. Long-term goals should answer the basic question, "Where do I want to be in five years and what do I have to do to get there?" Medium-range goals should address the issue of "Where do I want to be next year at this same time?" If you are under 25, you may want to use shorter periods, perhaps three years and six months.

Regardless of your age, short-term goals usually have to be broken down into more tangible tasks. First, each week should have concrete objectives that are attainable and provide for some progress toward the major goal. Second, each day should have a "to do" list to organize both personal and professional time. These lists do not have to be written out formally, but many of the most efficient corporate executives report doing so. They write their "to do" list prior to leaving the office, or later in the evening before retiring, or in the first few minutes after reaching the office. Allan Lakein, author of one of the best-selling time management books, suggested that the major difference between people at the top and people trying to make the top is that the ones at the top know how to use "to do" lists and make one up every day.[14]

The Pareto Principle.

The Pareto principle is named after an Italian economist and sociologist, Vilfredo Pareto, who lived during the late 19th and early 20th centuries. His notion can be summarized in the phrase *the vital few and the trivial many.* In general, the idea is that 20% of your goals contain 80% of the value. The remaining 80% of your goals account for only 20% of the value. To be effective in time management, invest time in proportion to value—in other words, in the few goals with much meaning. Problems appear when the trivial consumes a disproportionate amount of your time.

The way to solve this problem is to list the things you want to accomplish in the long-term, medium, and short-term periods. Arrange the list from most important to least important. Then distribute the bulk of your time along the few items at the top of your list. Thus, if your list for the next few months has 10 items, invest the most time in the first 2 or 3 and give less attention to the leftover. If the job permits, you may even leave some of them undone altogether.

Peter Drucker said that "Doing the right thing seems to be more important than doing things right."[15] The point is that you can be very efficient in what you are doing. But if you are doing the wrong thing, it is still a waste of time. You need to be working toward goals that are meaningful. The best way to know is to write out your goals and then sort them on the basis of what is important to you—priorities!

Goals set at one point in time do not stay valid goals for all time. Reevaluation is essential to avoiding working toward the wrong things. The story of Buzz Aldrin is a clear illustration of this point. Buzz Aldrin, one of the first astronauts to set foot on the moon, suffered a nervous breakdown shortly after his return to earth. He wrote an autobiographical account of his experiences and revealed what had happened. In essence, he forgot that there was life beyond the moon! He focused his attention so exclusively on going to the moon that he forgot to think about what he would do afterward. Many executives are just like this, as Merrill and Donna Douglass have pointed out. The executive devotes a lifetime to the company, collects some memento of the effort, and retires. "Within 18 months, they are dead. Why? Studies strongly suggest that these executives have much in common with Buzz Aldrin: They have no further goals to live for once they reach the end of their careers."[16]

Pruning and Weeding

The solution to diffusion is to prune out the unnecessary and weed out the unattainable. This may require that you focus on what specific tasks are required to reach the goal you have set. For example, many people engage in an incessant round of reading and filing memos, and then go through a panic of file cleaning when things pile up. Why file it in the first place? When you get memos announcing meetings or agendas, pitch them right after the meeting. Keeping copies of all correspondence is also a waste of time, especially if the letter was only seeking information.

Most importantly, learn how to say no to the requests for involvement in other activities. As nice as it might be to be all things for all people, it is better to be the best for yourself and your family even if it means being best in a more limited arena of activity. There is too much emphasis on the super-person. In general, trying to live up to such a fiction will only drain energy and lead to distractions that interfere with reaching the really important goals.

If you find that you are having difficulty saying no, examine the reasons. Is it fear of being left out or fear that you will be less liked? If so, put these hidden assumptions to a test. Recall the times you did say no and examine the outcomes. You will probably find that the results are not as disastrous as imagined. Or is the failure to say no due to lack of assertiveness: You want to say no, but can not seem to do it? Consider the possibility of an assertion-training class or book on assertion to help.

Getting Started: Breaking the Procrastination Habit

One of the most common causes of procrastination is that the job is viewed as so big and the available time so small that the job cannot be finished. So why start? The solution is to break the task down into smaller parts. Writing a paper or business report, for example, can be broken into several parts including background (library) work, reading, organizing, drafting, and rewriting. Even the background work can be broken down into smaller com-ponents. A 15-minute period here and there can be used to check on facts, figures, and resources. Once the job is viewed in this way, many more periods of time are seen as useful and getting started is easier.

Structure your work situation so that the cues will help get you started instead of adding to inertia and lethargy. Your office should be an office, not a lounge or recreation room. Work cues should facilitate attention without strain while minimizing distractions. It may be nice to have an office set up in a very cozy fashion. But too many nonwork cues, such as popular maga-zines and pictures of the family vacation, will only serve to sidetrack you. These cues become conversation pieces when other people come in, extend-ing the interruptions even longer. They cry out for attention at the most inopportune times, especially when the hard job is next on your list.

Finally, do not mix functions in your work area. If you must read to fall asleep, do so only in bed, never in your study chair. If you find yourself get-ting sleepy every time you try to read, you probably have gotten your cues mixed. Your mind is telling you that reading is a signal for going to sleep when you need to be alert. The general idea is to strengthen the cues that are most conducive to efficient work habits.

Concentrating: Zeroing In on Essentials

Getting started is only one part of the battle in effective time management. There are two other issues that must also be confronted. One is concentrating on the job long enough to get some whole unit or stage of the task done. The other is to stick with the task until it is done.

The ideas just discussed (controlling the cues in your work area and reducing distractions) will help you with concentration as much as with getting started. In addition, you may need to look at two other elements. First, people sometimes have difficulty working at any task for longer than a few minutes. If this is a recurrent problem, use the simple device of a clock and a self-contract to keep yourself at the task for a set period of time. Start off with a short period that is close to what you normally work. Then make a contract with yourself, such as "I'm going to work straight through for the next 20 minutes before taking a break." Gradually increase the amount of time by adding a minute a day. When you are able to concentrate on a task for at least an hour, consider yourself over the hump.

Second, some people try to work too long at a single task. The problem of short-term concentration is that it does not provide for continuity and rhythm, especially in complex tasks. The problem with long-term concentration is that it tends to produce fatigue, lower motivation, and reduced mental efficiency. The way to deal with this is to distribute work sessions and alternate tasks. For example, you can reward yourself with a short break, say 10 minutes, for every hour you work. During this time, you might do some more menial work, return phone calls, or idle down by closing your eyes and enjoying music on the radio. You might also switch tasks. The new content can help to keep motivation and interest at a high level over longer periods of time.

A major problem in the normal work environment, as discussed earlier, is dealing with the unscheduled interruption. There are several ways of managing these so that your blocks of time are not broken up. One simple technique is to make an appointment with yourself. If you can block out time on the calendar for your clients, you can also block it out for yourself. If you have an open door policy, stop this practice and put visits to your office on a more formal appointment basis. Or restrict the amount of time the open door policy is in effect. Then shut the door and focus. Be gentle but firm if people violate the Do Not Disturb sign. Also, do not feel guilty! You have a right to some privacy to complete your work and you can exercise a measure of control in that regard. If all else fails, consider using a second office either at work or at home.

Dealing with the chronic drop-in can be a problem. But there are some effective solutions. According to Rutherford, every time you respond to drop-ins with idle and pleasant chatter, you are signing an implicit or silent contract that encourages them to do it again.[17] In effect, you are giving them a license to interrupt anytime they want. This can be prevented by advising the person that you are in the middle of a project that needs to be completed and ask them to return later. Or suggest that you talk at the next scheduled break. Or ask if it is on business and suggest that another time would be more convenient for you. If the behavior persists, you can ignore the person until he or she gets the hint. Or you might tell the person bluntly that the behavior is disruptive and that you do not appreciate unscheduled visits.

Dealing with phone interruptions may be somewhat easier than with face-to-face confrontation. Ask your caller how much time the call will require and either call back or set a time limit. Use a receptionist to screen calls if possible. Perhaps the most effective technique is to simply *batch* calls, both incoming and outgoing. Designate certain periods of time that you will allow a phone call to go straight through and other times when phone calls are to be met with a "not available" response. Then set aside some time, perhaps one of your rest breaks, when you call back and make the calls you need to make of your own.

The technique of batching can also be used for handling your mail. Set aside one time interval when mail is opened and responses are provided where needed.

Staying With It: Marking Time and Progress

Perhaps the most effective way to keep yourself at a task is to provide some tangible reward or marker for completion of small steps. This can be done by having a checklist of the total project with each step listed separately. You can then check off each step as it is finished. A daily "to do" list is quite valuable for just this reason. A project calendar can also provide valuable feedback.

◆ HINTS FOR EFFECTIVE TIME MANAGEMENT

There are many suggestions for better use of time that do not conveniently fit in any of these categories. The next few pages present a potpourri of ideas culled from different sources that may prove helpful for one time management problem or another.

Using Transition or Commuting Time

In the United States, the average time to commute from home to job is approximately 45 minutes per day. In larger metropolitan areas, this goes up to approximately 75 minutes per day.[18] Added up over the period of a working year or even a working month, this amounts to a sizeable block of nonproductive time. If it is possible to treat the trip as down time (part of the relaxation you need to recover from the press of job duties) and if you are not falling behind at work, then you may not even need to change your commuting time. On the other hand, if you are finding it difficult to stay on top, then these moments might provide you with just enough time to take the pressure off at the office and at home. Some activities that can be carried out include learning new skills from tapes, dictating notes or ideas on both in-process and new projects, and thinking through time schedules for new projects.

Learning to Delegate

Delegating specific tasks to others can free a lot of time for a manager. If you find it difficult to delegate, consider whether there is some personal fear that is preventing delegating. Are you afraid that you will lose your position? Are you afraid that your peers will find out that there is not that much to your job after all? If you are able to pinpoint specific fears, then examine the logic of those fears. Get a friend to help if need be. If it is a lack of trust in the subordinates, examine the basis of that mistrust.

On the positive side, consider the fact that delegating puts you in the position of a teacher. You are developing skills and talent in others who might be able to carry on the work of the organization later on. Your legacy is then not just your work but a pool of talent that helps the entire company.

Internal Prime Time

Recall the concept of diurnal cycles and circadian rhythms. We each function on slightly different internal clocks that make us more efficient at certain times. Know your prime time, when you work the best, and try to structure work so that you do the most demanding work in synchrony with your prime time.

Also, study your sleep habits. Many people sleep more than they need to. The norm is 8 hours per night, but this may vary from 6 to 9 hours. There is evidence that sleep over 9 or 10 hours can have three bad results: It may lower your overall metabolic rate, leading to increased difficulty in maintaining a desirable weight; muscle tone may drop, leading to increased effort in carrying out normal tasks and reducing the ease with which you can exercise; and performance of the mental system may drop due to lethargy.

If you observe that you are sleeping more than 10 hours (the exception being when you are ill), a simple experiment will tell you whether you are sleeping more than necessary. Get up a half hour earlier for a few mornings. If you find that you are no more tired at the end of the day and do not feel the need to go to bed any earlier, you can probably get by without the half hour of sleep. This process can be repeated until you find the balance between sleeping enough and not wasting time sleeping. Even if you cut down, you should realize that you will not be cutting down on deep sleep, when the really important biological repair work is done. You will actually be reducing the amount of light sleep that occurs in the morning just before you are ready to wake up. On the other end, if you are already getting less than 6 or 7 hours of sleep, you probably should not cut any further. Very few people can get by on less sleep without doing their bodies harm.

Reading for Professional Development

In many technical and professional fields, it is necessary to stick to a routine reading program in order to keep up with important developments in the field. If you tried to read everything you would be overwhelmed. But even trying to read the bare minimum is a struggle much of the time.

One problem is the habit of reading word for word. On the average, a person will complete college reading at about 350 words per minute. However, repeated reading of very technical information leads to the habit of slower reading, a habit that then is carried over to reading a newspaper or novel. Surveys have shown that managers have a constant reading speed of about 250 words per minute, which does not change from one type of material to another.[19] At this rate, it takes anywhere from one to three minutes for each page of text. Even a 20-page article can consume an hour or more, far too much time to be able to keep up. But you do not need to read word for word to get what you need. This will be explained in a moment.

Speed-reading courses claim to be able to increase reading speed, to thousands of words per minute. But be assured that what is going on is not word-for-word reading. The visual system is physiologically incapable of processing information at that speed. These exaggerated claims have been shown to be based on a skimming procedure or on some systematic reading procedure (such as first and last sentence in each paragraph). The most often cited target for speed reading is 600–1,000 words per minutes. Even at this rate, you would still not be able to keep up.

There are ways to whittle the task down to manageable size. First, be selective of what you read. If you have summary or review journals, you may be able to keep up on the high spots of your profession. From the summaries, identify articles or books that contain the detailed information most critical to maintaining and developing your skills.

Then learn to read with an eye for the forest and not the trees. Develop the ability to scan material and pick out the basic details from an article without having to read the entire article. Most of the time, compulsive, word-for-word reading is based on the fear that something important will be missed. Also, there are some concepts from memory research that can work in your favor.

In general, much of the information you read is lost in the first 24 hours after reading. Only high spots, or story lines, are retained. So why not read that way from the start? Also, if you are reading word for word, you are overriding one of the great powers of the mind—its ability to fill in gaps. You do not need to read all the prepositions, for example, because the mind will just assume that they were there. The message will come through even if you have not read all of the words.

Another way of reducing the time for reading is to look for organizing themes in the author's style. Some authors provide the main idea at the beginning of a paragraph, elaborate in the middle, and summarize or provide transitions at the end. Therefore, you can often get the most important information by merely reading the first and last sentences of each paragraph. If material is highlighted in the middle, scan it on the way. Also, note other highlights such as lists of essential points and markers such as *first, second, third,* and *finally.*

Once Should Always Be Enough

Never handle paper more than once. How many times has a letter or memo come across your desk and you felt that you did not have the time to deal with it then? Each time you pick it up you follow the same sequence, though: Read it, think about it, decide what to do, decide not to do anything, wait until later, and repeat the sequence. Each time you add delays and excess mental baggage. If you do this even twice for each piece of correspondence, you can add as much as 25% to your work load. The work that you could accomplish in 8 hours will take you 10 hours or more. If you are taking work home, look at this aspect of your work behavior and consider whether change is needed.

Down Time and Idling

If you are too busy for relaxation, socializing, and exercising, you are just too busy. Down time is important for a change of both physical and mental pacing. It serves to refresh the body and revive the spirit. Too often, though, down time is counted as nonproductive, a waste of time. But the usual effect is that you are able to go back to work after idling and accomplish more in less time. Edwin Bliss suggested that being in good physical condition increases the percentage of working hours that are prime time.[20]

On the other hand, continuing to work under pressure usually has a snowball effect. Job performance gradually goes down, though often so insidiously that the real reason is overlooked. The conclusion erroneously drawn is that more work and harder work is what is needed and the snowball gets even bigger.

The idea is to obtain a balance between the necessity of work and the value of idling. If you spend 18 hours in front of the tube for sports or soaps, you might be overdoing on the idling end. But allow yourself a minimum of three to four hours at least two to three times a week when you can just shut everything out of your mind and let your mind rest. It may not be the most productive time of your life, but it can still contribute greatly to your overall satisfaction with life and work.

◆ SUMMARY

In this chapter, seven major time traps are identified. These were confusion, indecision, diffusion, procrastination, avoidance, interruptions, and perfectionism. Confusion stems from lack of a clear vision of where to go. Indecision is the inability to act decisively when required. Diffusion is being spread out so much that all efforts are less focused and efficient than they could otherwise be. Procrastination is an unnecessary delay in finishing a task. Avoidance involves a number of types of escape behaviors to avoid dealing with unpleasant duties. Interruptions result from the unscheduled drop-in, mismanaged phone calls, and self-initiated stops and starts that detract from continuity on the job. Perfectionism is compulsive overdoing beyond the point of value.

The major means of dealing with these errors in management are setting goals and priorities within goals. Also, using cue control for the work environment to increase concentration and reduce interruptions was discussed. Batching and handling routine chores on a mass basis at one time is a way of minimizing interruptions. Down time is important to maintaining mental and physical energy.

◆ NOTES

[1]Ferner, J. D. (1980). *Successful time management*. New York: Wiley, p. 12.

[2]Webber, R. A. (1972). *Time and management*. New York: Van Nostrand Reinhold.

[3]Bliss, E. C. (1976). *Getting things done: The ABC's of time management*. New York: Scribner's, p. 10.

[4]Carroll, L. (1966). *Alice's adventures in wonderland*. New York: Macmillan, p. 89.

[5]Rutherford, R. D. (1978). *Administrative time power: Meeting the time challenge of the busy secretary/staff assistant/manager team*. Austin, TX: Learning Concepts, p. 89.

[6]Kozoll, C. E. (1982). *Time management for educators*. Bloomington, IN: Phi Delta Kappa Educational Foundation, p. 13.

[7]Douglass, M. R., & Douglass, D. N. (1980). *Manage your time, manage your work, manage yourself*. New York: AMACOM, p. 235.

[8]Rutherford, *Administrative time power*, p. 28.

[9]Davidson, J. (1978). *Effective time management*. New York: Human Sciences Press, pp. 75–77.

[10]Davidson, *Effective time management*, p. 24.

[11]Marvin, P. (1980). *Executive time management: An AMA survey report*. New York: AMACOM, p. 7.

[12]Hummel, C. (1982). As reported in Posner, M. J. (1982). *Executive essentials*. New York: Avon Books, p. 21.

[13]Drucker, P. F. (1967). *The effective executive*. New York: Harper & Row, p. 575.

[14]Lakein, A. (1974). *How to get control of your time and your life*. New York: New American Library/Signet, p. 64.

[15]As cited in Bliss, *Getting things done*, p. 21.

[16]Douglass & Douglass, *Manage your time*, p. 79.

[17]Rutherford, *Administrative time power*, p. 33.

[18]Bliss, *Getting things done*, p. 19.

[19]Heyel, C. (1979). *Getting results with time management* (2nd ed.). New York: American Management Association, p. 69.

[20]Bliss, *Getting things done*, pp.33–34.

16

BEHAVIORAL HEALTH STRATEGIES: NUTRITION AND EXERCISE

*. . . running has given me a glimpse of the
greatest freedom that a man can ever know,
because it results in the simultaneous
liberation of both body and mind.*

Roger Bannister

A positive personal health program is just as much a part of stress management as relaxation training, autogenics, anxiety management, or cognitive restructuring. In essence, good health tends to increase resistance to stress by improving the person's capacity for responding to demands. This is true whether the demands are challenging and exciting or threatening and anxiety provoking.

Various statistics support the contention that Americans engage in a wide range of unhealthy behaviors including smoking, overeating, improper diet, lack of exercise, and excess use of drugs. For example, Americans take nearly 5 billion doses of tranquilizers to calm down, another 5 billion doses of barbiturates to unwind and sleep, and another 3 billion doses of amphetamines to perk up.[1]

Although close to 30 million Americans quit smoking in the decade between 1965 and 1975, mostly on their own,[2] approximately 35% of all adults still smoke. One figure that has been viewed with alarm is the large increase in the number of teenage girls and working women who now smoke, an increase that more than offsets the number of those quitting.

Our diets are loaded with an excess of fats and not enough carbohydrates. As a result, the frequency of obesity and coronary disease is much higher than need be. It is now estimated that nearly 80 million Americans are overweight.[3] And while a Gallup poll in 1984 showed that approximately 59% of the adult population engaged in daily exercise, over twice the number in 1961,[4] there are still many homes with a sedentary life-style. At the other extreme, among those who engage in physical exercise, far too many have an "Olympic syndrome," going into exercise programs too fast and too hard, pushing themselves to limits far beyond what is necessary for good health.

The purpose of this chapter, then, is to provide the basic principles for establishing and maintaining a good personal health program. There are many ways to construct such a program but the focus here will be on nutrition and exercise. Also, behavioral self-control techniques will be described that can be used to change a variety of unhealthy behaviors.

◆ EFFECTS OF STRESS ON METABOLISM AND DIET

Because stress has a generally arousing effect on the person, there is a potential for changes in both energy expenditure and energy intake. First, stress increases the rate of **metabolism,** the rate at which the body changes food supplies into energy. This leads to increased levels of sugar, free fatty acids, and lactic acid in the blood. The pituitary also indirectly affects the rate of metabolism. These effects include changes in water balance, suppression of the immune system, and increased carbohydrate and protein metabolism. The net effect of stress is that the body uses energy at a faster rate.

On the intake side, the pattern of eating may also change. Whether a person will be affected and how significantly his or her behavior will change depend on a variety of factors such as learning, emotionality, and personality. Some people learn that food is a means of escape when sad or depressed, while others learn that food is less desirable under these same conditions. The former may not only eat more, but may eat more frequently while under pressure. The latter may want to eat only subsistence meals or not want to eat at all. Externally controlled people are likely to respond by eating more, but internally controlled people are less likely to do the same.

When the pattern of responding to stress is to eat more and eat more frequently, a cycle may be established that leads to difficulty in controlling weight, if not to obesity. When the pattern is to eat less, especially such extremes as going without food for substantial periods, the body may be depleted of energy reserves at an even faster rate. When there is any dramatic change in eating patterns, look carefully at what is happening at work, at school, or in the family. It may be that some unresolved conflict has produced the change.

◆ EFFECTS OF DIET ON STRESS

While arousal can change metabolism and eating behavior, dietary practice can change sensitivity to arousing stimulation and environmental stressors. Thus, eating right is just as important as managing stress because vulnerability to stress increases with poor diet. There are two ways in which this happens.

First, excess amounts of sugars can deplete vitamins and minerals. This can have negative side effects since vitamins and minerals are essential to keeping many parts of the body, especially the nervous system, working properly. Depletion of some of the B vitamins (thiamine, niacin, and B_{12}, for example) increases nervous system reactivity, irritability, and nervousness. The bottom line is that you may be setting yourself up to respond to more events as stressful when you take in too many sweets.

Second, a number of foods commonly taken in large amounts have the potential to increase stress sensitivity. For example, coffee, cola, chocolates, and other products containing caffeine are among the most frequently abused beverage and food products in our society. One cup of coffee contains approximately 100–150 milligrams (mg) of caffeine (decaffeinated contains only 3 mg per 5-ounce cup).[5] As little as 250 mg can cause nervousness, insomnia, and headaches. It is now well known that caffeine acts as a stimulant to the central nervous system, has a tendency to charge up the autonomic system, and lowers the threshold for stress reactions. Stated in other terms, you are more likely to interpret an event as stressful if you have been on a diet loaded with caffeine, and you will probably respond in tense situations more quickly and strongly than if you had not been taking in so much caffeine. While these dangers occur with excessive use, the body appears to be able to handle lower levels with little or no negative side effects. Before delving into the next section on nutrition, you may wish to fill out the nutrition and diet scales provided in Self-Study Exercise 16.1.

Self-Study Exercise 16–1.   Health Behavior Profile for Nutrition and Diet

---

The following scale will help you compare your dietary practice to what is considered good practice. Instructions for scoring are provided at the end.

Circle the answer that most accurately describes your eating habits.

DAILY = Once or more per day
FREQUENTLY = Every week but not once per day
OCCASIONALLY = A few times each month but not once per week
SELDOM = No more than once per month

How often do you:	SELDOM	OCCASIONALLY	FREQUENTLY	DAILY
1. Eat fruits, vegetables, fiber?	1	2	3	4
2. Drink five or more cups of coffee in a day?	4	3	2	1
3. Eat fats, red meats, and dairy products?	4	3	2	1
4. Drink five or more soft drinks (diet or regular)?	4	3	2	1
5. Eat candies, sugars, pastries?	4	3	2	1

continued

continued	SELDOM	OCCASIONALLY	FREQUENTLY	DAILY
6. Take vitamin supplements?	4	3	2	1
7. Overeat at meals?	4	3	2	1
8. Eat between meals?	4	3	2	1
9. Eat while watching TV, reading, and so on.?	4	3	2	1
10. Skip breakfast?	4	3	2	1
11. Skip lunch?	4	3	2	1
12. Skip dinner?	4	3	2	1
13. Use crash diets to lose weight?	4	3	2	1
14. Take diet pills?	4	3	2	1
15. Use amphetamines to lose weight?	4	3	2	1

After you have completed the scale, go back and sum the values listed in the boxes you circled. Then circle the point on the scale below that corresponds to your total score. A high score suggests that your eating habits are fairly good. On the other end, a low score indicates there is some risk in your eating habits. If you have a score in the High Risk region, look back at the items checked that have values of 1 or 2. These items provide clues to some areas where a change in diet and nutrition habits may be warranted.

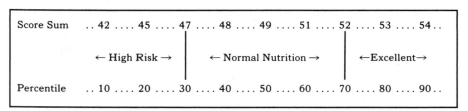

Score Sum	.. 42 .... 45 .... 47 .... 48 .... 49 .... 51 .... 52 .... 53 .... 54 ..
	← High Risk → | ← Normal Nutrition → | ←Excellent→
Percentile	.. 10 .... 20 .... 30 .... 40 .... 50 .... 60 .... 70 .... 80 .... 90 ..

The average score on this scale is 49.2 and the median is 49.5. The median indicates that 50% of the respondents scored higher than 49.5 and 50% scored below this. The scale has a reliability of .695, which is acceptable for this type of scale. This scale is not intended to be a comprehensive nutrition assessment and is provided for instructional purposes only.

◆ EATING RIGHT

Proper nutrition depends on eating the right foods in the right amounts. Nutrition research has shown that the adult human body must have 46 nutrients in order to be healthy and stay healthy. To maintain a constant weight, the average woman needs about 1,600–2,400 calories; the average man needs about 2,300–3,100 calories.[6] Table 16–1 provides the average

Table 16–1. Recommended Daily Energy Intake for Children and Adults

	Age (years)	Weight (pounds)	Height (inches)	Energy Needs (calories)
Youths	1–3	29	35	1,300 (900–1,800)
	4–6	44	44	1,700 (1,300–2,300)
	7–10	62	52	2,400 (1,650–3,300)
Males	11–14	99	62	2,700 (2,000–3,700)
	15–18	145	69	2,800 (2,100–3,900)
	19–22	154	70	2,900 (2,500–3,300)
	23–50	154	70	2,700 (2,300–3,100)
	51–75	154	70	2,400 (2,000–2,800)
	76+	154	70	2,050 (1,650–2,450)
Females	11–14	101	62	2,200 (1,500–3,000)
	15–18	120	64	2,100 (1,200–3,000)
	19–22	120	64	2,100 (1,700–2,500)
	23–50	120	64	2,300 (1,600–2,400)
	51–75	120	64	1,800 (1,400–2,200)
	76+	120	64	1,600 (1,200–2,000)
Pregnancy				+300
Nursing				+500

Note. Adapted from *Mayo Clinic Diet Manual* (p. 270) by Mayo Clinic, Committee on Dietetics (Eds.), 1981, Philadelphia: Saunders.

energy needs with ranges for children and adults of different weights and heights. To obtain the 46 nutrients, the normal adult needs to average *as a bare minimum* about 1,300 calories per day.[7] For these reasons, any diet that reduces to an extreme either the type or the quantity of food is dangerous in the long run and should be avoided.

The rules provided here are for the so-called normal adult, and suggested caloric intake levels are averages. Children and adults over 55–60 years of age differ in their requirements, as do pregnant and nursing women. Also, illness affects nutritional requirements. A person with a larger body and a strenuous job requires more calories than someone with a small body frame and a less physically demanding job. Finally, the intake does not have to match the standard exactly each day, but it should average out over a few days.

As noted earlier, the body requires 46 nutrients in order to work properly. These are distributed in six categories: water, carbohydrates, 9 proteins, fat, 13 vitamins, and 21 minerals. In these six categories, only carbohydrates, proteins, and fats contain calories. Calories provide the body with energy for internal processes and for muscular and brain work. But they also add body weight when consumed in excess. Carbohydrates are the least likely to add unwanted body weight, while fats are the worst offenders.

Water, vitamins, and minerals are essential to keeping the body functioning properly but do not contain calories. Most of these nutritional needs are readily met through natural food supplies. The challenge is to obtain the proper balance of foods so that all of the nutrients are supplied while keeping the calorie count at a level that will maintain your desirable weight.

The ideal diet should be 50% carbohydrates, 20% protein, and about 30% fat.[8] Unfortunately, the contemporary American diet is drastically out of balance, averaging 40% carbohydrates, about 15–20% protein, and nearly 40–45% fat.[9]

Carbohydrates: Filling Up, Not Fattening Up

Carbohydrates are complex food molecules made up of carbon, oxygen, and hydrogen—or, more simply, sugars. There are single-molecule sugars called monosaccharides, double-molecule sugars called disaccharides, and complex sugar molecules called polysaccharides. One simple sugar is glucose, the high-energy fuel in your bloodstream. Fruits and honey contain pure glucose, which can pass directly into the bloodstream for fast energy. Foods such as bananas and oranges also contain simple sugars, but they must be converted into glucose in order to be used by the body. This is true of all the other sugars as well. Common table sugar and milk are sources of double sugars, while corn, beans, and potatoes are sources of complex sugars.

Carbohydrates provide the primary fuel for exercise, labor, and brain work. The brain actually depends on a continuous supply of glucose to work properly. It cannot reserve or hold back fuel for later use. This is why a good breakfast is important to starting the day off right. If you do not eat in the morning, the brain does not have the immediate energy it needs to work properly. The muscles, though, are able to save up glucose in a type of energy bank to be withdrawn when needed. In its stored form, glucose is called glycogen.

In addition to providing a quick source of energy, carbohydrates fill you up more quickly with fewer calories than any other food. Therefore, you will have a tendency to feel full more quickly and stop eating sooner when you eat carbohydrates.

One of the most important benefits comes from carbohydrates that are high in fiber or cellulose content. These are the so-called complex carbohydrates, which are made up of millions of sugar molecules. Two characteristics of high-fiber foods make them valuable to a healthy diet. First, high-fiber foods do not break down in the digestive system as readily as other foods. In fact, the upper intestine cannot break down fiber at all. Since they cannot be broken down, they cannot be absorbed into the body. As a result, you do not have to worry as much about adding weight when eating high-fiber foods.

Second, fats bind to fiber. If there is some fiber in your stomach when fat is added, some of the fat will latch on to the fiber and pass out of your system as part of the body's waste. When you eat something that has high fat content, like a richly marbled steak, eat it with fiber to reduce the amount of fat that gets into the system.

Common foods containing carbohydrates are vegetables, fruits, and whole grains. When you think you just have to have a snack before the next meal, instead of grabbing for the potato chips, which have high fat content, eat an apple or celery or carrots. This will reduce hunger, provide energy, and add fiber to the digestive tract.

The Proteins

Proteins may be the most overrated food in the American diet. There seems to be a common belief that protein provides strength and that the best source of protein is meat. In fact, strength is developed through exercise and the best source of energy for exercise comes from carbohydrates. The idea that the vegetarian must be inherently weaker than the meat-eater is an unfortunate stereotype and inaccurate belief.

Further, protein is *not* a source of quick energy. It has to be converted before it is useful. While there are calories in protein, it seems to be the last foodstuff converted to energy after the carbohydrates and the fats. The body uses protein only during periods of severe starvation or dieting.

Proteins are the basic building blocks for all the tissues in your body. Hair, skin, eyes, muscles, and organs are all built with protein in combination with other materials. Even the enzymes that regulate body functions are proteins. In the human body, proteins are made of 21 different amino acids. The body is capable of manufacturing 12 of the 21 amino acids by itself, but the other 9 have to come from the diet.

Protein can be obtained from a variety of sources. It is most commonly obtained from animal sources such as poultry, eggs, fish, lean meat, cheese, and milk. It is also available from many plant sources such as cereals, nuts, beans, and leafy vegetables. There is no need to eat any meat at all to obtain all the protein you need. Gabe Mirkin noted that you can get virtually all the protein you need in two large glasses of milk or in 12 ounces of corn and beans per day.[10]

During periods of intense stress, illness, infections, and injury, the body may increase its demand for protein by as much as 100%. Intense exercise and body building may have the same effect.[11]

Good Fats and Bad Fats

If proteins are the most overrated food, fats may be the most misunderstood. Fats are often feared because of the association with obesity and coronary difficulties. In spite of this, fats are the most overused if not abused foods. As noted earlier, fats constitute about 45% of the American diet, although the maximum should be about 30%. The average male should carry no more than 15% body fat and the average female should carry no more than 25% body fat. Yet the average American carries much more, a type of excess baggage with harmful side effects. A male 45 years of age carrying 25 pounds of excess fat has a life expectancy reduced by 25%![12]

At the same time, fats are essential to a healthy body and, in the final analysis, to survival. Fat is a storehouse of energy and fluids for the body to draw on whenever it needs. Fat converts to energy much more quickly than protein does. It is essential to vitamin transport. The ability of the immune system to protect the body against viruses and bacteria is also dependent on the presence of fat. Finally, fat is one major way in which the body protects itself against cold.

Most of the danger from fats comes from the deposits of cholesterols in the bloodstream and the buildup of yellow fat on the body. First, excess calories may be converted by the liver to a type of blood fat called cholesterol. There are two kinds of cholesterol called lipoproteins. One is a good type of fat, and the other one is bad fat. The good type of cholesterol is called high-density lipoprotein, or HDL for short. The bad cholesterol is called low-density lipoprotein, or LDL. Coronary attacks are associated with a high concentration of LDL; persons with high HDL tend to have fewer attacks.

HDL serves to keep the arteries clean and elastic. In contrast, LDL embeds itself in the arterial walls, beginning to narrow and harden the artery so that blood can only pass with much greater effort for the heart and much higher pressure in the arteries. Those who exercise consistently carry more of their cholesterol as HDL, the good lipoprotein, while sedentary people carry more of their cholesterol as LDL.[13]

Second, excess calories are stored in a type of fat called yellow fat. This is the harmful fat. If you could expose the fatty tissue just beneath the skin, such as in the fold of fat around your waistline, you would find yellow fat.

Fat is consumed in butter, oils such as those used in fast food frying, salad dressings, ice cream, and fatty meats such as bacon. It is now thought that the best way to control the problems caused by fats is to reduce the intake of all kinds of fats and to maintain a regular exercise program.

◆ VITAMINS: USE OR ABUSE AND ADDICTION?

In recent years, a variety of vitamin supplement diets and therapies have been publicized that advocate megadoses of some particular vitamin. The extent of vitamin consumption is indicated by the $1.4 billion spent by U.S. consumers in 1984.[14] The rationales for vitamin diets vary. One line of thinking is based on the age-old observation that vitamin deficiencies cause extremely serious physical problems—pellagra and scurvy, for example. If a little supplement is advisable to keep this from happening, then a lot of the supplement must be even better. This argument does not consider what vitamin poisoning can do to the body.

Another argument is that vitamin guidelines are established as minimums and do not take into account variations in size and health of the individual. Larger people and sick people certainly must need more vitamins. Therefore, as the argument goes, we should look at nothing less than an "average" allowance, which must be larger than the listed minimums. This argument, however, does not consider the vitamins obtained from daily food. A balanced diet is able to supply most of the vitamins you need at the levels you need. If you then supplement your diet with common vitamins providing 100% of the daily requirement, you may be taking in around twice what is needed.

Perhaps the most difficult argument to refute is the one that says, "I was really sick with _____ and I took _____ and got better right away." Fill in the blanks with "a cold" and "vitamin C" and you have the argument made famous by Linus Pauling. Unfortunately, this argument does not consider the **placebo effect,** the fact that if a person *believes* a treatment will be effective, there is increased likelihood that it will indeed be effective. This belief can be sufficient to marshal the body's natural healing powers.

This issue can be addressed by using an experimental design called a double blind. In a **double-blind study,** the subjects do not know what treatment they are getting, and the experimenter does not know either. In vitamin studies, subjects might be getting a placebo that looks and tastes like the real thing but is chemically inert. A review of studies on vitamin C and the frequency and duration of colds failed to show any practical significance and few statistically significant results. Among the best-designed studies, 50% showed no significant results and the remaining less carefully designed studies showed such small differences as to be of virtually no importance.[15]

In contrast to the alleged positive effects of megadoses of vitamins, relatively little attention has been devoted to the dangers of vitamin overdose. Charles Marshall, though, has documented the hidden dangers of vitamin overdoses. He noted that the practice of taking vitamin supplements has turned into a pattern of abuse based on the mistaken notion that more is better. This is often combined with a false security that translates to "I take so many vitamins I don't have to worry about the rest of my diet."[16] He also noted that some vitamins can be addicting, and there will be withdrawal symptoms if the dosage level is reduced drastically or cut altogether. A few of the dangers are noted here, as documented by Marshall.

Large doses of vitamin A produce so many negative effects that time does not permit reporting them all. The list includes loss of appetite, weight loss, loss of hair, anemia, blurred vision, extreme drying and thickening of the skin, dry and cracking lips, canker sores, increased brain and spinal fluid pressure with headache, irritability in children, and birth defects in children born to mothers who took megadosages during pregnancy.[17]

There are no known toxic effects from the B complex vitamins, although some unpleasant side effects may occur from too much niacin.

Vitamin C—much heralded for its ability to prevent, or at least reduce, colds and flu—is probably one of the most abused vitamins in American society. In 1976 Americans paid $80 million for vitamin C supplements.[18] While the recommended dietary allowance for vitamin C is 60 mg for both men and women,[19] the average daily consumption was 125 mg in 1983.[20] And, following advice from "experts," many people take as much as 2,000–4,000 mg per day. The dangers from megadoses of vitamin C are extensive. The most common side effect is diarrhea. Other dangers are complications in pregnancy (including spontaneous abortion), lowered sperm count, increased uric acid excretion, decreased tolerance for low oxygen levels, interference with urine tests for sugar and stool tests for blood, decreased resistance to bacterial infections and tumors, and damage to tooth enamel.[21]

Overdoses of vitamin D can cause loss of appetite, nausea, headaches, and depression. Long-term use may result in calcification of soft tissues and kidney failure. Excessive urination and diarrhea or constipation may also occur. When the kidneys become involved, high blood pressure, increased levels of blood cholesterol, and heart damage can follow, in some cases with fatal results.

Although the specific role of vitamin E is still uncertain, Americans spend approximately $100 million each year on it. Their interest is apparently based on early observations in laboratory rats that vitamin E confers increased sexual vitality and longevity. Such effects have not been demonstrated in humans and the studies with rats are far from convincing. Megadoses of vitamin E are known to result in elevated blood triglyceride levels in women and a reduction in thyroid hormone in both sexes. Laboratory studies of animals overdosed with vitamin E show actual thyroid gland damage. Could such damage be the cause of reduced thyroid hormone production in humans?

In addition to the potential dangers from megavitamin therapy, there are physiological and practical reasons to avoid such excesses. Physiologically, the body acts like a reservoir that can hold only a certain amount of a vitamin before overflowing. In the case of vitamin C, the body can hold only about 1,500 mg. If the body's reservoir is close to full (as it usually is), when you take a 1,000-mg pill the body does what a reservoir does. Some of the old goes out with some of the new, and some of the old and some of the new stay in the body. About 500 mg of the new vitamin is absorbed into the body store, while about 500 mg is lost in stools and another 500 mg is lost in urine. The body's ledger sheet for vitamin C is balanced. Practically, then, you are spending your hard-earned money to pass stools and urine rich in vitamin C.

In sum, megavitamin therapy has not proven beneficial and it can produce dangerous side effects. The body cannot possibly use the huge amounts of vitamins some are pumping into their bodies. And it is largely a waste of money.

◆ EATING LIGHT

This could well be called the age of diets and dieting. You can find dozens of different diets, any one of which claims to have the secret to help you take off and keep off excess pounds. Gabe Mirkin reported that over $10 billion dollars is spent each year by nearly 20 million Americans on reducing diets.[22]

First, any diet program that focuses solely on what goes in (calories) without discussing what goes out (energy expenditure through exercise) should be viewed skeptically. In order to lose weight and keep it off, you need to change the balance in the equation of input and output. You must burn more calories than you take in.

There are several dangers inherent in programs that focus solely on the input side. One danger comes in diets that reduce calories to the extreme. Such diets generally cannot provide the balance of six nutrients needed by the body. Gabe Mirkin suggested that your diet should never go below 1,000 calories if you are not exercising, and the intake should stay above 1,300 calories if you are.

Another danger is that dieting takes off muscle tissue, not fat. On the other hand, by exercising you remove fat but tone muscle. You are getting rid of what you need to lose and keeping what is more important. Resist the temptation to forego exercise in order to reduce caloric intake. In general, this practice is self-defeating, whereas proper exercise is one of the most effective methods for obtaining weight loss, especially by getting rid of yellow fat.

The final difficulty is that restricting your diet may actually work against weight loss. This is because the body "reads" reduction in food as an extreme privation or starvation event. It responds by slowing everything down, a conservation strategy that retains fat instead of discarding it. Only dangerously low calorie diets will cause your body to draw out of the protein and fat reserves so that weight loss occurs.

There is one body change that may cause confusion at the beginning of a program emphasizing weight loss through exercise. Muscles are denser than fat, and thus weigh more than fat for the same volume. Even though you are burning off fat during exercise, you may not see a change on the scales, and in some cases you may even see a weight gain. This should not be cause for alarm. It is better to carry weight in the form of conditioned muscle than in the form of fat debris loaded under your skin and floating in your blood. It is not weight per se but percentage of body fat that is dangerous.

To summarize, if you must diet, observe the following guidelines:

1. Keep caloric intake above the minimum so that you obtain all the essential food groups.
2. Combine dieting with exercise that burns off more calories than you consume.
3. Keep food intake balanced in the proportion of 50% carbohydrates, 20% protein, and 30% fats. If you cut anything further, it should be fats.
4. Avoid diets that require a dangerously low caloric intake for any period.
5. Avoid diets that eliminate all of one type of food or suggest excessive amounts of a particular food.
6. Do not assume that vitamin supplements can take the place of carbohydrates, proteins, or fats. Vitamins contain no calories whatsoever.

◆ EXERCISE, HEALTH, AND STRESS

The benefits of exercise cannot be overemphasized, and its necessity should not be underestimated. Before the dawn of the industrial–technological soci-

ety, getting enough exercise was rarely an issue and diet clinics were unnecessary. Daily life was taken up with the incessant struggle for existence.
Now, however, virtually every chore that once demanded physical activity
has been mechanized or streamlined to reduce effort and thereby much of
the associated physical benefit. Even getting up to change the TV channel
has been automated! In this climate, it is little wonder that people are on a
continuous dieting treadmill. Even a very low calorie diet will probably put
weight on because the input of calories is not balanced by the output of
energy.

Self-Study Exercise 16–2.   Health Behavior Profile for Exercise

---

This profile is intended to help you determine the adequacy of your current
physical activities and/or exercise program. Read the instructions before completing
the profile. Instructions for scoring are given at the end along with the necessary
information on how to interpret your own score.

Indicate the level of your participation in any of the listed activities by circling
the appropriate boxes below.

AEROBIC = Four or more times per week
FREQUENTLY = Two or three times per week
WEEKLY = About once per week
MONTHLY = About once per month
NEVER = Almost never

How often do you participate in:	NEVER	MONTHLY	WEEKLY	FREQUENTLY	AEROBIC
1. Swimming	0	1	2	3	4
2. Walking (one mile per day)	0	1	2	3	4
3. Hiking or backpacking	0	1	2	3	4
4. Gardening	0	1	2	3	4
5. Bicycling	0	1	2	3	4
6. Calisthenics, aerobics, dance exercise	0	1	2	3	4
7. Racquetball, tennis	0	1	2	3	4
8. Canoeing or boating	0	1	2	3	4
9. Water or snow skiing	0	1	2	3	4
10. Hunting or fishing	0	1	2	3	4
11. Golfing	0	1	2	3	4
12. Team sports	0	1	2	3	4

13. Running (five or more miles per week)

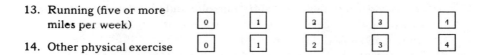

14. Other physical exercise

After answering all 14 questions, *sum* the values in all the circled boxes. Then, *count* all the boxes with the value of 1 or more. *Divide* the *sum* by the *count*. This is your **aerobic index**. Finally, locate your aerobic index on the scale below. A low aerobic index suggests that you are not getting enough exercise. A high aerobic index suggests that your pattern of exercise is fairly good. If you have a score at the high-risk end of the scale, you should think about how to begin a consistent exercise program that will place you in the normal, if not excellent, range.

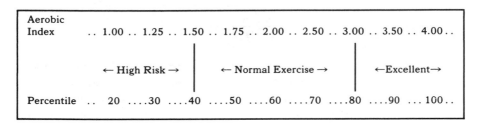

Physical Benefits of Exercise

Physical exercise has a wide range of positive effects for the body. These include the following:

1. Increased respiratory capacity.
2. Increased muscle tone (anaerobic exercise).
3. Increased strength in bones, ligaments, and tendons.
4. Improved cardiovascular functioning (aerobic exercise).
5. Reduced risk of heart disease.
6. Improved circulation.
7. Reduced cholesterol and triglyceride levels.
8. Increased energy.
9. Improved sleep and reduced need for sleep.
10. Increased rate of metabolism.
11. Reduced body weight and improved fat metabolism.
12. Reduced risk of injury from slips, falls, and so forth.
13. Slowed-down aging process.[23]

Mental Benefits of Exercise

Many athletes report a variety of mental benefits accompanying involvement in physical activity. There is, for example, a **runner's euphoria**, a feeling of elation, spiritual ecstasy, or transcendence so powerful that achieving the same state again almost becomes a goal in its own right. Thus it serves as a powerful incentive to continue the activity. Short of this type of peak experience, exercise has a number of other benefits:

1. Increased feelings of self-control, independence, and self-sufficiency.
2. Increased self-confidence.
3. Improved body image and self-esteem.
4. Mental change of pace from the pressures of work, even when work is physical.
5. Improved mental functioning, alertness, and efficiency.
6. Emotional catharsis or cleansing out of tensions from interpersonal conflict and job stress.
7. Reduced overall levels of stress.
8. Relief from mild depressions.

◆ PREPARING FOR EXERCISE

Preparing for exercise can be as important as the actual exercise. Think of each exercise session as divided into three distinct periods: warm-up, exercise, and cool-down. Whatever the sport, schedule a 10–20-minute *warm-up* period prior to the main workout. During this time, do some easy stretching and limbering routines. The goal is to bring your body temperature up slowly and get your muscles ready for more demanding activity later on. If bicycling, set an easy pace for the first mile or two before increasing the pace. If you are a runner, do some light calisthenics or equivalent before starting. But never go full speed from the start.

After completing an exercise session, also allow 10–20 minutes for cooling off. The longer and harder the workout, the longer you will probably need for cooling down. Just taking a brisk walk may be enough, but light calisthenics can also be used. If you do not cool down properly, the muscles may become congested with increased blood flow. Ketones, or poisons, may build up in your blood, producing pain and discomfort, such as cramps.

Finally, if you are just beginning an exercise program or are deciding whether to do so or not, remember that an exercise program must be considered as a developmental process. Start off with light exercise in relatively short sessions. As your fitness improves to a degree that is adequate for your sex and age, you can increase the intensity and the length of the sessions.

Later on, exercise should be viewed as being primarily for *maintenance,* not progress. Avoid the idea that you have to be constantly making progress to some higher level, lifting more weights, playing more games, running more miles, or running faster. There are limits to what the human body can accomplish, what it can endure, what you personally can do. Continuous progress is ultimately impossible. At some time, you will reach a plateau and find that you can go no further. That is the time to consider maintaining what you have gained. To think otherwise is largely self-defeating and may be downright foolish. As others have pointed out, fitness is not a ribbon achieved in competition. It is a road you travel all your life. After reaching speed, you do not have to keep on accelerating. Rather, you should travel at a safe and constant speed.

◆ EXERCISING FOR FITNESS

There are relatively few rules to guide an adequate exercise program, but they are important. First, the exercise program should aim for aerobic fitness more than strength. **Aerobic fitness** is "the ability to take in, transport, and utilize oxygen."[24] Building up muscle strength through body-building routines may be acceptable if a hard body is your primary goal and you are also involved in some other exercise that builds cardiovascular fitness. But body-building routines are, for the most part, **anaerobic** (meaning "done without air"). Even though the muscles are toned and strengthened by such routines, heart rate and respiration are not significantly increased for any length of time. Thus, programs of this nature do very little for cardiovascular fitness.

Second, to achieve aerobic improvement, four factors may be varied. These are frequency, type, duration, and intensity of exercise. How effective your exercise program is over the short run and how well you maintain it over the long haul depends on the interaction of these four.

How Often to Exercise?

The general rule is to exercise at least three times each week, preferably four, in order to obtain aerobic improvement. Anything less than this will produce as much or more loss in the off days as you gain on exercise days. Anything more than this may wear down your body. When this happens, you will feel gradually increasing fatigue and you may lose motivation for exercise. If you absolutely must exercise more than four times per week, do what professional athletes do. Schedule the major workouts on roughly an every-other-day basis. Schedule light workouts on the off days. You might even use a different type of exercise on the off days to provide some variety and maintain motivation.

What Exercise Is Best?

Entire books have been written on the specific forms of exercise and how good or inadequate they are. This section is only intended as a summary of some of the most important findings. Whatever type of exercise you choose, it should fit sensibly into your life-style and be within reach of your physical capacities.

One method of rating different types of exercise uses the number of calories burned in the course of one hour of exercise. Table 16–2 is such a table. This table contains some rather interesting bits of information. For example, note that rapid walking burns more calories than even swimming or running. The moral is simple enough: You do not have to engage in very intense and demanding sports, such as a marathon, in order to achieve aerobic fitness. In fact, an activity that burns in the vicinity of 200–300 calories per hour is sufficient if you do it consistently three or four times per week.

Table 16–2.   Energy Expenditure per Hour During Different Types of Activity for a 70-Kilogram Man

Form of Activity	Calories per Hour
Sleeping	65
Awake, lying still	77
Sitting at rest	100
Standing relaxed	105
Dressing and undressing	118
Tailoring	135
Typewriting rapidly	140
Light exercise	170
Walking slowly (2.6 miles per hour)	200
Carpentry, metal working, industrial painting	240
Active exercise	290
Severe exercise	450
Sawing wood	480
Swimming	500
Running (5.3 miles per hour)	570
Very severe exercise	600
Walking very fast (5.3 miles per hour)	650
Walking up stairs	1,100

Note. Adapted from *Basic Human Physiology: Normal Function and Mechanisms of Disease* (p. 737) by A. C. Guyton, 1977, Philadelphia: Saunders.

Also note that just walking slowly burns about 200 calories per hour. Moderate aerobic exercise uses about 300 calories per hour. Measured against this norm, many activities provide adequate aerobic fitness. For example, a brisk two-mile walk at approximately three miles per hour is all that most people need. There is no investment in equipment, no expensive club membership fees, no fear of embarrassment, no competition, and relatively little worry about overdoing.

In general, such activities as running, bicycling, swimming, or aerobic exercise classes are cited as the most beneficial. Home treadmills and exercise machines provide adequate exercise where time and access are problems. And jumping rope is one of the simplest yet best forms of aerobic exercise. It is cheap, can be done virtually anywhere, and can be varied in intensity and length of time. Another simple exercise can be varied out on a set of stairs. It is similar to the "step-up" test for cardiovascular fitness. Just step up two or three steps and back down, and repeat. Doing this for just 15 minutes at a continuous pace is roughly equivalent to walking three miles slowly.

How Long Should an Exercise Session Last?

Developing aerobic fitness can be accomplished by increasing the length or the intensity of the workout or both. However, very severe workouts can be dangerous for a variety of reasons. You are more likely to have muscle strains, tears, ankle sprains, and assorted other injuries as the intensity of the workout increases. Severe workouts should never be attempted when you are first beginning an exercise program. In addition to the reversible injuries just described, more serious outcomes can occur, such as heart attacks. If a choice is to be made, opt for slightly longer workouts of moderate demand rather than shorter workouts of very severe demand.

To understand how long and how intense exercise should be, it may help if you gain perspective on what the end result is to be. To be fit means three things: The muscles are conditioned well enough to carry on work; the lungs have the capacity to take in air to supply to the heart and muscles; and the heart can increase its capacity (beats and volume) to meet the demands of work and exercise. While anaerobic exercise will help achieve fitness in the first sense, only aerobic exercise will meet all three criteria at the same time.

To focus on the lungs and heart first, consider these facts. The average person has a resting heart rate around 70–75 beats per minute (bpm). A finely conditioned athlete has a resting pulse of 60 bpm, sometimes even lower. A person whose life-style has been sedentary is more likely to have a resting pulse around 80–90 bpm. In addition, the person with a sedentary life-style has a heart that cannot respond to demand as readily as the tuned heart. This difference between the conditioned and the "deconditioned" heart means that the heart must beat about 30,000 more times each day for the person who is out of shape! In the course of a lifetime, that is a lot more work for the heart and the reason some hearts give out sooner.

But the heart can beat much faster than the 70-bpm average. In fact, it can beat as fast as 200 bpm or more. The ability to work with minimum strain is dependent on how much the heart rate can be raised and sustained over a period of time. Aerobic exercise gradually increases the rate at which your heart can work. But it also gradually decreases the resting pulse so that your heart does not have to work so hard when you are physically inactive.

The general rule is that your exercise should increase your heart rate to between 60% and 80% of the maximum capacity for your age. The maximum capacity can be obtained by subtracting your age from 220. If exercise does not increase heart rate above 60%, or about 115 bpm for the 30-year-old ($220 - 30 = 190 \times 0.6 = 115$ bpm), little or no progress will be made toward aerobic fitness. If you are 30 years old, the upper limit for aerobic exercise is about 152 bpm ($220 - 30 = 190 \times 0.8 = 152$ bpm). Table 16–3 provides maximum heart rates calculated for different ages with the minimum and maximum ranges for aerobic exercise. Note that the value given for each age is the average for that age. Depending on a number of factors, the value may vary more than 10 bpm plus or minus the listed value. These ranges are also provided in Table 16–3.[25]

You can get all you need from a one-hour workout of moderate intensity that includes warm-up and cool-down. The real benefit for cardiovascular improvement, though, comes from the 20–30 minutes in the middle when the heart rate is raised above its normal resting rate to somewhere between minimum and maximum, as just calculated. How much the heart rate is raised determines the quality of the exercise. Low-intensity aerobic effort raises the heart rate to no more than the minimum (115 bpm for the 30-year-old). Moderate-intensity aerobic effort occurs when the heart rate is raised

Table 16-3.   Maximum Heart Rate by Age with Maximum Training Heart Rate and Minimum Training Heart Rate for Aerobic Fitness

Age	Maximum Rate	Range	Maximum Training Rate	Minimum Training Rate
10	210	200–220	168	126
15	205	195–215	164	123
20	200	190–210	160	120
25	195	185–205	156	117
30	190	180–200	152	114
35	185	175–195	148	111
40	180	170–190	144	108
45	175	165–185	140	105
50	170	160–180	136	102
55	165	155–175	132	99
60	160	150–170	128	96
70	150	140–160	120	90
80	140	130–150	112	84

Note. The range given for the maximum heart rate is provided as an indication of individual variability. The upper limit may be safely reached by individuals in better condition, but *the lower limit may be the upper limit of safety for those not in good condition.* Also, the high and low range concept should be carried over to both the maximum and minimum training rates. To do this, multiply the range values by 80% for maximum training rate and by 60% for minimum training rate.

above the minimum but not above about 70% (between 115 and 135 bpm). Heart rates between 70% and 80% reflect a high-intensity aerobic effort.

How Hard to Exercise: The "No Pain, No Gain" Myth

How hard you should exercise depends on what your goals are for the exercise and what your current level of conditioning is. While some exertion is necessary to develop fitness, too much exertion can be physically damaging. This is especially true in the early stages of exercise. If your goal is to get and keep an adequate level of fitness, then moderate workouts are probably all you need. If you are a born competitor in search of excellence and the chance to prove just how good you are, a more strenuous level of exercise may be warranted. But do not depend on the competition motive to sustain a long-term exercise. In fact, attitudes that focus on competition and proving oneself may be the greatest barrier to getting a larger number of people to engage in safe but adequate exercise.

Work into the exercise program slowly if you have been out of shape for any period of time. It usually requires several weeks of low-intensity exercise and several more weeks of moderate exercise before the body is able to profit from very strenuous workouts.

In any case, far too much emphasis has been put on competition and the notion of "no pain, no gain." The Olympic syndrome mentioned earlier is the idea that the exercise, to be useful, must lead to the pinnacle of success. That may be acceptable for the athletically gifted young. But for the average adult, a more modest and attainable goal should suffice. Exercise should be fun, and contrary to what some may say, it does not have to be painful in order to be helpful. This should already be clear from the fact that brisk walking and 30 minutes of moderate aerobic exercise are sufficient for cardiovascular fitness. Indeed, Brian Sharkey has reported research showing that a daily five-minute, 100-calorie-burning workout is sufficient to provide progress to aerobic fitness.[26] After a few weeks, move up to the 300-calorie range. Later on, if you wish, move up even higher. If you are exercising in part to control weight, then workouts should be in the 300-calorie range.

◆ BARRIERS TO EFFECTIVE EXERCISE

Given all the proven benefits of exercise, it may seem surprising that more people do not establish exercise programs. But there are many attitudes and perceptions that probably keep many people from it. Two such attitudes have already been mentioned, society's obsession with competition and the Olympic syndrome. It should be clear from the foregoing discussion that you do not have to run a marathon to achieve good health. Select an exercise that is right for you, set your own standards, and see them through. Also, know the limits of your physical capabilities and stay within them.

Another attitude that prevents exercise is the perception of lack of need. This is the person who says, "I'm in as good shape as anyone else if not better." While that may be true to some extent, it is not an excuse to keep from engaging in a regular program of exercise. If your physical activity does not meet the criteria for aerobic fitness given earlier, you need exercise no matter how fit you feel.

There is also the excuse that exercise programs cost too much. As noted before, there are several types of exercise that cost virtually nothing yet provide all the physical conditioning needed. Another related excuse is that exercise takes too much time or competes with more important activities. Three or four hours per week given to physical health is actually less than 4% of the total waking time for one week. It is probably less than the average time spent watching TV in one week. Even TV time can be used for calisthenics, jumping rope, or riding an exercise bicycle. In the final analysis, what is more important than keeping your health?

Some people also feel that they will be embarrassed if they go to an exercise class or take up some sport involving any degree of competition. There are a number of ways around this. For example, get a friend who is in about the same shape to exercise with you. Also, in classes such as aerobic dance, remember that there are usually people who have taken the classes before and are there now for the purpose of keeping fit. You should not compare yourself to them. In most cases, you will find far more support and encouragement for trying than anything else.

Finally, there is a tendency to exaggerate a failure. Whether this is because of not having reached some goal or because of missing a practice session, a single failure leads to quitting. There will be setbacks in any exercise program. There will be times when you do not feel well and cannot run as far or as fast. These should be taken in stride as part of the process. In fact, it helps to take a flexible attitude toward exercise. You do not have to do the same thing all the time. You do not have to run farther and faster each and every time. Allow your exercise to vary with mood and condition—just keep exercising.

◆ MARATHON RUNNING: THE MYTH OF CORONARY IMMUNITY

Space does not permit anything more than a brief statement about one of the more unfortunate myths to develop in recent years. This is the idea that if you can run a marathon, you will achieve a form of immunity to coronary disease. The myth is unfortunate because of the number of people who have pursued the dream of immunity too fast, too hard, with too much pain. This idea has been shattered by the deaths of a number of runners who were in peak condition but died anyway, some even during the course of running. The best-known case is the death of Jim Fixx, the author of a popular book on running.[27] In general, vulnerability to coronary disease results from a number of factors, including genetic endowment, diet, and exercise. Exercise itself does not reverse the effects of genetic endowment. It may help someone at risk to live a healthier life, but it does not remove risk altogether.

◆ EXERCISING FOR WEIGHT CONTROL

As noted earlier, exercise can be an important asset to a weight-loss program. In fact, attempts to reduce weight that do not include some form of exercise are generally less effective, if not doomed to failure outright. Exercise speeds up a sluggish metabolism, causing the body to burn calories at a faster rate. This effect carries over beyond the period of activity. Your body will burn calories at a rate about 10% faster for as much as four to six hours after exercising.[28] In fact, your metabolism will be slightly higher, even while you are resting and sleeping, than if you are not exercising.

◆ PRECAUTIONS FOR EXERCISE PROGRAMS

There are a few precautions to consider before starting an exercise program. First, it is now recommended that anyone over 35 years of age obtain a thorough medical exam prior to beginning. The longer it has been since you last exercised the more crucial this precaution is. The exam should probably include some form of stress test in addition to the routine checks. Therefore, do not hide the purpose of the exam from your physician. To do so will only defeat the purpose. Also, if you have had any back or heart problems, by all means obtain a medical checkup before starting the program.

Remember the warm-up and cool-down periods before and after exercise. Finally, make sure that you have taken in both fluids and calories to sustain physical exercise. Lack of either can produce physical problems during the exercise and more fatigue. The hotter the weather, the more the fluid intake is important. The longer the workout you plan, the more muscle energy you need.

◆ BEHAVIORAL SELF-CONTROL: PRINCIPLES FOR STICKING WITH IT

In this section, some basic principles of behavioral self-control will be provided. These principles have been developed in clinical studies aimed at helping people to do the very things discussed in this chapter—that is, to reduce weight and engage in consistent exercise. Nonetheless, the ideas presented here can be extended to cover a variety of other unhealthy behaviors such as smoking.

Set Attainable Goals

There are two elements to this principle. First, you need to know exactly where you want to go with your program. And second, you need to make sure that you can get there. If you want to lose 25 pounds or exercise three times per week each week of the year, make it crystal clear. Such goals as "I want to look better" or "I want to get in shape" are so general that you can lose all sense of how to get there.

In regard to the second issue, there is no point in setting a goal of losing 50 pounds if you only need to lose 25 and losing more could actually be dangerous. Also, don't try to run a four-minute mile or a two-hour marathon. These are goals for the professionals. Be happy even with a modest achievement.

Break the Long-range Goals Down into Short-term Goals

In addition to saying where you want to get, set goals that mark progress for the trip there. Do not think in terms of losing 25 pounds or 100 pounds or running a marathon. Think instead of losing 2 pounds or 5 pounds or running a three-meter race. You can be even more specific than this. If you want to lose 25 pounds, over what period of time will you do it? And how much do you want to lose this week and next week in order to make the goal? In this way, cut up a big trip into little parts. You can keep track of your progress more easily, and you are more likely to stay motivated and keep at the program because you can see that you are making gains.

Provide for Observable Progress Reports

It is important that you see the progress you are making. In behavioral terms, this is called self-monitoring. There are any number of ways to count or measure your own behavior. You can count the frequency of repetitions in an exercise routine. You can time how long it takes you to bicycle a certain distance. A weight record can be filled out each day. A daily log can be checked to indicate the exercise you carried out. A record of eating behavior should record what you eat in calories, when you eat, what other activities are going on while eating, and who is present. Whatever the method, make your behavior and progress clearly visible.

One of the most popular records is a calendar. The behavior you are trying to change is recorded directly on the calendar. It is sometimes helpful to translate this record to a simple chart or graph. In addition to the positive feedback you get from seeing your progress, you may also be able to see patterns (weight gains over the weekend that slow down progress) or detect problem areas in your program. Most of the popular commercial programs use such charts.

Making the chart public or semipublic can also help to maintain motivation. A public chart almost becomes a contract with the viewers that you will succeed. You draw upon powerful sources of social approval as you progress and gentle reproof when you let down. The chart does not have to be public in the literal sense; it can be made visible to the people in your division at work or to your inner circle of friends.

Provide Yourself with Some Tangible Rewards

If you meet certain short-term goals, there ought to be some reward. Perhaps you could agree with your spouse to set aside a certain amount of money to buy some personal nicety when a goal has been reached. Buy some clothing you have been wanting or a record to add to your collection. This approach is called a contingency contract, in formal terms.

In addition to specifying the positive side, you can also agree on some fine or punishment that will occur if the goal is not met. For example, say that you are going to lose a pound each week for a month and the positive reward will be a sweater. If you do not meet that goal, the money will go to something that you really do not like, such as support of a politician or organization that you cannot stand.

Identify and Control Environmental Stimuli

One of the most important parts of self-control is sorting out the environmental events or stimuli that support your bad habits. For example, a chart of eating habits, as described earlier, may reveal that heavy eating occurs most when you are alone. Or a similar analysis may show that continuous snacking occurs while you watch TV.

The general rule is to change the environment in a way that reverses the relationship. For example, you can engage in behavioral restrictions. Eat only in the kitchen, and do not move the TV into the kitchen to circumvent the rule! If you find that you do not exercise once you get home because of distractions, take your workout gear with you. Some people schedule a walk as part of their lunch break. Others take a longer break to go to the local health club and work out. This is an excellent idea since it serves as a good change of pace and a type of recharging for the balance of the day. Still others schedule a workout at the club or park on their way home from work. Any of these tricks may break the pattern of negative stimulus control at home.

Make the Routine Habit Forming

Whatever exercise you choose, get into a routine and stay with it. When the schedule gets tight, one of the first things to go seems to be exercise. You need to resist this temptation, especially early in your program. If you work out consistently for a while, you should find that the consistency is habit forming. In fact, there may be tension when you break this new habit. That is as it should be.

Use Nonproductive Time for Double-timing

Some people complain that they do not have the time for exercise, yet they spend many hours watching TV. Turn that nonproductive time into fitness time. For example, you can do calisthenics such as situps or pushups and never miss a heartbeat of "Dynasty" or "Monday Night Football." Why not skip rope to "Late Night with David Letterman"? Obviously, you could also watch an exercise class. If that is your forte, by all means do it and relax at the other times. But if your analysis of time shows significant nonproductive time, look for ways of double-timing and turn those sedentary hours into profitable fitness hours.

Even if your quiet times at home are filled with productive activities such as reading and corresponding you can still work in some effective exercises to move you in the direction of fitness. Take a break from your creative pursuits to work on an exercise bike, for example. In fact, you may find that the mind continues to work on a problem that had you stumped. While you are exercising, the solution may occur and you will be able to return to your activity energized in more ways than one.

One word of caution is in order. Many people do have only a few leisure hours available. If you watch TV sparingly and that for specific reasons such as self-development or just relaxation, do not feel guilty about using it for that purpose. By all means leave that time clean and uncluttered by exercise. But look for ways of freeing up the rest of your schedule to provide the time you need for fitness.

◆ SUMMARY

In this chapter, the basic elements of sound nutrition, diet, and exercise have been described. The general principles in each area are relatively straightforward as established by a solid line of research. In regard to nutrition, first try to balance your diet with more carbohydrates and fewer proteins and fats. The percentages should be about 50%, 20%, and 30%, respectively. Second, increase the amount of fiber in your diet because fiber helps to remove fat and helps you feel full, thus reducing the tendency to overeat. Third, reduce the amount of saturated fats, sugars, and salt. Finally, resist the temptation to use megadoses of vitamins. In general, your body cannot absorb vitamins above a certain point. Any more than that will simply be passed off through urine and stools.

If you feel that you need to diet for health reasons, first plan your dieting program around an exercise program. This is the most effective way to lose weight since exercise will help you burn off more calories even when you are not exercising. Second, avoid extreme diets that either reduce calories to a very low amount or exclude all of one kind of food. Third, keep the calorie count above 1,300 especially if exercising. Fourth, trying to lose a large amount at one time can be very dangerous to your health. Think in terms of a program of losing at most about one pound per week. And think in terms of maintaining an altered eating life-style coupled with exercise after the weight loss has been achieved.

Any fitness program should consider an exercise that is within your physical capabilities and fits comfortably into your professional and family pattern. Exercise does not have to be painful, expensive, excessively time-consuming, or glamorous to provide benefits. Once you have selected an appropriate exercise and set a schedule, make that schedule habitual. Always carry out a warm-up before commencing hard workouts, and be careful to cool down slowly. The most intense exercise should raise your heart rate to somewhere between 70% and 80% of your resting heart beat. Avoid the Olympic syndrome. Also remember that there has to be a limit to what you can achieve. Avoid the notion that you must always be improving. After you have reached an adequate level of fitness, shift your program to one of maintenance.

◆ NOTES

[1]Posner, M. J. (1982). *Executive essentials*. New York: Avon Books, p. 153.

[2]Schachter, S. (1982). Recidivism and self-cure of smoking and obesity. *American Psychologist, 37,* 436–444.

[3]Mirkin, G. (1983). *Getting thin*. Boston: Little, Brown, p. 3.

[4]Gallup, G., Jr. (1984). *The Gallup poll: Public opinion 1984*. Wilmington, DE: Scholarly Resources, pp. 112, 113.

[5]Mayo Clinic, Committee on Dietetics (Eds.). (1981). *Mayo Clinic diet manual.* Philadelphia: Saunders, p. 297.

[6]Mayo Clinic, *Diet manual,* p. 270.

[7]Mirkin, *Getting thin,* p. 110.

[8]Mayo Clinic, *Diet manual,* p. 301.

[9]Mirkin, *Getting thin,* p. 114.

[10]Mirkin, *Getting thin,* p. 123.

[11]Gutlin, B., & Kessler, G. (1983). *The high-energy factor.* New York: Random House, p. 120.

[12]Mirkin, *Getting thin,* p. 34.

[13]Gutlin & Kessler, *High-energy factor,* p. 95.

[14]U.S. Bureau of the Census. (1985). *Statistical abstract of the United States: 1986* (106th ed.). Washington, DC: U.S. Government Printing Office, p. 783.

[15]Marshall, C. W. (1983). *Vitamins and minerals: Help or harm.* Philadelphia: Stickley, pp. 122–132.

[16]Marshall, *Vitamins and minerals,* pp. 20–21.

[17]Marhsall, *Vitamins and minerals,* p. 50.

[18]Mirkin, G., & Hoffman, M. *The sports medicine book.* Boston: Little, Brown, p. 72.

[19]National Research Council, Food and Nutrition Board. Committee on Dietary Allowances. (1980). *Recommended dietary allowances* (9th rev. ed.). Washington, DC: National Academy of Sciences, p. 186.

[20]U.S. Bureau of the Census, *Statistical abstract,* p. 122.

[21]Mirkin, *Getting thin,* pp. 114–115.

[22]Mirkin, *Getting thin,* p. 17.

[23]Harris, R., Frankel, L. J., & Harris, S. (Eds.). (1977). *Guide to fitness after fifty.* New York: Plenum Press.

[24]Sharkey, B. J. (1984). *Physiology of fitness: Prescribing exercise for fitness, weight control, and health* (2nd ed.). Champaign, IL: Human Kinetics, p. 3.

[25]Sharkey, *Physiology of fitness,* p. 171. Sharkey's findings, based on a sample of 2,500 people, was that the range was plus or minus 12.

[26]Sharkey, *Physiology of fitness,* p. 42.

[27]Fixx, J. F. (1977). *The complete book of running.* New York: Random House.

[28]Mirkin, *Getting thin,* p. 50.

APPENDIX:
ANNOTATED GUIDE TO
STRESS AND COPING TESTS

Because of an increasing demand from the public sector, more and more coping techniques, including assessment procedures, are being made available for personal use. Self-rating scales seem to provide a service previously thought attainable only in a clinical setting.

Unfortunately, most self-help tests provide little evidence to support their advertised claims except **face validity**, the *appearance* of measuring what they said they were measuring. Let the buyer beware—the promise of self-help tests may be more apparent than real!

◆ TESTING THE INTEGRITY OF TESTS

Most scientific disciplines have established internal standards for measurement procedures that are considered acceptable. The two most important such standards are reliability and validity.

Reliability

In technical terms, a test is **reliable** if it gives the same results every time. If an intelligence test showed that a child was a genius on one day, average another day, and mildly retarded another day, you would have every reason to doubt the integrity of that test. Such a test would be unreliable.

Validity

A test is **valid** if it measures what it is supposed to measure. Most of the time, we are concerned about *construct validity,* where **construct** refers to a group of traits or personal characteristics that are guessed at rather than seen directly and concretely. Intelligence is a construct. It cannot be directly seen or measured. We have to make educated guesses both about what intelligence is (a difference in quality) and about degrees of intelligence (a difference in quantity).

Four different classes of scales have been developed to help measure stress and personal health. These are assessment of current level of stress, assessment of health risks, evaluation of stress-coping skills, and assessment of life-style. The type of information provided by each can be invaluable in determining what risks are most prominent, what coping skills are most in need of strengthening, and what health behaviors are most in need of changing. The following is an annotated bibliography of some of the most commonly used stress and health tests.

◆ STRESS TESTS

Stress tests provide two types of information: the *sources* and the *types* of stress. Stress tests help to identify whether stress is occurring on the job, at home, or in personal and professional relationships, and so on. Once the source is localized, attention can be devoted to pinning down the nature of stress. A large number of tests have been introduced that claim to measure some facet of stress; only a representative sampling can be presented here. Several entries are review articles covering particular types of assessments.

Stress Measured as Anxiety

1. **Taylor Manifest Anxiety Scale (TMAS).** Taylor, J. A. (1953). A personality scale of manifest anxiety. *Journal of Abnormal and Social Psychology, 48,* 285–90. The Taylor Manifest Anxiety Scale, derived from the world-renowned Minnesota Multiphasic Personality Inventory, has generated literally thousands of research articles.
2. **Hamilton Anxiety Scale (HAS).** Hamilton, M. (1959). The assessment of anxiety states by rating. *British Journal of Medical Psychology, 32,* 50.
3. **State–Trait Anxiety Scale.** Spielberger, C. D., Gorsuch, R. L., & Lushene, R. E. (1970). *Manual for the State–Trait Anxiety Inventory.* Palo Alto, CA: Consulting Psychologists Press.
4. **Self-rating Anxiety Scale (SAS).** Zung, W. W. K. (1971). A rating instrument for anxiety disorders. *Psychosomatics, 12,* 371–379.
5. Borkovec, T. D., Weerts, T. C., & Bernstein, D. A. (1977). Assessment of anxiety. In A. Ciminero, K. Calhoun, & H. Adams (Eds.), *Handbook of behavioral assessment* (pp. 367–428). New York: Wiley. This review of anxiety assessment in 1977 found 191 references to different scales (there may have been even more).
6. Zung, W. W. K., & Cavenar, J. O. (1980). Assessment scales and techniques. In I. L. Kutash, L. B. Schlesinger, and associates (Eds.), *Handbook on stress and anxiety* (pp. 348–363). San Francisco: Jossey-Bass. This includes a review of some of the most frequently used stress and anxiety measures along with some critical analysis of the research supporting the different measures.

Stressful Life Events

1. **Social Readjustment Rating Scale (SRRS).** Holmes, T. H., & Rahe, R. H. (1967). The Social Readjustment Rating Scale. *Journal of Psychosomatic Research, 11,* 213–218.

2. **Schedule of Recent Experiences.** Holmes, T. H., & Rahe, R. H. (1967). *Schedule of Recent Experiences.* Seattle: School of Medicine, University of Washington.

3. **Life Experiences Survey (LES).** Sarason, I. G., Johnson, J. H., & Siegel, J. M. (1978). Assessing the impact of life changes: Development of the Life Experiences Survey. *Journal of Consulting and Clinical Psychology, 46,* 932–946. A 47-item scale that taps many of the same events as the SRRS but with some differences.

4. Monaghan, J. H., Robinson, J. O., & Dodge, J. A. (1979). The Children's Life Events Inventory. *Journal of Psychosomatic Research, 23,* 63–68.

5. **The Hassles Scale.** Kanner, A. D., Coyne, J. C., Schaefer, C., & Lazarus, R. S. (1981). Comparison of two modes of stress measurement: Daily hassles and uplifts versus major life events. *Journal of Behavioral Medicine, 4,* 1–39. Based on the idea that "it's the little things that count," the scale assesses daily hassles such as losing the car keys, not having enough money at the end of the month, too many interruptions, not enough time with the family, and not enough time for family and personal pursuits.

6. Forman, B. D., Eidson, K., & Hagan, B. J. (1983). Measuring perceived stress in adolescents: A cross validation. *Adolescence, 18,* 573–576. A life-events scale for adolescents based on the life-change concept.

Assessing Type A Behavior

1. **Jenkins Activity Survey (JAS).** Jenkins, C. D., Zyzanski, S. J., & Rosenman, R. H. (1965). *Jenkins Activity Survey.* New York: The Psychological Corporation. This is probably the most notable Type A scale in paper-and-pencil format with objective scoring.

2. **Structured Interview (SI).** Friedman, M., & Rosenman, R. H. (1974). *Type A behavior and your heart.* New York: Knopf, pp. 82–85. This was the first clinical method of diagnosing Type A behavior, consisting of 26 questions presented by a trained interviewer.

3. Chesney, M. A., Eagleston, J. R., & Rosenman, R. H. (1981). Type A behavior: Assessment and intervention. In C. K. Prokop & L. A. Bradley (Eds.), *Medical psychology: Contributions to behavioral medicine.* New York: Academic Press. Chesney and her colleagues note that at least six other Type A scales have been developed. They provide a critical review and references for alternatives.

Assessing Work Stress or Job Burnout

1. Berkeley Planning Associates. (1977). Project management and worker burnout. In *Evaluation of child abuse and neglect demonstration projects* (Vol. 9). Springfield, VA: National Technical Information Service. A burnout scale based on the concept of job alienation.

2. **Staff Burnout Scale (SBS).** Jones, J. W. (1980). *The Staff Burnout Scale for health professionals.* Park Ridge, IL: London House. Builds on Maslach's conceptual base, but expands the range of items to include behavioral and physiological items. Includes a social desirability scale to detect when an individual may be responding to social pressure.

3. **The Maslach Burnout Inventory (MBI).** Maslach, C., & Jackson, S. E. (1981). *The Maslach Burnout Inventory.* Palo Alto, CA: Consulting Psychologists Press. Provides four subscales: emotional exhaustion, personal accomplishment, depersonalization, and involvement.

4. **The Tedium Scale.** Pines, A., & Aronson, E., with Kafry, D. (1981). *Burnout: From tedium to personal growth.* New York: Free Press.

5. Veninga, R. L., & Spradley, J. P. (1981). *The work stress connection.* Boston: Little, Brown. Used a self-rating scale, though not self-scoring, in a national survey of job stress. The scale is published in the book and may be sent in for scoring.

6. Shinn, M. (1982). Methodological issues: Evaluating and using information. In W. S. Paine (Ed.) *Job stress and burnout: Research, theory, and intervention perspectives* (pp. 61–79). Beverly Hills, CA: Sage Publications. Shinn identified five "published" burnout scales in this review.

◆ HEALTH STATUS INDEXES

Health status scales seek to determine how well you are right now or have been in the very recent past. They may also try to assess genetic load and recurrent physical health problems. **Genetic load** can be thought of as a tendency to break down physically in a certain way if stress threatens. Health risk is usually determined by evaluating family history. The more often a family has had a certain disorder, the more likely it is that offspring of the family will experience the same disorder.

1. **Cornell Medical Index (CMI).** Broadman, K., Erdmann, A. J., Lorge, I., & Wolff, H. G. (1949). The Cornell Medical Index: An adjunct to medical interview. *Journal of American Medical Associa-*

tion, 140, 530–534. The CMI was intended to provide the physician with a quick, comprehensive overview of the health status of a patient to guide further diagnostic or treatment decisions.

2. **Social Assets Scale.** Luborsky, L., Todd, T. C., & Datcher, A. H. (1972). A self-administered social assets scale for predicting physical and psychological illness and health. *Journal of Psychosomatic Research, 17,* 109–120. This scale is based on the observation that high social assets, such as education and occupation, are associated with symptoms best described as turning against oneself. Low social assets, on the other hand, are presumably associated with symptoms of turning against others, as shown by assaultive behavior.

3. **Sickness Impact Profile (SIP).** Gilson, B. S., et al. (1975). The Sickness Impact Profile: Development of an outcome measure of health care. *American Journal of Public Health, 65,* 1304–1325. The SIP is intended to determine limitations that result from sickness.

4. **Index of Well-being (IWB).** Kaplan, R. M., Bush, J. W., & Berry, C. C. (1976). Health status: Types of validity and the Index of Well-being. *Health Services Research, 11,* 478–507. The most sophisticated health status index, which provides both a health status measure and an optional prognosis measure.

◆ COPING SKILLS ASSESSMENT

An argument can be made that virtually anything that helps the person cope is by definition a coping skill and therefore should be studied. Practically speaking, though, a common core of personal characteristics thought to be important to coping has emerged in assessment instruments. These include assertiveness, competence, and locus of control.

Assertiveness

1. **Gambrill–Richey Assertion Inventory.** Gambrill, E. D., & Richey, C. A. (1975). An assertion inventory for use in assessment and research. *Behavior Therapy, 6,* 550–561. This is probably the most frequently used assertion inventory. The scale can help point out areas where more assertive behaviors need to be developed.

Locus of Control

1. **Locus of Control.** Rotter, J. B. (1966). Generalized expectancies for internal versus external control of reinforcement. *Psychological Monographs, 80*(Whole No. 609, 1–28). Of all the personal characteristics thought to be related to stress, locus of control is perhaps the most frequently measured.

2. **Multidimensional Health Locus of Control (MHLC).** Wallston, K. A., Wallston, B. S., & DeVellis, R. (1978). Development of the Multidimensional Health Locus of Control (MHLC) scales. *Health Education Monographs, 6*, 160–170.

Competence

1. Zeitlin, S. (1982). Assessing coping behavior in children with learning disabilities. *Exceptional Child, 29*, 43–51.
2. Ventura, J. N., & Boss, P. G. (1983). The Family Coping Inventory applied to parents with new babies. *Journal of Marriage and the Family, 83*, 867–875. A specific coping scale developed to study how parents cope with the arrival of a new baby.
3. **CHIP—Coping Health Inventory.** McCubbin, H. I. (1983). CHIP—Coping Health Inventory for Parents: An assessment of parental coping patterns in the care of the chronically ill child. *Journal of Marriage and the Family, 45*, 359–370.
4. Litman, G. K., Stapleton, J., Oppenheim, A. N., & Peleg, M. (1983). An instrument for measuring coping behaviors in hospitalized alcoholics: Implications for relapse prevention treatment. *British Journal of Addiction, 78*, 269–276.
5. Stone, A. A., & Neale, J. M. (1984). New measure of daily coping: Development and preliminary results. *Journal of Personality and Social Psychology, 46*, 892–906. This is a measure of coping with daily problems that seems to measure general coping skills.

◆ ASSESSMENT OF LIFE-STYLE RISKS

Life-style simply refers to a pattern of behaviors more or less under personal control that can directly or indirectly affect health, longevity, and stress. Such behaviors are also frequently referred to as *self-defeating behaviors* or *high-risk behaviors*. Assessments of this nature aid the person in planning a personal health program and in sustaining motivation for life-style change. Life-style assessment can help you focus on specific behavior patterns that are most in need of change.

1. **Health Hazard Appraisal (HHA).** Safer, M. A. (1982). An evaluation of the Health Hazard Appraisal based on survey data from a randomly selected population. *Public Health Reports, 97,* 31–36. Four factors are combined in this scale: personal risk factors, physiological measures, and personal and family health history. The scale provides information on what the likelihood of death would be if the person modified certain high-risk behaviors.

◆ COMPUTERIZED STRESS ASSESSMENT

One recent development in stress scales is the computerized stress and life-style assessment. Such products may be as broad as coping with stress or as narrow as a diet analyzer. A word of caution is in order. These instruments are frequently aimed at capitalizing on the popularity of computers and are not the result of well thought out research programs. Reliability and validity information is not readily available, if it exists at all. Finally, there may be no more than "advertising" information that implies, but does not demonstrate, a scientific basis for development of the program. For example, such statements as "based on well-known clinical procedures," "expert systems software," or "gives a scientifically accurate personality profile" are no more than advertising jargon.

On the other hand, certain packages, such as nutrition and diet packages, can be used with some degree of confidence since the basis for calculating these factors is more straightforward. In any case, before you purchase one (such programs cost between $30 and $300), seek as much information on the program as possible. It might also help to check with a local computer dealer to see if a demonstration can be arranged.

AUTHOR INDEX

SUBJECT INDEX

CREDITS

Photo Credits:

p. 5: AP/Wide World Photos, **p. 18:** © Karsh, Woodfin Camp & Associates, **p. 190:** AP/Wide World Photos, **p. 304:** Jerry Berndt/Stock Boston

Figure Credits:

Figure 2.2 (p. 25): adapted from *The Stress of Life,* by Hans Selye. Copyright © 1956 by McGraw-Hill Book Company. Reprinted by permission.

Figure 3.5 (p. 48): from *Basic Human Physiology: Normal Function and Mechanisms of Disease,* by A. C. Guyton. Copyright © 1977 by W. B. Saunders. Reprinted by permission.

Figure 3.6 (p. 54): from "Aids Risk Group Profiles in Whites and Members of Minority Groups," by R. Bakeman, J. R. Lumb, R. E. Jackson, and D. W. Smith. Reprinted by permission of *The New England Journal of Medicine, 315*(3), pp. 191–192, 1986.

Figure 5.1 (p. 103): adapted from Figure 5.1 in *Issues and Approaches to the Psychosocial Assessment of the Cancer Patient,* by I. Barofsky. Copyright 1981 by Academic Press. Reprinted by permission.

Figure 5.2 (p. 108): reprinted by permission, from *Journal of Studies on Alcohol, 44,* pp. 395–428, 1983. Copyright by Alcohol Research Documentation, Inc., Rutgers Center of Alcohol Studies, New Brunswick, NJ 08903.

Scattered quotes in Chapter 5 adapted with permission of The Fress Press, a Division of Macmillan, Inc. from *Contemporary Theories About the Family,* Volume I, edited by Wesley R. Burr, Reuben Hill, F. Ivan Nye, Ira L. Reiss. Copyright © 1979 by The Free Press.

Figure 6.1 (p. 124): adapted from "The Family Stress Process: The Double ABCX Model of Adjustment and Adaptation," by H. I. McCubbin and J. M. Patterson. In *Marriage and Family Review, 6,* pp. 7–37, 1983. Reprinted by permission.

Figure 9.1 (p. 185): adapted from "A Reinforcement Model of Evaluative Responses," by D. Byrne and G. L. Close. In *Personality: An International Journal, 1,* pp. 103–128, 1970.

Figure 9.2 (p. 188): from *Environmental Psychology,* 2nd Edition, by Jeffrey D. Fisher, Paul A. Bell, and Andrew Baum. Copyright © 1984 by CBS College Publishing. Copyright © 1978 by W. B. Saunders Company. Reprinted by permission of CBS College Publishing.